Maya History and Religion

UNIVERSITY OF OKLAHOMA PRESS : NORMAN

J. Eric S. Thompson

Maya
history
and
Religion

BY J. ERIC S. THOMPSON
Ethnology of the Mayas of Southern and Central British
Honduras (Chicago, 1930)
Archaeological Investigations in the Southern Cayo
District, British Honduras (Chicago, 1931)
Mexico before Cortez (New York, 1933)
Excavations at San José, British Honduras (Washington, 1939)
Maya Hieroglyphic Writing: An Introduction
(Washington, 1950; Norman, 1960)
The Rise and Fall of Maya Civilization (Norman, 1954, 1966)
Thomas Gage's Travels in the New World (ed.) (Norman, 1958)
A Catalog of Maya Hieroglyphs (Norman, 1962)
Maya Archaeologist (Norman, 1963)
Maya History and Religion (Norman, 1970)

INTERNATIONAL STANDARD BOOK NUMBER: 0–8061–0884–3
LIBRARY OF CONGRESS CATALOG CARD NUMBER: 72–88144
COPYRIGHT 1970 BY THE UNIVERSITY OF OKLAHOMA PRESS, PUB-
LISHING DIVISION OF THE UNIVERSITY. COMPOSED AND PRINTED AT
NORMAN, OKLAHOMA, U.S.A., BY THE UNIVERSITY OF OKLAHOMA
PRESS. FIRST EDITION.

Contents

Illustrations

MAPS

Maya History and Religion

CHAPTER I

Putun (Chontal Maya) Expansion
in Yucatan
and the Pasión Drainage

INTRODUCTION

This first chapter, because the thesis is new and so must be supported with detailed argument, may seem to a fair proportion of readers like driving over a succession of clover-leaf intersections with all destinations and route numbers hidden by driven snow. Let them take heart; the route is clearer ahead and, as signs along those concrete curves, here is a summary of the main arguments:

1. The Putun, also called Chontal Maya, were a thrusting group, strongly affected by Mexican-speaking neighbors, whose home was in southern Campeche and in the huge delta of the Usumacinta and Grijalva rivers of Tabasco. Their home was peripheral to the great development of the Maya Classic period, and there is little evidence that they were abreast of the great advances in art, architecture, and astronomy of their neighbors east and northeast of them.

2. Because the Putun, as the seamen and sea traders of Middle America, controlled the sea routes around the Peninsula of Yucatan, a branch of them, called in Yucatan the Itza, established themselves in the island of Cozumel on the opposite side of the peninsula and, crossing the channel, acquired a beachhead at Polé on the

3

mainland. Thence they penetrated inland, conquering a number of centers including Chichen Itza (A.D. 918).

3. Having established themselves at Chichen Itza and opened overland communications with their homeland in southern Campeche, and being almost bilingual and deeply under Mexican influence, they were ready to receive Quetzalcoatl-Kukulcan fleeing from his enemies in Tula (probably A.D. 987). This second group, entering from the west, brought stronger Mexican influences, with those of Tula dominant.

4. At a somewhat earlier date other Putun groups, probably from Potonchan at the mouth of the Grijalva River, established a trading base at the strategic site of Altar de Sacrificios, where the Pasión and Chixoy rivers meet to form the Usumacinta (ca. A.D. 800). Even earlier (A.D. 730–50) what was probably another Putun group won temporary control of Yaxchilan.

5. From Altar de Sacrificios the invaders, pushing farther up the Pasión, conquered Seibal (ca. A.D. 850), an important Classic-period site, and pushed on to Ucanal, almost on the British Honduras border and in the Belize River drainage.

6. After the abandonment of the ceremonial centers and the overthrow of the Maya nobility, including the newly arrived Putun leaders, the remnant of the Putun established themselves south of the Pasión, naming their land Acala or Acalan, "Land of the Canoe People," after their original homeland in the Grijalva-Usumacinta delta. There, under the loose designation Lacandon, they maintained their independence until 1695, with their largest town, renamed Dolores by the Spaniards, just north of the great bend of the upper Lacantun River.

7. Between A.D. 850 and A.D. 950 this once peripheral people controlled, in part or absolutely, northern Tabasco, southern Campeche, Cozumel, Bakhalal, and Chetumal along the east coast of the peninsula; Chichen Itza and probably other centers in central Yucatan; and, for a short while, much of the Pasión drainage as well as Ucanal in the Belize drainage. The expansion of this

4

The Civilization of the American Indian Series

Introduction

Archaeology is the study of dead cultures. The word has romantic connotations and perhaps for that reason has come to be loosely used in speaking of the Maya as though their archaeology and their whole history were one and the same thing. Nothing could be farther from the truth. What the spade, trowel, and whisk broom of the excavator contribute is only part of the still-accumulating knowledge of the history, daily life, and thought processes of that remarkable people.

Maya culture, like, for instance, that of the Jews, is still very much alive; one sees the present in the past and the past in the present. It would be absurd to publish under some such title as "Jewish Civilization" a book on excavations at Jerusalem, Jericho, and other sites in Palestine without reference to Jewish written history and literature. It is equally illogical to treat of the Maya without recourse to the mass of information forthcoming since their culture came under European observation; an ounce of documents is worth more than a peck of artifacts. On the other hand, archaeology can supplement or even correct faulty tradition or history of the early periods.

From that moment of first contact with the outside world on

March 1, 1517, when some thirty Maya were dined and wined—
one wonders how the Maya palate, attuned to their harsh mead
tipple, *balche*, reacted to the wine of Castile—on board the flagship
of Francisco Hernández de Córdoba off Cape Catoche, the white
man has recorded his observations of Maya life. On March 2 the
Spaniards went ashore, and banqueting gave place to battle. While
the soldiers fought, Córdoba's chaplain brought away from a
Maya temple, hard by the scene of action, idols of pottery and
wood decked with diadems and ornaments of low-grade gold. His
was the first record of Maya religion; his comrades', that of the
dress, weapons, and tactics of Maya warriors.

The student supplements those first reports with the writings
of Spanish churchmen and officials and the countless reports on
the administration of the new lands sent to Spain to feed the
bureaucratic appetite and weigh down the shelves of government
archives. He may wade through tedious and lengthy histories
of the activities of Franciscans and Dominicans in Mexico and
Guatemala in search of the occasional chapter or even aside containing some hitherto unreported ethnological detail or naming
the Maya language or dialect then spoken in a town which later
ceased to be Maya speaking. He can take the information thus
laboriously gleaned and perhaps use it to elucidate some obscure
passage in a Maya historical document or even some detail of
sculpture.

Unknown documents adding greatly to our information on
the Maya are constantly being brought to light. Scholes' discovery
of the Paxbolon and related papers brought us knowledge of the
activities of the Putun Maya and the story of the evangelization of
southwestern Campeche (on which I have drawn heavily in chapters one and two), previously an almost completely blank spot
on the map; and his discovery of the Tovilla report, also in the
archives at Seville, supplied data to correlate the calendar of the
Manche Chol of southeastern Petén with our own, a matter on
which not even the most optimistic Maya student had ever expected to have the slightest information.

Ethnologists working in the twenties and thirties among Maya
communities unearthed invaluable survivals of the old paganism—
religious ceremonies and beliefs, old customs, myths, and so on.

Less than fifty years ago no one dreamed that some Maya communities not only retained the old sacred almanac of 260 days, but were still regulating their lives by it. Again, the custom of piercing the septum of the nose and inserting an ornament in the hole was known from a study of Maya reliefs and from the writings of sixteenth-century observers to have been a Maya practice, but only in recent years has the custom been noted as still in force in one remote Maya group.

Such discoveries in colonial documents and in modern ethnological research are made because Maya culture did not die with the Spanish Conquest; it still persists. The Maya, an ultraconservative, deliberately conserved the past. Maya antiquarians set themselves the task of preserving their cultural heritage. Thanks to them we have such inestimably rich sources as the Books of Chilam Balam in Yucatan and the Popol Vuh of the Quiche of highland Guatemala. Written in native languages but employing the Spanish alphabet and writing, they preserve a wealth of detail on Maya religion, history, and myth.

For the Maya, the shock of the Spanish Conquest was devastating; his old religion was proscribed, he was uprooted and gathered into towns so that he could be instructed in Christianity and kept under surveillance lest he slip back into heathenism, and he was placed under the domination of a people of a different race who neither knew nor were interested in Maya ways.

One thing was unchanged: the peasant who had been forced to build temples and pyramids to the old gods now toiled at pulling them down and erecting on their foundations churches and friaries which in their size and commodiousness would have shocked Saint Francis. Yet the onslaught was not fatal to Maya culture. The old religion went underground; the friars were too few to keep a strict control on their resentful flocks, and, indeed, seldom having a deep insight into native ways, were for the most part little aware of what was going on under their noses, let alone of the pagan ceremonies being performed in remote forest clearings to propitiate the old gods who sent the rains.

How successful Maya resistance was to many of the new ways shows up particularly in the way the Maya clung to their language —and culture and language are knit together. As late as 1766, commissioners sent to report on conditions in Yucatan and Campeche (Scholes et al., 1936–38, Vol. 3, ch. 153) complained: "In all the towns en route from Carmen to Campeche and thence to Mérida we did not have the pleasure of hearing a single Indian speak Spanish." They had to take an interpreter with them.

Until the present century the Yucatec-Maya language seemed almost as firmly entrenched, except in the largest towns, as the commissioners had found it; but in the past few decades radio, schools, the building of roads with concomitant bus services, and growth of a national spirit have brought to the Maya peasant awareness of what is going on outside his small community (p. 162). The process of integration accelerates; old ways and the old speech are its victims. Survivals, so far as they relate to the spiritual side of Maya culture, are melting like snow in the hot rays of technological materialism. I sometimes recall the horse-drawn bus and hansom cab of my childhood; I dread the thought that I may yet recall a Maya way of life which has also fallen a victim to "progress."

Maya culture, then, has a continuity from the first centuries of the Christian Era to the present day; the correlation of all the data from colonial writings and observations of survivals among the present-day Maya with the information archaeology yields alone will give us a true picture of Maya life. Admittedly, there are dangers in this approach: Maya culture was never static, but, in view of Maya conservatism, the danger of error in interpreting past history from colonial or present-day practices is diminished. Furthermore, some knowledge of medieval Spanish customs and traditions is necessary. Modern rites which stem from Spanish usage have been ascribed to the Maya.

At present, Maya studies suffer from imbalance. On the one hand, many archaeologists seldom lift their eyes from their excavations to see how colonial sources can supplement their findings, or are content to satisfy their curiosity with Landa's account of the Maya. A fantastic amount of time and effort is spent in labeling pottery with what are for the most part uncouth, unpronounceable names (some taken from Spanish not even correctly spelled). The report on one smallish site contains no fewer than 177 named varieties; another, on the partial excavation of three mounds, adds some 80 names, nearly all of which are tongue-twisting polysyllabic Nahuatl. Archaeology is in mortal danger of losing itself on the bypaths of abracadabra. There is precious little difference between the Maya medicine man mystifying his patients with muttered incantations and the ceramicist awing his scant congregation with still more esoteric names. However, senescent failure to adjust to new techniques may well have prompted my stricture.

On the other hand, the social anthropologist of today is not primarily interested in survivals of Maya practices as were men of an earlier generation, such as Sapper, Tozzer, La Farge, Termer, and Goubaud. Generally speaking, the problems that interest him are related to the functioning of a somewhat primitive community in an era of change. His thoughts are perhaps directed to parallel or contrasting change in some African or Italian group confronted by similar need for adjustment. Naturally, he has every right to choose his objectives and shape his studies thereto, but for the student interested in Maya culture as a continuing entity from its beginnings to the present day such investigations are tangential.

The ethnohistorian seeks to correlate data from colonial writings and observation of the modern Indian with archaeological information in order to extend and clarify the panorama of Maya culture. He is alert to spot some detail in a colonial or present-day source which bears on an archaeological problem and vice versa. Here is an illustration of that process.

In a lengthy footnote on page 37 of Scholes' and Roys' scholarly *The Maya Chontal Indians of Acalan-Tixchel* discussing the origin of the word Tabasco, the authors establish that the name of the ruling family in the great Putun settlement of Potonchan, at the mouth of the Usumacinta River, was given by the Spaniards as Cipaque, a corruption of Cipacti, the first of the twenty Mexican day names. On a stela showing strong "foreign" influences at Seibal, far up the Pasión, tributary of the same Usumacinta River, Cipacti glyphs stand above portraits of two rulers. The rest of the text is in standard Maya glyphs. I was already convinced, contrary to opinions emitted by colleagues, that the invaders who had won control of Seibal were those same Putun (alias Chontal) Maya who had been strongly influenced by Mexican neighbors. Here, then, in a passing citation of an obscure, unpublished document examined by Scholes in Seville's Archives of the Indies, was confirmatory evidence that the Cipacti rulers of Potonchan had gained control of Seibal (p. 41). The reference had solved a problem which the archaeologist could never have hoped to have answered on the strength of what his excavations produced.

The process can be reversed: the "ceremonial center" pattern of many present-day Maya groups in the uplands of Guatemala and Chiapas, in which the people who live scattered over the surrounding country flock into the town center, semi-deserted at other times, for religious and political occasions, markets, and jollifications, is a direct continuation of the archaeological picture (Thompson, 1966:70). Throughout highland Guatemala and Chiapas, the Maya place yellow flowers, such as calendulas or marigolds, on graves, above all during the highly paganized celebration of All Souls' Day. This custom can be traced back to early colonial times, when, one writer informs us, mourners customarily anointed themselves with yellow ointment. In fact, the rite goes much farther back in time; yellow was the color assigned by the ancient Maya to the south, the region over which the death god and his spouse presided, and the death god himself is often painted with yellow spots. Here then, archaeology explains what might have seemed a puzzling custom.

Even everyday Maya language is a preserver of the past, for custom may be imprisoned in language like fly in amber.

The Maya used very large numbers of what are termed numerical classifiers. We have a few in English, but nothing comparable to Maya: eight loaves of bread, three flights of birds, six head of cattle, or two servings or helpings of chicken à la king. Maya numerical classifiers at times are based on shape. *Dz'it*, for instance, is the numerical classifier for long thin objects; you ask for 2 *dz'it* candles, 6 *dz'it* corn on the cob, 4 *dz'it* bananas, 1 *dz'it* cigarette, 1 *dz'it* cotton thread, and so on. As time was thought to be a journey on a road stretching to infinity, periods of time were also long and thin, and the Maya spoke of 1 *dz'it* year or 1 *dz'it* katun. The Maya made their categories on visual grouping and then drew on their imaginations to enlarge them.

Ac was a numerical classifier for what we might call hollow objects: houses, churches, canoes, caves, holes in the ground, troughs, vases; but which the Maya also saw from inside looking out, as spaces enclosed by walls. (*Ac* was classifier of another group—seated or sat on objects—because *ac* is the root of words meaning "seated," but that is the result of chance convergence and need not detain us).

Among objects in the *ac* classifier group were milpas and towns. Illogical? Not a bit; a milpa is a clearing in the forest, a hollow space surrounded by living walls of tall vegetation. The same is true of the town or small settlement; it, too, is a clearing in the forest, a cockleshell afloat in a green sea which, if not kept at bay, may swallow it as the waters engulfed Pharoah's chariots. Such a fate many a Maya town, ancient and modern, has suffered.

Our examination of this humble two-letter suffix has given us a glimpse of the Maya in the imagination of their hearts, but there is a lot more to it than that. Some students refuse to accept the proposition that Maya civilization was based on slash-and-burn milpa agriculture, believing that the wasteful system could never have supported the numbers needed to build and sustain the great ceremonial centers. Our modest *ac* is a strong counterargument. It was current in the sixteenth century but is probably not a proto-Maya term and so probably came into use when Maya civilization was going strong, but it could have been adopted only to describe cornfields which were forest clearings. It is evidence that the Maya lowlands were never a sort of Kansas-*cum*-Nebraska with howler monkeys and jaguars cowering in nature reserves.

The same deduction concerning landscape during the Classic period may be made from the use of *ac* for counting towns or settlements.

From such specific instances, we may conclude that speech supplies more bright-hued thread with which to weave our pattern. These illustrations, too, disclose a second secret: research's greatest joy lies in the power it gives us to set in an over-all design those scraps of information absorbed quite unconsciously and tucked away in some dark cupboard of the mind, whence they will tumble out, like children's building blocks, when needed.

The studies which follow are, so to speak, vocal scores with parts for archaeology, ethnology, colonial documentation, and so on as in a madrigal or, for that matter, a barbershop quartet; we can not permit archaeology, like some nineteenth-century prima donna at a recital, to be the sole performer. This, of course, is the approach of the ethnohistorian. If I seem to lay too much emphasis on colonial sources, it is because they are generally the least utilized, and, in most of the topics here touched on, documentary and ethnological data are far weightier than the archaeological.

In chapter 1, which treats of the Putun Maya, hitherto called the Chontal Maya, Spanish sources are used to support a new analysis of Maya accounts in the Books of Chilam Balam treating of the "Mexican" conquest of Chichen Itza. That material is expanded from what the Paxbolon papers have to say about pre-Conquest aggrandizement of the Putun. All this had to go on the archaeological canvas, together with a regrouping of the principal actors in Yucatan history, against a background of the Putun as *the* seafaring traders of Middle America. To get away from this metaphor before the paint from the canvas gets in the writer's ink, this interpretation of history called for a fresh scrutiny of murals at Chichen Itza. As in any shifting of the configuration of history, the writer is faced with the decision of what data are significant.

In the second half of the chapter, facts from colonial sources are marshaled to explain the appearance toward the close of the Classic period of non-Classic elements at two sites on the Pasión River, as the upper Usumacinta is called. Documentary evidence again helps archaeology to the shrine of Clio.

In recent years, historians, particularly at the University of California, have interested themselves in the almost incredible drop in Indian population of Central Mexico which immediately followed the Spanish Conquest. Chapter 2 deals with the equally catastrophic depopulation of the Maya Central area. Great sweeps of the rain-forest lowlands were left almost uninhabited largely because of the spread of newly introduced diseases, in particular malaria, hookworm, yellow fever, smallpox, and influenza. The effect was as though multiple Hiroshima clouds had mushroomed over the area. The story is reconstructed from historical documents, medical reports, and some ethnological observations.

The old idea that those areas had remained largely uninhabited from the time the great ceremonial centers were abandoned at the close of the Classic period is shown—and here by archaeological evidence—to be false, a conclusion which gives me uncommon satisfaction, for that is what I had preached to deaf colleagues for forty years until the glad tidings I so long shouted from the mountaintop had become a sort of buzzard's croak by a cesspool.

In a frankly theoretical conclusion to that chapter, I look for a parallel between events in that area after the Spaniards came and what may conceivably have happened there some seven centuries earlier, when the ceremonial centers and the whole apparatus of oligarchic government came to an end.

Chapter 3, also focusing on the archaeological postcontact period, defines the eastern boundary of the Maya at the time of the Spanish Conquest, but again I have gingerly dipped a foot in the cold, deep waters of theoretical reconstruction of earlier history. Here, too, a diligent search of the scriptures had a little assistance from archaeology.

The use of tobacco, subject of the next chapter, illustrates what happened to what was almost an element of religion in Maya eyes when it became part of Spanish or, for that matter, all Western culture.

Tobacco among the Maya had a very important role in religious life; it was an important element in the prevention and cure of disease, in some parts was deified, and was an element which united the community. Its pleasure-giving qualities seem in Maya eyes to have been quite subordinate to its other functions. Yet when tobacco was taken over by the Spaniards it was only as a commodity which gave pleasure to the individual; all the Maya ritualistic and community associations were shed. This process was in line with Spanish secularization of those cultural elements of the conquered natives which they absorbed. Maize was no longer the beloved and sacred staff of life; it became for the conqueror an item of tribute and commercial transactions. Cacao suffered the same degradation. Conversely, the Maya and their neighbors tended to sanctify alien cultural traits which they accepted, if there was half a chance to do so. Nothing illustrates this better than the ceremony, taboos, and position in society accorded to that Old World feature, godfatherhood. The relationship between a man—and his wife, too—and the godfather of his child was completely transmuted when it was accepted by the Maya. An element of Spanish culture as secular as religious was exalted by the Maya beyond all recognition. One has only to read Ruth Bunzel (1952:154–62) to realize the solemnity and ritual which surrounds this relationship. Similarly, the Spanish *cofradías* (religious brotherhoods) have taken on a far deeper religious and social significance on being adopted by the Maya than they ever possessed in the peninsula, but the charitable side of such organizations has been rejected by Maya borrowers. Again, the *vara*, or wand of office of local functionaries, which in Spain is a badge of office, is almost deified by the Maya and other Indian groups as far distant as Peru.

Even the horse which so amazed the natives at first contact was received into Maya religion. Cortés' horse, left behind disabled by a splinter in its hoof, was presented with bouquets of flowers, a common form of religious offering, and was given birds (probably turkeys) and meat either as food or in sacrifice. A stone statue of the horse was set up in one of the temples and became one of the principal gods under the name Tzimin Chac, "Tapir Lightning" (the Maya named the horse "tapir," the animal closest to it in appearance; "lightning," because the Maya at first thought the horse was discharging lightning when the man on its back fired his gun). The thigh bone of the original horse seems to have been preserved in another temple.

The supposed association of the horse with firearms was one of the reasons which led the Maya to conceive of the Chacs, gods of rain and lightning, as riding on horses, a belief they still hold. Thus, the horse, in Spanish eyes man's servant, became in Maya belief his lord.

The way the Maya took like ducks to water to the Mediterranean categories of hot and cold for all foods and to the beliefs surrounding evil winds and the evil eye are other instances of how Maya mentality refashioned Old World concepts in a context which, while not precisely religious, was that of religion's stepsister, witchcraft. Reactions arising from the domination of one culture by another tell us much about each.

Trade relations, discussed in chapter 5, bring home the economic side of Maya life, for if much of this book gives the impression that the Maya took very much to heart—admittedly out of context —"Thou shall not live by bread alone," it is well to recall that no civilization achieves greatness without extensive interchange of products.

Archaeology supplies the data on trade in durable objects from the Formative period, before the birth of the speaker of those words, to the start of the sixteenth century. Columbus' dramatic encounter on his fourth voyage with a laden trading canoe marks the start of the contact period; a chance reference in a seventeenth-century Manche-Chol dictionary to the source of local salt provides the excitement of discovery in an unexpected place; and the colorful markets in highland towns of Guatemala bring the story to present times.

The final chapters outline Maya religion and myth, major preoccupations of that people. The three concerning religion are largely confined to the lowlands to avoid creating bewilderment with innumerable names of deities and overlapping in their functions. Here, alas, Spanish sources are not as satisfactory as they might have been; Franciscans and Dominicans were united, with few exceptions, in dismissing Maya gods under such collective terms as idols or demons. From their point of view they were right; Sahagún's interest in Aztec religion led him into serious trouble with his brethren. On the other hand, the Books of Chilam Balam and, above all, Ritual of the Bacabs supply innumerable names but almost no explanation of their functions and relationships. That is understandable; their authors did not write with modern students in mind.

It has been said, with truth, that man makes his gods in his own image. So, by looking at Maya gods we can see mirrored the character, mentality, and outlook of the Maya, which, I take it, is our enterprise. In their prayers, sacrifices, and other rites the Maya bared their souls to their gods; they bared them also to us if we have understanding. I have not slighted the reader's intelligence by constantly calling attention to this. Like the traveling salesman's new coat, not openly entered in his expense account, it is there all the same.

To say that there were two Maya religions—one of the ruling class, the other of the peasant—would be a gross exaggeration, but there were certainly very important differences in the attitudes and beliefs of the two groups which I try to emphasize. We have much information on those of the peasants because, to a considerable extent, they survived through the Colonial period and even to our day. In contrast, the beliefs and practices of the ruling class died when the ruling class ceased to think as Maya.

The Franciscans knew what they were about when they made themselves responsible for the education of the sons of the old nobility and priesthood; the ways and beliefs of the ancient regime became as irrelevant to a generation of mission-educated Maya as did precedence and ceremony at the court of George III to the westward-looking America of Andrew Jackson.

Consequently, information on the cults of the ruling class, notably those of Itzam Na, Kukulcan, and Venus deities, is scant. In reconstructing that of Itzam Na, I lay myself open to the charge of having built with too few factual bricks and laying them in a mortar perhaps dangerously diluted with the sand of speculation, particularly in suggesting that during the Classic period the worship of Itzam Na approached monotheism among the ruling class.

I take shelter in the obscurity surrounding an adequate definition of monotheism. The term, for instance, is applied to Christianity which, in fact, during most of its history has accepted a division of powers between God and Satan. Itzam Na seemingly shared powers with, or delegated them to, certain minor deities who were his underlings. Another difficulty is that, strictly speaking, Itzam Na is four beings in one, and those four are of reptilian, not human, nature. In using expressions such as "approach" monotheism, I am endeavoring not to equate the Itzam Na cult with true monotheism but to show that in my opinion (and, incidentally, that of Maya colonial writers who defined the period when it was dominant as one in which idolatry was unknown) the Maya ruling class had reached a stage closer to monotheism than to polytheism.

Let me confess here what will soon be obvious: I do not belong to the "Let the facts speak for themselves" school. In a book such as this there is not room for all the facts, let alone the hints and whispers of facts which outnumber certainties in most Maya sources. Having spent my working life trying to sort them out, I feel I should have a claim to pick for the reader the most pertinent. Prejudice may lead to a wrong deduction now and again, but such errors are better than bogging down in an unbounded welter of pros and cons. History without a little prejudice is dull as ditch-water; naturally, if you oversalt the dish you ruin it.

So far as my observation goes, mainly graduate students hew to the line of impartiality in historical studies. I suspect with their restricted and secondhand knowledge that is the only course open to them. Like soiled blue jeans, acne, and a taste for pizza, that attitude should be discarded with intellectual adulthood. Alas! Some never summon the courage to do so.

Perhaps in this matter of near monotheism I have been swayed by my affection for the Maya, but, there again, is monotheism naturally superior to polytheism? I have had the doubt in the back of my mind, so perhaps all I wanted was to be a shade sensational.

The final chapter gives us another insight into how the Maya thought; they tell of themselves as they tell of creation. Those myths also affirm the essential unity of Middle American culture. Such stories were—and still are—told around campfires and among men passing the night in vigil, segregated from their wives to ensure continence, before some agricultural rite. Many, no doubt, were spread by merchants from distant lands paying for hospitality with a story, as troubadours once sang for their suppers.

This book is a culling from the labors of many friends. Some, like Landa, Remesal, Ximénez, and Oviedo y Valdés, wrote in the sixteenth, seventeenth, and early eighteenth centuries; others, like Roys, Scholes, and La Farge, are among the giants of this century. All were filled with a compelling urge to record, to the best of their several abilities, what they knew of the Maya. A score of flames from midnight oil have burned to the spirit of research and have, I trust, illumined my desk as I have tried to guide my pen to follow the flowing lines they wrote. At times I have muttered at their failure to impart some vital fact within their knowledge, but, there, one may murmur a friendly grumble at friends even if they have departed this life three or four centuries ago. I like to think they have mellowed my thoughts and my pen. As T. S. Eliot put it, "The communication of the dead is tongued with fire beyond the language of the living."

A word about citations of sources: This book is directed to both *aficionados* and students; the former regard a surfeit of references as savoring of pedantry, whereas students already know the sources of many statements or can locate them in a well-annotated reference book such as A. M. Tozzer's edition of Landa. Having in mind an old friend and colleague who supplied the ghastly total of twenty-eight hundred footnotes to the first two volumes of a bulky report, I have tried to steer a middle course. Citations are confined to obscure sources, and in a few places where they come thick and fast they are grouped in a single footnote. Even so, since much of the material derives from out-of-the-way reports, citations are overly numerous. Samuel Johnson, writing on this very subject of footnotes, pithily remarked, "The mind is refrigerated by interruption."

I am very grateful to the Council of the Royal Anthropological Institute for gracious permission to reprint, as chapter 2, the Huxley Memorial Lecture, delivered in 1966 and published in the *Proceedings* of the Institute for that year. Minor changes have been made.

I am also indebted to my old friend and colleague Dr. Alberto Ruz L., director of the Seminario de Cultura Maya, National University of Mexico, for his kindness in permitting republication of the chapters on Maya trade and creation legends which appeared in *Estudios de Cultura Maya*, Vols. IV–VI, a much appreciated gesture.

Finally, I am under a deep obligation to J. P. Elsden, who, since retiring as headmaster of the Boys British School, Saffron Walden, seems to have divided his time between running the local golf club and drawing with infinite patience and care maps of the Maya area. He drew not only the maps for my *Maya Archaeologist* but also those illustrating chapter 2, "The Maya Central Area at the Spanish Conquest and Later: A Problem in Demography," and chapter 3, "The Eastern Boundary of the Maya Area: Placements and Displacements." They are a vital contribution to this book.

Ian Graham most generously found time to draw the map of the Spanish *entradas* for the conquest of what was later called Dolores before setting forth on one of his own annual *entradas* into the Maya rain forest. Still more, his drawing of a chief, found on an earlier *entrada*, breathes nobility and life into the title page.

J. ERIC S. THOMPSON

Harvard, Ashdon,
Saffron Walden,
Essex, England
March, 1969

Pronunciation
and
Place Names

Maya pronunciation of vowels is modeled on Spanish: *a*, between that of *cat* and *father*; *e*, clipped, between that in *bet* and *grey*; *i* as *ee* in *knee*; *o* as in *pomp*; *u* as *oo* in *good*, but as *w* before other vowels. Consonants are as in English except *c* is always hard, and *x* is pronounced as our *sh*. *K*, *p*, and *t*, when followed by an apostrophe, are ended by a quick closing of the glottis, which produces a short explosive sound something like the barked command of a top sergeant. The consonants *d*, *f*, *j*, *r*, and *v* are absent in Yucatec and most lowland Maya languages, but Chorti is distinguished from Chol(ti) by the substitution of *r* for *l* (*ti* is "mouth," hence "speech"; milpa is *chor* in Chorti, *chol* in Chol[ti], so both names mean "milpa makers' speech"), and highland Maya languages generally use *r* where lowlanders use *l*. Final *e* is pronounced in all Spanish and Maya words; *qu* has *k* sound in Spanish before *e* and *i*, and that applies to native place names such as Quirigua and Quezaltenango.

To avoid utter confusion, the spelling of Maya words in this book has been standardized; half a dozen linguistic alphabets have been converted to the accepted canons of Maya literature; *dz'*, *p'*, and *t'* replace reversed *c*, *th*, and *pp* of early writers.

Ix or *X* is the female gender prefix in Yucatec; an *sh* sound. This the Spaniards in the sixteenth and seventeenth centuries wrote as *ix*, having had difficulty in pronouncing a sibilant before a consonant, but later they tended to write it as a plain *x* prefixed to the word with which it belonged. Thus both *ix ku* and *xku* are correct ways of writing "goddess' in Maya, although the latter more closely produces the sound. The old spelling is retained only where it is well established in the literature, for example in the case of Ix Chel. This indicator of female gender is also prefixed to some names of insects, reptiles, and plants, more or less at hazard, it would appear, and without any reference to sex.

Ah or *H* is an aspirate which is the male prefix in Yucatec. This the Spaniards first wrote as *ah*, again having difficulty, this time with a prefixed aspirate, in coping with an unaccustomed sound. Later they wrote it as *h*, which is closer to the actual sound. The same problem arises; some terms—for example *ah kin*, "priest"—are too strongly established in the literature to be changed now. Thus *ah* and *h* occur together. This prefix also expresses ownership or close relationship, and then applies to both men and women; *zi*, "firewood," *ah zi*, "man who gets firewood"; *con*, "to sell," *ah con*, "seller"; but *zac*, "loom," *ah zacal*, "a woman who weaves"; *icham*, "husband," *ah icham*, "woman who has a husband."

Place names in Yucatan are nearly all Maya, whereas in the highlands of Guatemala and adjacent El Salvador they are mainly Nahuatl (Aztec and related tongues). The reason for the latter arrangement is that Alvarado conquered Guatemala with the help of Nahuatl-speaking Indians of Tlaxcala, Central Mexico. They passed on to the Spaniards the Nahuatl place names, not the Maya ones. Place names ending in *an*, *ango*, *co*, *pa*, or *te* are usually of Nahuatl derivation. Accents are confined in this book to Spanish personal and place names.

Examples:

Uxmal	Oosh'mal	Uaxactun	Wash-ac-toon'
Yaxchilan	Yash'cheelan'	Chichen Itza	Chee-chen' Ee-tza'
Pusilha	Poo'-seel-ha'	Tixchel	Tee-shchel'
Quirigua	Kee-ree-gwa'	Ahau	A-how'

peripheral group at the close of the Classic period into the former heartland of Maya culture is comparable to Macedonian aggrandizement at the expense of Classic Greece when the latter was past its cultural peak.

Now for detail.

THE HOME AND CULTURE OF THE PUTUN

Chontal (from the Nahuatl *chontalli*, "foreigner") designates three or perhaps four distinct linguistic groups, including the Maya of Tabasco, a source of much confusion (a recent survey of the physical characteristics of the Maya peoples included the Chontal of Oaxaca). Accordingly, I shall here refer to the Chontal Maya as Putun, the name which at least a part of this group applied to themselves. The sixteenth-century ethnologist and linguist Ciudad Real (1873, 2:393) writes that the Chontal Maya of Tixchel, formerly of Itzamkanac, spoke a language called *putunthan* (*than* means "language") or Chontal. Berendt (n.d.), following Galindo, confused the situation by applying *putun* both to the Chontal Maya of Tenosique, Zaquila, and other places, and to the Palencano Chol.

At the Spanish Conquest, Putun territory stretched from the Río Copilco, not far west of the great Maya site of Comalcalco, across the deltas of the Grijalva and Usumacinta, the Laguna de Términos and the Candelaria basin; and north along the coast almost to Champoton (Roys, 1957:167). Inland, Putun control reached at least as far as Tenosique, on the Usumacinta, and beyond Itzamkanac, on the Candelaria River, in southern Campeche (Scholes and Roys, 1948). A line drawn south from Itzamkanac would pass slightly east of Yaxchilan. Nahuat-speaking towns mingled with Putun in the Grijalva delta (Map 1). Nahuat is a dialect of Nahuatl (the latter spoken by the Aztec and their neighbors in Central Mexico) which uses *t* for Nahuatl *tl*. These Nahuat towns probably long antedate Toltec expansion, but may have facilitated it.

The Grijalva-Usumacinta delta is in large part low semiswamp, unsuited for cultivation and thinly populated; the raised banks

5

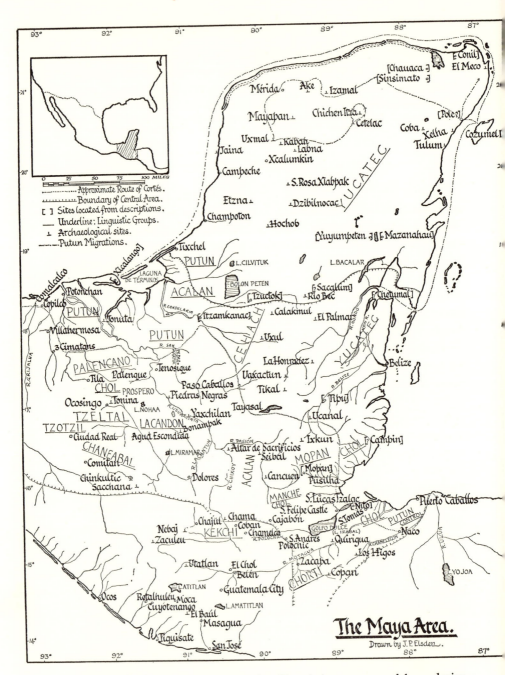

The Maya Area.

Drawn by J.P. Elsden.

Map 1.—The Maya Area. Showing linguistic groups and boundaries of the Central area, invasion routes of the Putun and Cortés, and locations of abandoned towns. (*Drawn by J. P. Elsden.*)

of streams support most of the dwellings. From an airplane, one views a vast green desolation broken by innumerable ponds, swamps, and sinuous, muddy streams which the almost imperceptible gradient does little to speed. In the rainy season floods are everywhere. It cost Cortés infinite labor to cross this area on his march to Honduras; the modern railway to Yucatan swings seventy miles inland to avoid it. The Candelaria basin is far less swampy.

The natural transport was and still is by water, and that was an important factor in the economic advance of the Putun. The Nahuatl traders from the Valley of Mexico were not sailors—that network of streams, swamps, and backwaters was navigable only by those who had mapped them in memory from childhood—and all the evidence indicates that at certain exchange points the Culhua-Mexica merchants handed over to the Putun their cargoes to be carried thence by water. There was a regular sea trade, controlled by the Putun, which circled the peninsula of Yucatan from the delta lands and the Laguna de Términos to the Sula Plain of Honduras, with numerous ports of call en route. The Putun were the Phoenicians of the New World.

Perhaps the chief Putun town was Potonchan (note *poton* [*u-o* interchange as in Toltec-Tultec, Olmec-Ulmec, Tochtlan-Tuxtla, and the like] and probably *chan*, "snake": "Putun snake?"), almost opposite Frontera (now Alvaro Obregón), at the mouth of the Grijalva (Scholes and Roys, 1948, Map 3). It was at Frontera that Cortés won a hard-fought battle, small quantities of gold, and his Indian mistress-interpreter Marina, whose knowledge of Putun and, through that, related lowland Maya tongues, as well as Nahuatl, was of stupendous value to Cortés.

Better known, thanks to the Paxbolon papers (Scholes and Roys, 1948) discovered by the senior author in Seville, is the Acalan branch of Putun. The capital of this Chontal-Maya group, as the authors term them, was Itzamkanac, which they show was on the present-day Candelaria River, known to the Nahuatl as the Acalan River. The Nahuatl similarly referred to the province and its capital as Acalan, "Place of Canoes," a reference to the livelihood of those indomitable traders. It is known that these Acalan Putun had a trading post at Nito, Guatemala, on the other side of the Yucatan Peninsula, just about where the present Livingston stands at the mouth of the Río Dulce. Here, Cortés wrote (Mac-Nutt, 1908, 2:264), the Acalan Putun occupied a whole quarter of the city with the brother of the ruler of Itzamkanac as a sort of viceroy.

Itzamkanac was too far up the Candelaria to have served as a convenient port for transshipment, and for that reason it is not unlikely that the great port of Xicalango, on the point of land enclosing the western arm of Laguna de Términos, was controlled from Itzamkanac, as was, without much doubt, the bay itself. There was a Nahuatl colony at Xicalango, but I think it comprised only those engaged in buying and selling and such activities as preparing through bills of lading for the Yucatan-Honduras sea route.

Potonchan, in contrast, probably controlled the Usumacinta trade; the Nahuat-speaking Cimatan towns perhaps traded with the Zoque and the inhabitants of the highlands of Chiapas.

The Putun language is quite close to the Chol dialect spoken around Palenque; it differs from Yucatec perhaps a little less than Portuguese from Spanish (the Spaniard Aguilar, several years captive in Yucatan, transmitted in Yucatec Cortés' orders to Putun-speaking Marina, who, in turn, translated them into Nahuatl). The fact that one of Putun speech could make himself understood from the mouth of the Usumacinta to the mouth of the Chamelecon because of the minor linguistic changes gave the Putun merchants a second great advantage over their Culhua-Mexica rivals—the first advantage, their seamanship, has been mentioned.

Personal names indicate a strong intermingling with a people of Nahuat speech, some of whom pretty clearly formed ruling dynasties among the Putun. No less than eleven of fourteen known Putun personal names from the Chontalpa (i.e., the area of the deltas) appear to be of Nahuat origin, and these include six day names of the Nahuat calendar, but without the essential numbers (Scholes and Roys, 1948:61–64). Among the Acalan Putun, Scholes and Roys estimate that about one-third of the personal names may be of Nahuat derivation, and these include Nahuat day names, again without the essential attached coefficient. In one instance, there is a Maya calendar name together with a numerical coefficient, Bolon Lamat, but one suspects for this solitary case some different ancestry.

As for Potonchan, Scholes and Roys (1948:37), in a fine feat of detection, established that two decades after the Conquest the ruler was Francisco Zipaque, who had succeeded Hernando Azbaque. This, they convincingly showed, was a corruption of Acipac, which with locative affixes, Putun *ta* and Nahuatl *co*, reappears as the geographical entity Tabasco.

Cipaque, which seems, then, to have been the family name of the Potonchan dynasty, is surely the Nahuatl day name Cipactli, first of the twenty days. This acquires greater importance for, as we shall see, Cipactli signs with coefficients appear almost surely as name glyphs of foreign intruders at Seibal (p. 41). This is reminiscent of the claims of a Nonoualco ancestry by groups in Yucatan, including the Xiu.

The little information on Putun political organization comes again from the Acalan branch (Scholes and Roys, 1948:54, 78–87). Succession in the ruling group was from father to son or to a younger brother of the deceased presumably when the son was too young. That younger son then succeeded his uncle, thereby restoring the principle of primogeniture. Itzamkanac was divided into four quarters, a device found in many parts of Middle America. It may have been of Mexican origin, but the terms to describe it, *tzuc* or *tzucul* with relationship suffix *-ul*, are Maya; they are used to name the four divisions of the invading Itza in the Chilam Balam of Chumayel (Roys, 1933:139). The first Acalan Putun were led by four chiefs under a fifth, Auxaual, who settled in the Tenosique region.

Material on Putun religion is scant. Except for Kukulchan (the Kukulcan of Yucatan: Putun *ch* corresponds to Yucatec *c*), the few deities mentioned are Maya, among them being Ikchaua, the great merchant god, whose cult was spread (by the Putun?) over much of the Maya area, and Ix Chel, the moon goddess and patroness of medicine, weaving, and childbirth, whose cult was also widespread.

Few Putun-speaking villages now remain, and little is known of their aboriginal culture. Blom and La Farge (1926–27:141–45,

9

465–78, 487–502) give a few ethnological notes and linguistic material on a village near Macuspana where the Putun dialect is called Yocotan; two or three myths have been recorded; and that genial former buccaneer, Dampier, who spent some time logging in their territory, adds scanty ethnological details.

THE PUTUN ITZA IN YUCATAN

In recent years there has been fairly wide acceptance for placing the start of Mexican influences at Chichen Itza at 10.8.0.0.0, Katun 4 Ahau (A.D. 968–87 in the Goodman-Martínez-Thompson correlation, in which all dates are given unless otherwise stated) partly because that is the first occurrence of a katun 4 Ahau, traditionally associated with Kukulcan's arrival, after the last surely dated monument of the Classic period which records a date 10.2.9.1.9 falling in a tun 10 of a katun (10.3.0.0.0) 1 Ahau (Roys, 1933:204; Thompson, 1937:190; Morley, 1946:87; etc.). On the other hand, Andrews (1965:313) has Toltec influence at Chichen Itza "somewhere in the period A.D. 900–1100," corresponding to approximately 10.17.0.0.0 to 11.7.0.0.0 in the Spinden correlation which he now prefers, or 10.3.10.0.0 to 10.13.10.0.0 in the Goodman-Martínez-Thompson.

Opinion now favors an earlier appearance of marked foreign influence in Yucatan in general and Chichen Itza in particular (e.g., Proskouriakoff, 1951). Mexican influences intrude at Uxmal and other Puuc sites, notably Kabah, which most students accept as Late Classic period with perhaps a continuance a few decades after 10.4.0.0.0. A recently announced Carbon–14 date of A.D. 870±100 for wood associated with Mexican-type vessels of Tlaloc and Xipe in the Balankanche caves near Chichen Itza (Andrews, 1965:313) is best explained by Mexican groups there before 10.8.0.0.0.

The dating problem and a sharpened interest in the Acalan Putun following publication of the magnificent Scholes and Roys study (1948) of that region led me to look with increasing favor on an idea with which I have long toyed, namely that Itza were of Putun or, as I then called them, Chontal-Maya stock (Thompson, 1945:12; 1954:99–100). Still later this idea was considerably expanded (Thompson, 1966:119, 128). The time has come to detail the facts and interpretations on which this reconstruction of history was based. In brief, the ideas now advanced are these:

1. Two foreign groups established themselves at Chichen Itza. First came the Itza, perhaps in A.D. 918. They were followed by Kukulcan and his retinue about A.D. 980. Landa, it will be recalled, wrote that his informants were uncertain whether Kukulcan came before, after, or at the same time as the Itza.

2. The Itza reached Chichen Itza from Cozumel, and the invasion route, starting at Polé, port for Cozumel, given in the Chilam Balam of Chumayel, refers to that invasion of A.D. 918 (Map 1).

3. The Itza are identified as Putun (Chontal Maya) by the names applied to them, Putun and Ah Nun, and because they are closely associated with Chakanputun, "Savannah of the Putun," seemingly their homeland. Furthermore, an invasion by sea, as indicated by the starting point and by murals at Chichen Itza, agrees with the historical role of the Putun as seafarers.

4. Such a reconstruction of Itza arriving via Polé, on the east coast, and Kukulcan from the west, as Landa recounts, is in agreement with the tradition of the big and little descents, as mentioned by Lizana (1893:3–4). It will be recalled that the tradition tells of a large-scale invasion from the east, a smaller one from the west.

The story of the arrival of the Itza at Chichen Itza after long wanderings in Yucatan is given in the Chilam Balam of Chumayel (Roys, 1933:70–73). The point of departure is not named, but the first place reached was Polé, on the northeast coast, and as that was the port through which traffic to and from Cozumel passed, it is a reasonable conjecture that Cozumel was the point of departure. In any case, the invaders came by sea and therefore must have been seafarers. After a great westerly sweep over northern Yucatan, the migration ends at Cetelac, about thirteen miles south of Chichen Itza, which Roys (letter of 1954) thought to have been the western terminus of the Coba causeway. He felt reasonably confident that the town of Yaxuna was founded after A.D. 1790 and on the (disputed) border of the southern Cupul with Sotuta (Roys, 1957:126), which may be significant.

This is followed by what Roys judged to be another migration, but the point of departure is close to Cetelac, and I am inclined to look at it perhaps as a branching off of one or more of the Itza divisions. The migration seems to end at Tizip (unlocated), the next stop after Dz'oyola, close to Ichcanziho (Mérida). There follow references to an assembly at Ichcanziho and to other places, after which the story switches to Chichen Itza, the assembling of the tribute at Cetelac, and the beginning of the rule of the chiefs— presumably the Itza, although not specified—events assigned to both Katun 11 Ahau and Katun 13 Ahau. The building of the house of the ruler "on high" and the construction of the stairway (*u pakal yebal*, "the cementing together of the stairway," which implies that the staircase was of stone) refer, I am inclined to believe, to the building of the inner Castillo at Chichen Itza. References to Hunac Ceel in this context are, I believe, anachronistic.

The well-known Valladolid lawsuit of 1618 (Brinton, 1882: 114–18) throws light on the above Itza migration. One witness testified concerning a group which had come from the kingdom of Mexico. Some established themselves at Chichen Itza, where they built the very sumptuous buildings; others went south and established themselves at Bacalar (Bakhalal); and still others, whose leader was Cacalpuc (Zacalpuc), went to settle in the coastal region to the north. It fell to a certain Cupul to settle at Chichen Itza, and all obeyed him as lord. Those of the island of Cozumel were his subjects also.

A second witness almost repeats the above testimony save that he states that the invaders were led by four members of the same family: one settled at Chichen Itza, another at Bakhalal, the third on the north coast, and the fourth on Cozumel. All brought settlers with them and were lords for many years. One of them, called Tan-u-pol Chicbul, "He with a *Ch'icbul* ['groove-tailed *ani* bird,' according to Roys] on the Front of his Head," was supposed to be related to Moctezuma. This description reminds one of the "Mexican" warriors on reliefs and paintings at Chichen Itza whose badge is a bird set head down on the front of the headdress.

The starting point of these invaders is given as the kingdom of Mexico, a wide term referable to any part of Mexico outside

12

Yucatan and Campeche, and which might well signify the Chontalpa of Tabasco.

Landa (Pérez Martínez, 1938:216) has what seems to be a variant of the above: Three brothers came to Chichen Itza from the west (*sic*) and gathered there a great settlement of peoples and races, whom they ruled for some years in great peace and justice. They were devoted to their god and erected many attractive buildings, including the largest there, of which Landa gives a sketch from which, with his description, it is quite clear that he refers to the later Castillo. They came without women. The Indians said that one later left the land by way of Bakhalal. Those who ruled afterward became so one-sided in their tyrannical, dissolute, and unrestrained conduct that the people put them to death and abandoned the site.

There is historical evidence that Cozumel and Bakhalal, mentioned in the above stories as strongholds of the Itza, in fact were under Putun Acalan dominance. In the Paxbolon papers (Scholes and Roys, 1948:383) it is recorded that the ancestors of the rulers of Itzamkanac had come from Cozumel. The leader was Auxaual, and he was accompanied by four chiefs. Furthermore, Ix Chel was the chief deity of Cozumel and one of the most important of the Putun. Bakhalal—there is little reason to identify this ancient territorial designation with the present town founded by the Spaniards—was, I think, part of Chetumal province and an important trading center which also appears to have come under Acalan-Putun control, for it paid tribute at one time to the ruler of Itzamkanac (Scholes and Roys, 1948:385).

The story of the Itza conquest of Chichen Itza is in a song in the Chilam Balam of Chumayel (Roys, 1933:114–16). Two details of this lament are of outstanding interest. First, in an obscure sentence there is a reference to the Putun. Roys translates this, "Who am I among the people of Putun?" the context implying that the Putun were the conquerers of Chichen Itza.

More important, the date of the conquest of Chichen Itza is given as 1 Imix on which the ruler was seized, and 2 Akbal 1 Yaxkin when they, "our enemies," surely the Itza, came. The date 2 Akbal 1 Yaxkin occurs every fifty-two years. Its first oc-

13

currence after the last lintel of the Classic period was carved was 10.4.9.7.3, 2 Akbal 1 Yaxkin, April 26, A.D. 918; the next occurrence of the date would fall in A.D. 970.

The earlier reading is preferable if the gap at the end of the Classic period is to be closed. It also finds some support in the fact that the date falls in a tun 11 Ahau associated with the Itza migration. There is also a statement that the tribute which was introduced by the Itza at Chichen Itza was handled in Katun 11 Ahau. There is a good possibility that through an error of the colonial scribe 11 Ahau was identified as a katun date instead of a tun date. That the two accounts, the migration and the song, refer to the same invasion is clear from the fact that Mizcit Ahau is referred to as the leader in the song, "We were [as] tame animals [to] Mizcit Ahau," and the only person named in the account; and in the Itza migration is prominent among a number of people: "The sweeper who swept the lands was Mizcit Ahau." This is a pun, for *miz* is "to sweep," although Mizcit is almost surely a Nahuat name, probably referable to the mesquite bush. In a parallel passage (Roys, 1933:65), Mizcit Ahau swept the leagues (of the roads) at Uuc-hab-nal, which, as Roys has suggested, is in all probability an old name for Chichen Itza. Again the event was placed in a katun 11 Ahau (error for Tun 11 Ahau?).

The alternative position, 10.7.2.2.3, 2 Akbal 1 Yaxkin, A.D. 970, does fall in a katun 4 Ahau, the katun associated with Kukulcan, but there is no mention of Kukulcan in the sources discussed above, nor of 4 Ahau either. Moreover, we are working on the hypothesis that the Itza came before Kukulcan. It must be emphasized that these historical narrations are badly garbled—for instance, Ah Mex Cuc, probably ruler of Chichen Itza some three centuries later, appears in the story and is associated with what may be the history of the construction of the Castillo.

Some reasons for identifying the Itza with the Putun have been mentioned above; these, together with others not discussed, are:

1. The Itza migration opens with the arrival of the invaders at Polé, terminus of the cross-channel route from Cozumel. The point of departure is not given here or in the description of the second leg or divergence of the migration, but one may assume that it was Cozumel, known to have been at one time under Putun

control and from which the Putun migrated to re-establish control in Tabasco (Scholes and Roys, 1948:383). Pilgrims came to the shrine of Cozumel dedicated to Ix Chel, a goddess shared by Putun and Yucatec Maya, from Tabasco, Xicalango, and Campeche (*Relaciones de Yucatán*, 2:54). In fact, as Roys has suggested, these were probably for the most part merchants who combined trading with pilgrimage, as is still the practice in Mexico and Guatemala. From their points of departure one may conclude that they were in large part Putun, whose maritime commerce en route from Tabasco to the Bay of Honduras doubtlessly served Cozumel, an important distributing center for the salt from the beds to the north. Clearly, Cozumel was very closely linked to the Putun on the opposite side of the peninsula.

2. Murals on the walls of the Temple of the Warriors, Chichen Itza (Morris, Charlot, and Morris, 1931, Plates 139, 146–49, and 159), and scenes on gold disks recovered from the cenote show that the invaders came by sea. Varieties of fish are clearly marine, not freshwater, species. Furthermore, there are no large bodies of water in northwestern Yucatan. As we have seen, the Putun were the seafarers of the Caribbean shores of the Maya area. It is a fair conclusion that these murals represent sea traffic and coastal raids by the Putun if the Itza are correctly identified as Putun (Plate 3*a*).

3. The invaders are specifically named Putun in the song of the seizure of Chichen Itza already cited (Roys, 1933:115).

4. Chakanputun is very closely associated with the Itza. They came from there and they returned thither. Chakanputun has been identified with Champoton, on the coast south of Campeche, but the identification has been challenged, and to me seems improbable. Chakanputun signifies Putun province (cf. *holchakan*, "boundary of province") or Putun savannah. That is, the Putun invaders came from the province of Putun or, less probably, the savannah of the Putun. Chanputun, the old form of Champoton, was translated "stinking place," an identification Roys (1957:167) doubted. *Chan* in Putun and allied languages means "snake," whereas *chaan* is "sky." Potonchan, the great Putun capital at the mouth of the Grijalva, is merely Chanputun (Champoton) reversed, for *o* and *u* were often interchanged when native words

were hispanicized. The fact that the Itza came from the province of Putun is excellent confirmatory evidence that they were Putun. Bakhalal, another place closely associated with the Itza, was on the borders of, or inside, the province of Chetumal (Chactemal) which at one time paid tribute to the Putun of Itzamkanac, and in that neighborhood a dialect similar to that of Campeche was spoken (Ciudad Real, 1873, 2:468). Putun settlement there, in accordance with the Valladolid lawsuit, would explain this.

5. The Itza are frequently termed *ah nunob*, "those who do not know the language of the land, stammerers or stutterers." There is also a Putun word *num*, "to pass from place to place," with *nunum*, "a vagabond, one without fixed abode," its Yucatec equivalent. Both meanings would apply to the Putun. As the term was, I believe, never used for the Spaniards, who were called *dz'ulob*, the distinction probably indicates that *nun* referred to a speaker of an allied language, applicable to Putun which was quite close to Yucatec. As to the alternative meaning, the Putun, like the fairies in *Iolanthe*, were forever "tripping hither, tripping thither; nobody knows why or whither."

An alternative and speculative explanation would connect the word with Nonoualco, the Nahuatl name for the Chontalpa. Charles Dibble calls my attention to Garibay's (1958:120) derivation of this from Nahuatl with the meaning "in the inhabited place." It is a strange coincidence, if no more, in view of the common interchange of *u* and *o* (*tulteca, tolteca; ulmeca, olmeca*; etc.), that the *Ah nun* may have come from Nonoualco. In any case, the term indicates that the Itza did not speak Yucatec, but what was probably a closely allied tongue.

6. Ralph Roys called my attention many years ago to a very important point: the Yucatec Maya placed the title *ahau* before a chief's name, as Ahau Cocom, Ahau Pech, and so on, whereas the Acalan Putun, as the Paxbolon documents made clear, placed *ahau* after the chief's name, for example, Palocem Ahau and Mututzin Ahau. In the song of the conquest of Chichen Itza by the Putun, so named, the leader of the invaders was called Mizcit Ahau, and this title is repeated in the account of the migration which terminated in the seizure of Chichen Itza by the Itza (Roys, 1933:74). Hunac Ceel, never regarded as a true native son of

Yucatan, has *ahau* after his name in the prologue to the above-mentioned song (C. B. Chumayel MS:58) although, in fact, he almost certainly lived long after that event. This postpositioning of *ahau* is further evidence that the Itza were Putun or of some related southern group.

7. A peaceful scene in a mural of the Temple of the Warriors shows warriors in canoes passing a shore village. The huts have their single doorways not in the center of the façade, as is the universal custom in Yucatan, but at the side (Plate 3*a*). It is true that much of the mural has been reconstructed, but the colors on the surviving fragmentary pictures of huts strongly support the reconstruction, which is less obvious from the black and white sketches. This type of hut appears to be similar to an illustration of one from Naranjal, on the upper Candelaria, said to be typical of Candelaria settlements (Andrews, 1943, Fig. 25*b*). It will be recalled that Naranjal is only a few miles upstream from the supposed site of Itzamkanac, capital of the Acalan Putun.

However, the huts of the Warriors mural may have the doorway recessed so that one corner of the façade forms a sort of porch or veranda sheltered by the thatch of the main roof. I saw huts of that kind with an inset corner porch with the doorway in its back some three decades ago in the Tzeltal village of Amatenango. The type is unusual.

Wauchope (1938, Figs. 13, 36) illustrates examples at San Lucas Tolimán and Cuilapa, Santa Rosa, both in the Guatemalan highlands. Of particular interest to our discussion is a plan given by Andrews (1943, Fig. 5*b*) of a house site, presumably pre-Columbian, having a similar inset porch at the corner of the front with a doorway in its rear leading into the main room. This is at Las Ruinas, a few miles northwest of Cilvituk, which may have been within Acalan-Putun territory; at least, it can not have been far outside. Wauchope, in correspondence, calls my attention to a house site at Chichen Itza (*op. cit.*, Fig. 51, *3*) which might conceivably fall in this same category, but it is hard to decide the point; I am inclined to think it is not the same.

All in all, this mural appears to show Putun warriors voyaging by a coastal village which, from the type of hut, was probably Putun or inhabited by some other group on the Campeche-Tabasco coast. Perhaps the scene represents the departure of the Putun warriors on their long voyage which was to end with the conquest of Chichen Itza and other places in Yucatan.

The same type of hut with a door or porch and door at one corner occurs in the mural which once covered the south half of the west wall of the Temple of the Jaguars and Shields. This was copied by T. Maler (Willard, 1926: opp. 216; and reproduced in Tozzer, 1957, Fig 60) and Adela Breton (facsimiles in Bristol City Museum and Peabody Museum, Harvard University). Individual figures appear in Seler (1902–23,5:337–42). The mural—or rather the whole save a strip at the bottom—represents an attack on a village.

The attackers have certain "Toltec" features—notably, back shields or mirrors, knee and ankle fur bands, and, in some instances, "Toltec" headdresses—but some have feathers projecting from the small of the back, a feature usually regarded as Maya. The two chiefs (Seler, *op. cit.*:338–39) have huge feathered serpents entwined around them in typical "Toltec" presentation, and one has the blue bird insigne set in the front of his turquoise headdress. Both carry round shields, a somewhat rare element of "Toltec" costume. One is decorated with fourteen circles, and the other with eleven squat crescents. Shields of this type adorn the façade of the Temple of the Jaguars and Shields, and a similar shield is carried by the "Toltec" warrior of Gold Disk F from the cenote. Moreover, one of the chiefs has the feather decoration projecting from the small of his back.

Without going into further detail, it is clear that the attackers are dressed as "Toltec" of an aberrant type so far as Chichen Itza is concerned.

The defenders of the village, on the contrary, are birds of another feather. In contrast to the Yucatec Maya, they use spear-throwers and darts. They wear spherical turbans, generally white, which reminded Seler of headdresses of figurines from Jonuta and Campeche. From these rise two blue feathers. The warriors wear white tunicles, and, for the most part, do not have the "fur" bands at knee and ankle which distinguish "Toltec" warriors. Their legs and feet are bare or they may wear white sandals. They brandish round shields with a crescentic device, but both the colors and the fact that there is a single crescent are in contrast to the attackers' shields. Some wear the feather projection in the small of the back.

The extraordinary feature about the defenders is that the leaders and some of the rank and file carry back banners *(pamitl)* such as distinguished Mexican warriors wore (cf. Seler, *op. cit.*, 2:568–71). So far as I know, no such back banners have been reported elsewhere from the Maya area. The defenders, clearly, are neither Yucatec Maya nor "Toltec," but some other group which was Mexican speaking or highly Mexicanized in view of the back standards.

One can only conclude that the mural commemorated an attack by Putun Itza nowhere in the vicinity of Chichen Itza, but probably in Tabasco, where Putun, Zoque, and Mexican-speaking groups lived alongside one another. I think the ethnic identifications on the murals and reliefs of Chichen Itza have been over-simplified; there are surely more than two and may be as many as five groups involved.

The beehive huts at the base of this mural also point to activities outside the Yucatan Peninsula, where round huts are unreported (Wauchope [1938:234] notes that Lundell's round foundations at Chakantun, between Tayasal and the Pasión, are, in fact, apsidal or dumb-bell shaped), although round temples, probably reflecting specific cults, have a sporadic distribution.

The huts of the Huaxteca are round (Schuller, 1924:143), and du Solier (1945) notes a very high proportion of round ceremonial substructures which would indicate that the round hut was probably a pre-Columbian feature of Huaxtec life. However, there now is and almost certainly was in post-Classic times a huge gap between the two branches of the Maya family. Unfortunately, we know almost nothing of ancient house types at the bottom of the Gulf of Mexico. Whatever the answer may be to this problem, the village at the top of the mural is not Yucatec, but the huts with the door or perhaps porch at the side seem to indicate their inhabitants lived in the crescent from Campeche to the Coatzacoalcos River.

One may well ask why scenes possibly representing battles in the southwest of the Maya area should be shown on frescoes at

Chichen Itza. The answer, I think, is that the Putun controlled a huge area, probably with two or more capitals—one in Chakan-putun, a second in Chichen Itza, and perhaps a third at Potonchan or some other center in the heart of the Chontalpa. It would be a situation somewhat comparable to the Roman Empire with capitals in Rome and Constantinople, each, in turn, dominant. The Maya chronicles make it abundantly clear that the Itza, when they conquered Chichen Itza and settled in Cozumel and probably the Chetumal-Bakhalal area, did not relinquish control of their old territory; there were constant journeyings to and from Chakan-putun (Putun province and perhaps the name of the capital as well). Even Nonoualco may have been partly under their control. Thus, a mural of a victory in Tabasco might well adorn a building at Chichen Itza, a regional capital. This large strip of Putun territory, as we shall see, made easy the arrival of Kukulcan and Toltec influences in north central Yucatan after the Itza had gained control of Chichen Itza. On leaving "Mexico," he and his followers entered Putun territory; Xicalango was probably the gateway through which Mexican influences reached Yucatan at least as early as the tenth century. He was not entering *terra incognita*; trade, travelers, and individuals almost surely had followed that route long before Kukulcan set forth on his travels.

8. In the Books of Chilam Balam, the Itza are continually reproved for their erotic practices in terms such as "the unrestrained lewd ones" and "The foreigners . . . brought shameful things when they came. They lost their innocence in carnal sin . . . of Nacxit Xuchit, in the carnal sin of his companions." There is evidence of what appear to be erotic practices in the Mexican period at Chichen Itza (phallic cult in Yucatan appears to be a somewhat earlier introduction, p. 319). In the late Mexican structure 5C3, the Temple of the Little Heads (Vaillant, 1933; Ruppert, 1952, Fig. 145), the loin cloths of the two large Atlantean figures which once supported the inner soffits of the vaults are deliberately set to one side so as to expose the genitals. Again, on the pilasters of the doorway of the Mercado, leading from the gallery to the patio and focus of all attention, are richly clad persons, but bereft of loin cloth; the contrast of lavish headdresses, necklaces, anklets, and the like with the exposed genitals is obviously deliberate (Ruppert,

1943, Figs. 19, 20). In both buildings these erotic sculptures mark the entrance to an inner room. I think representations of prisoners can be eliminated since nowhere are there bound limbs and two of the Mercado men are armed. If these sculptures do not serve to humiliate enemies, they can only depict the preliminaries of erotic rites such as the Yucatec Maya so deplored among their Itza conquerors.

Apart from phallicism, a very different matter, one of the few reports of eroticism comes from Laguna de Términos, in Putun territory. On the Grijalva expedition, among pottery idols (effigy incense burners?) and braziers found on what is now Isla Carmen, were two wooden figures, one representing two men engaged in sodomy, the other a man holding his genitals in both hands (Oviedo y Valdés, 1851–55, bk. 17, ch. 17). Díaz del Castillo locates these pieces in Cabo Catoche, but it is doubtful that he was an eyewitness, whereas Oviedo y Valdés' informant appears to have been quoting from a diary. The peoples of coastal Vera Cruz had an evil reputation for homosexuality, whereas an erotic figurine from near Alvarado (Bartres, 1908, Plate 48) illustrates what the Maya said of the Itza: "They twist their necks, they twist their mouths, they close their eyes, they slaver at the mouth." The Putun may have adopted such practices from neighbors to the northwest. However, the argument here advanced is far less weighty than points 1 through 7.

9. A point to bear in mind, although it is hard to assess its cogency, is that Itzamkanac, the capital of the Acalan Putun at the time of the Spanish Conquest, incorporates the term Itzam, which is very close to Itza. Itzam is part of the names of more than one Yucatec god (Itzam Na, Itzam Kauil, Itzam Cab Ain). *Itzam* is given as meaning "lizard" in the Vienna dictionary; according to Martínez Hernández (1912:170) the term is—or rather was when he wrote—still applied by old fishermen to the whale. Among the Lacandon, Itzam Noh Ku, "Itzam the Great God," is god of hail, lord of Lake Pelha in which he dwells, and, according to a recent source, lord of crocodiles (Bruce, 1967). Itzam is a Pokom deity (Miles, 1957:748) and, among the Kekchi of the Alta Verapaz and southern British Honduras who claim him as both male and female, he is a world directional mountain deity (Thompson,

1930:58–59). This wide distribution of Itzam as the name of a deity blunts the edge of the above argument.

KUKULCAN AND TOLTEC INFLUENCES AT CHICHEN ITZA

Accepting on the strength of the above arguments that the Itza were Putun (Chontal Maya) and that they invaded Yucatan via Polé and seized Chichen Itza in A.D. 918 (10.4.9.7.3, 2 Akbal 1 Yaxkin), the apparently quite separate problem of dating the influx of Tula influences linked to the actual or mythical arrival of Kukulcan remains.

The scheme combining Toltec and Yucatec traditions advanced nearly three decades ago (Thompson, 1941:102–103) seems still to cover the situation. According to Mexican tradition, notably the *Anales de Cuauhtitlan* (Chimalpopoca, 1945:11), Quetzalcoatl reached the Gulf coast, became Venus, and died when the planet arose at heliacal rising four days after inferior conjunction in a year 1 Acatl. This series of mythical events is thought to cover Quetzalcoatl's visit to Yucatan, but it is rather generally agreed that these occurrences must be moved forward two calendar rounds of fifty-two years each from the position assigned them in the *Anales de Cuauhtitlan*, namely to A.D. 987, if the records are referable to the Mixtec system, to A.D. 999 according to the Mexican system (Jiménez Moreno, 1952:224).

The historical material in the katun prophecies in the Books of Chilam Balam is more reliable than the chronicles which may well have been compiled from various sources in the eighteenth century. Katun 4 Ahau of the second series of katun prophecies (Roys, 1933:161) is devoted to the coming of Kukulcan, alias Quetzalcoatl (what had happened in the past was expected to happen when a katun of the same name came to power), and of the Itza:

> Katun 4 Ahau ... is established at Chichen Itza. The settlement of the Itza shall take place. The quetzal [symbol of Kukulcan] shall come, the green bird shall come ... Kukulcan shall come with them for the second time. The word of God; the Itza shall come.

However, Katun 4 Ahau of the first series makes no direct men-

22

tion of the Itza or of Kukulcan, but "there shall arrive the quetzal" and "there shall arrive Christ." The quetzal, of course, was intimately associated with Kukulcan; whether the Maya came to confuse Christ with Quetzalcoatl because both were expected to return to reign over the people is open to argument. Leaving that matter unsettled, we may note that in the second Chronicle of the Chilam Balam of Chumayel, which Roys (1933:139n.) remarks is in fact a song or chant rather than a chronological record, Katun 4 Ahau is the katun of the discovery of Chichen Itza and of both the great and little descents by implication. We are informed that they came in four divisions, and that they were called Itza when they settled at Chichen Itza. The four (possibly five) places from which the four divisions set forth are named and are assigned to world directions. One, that to the west, is called Holtun Zuiua. *Holtun* appears to be a Putun word signifying "harbor" (Scholes and Roys, 1948:81), and Holtun was the Putun name for Puerto Escondido, on the northern arm enclosing Laguna de Términos. *Zuiua* is a term, apparently Nahuatl, very closely associated with the Mexican or Mexicanized invaders who claimed Toltec descent. Holtun Zuiua, therefore, suggests a port in Chontalpa, where Mexican (Toltec) and Putun cultures met. There is mention of a Holtun Itza on the east coast, seemingly in the Bakhalal-Chetumal region (Roys, 133:146n.), where, as we have seen, Putun influences were fully developed. One of the other points of departure was Canhek Uitz, Bolonte Uitz, "Four-peaked Hill, Nine Hills." In a fresco on the east wall of the Temple of the Jaguars and Shields (Willard, 1926:221), warriors are seen scrambling up and down forest-clad peaks. On the design shown there are four peaks; if this was the total number the scene might represent the point of departure, Canhek Uitz, with which Bolonte Uitz, "Nine Hills," is associated. Their direction was the south. As Roys has noted, there is a site called Nueve Cerros on the Chixoy River, a famed center for salt working, probably once in Putun control. (p.291).

The chronicles have nothing to say of the arrival of Kukulcan, but from the other sources quoted we saw that he was believed to have come in a katun 4 Ahau and, according to the Mixteca system (adjusted by an agreed addition of 2x52 years), to have reached the Gulf Coast in A.D. 987. In fact, a katun 4 Ahau ended in November, 987.

If Kukulcan came to Putun territory at the bottom of the Gulf of Mexico, perhaps to Chakanputun itself (he is said to have left by Chanputun), and was well received by the already strongly Mexicanized Putun, the difficult problem of how he reached Chichen Itza—for surely he did not wander forth into the unknown with only a small band of followers—is more easily explained. It then became merely a matter of moving from one province of the Putun "Empire" to another.

I would suggest that Kukulcan was accompanied to Chichen Itza in Katun 4 Ahau by a second group of Putun Itza, more strongly influenced by Tula than the Putun Itza invaders of A.D. 918 (in Tun 10 of Katun 10 Ahau). Possibly the doubts Landa reported regarding whether the Itza conquered Chichen Itza with Kukulcan or before or after his arrival arose from two groups of Itza having come, one before and one with Kukulcan. After all, those events were six centuries in the past when Landa gathered his information. I would further suggest that the first Putun Itza erected the inner Castillo at Chichen Itza which is entirely free of feathered-serpent decoration, whereas the overwhelming Tula influences were introduced by Kukulcan and the second lot of Putun Itza. The first Putun Itza, invading from Polé, were credited with "many sumptuous buildings"; the second lot probably built the outer Castillo.

One final point: the Itza arrival is tied to Katun 8 Ahau, and that of Kukulcan to Katun 4 Ahau. In fact, if our reconstruction of the date of the first invasion is correct (10.4.9.7.3, 2 Akbal 1 Yaxkin), that took place in Tun 10 of the preceding Katun 10 Ahau. The explanation may lie in the fact that the incoming katun took office halfway through the previous katun, so Katun 8 Ahau would have entered slightly over two hundred days after the above date. The ceremonial installation (date chosen by divination?) of their ruler—Mizcit Ahau (?)—may have been some time later, after Katun 8 Ahau assumed power. Katun 8 Ahau was *the* katun of warfare, conquest, and change: in the next Katun 8 Ahau Hunac Ceel seized Chichen Itza and drove out the Itza, and, we are told, "for thirteen folds of katuns they had dwelled there."

The following Katun 8 Ahau witnessed the destruction and abandonment of Mayapan. It is possible that later writers of prophecies, taking a sacerdotal license, shifted the Itza conquest those few years to have it fall in Katun 8 Ahau, traditional katun of conquest, and also to bring the event into agreement with the tradition that the Itza occupation of Chichen Itza which ended in Katun 8 Ahau had lasted thirteen katuns. The magic of numbers probably meant more to them than pinpointing historical events.

PUTUN INCURSIONS INTO THE UPPER USUMACINTA AND PASIÓN DRAINAGES

In the second half of this chapter reasons are given for attributing to the Putun the strong foreign influences long recognized as marking the closing phases of certain Classic Maya sites in the Pasión drainage, notably Seibal and Altar de Sacrificios.

The main arguments for this thesis are these:

1. The Putun were long established in the estuaries of the Usumacinta and Grijalva rivers, and on geographical grounds were well situated for wielding such influences.

2. Putun groups were established some distance up the Usumacinta River in the fifteenth century, and there is little reason to suppose they were not there considerably earlier.

3. The Putun were traders and at the same time expansionists who thrust into many other parts of the Maya area at the close or shortly after the end of the Classic period. It is accordingly logical that they should have penetrated into the even more accessible upper Usumacinta and Pasión valleys.

4. The Putun had intermarried with Mexicans, had absorbed much Mexican culture, and were immediate neighbors of Mexican-speaking groups and therefore qualify as transmitters of Mexican influences to those areas.

5. Two Cipacti glyphs, possibly or even probably name glyphs, are inscribed on Stela 3, Seibal. Cipacti was the name of the ruling Putun family at Potonchan.

6. Sculptural details at Seibal and sites to the north are strongly reminiscent of Putun Itza motifs at Chichen Itza.

7. Earlier influences attributable to Campeche, largely in Putun control, appear earlier in Yaxchilan.

25

8. The presence of huge quantities of Fine Orange and Fine Gray pottery mark the final occupation of Altar de Sacrificios, a strategic trading and distribution center. These could well indicate Putun influences or occupation because those wares were probably made in or near Putun territory.

9. A group of settlements south of the Pasión in the sixteenth century was known as Acalan or Acala, precisely the same term as that applied to the Putun group of Itzamkanac. It must be more than coincidence, in view of the above points, that there was an Acalan between tributaries of the upper Usumacinta, and a province of Acalan on the Candelaria River known to have held positions on the lower Usumacinta and whose people were leading traders and expansionists. As we shall see, there are reasons for concluding that the groups in eastern Acalan had been affected in the past by Putun influences from the Gulf of Mexico.

The first four of the above points are, I think, generally acceptable. The settlements of Putun on the lower Usumacinta are reviewed by Scholes and Roys (1948:24–27, 317, 438–46), who note that Tenosique (ancient Tanotz'ic) was both Putun (Chontal-Maya) speaking and, late in the sixteenth century, the frontier Christian town. Tenosique was still Putun speaking in the opening decades of the nineteenth century and later, but there was confusion because Galindo (1832) wrongly applied the term *puctunc* to Palencano Chol, which, indeed, is close to Putun. Berendt, in his notebooks, comments on Galindo's paper, noting that Putun was therefore another name for Palencano Chol, and observes that some of the old inhabitants of Tenosique, now intermingled with Maya Yucatec immigrants, were of Putun speech. He also assigns Montecristo and Saquila (ancient Iztapa to those of Nahuatl speech?) to his Putun group. Names of persons in early colonial Tenosique, as in other Putun groups, were mixed Maya and Nahuat—a point, as we shall see, of very considerable importance.

I therefore call attention to the Scholes and Roys evidence that the Usumacinta, as far upstream as Tenosique, last of the civilized towns, was Putun in the sixteenth century, and note that there is evidence that Tenosique was still Putun speaking in the early nineteenth century. Most important of all, in Tenosique the Putun names are of mixed Maya and Nahuat derivation.

EASTERN ACALAN AND "LACANDON" IN THE COLONIAL PERIOD

Concerning the inhabitants of the large rain forest area south of the upper Usumacinta and the lower Pasión, information is little and what there is has been poorly co-ordinated. The most detailed ethnographical picture is that of the town seized by the Spaniards in the spring of 1695 and renamed by them Nuestra Señora de Los Dolores (henceforward referred to as Dolores). The invaders entered in two divisions, both well documented. The fullest information comes from the official diary of the expedition under Presidente Jacinto de Barrios Leal, kept by Pedro Álvarez de Miranda (Ximénez, 1931–33, bk. 5, chs. 60–62). Entering from Ocosingo, the army marched along a river which must have been the Jataté, reaching a position south of Lake Miramar, from which a reconnaissance party went forward to survey the lake, for it was on one of its islands that earlier expeditions had found the Lacandon. However, the 1695 expedition found no evidence of occupation. This news disconcerted Barrios, and his party was uncertain whither to turn. At that point the army captured a Lacandon who led them to the chief Lacandon town. This lay thirteen leagues to the southeast from their camp south of Lake Miramar. A large river, presumably the Azul, had to be crossed. In a straight line the distance from the camp would place the town on the Lacantun River a little below its junction with the Ixcan (Map 2).

Data on the second prong of the *entrada* (Villagutierre, bk. 4, chs. 10–14) which started from San Mateo Ixtatan, in the Cuchumatanes, located the Lacandon town in the same place. The route followed the San Ramón and then the Ixcan, into which the former flows, just above the junction of the latter with the Lacantun. The Lacantun was crossed close to where the waters of the Ixcan mingled with it. From there a few hours travel in an unspecified direction, but probably following the Lacantun eastward, brought the missionaries who had gone ahead of the army to the Lacandon town. A third contemporary source (Villagutierre, bk. 6, ch. 6) informs us that the Lacantun was close to Dolores.

There can be no serious doubt that Dolores lay in the great bend of the Lacantun, a few miles downstream from where the Ixcan flows in, about forty miles due south and perhaps forty-four miles

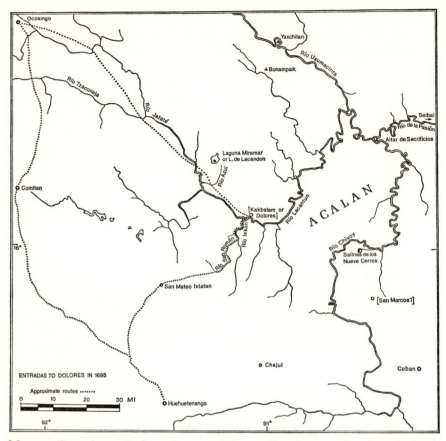

Map. 2—*Entradas* to Dolores in 1695. The smaller force under Captain Rodríguez took forty days to reach Kakbalam from San Mateo Ixtatan. The main force under President Jacinto de Barrios left Ocosingo on the same day (February 28). Scouts finding no evidence of occupation at Lake Miramar, the army pushed on, reaching Kakbalam after fifty days. The town was renamed Dolores because it was sighted on Good Friday. *(Drawn by Ian Graham.)*

southwest of Altar de Sacrificios, where the Chixoy unites with the Pasión to form the Usumacinta, and thirty-one miles west by north of Salinas de los Nueve Cerros, the famed salt deposits on the Chixoy River.[1] From a captured Lacandon the invaders learned

[1] Frans Blom (Blom and Duby, 1955–57:210–15) supposes that the expedition from San Mateo Ixtatan, passing down the San Juan (although the account mentions the San Ramón), crossed the Lacantun, and made northwest for Lake

28

that there was a second large town and three small ones (Ximénez, 1931–33, bk. 5, ch. 62), the names of two of the smaller ones seemingly Mop and Peta. The names of the principal chiefs have survived and will be discussed below.

A very important source on the Indians of Dolores was a young Indian from Chajul, an Ixil village near Nebaj, who was captured by raiding Lacandon about 1608 when he was about nine years old, and who spent about twenty-two years among them before escaping back to his native Chajul. In fact, Chajul was the nearest highland settlement to the location we have given Dolores; it lies forty-four miles directly south. Tovilla (1960, bk. 2, ch. 8) interviewed him.

The Lacandons had two towns, eight leagues apart, named Culuacan and Cagbalan (also written Caguatan and Cagabalan—probably Kak Balam, "Fire Jaguar"). The first town was of 140 multiple-family houses and was under four chiefs, whom the informant named; Cagbalan was of 300 multiple-family houses, and was also ruled by four chiefs called Cabnal, Tunhol, Tuztecat, and Chancuc. The men of these towns carried on some trade with the Indians of Tabasco (along the lower Usumacinta?), and went to certain distant salt deposits which from subsequent information proved to have been the salt works of Los Nueve Cerros on the Chixoy, about thirty-eight miles north-northwest of Coban.

The same names of chiefs as those given above, allowing for poor transcription, are found in accounts of the settlement of Dolores in 1695. Moreover, in the account of the Villa Vicencio *entrada* of 1586, a Lacandon prisoner informed about the group (*parcialidad*) of Cabenal (*sic*), which, he stated, was situated some eight to ten leagues east of Lake Miramar (Morales Villa Vicencio, 1937:144).

Cabnal was the head chief 110 years later at the Barrios *entrada*.

Miramar. There, apparently, they rounded up the Indians and settled them in a new town, named Nuestra Señora de Los Dolores, which Blom would locate either at the position I suggest or between the Lacantun and the Azul. The sources make it perfectly plain that Dolores was a native town renamed by the Spaniards without any change of position. The point is important, because it establishes that Dolores had nothing to do with the *peñol* of Lake Miramar, which had ceased to function as a Lacandon center by the latter part of the seventeenth century, and probably since the place and its milpas were razed for the second time in the Villa Vicencio campaign of 1586.

Indeed, to this day Capnal is the name applied to the Lacandon by the Indians of Santa Eulalia in the adjacent highlands of Guatemala, although they no longer know why. Beyond doubt, Cagbalan was renamed Dolores.

Clearly, then, the same names were assumed by chiefs generation after generation. The names as given by the Indian of Chajul are listed below, together with the variant forms reported in 1696 in parentheses with Vil, Val, or Mar to indicate the source: Villagutierre y Soto-Mayor; Valenzuela, whose *relación* was published in García Peláez (1968) and was probably used also by Villagutierre; and the letter of Fray Margil of 1695 from Dolores (Tozzer, 1913).

Cabnal (Val and Vil; Cabenal, Morales Villa Vicencio); Tuztecat (Tuxtecat, Val; Tustecat, Vil and Mar); Tunhol (Tutinol, Mar; Tpxnol, Val and Vil); Chancuc (Chancut, Vil; Chaucut, Val); and Cucit Cazqui were the four chiefs and high priest of Cagbalan according to the Chajul Indian. Those of Culuacan were Bibaao; Julamna (Julabna, Mar; Sulabna, Val; Sirlabna, Vil); Acchicel (Chichel, Mar, Val, and Vil); Cagtei; and the priest Cuichilaquin Aeque Urabal or Anabal. Other names reported are Polon (Val and Vil); Tzactzi (Mar; Tzatzi, Val; Tzatzis, Vil); Itzquin (Mar; Izquin or Isquin, Vil; Quin, Val); and Buban (Val and Mar; Kim-Bubari, Vil).

A few corrections are permissible: Polon is surely Bolon; Bibaao, Bib Ahao; Cagtei may be Kakte, equivalent of Yucatec Kakche, "ebony tree"; and Aquin is surely Ah Kin, "priest" in Yucatec. In addition, there are two names of individuals from the *peñol* of Lake Miramar reported by the Villa Vicencio expedition —Coatek or Coatec or Coate, and Ocelo, pretty clearly Coat and Ocelot—both Nahuat day names and both recorded among Acalan-Putun day names. Also, the chief of the Lacandon town of Puchutla, razed by the Spaniards in the sixteenth century, was Cham-Ahhoal (Chan Ahao, "snake lord?"), which again follows the Putun tradition of Ahau after the name.

Of the above names it may be quoted that:

1. As has been remarked, those of chiefs were passed from generation to generation.

2. Many are composed of two words: Cabnal (*cab*, "earth,"

and *nal*, "elote?"), Chancuc (*chan*, "snake," and *cuc*, "feather?"), and others.

3. Some names are Maya, but a few are of Nahuat derivation: Tuztecat or Tuxtecat (day names Tochti, "rabbit," and Eecat, "wind"?); Izquin (Itzcuinti, "dog," also a Nahuat day name); Coate and Ocelo (Nahuat day names Coat, "snake," and Ocelot, "jaguar").

4. *Ahao* follows the name, in contrast to Yucatec precedence. All four features are typical of Putun peoples. The Putun Itza, for instance, used compound names, and chiefs' names became inherited titles (note Canek, a dynasty of the Itza at Tayasal). A mixture of Maya names and Nahuat day names is typical of the Putun of Acalan-Tixchel and the Putun of the Chontalpa, as already noted, and the placement of *ahao* or *ahau* after the name is again a Putun feature (shared by their neighbors the Manche Chol).

It is worth bearing in mind that personal day names are not typical of the Nahuatl peoples of the plateau of Central Mexico, which would suggest that these day names of the Putun were taken over from a Nahuat group of the Gulf Coast area and not from distant Tula. The *t* substituted for *tl* supports that suggestion.

The place names are of considerable interest: Cagbalan (Kak Balam?) is Maya, but Culuacan is as Nahuatl as cherry pie is American, and comes to us from an informant who spoke no Nahuatl. With regard to the sixteenth-century names of Lacandon towns near (west and north?) the *peñol* of Lacandon (Lake Miramar), Puchutla and Tupiltepec, one must bear in mind the distinct possibility that as Nahuatl-speaking auxiliaries, as well as Chiapanec Indians who would have used Nahuatl as lingua franca, were the backbone of those early *entradas*, Maya names for those settlements might have been passed on to the Spaniards in Nahuatl translation, although the fact that the river (the Jataté?) flowing close to Tupiltepec was known as the Tupiltepec River carries some weight in deciding this difficult problem. Apparently Culuacan, flourishing about 1630, had been replaced by the towns called Peta (Margil has Pecta) and Ebula in 1695, for Margil lists their chiefs, and his names in part correspond to those given for Culuacan at an earlier period. At any rate, we have the same mixture of

Nahuat and Maya in place names as already noted for personal names.

The culture of the people of Dolores seems to have been purely Maya, but, like some present-day Lacandon, they pierced the septum of the nose, a custom perhaps introduced into the Usumacinta drainage from outside in late Classic times. That the language was Chol seems to be established beyond much doubt (the only surviving Manche-Chol vocabulary and *arte* was used and probably transcribed by Fray Margil and his colleagues at Dolores; another source speaks of the language of Dolores as a mixture of Yucatec, Chontal, and Tzeltal, a fair enough description of Chol). It must be emphasized that Lacandon in the colonial period was a geographical, not a cultural or linguistic, term, and that the present-day Lacandon are surely descendants of later immigrants into the country who probably absorbed the remnants of the earlier inhabitants and may have taken over some of their customs.

EASTERN ACALAN: MARTYRDOM OF FATHERS VICO AND LÓPEZ (1555)

We must move back 150 years for the early background of the "Lacandon" of Dolores.

The province of Acalan according to Villagutierre y Soto-Mayor and León Pinelo) or Acala (according to Remesal and the two writers, Ximénez and Tovilla, who drew their information from him) was a poorly defined area north or northwest of Coban, Alta Verapaz. The spelling Acalan is more likely to be correct, for it was used by the official historians, and a final consonant is more likely to drop off than to be added. The people are sometimes called Acalan or Acala, but more frequently are referred to as Lacandon. After A.D. 1600 or thereabouts the name of Acalan disappears, and the people are called Lacandon.

Acalan first appeared in the literature when the Dominicans, in 1550, sent a mission from Coban to convert the Acala. Fathers Tomás de la Torre and Domingo de Vico traveled several days through swamps and forests to the province of Acalan, and spent some months there. Father Vico was able to preach to them in their native tongue because he had previously served among Chol communities around Golfo Dulce (Remesal, 1932, bk. 9, ch. 2).

Many were baptized, and at a later period these were gathered in a village named San Marcos, which lay north or northwest of Coban and was referred to as the first town of Acalan. This Fr. Vico, later appointed prior of Coban, continued to serve between other duties. The location of the village is uncertain; I suspect it lay somewhere west of the present village of Chisec. Tovilla (1960, bk. 2, ch. 4) placed it ten leagues north of Coban, but from a letter to the Audiencia in Guatemala of the same date (1631) we learn that the Indians of San Marcos were well acquainted with the Chixoy Valley and acted as paddlers and guides to an expedition which penetrated to the Salinas de los Nueve Cerros (Ximénez, 1931–33, bk. 4, ch. 69). By one of fate's strange quirks, a party of Lacandon, which included the young Indian captive from Chajul, mentioned above, had gone to those same salt mines to extract salt and there spotted the advance party of Spaniards, including Father Morán, author of the Chol dictionary also mentioned above. The Lacandon discussed attacking the small party, but stayed their hands.

From this association of San Marcos, "first town of Acalan," with the middle Chixoy Valley, I am inclined to see Acalan as perhaps once occupying the quadrilateral area between the Chixoy or Salinas River on the west, the Cancuen on the east, the Pasión on the north, and the beginning of the highlands immediately north of Coban on the south.

In 1555, despite many reports of unrest among the Christian Acalan of San Marcos, Prior Vico, accompanied by a young Dominican Fr. Andrés López, returned on a mission to the town. Apparently the non-converted, angered by fear of encroachments of Spanish rule, revolted, and with the aid of a group described as neighboring Lacandon, but almost certainly fellow Acalan, murdered the two Dominicans, captured and sacrificed on the spot a young acolyte, and slew some thirty of the Christian Indians from Alta Verapaz who had accompanied the fathers (Remesal, 1932, bk. 9, ch. 7).

The poignant account which Remesal (bk. 10, ch. 7) wrote of the martyrdom of the two friars covers a sequence of incidents of tense drama. Apart from the courageous faith shown by the victims, there is the problem for the ethnohistorian to assess: were the

Indians playing with their victims, as cat with mouse; was the succession of incidents, comparable to moves on a chessboard, part of a regular pattern of behavior (note, for example, the temporary pause in the fighting when the acolyte is sacrificed, as though that were standard procedure in the ritual of attack); or was nothing planned beforehand?

Fr. Alonso de Vayllo was to have accompanied Prior Vico on this mission, but he came down with fever; Fr. Andrés López was chosen in his place. This young Spaniard, when he first came to the New World, was "strong and robust, the bravest of the brave, and stronger than any other Spaniard in the Indies, as the *alcaldes* and half the population of Ciudad Real [capital of Chiapas] could bear witness, for all of them were unable to take him prisoner in certain knife fights which he had there with a neighbor." He turned over a new leaf, joined the Dominicans, and had been priested shortly before this mission in late November, 1555.

In view of the reports of serious turmoil at San Marcos, Don Juan, Indian governor of Alta Verapaz, tried without success to persuade Fr. Vico to allow him and a band of three hundred Christian Indians to serve as escort. They were ordered to return to Coban, and Fr. Vico collected the swords and shields of the thirty or forty Indians who remained. The San Marcos Indians who had, it was claimed, sent to call Lacandon Indians to their aid showed evidence of unquiet and hostility. They assembled in the town in great numbers but made no overt move of hostility.

The two friars, fearing that the fate against which they had been warned was about to overtake them, spent the night in prayer in a hut. When the morning star rose (note the expression, clearly from the lips of the Indian informant), Fr. López suggested to his companion that now that the night was nearly passed it was clear the Indians did not plan to attack them and so, with his superior's permission, he would go to another hut to get some sleep. His request was granted.

Father Domingo continued praying. At dawn one of his Coban Indians came to the door to warn him that the Indians had fired the thatch of his hut, and, although the fire was slow because the thatch was green, he must soon leave. The Indian, a courageous man, said to the prior, "Give me one of the swords you have below your bed, and I give you my word to get you and Father Andrés out of here to safety despite the thousand Indians waiting for you." Father Domingo told him to make his escape, that he and Father Andrés would stay; that God, if He so willed, would save them. The Indian returned a second and third time, then, at Father Domingo's direct orders, taking sword and shield, he dashed forth, and, amid a shower of arrows, broke through and escaped with light wounds.

When it was fully light, Father Domingo went out into the plaza where the Indians were congregated. They made way for him—Remesal says they did not come in contact with him because of the heathen belief that one who came close to a priest would immediately die. They began to shoot their arrows at him, but without hitting him. He entered the church, knelt down, and commended his soul to his Maker. A little later, seeing that the church, too, was afire, he came out and began walking among the Indians, asking them why they sought to kill him. More arrows were the only reply. One pierced him in the throat, at which, in a loud voice, he called on the name of Jesus.

This cry awoke Father Andrés, who, coming to the door of his hut to ascertain what had happened, received an arrow in his chin. As though it were no more than a mosquito bite, the young priest pulled out the arrow, wiped away the blood, and ran down to succor his companion who lay bleeding on the ground. With the help of an Indian acolyte Father Domingo had brought with him, Father Andrés moved him against a wall, and, although bleeding profusely from his own wound, knelt down to help his superior to die. One of the youthful acolytes stood in front of the fathers to defend them from the arrows which continued to rain on them. Apparently, on orders from their chief, the Indians closed in, seized, dragged off, and immediately sacrificed the youngster in the usual manner by removing his heart.

The shooting then ceased, and the Indians moved off to kill the horses. During this brief pause Prior Vico breathed his last. It was the eve of the Feast of St. Andrew, to whom Father Domingo had always shown great devotion and on whose day he had had a premonition he would die. It was also, of course, the eve of the saint after whom Father Andrés was named.

Father Andrés, seeing that his companion was dead and he was alone, went to the room, collected a maize cake, a drinking gourd, and his breviary; and, after a halt for prayer, set off slowly for Coban, with blood flowing from his wounds, as though he felt that if an Indian could break through the enemy ranks, he, with all his strength, could do likewise. A troop of enemy Indians came upon him, and a shower of arrows multiplied his wounds so that he seemed bristling with arrows; and there, on the trail to Coban, he died. Some of the Coban Indians, including three of the acolytes, broke through and reached Coban safely, but about thirty of them were slain.

THE EASTERN ACALAN MOVE WEST

Four years later, in 1559, when a Spanish force entering from Comitan attacked the Lacandon on their island fortress on Lake Miramar, Don Juan, the Indian governor, led an expedition from Coban to revenge the deaths of his old friend Fr. Domingo de Vico and his companion Fr. Andrés López. They attacked the Acalan stronghold which lay at the back, that is, east, of the *peñol* of Lake Miramar. No less than 80 of the Indian leaders supposed to have been involved in the deaths of Frs. Vico and López were hung, and 180 prisoners were taken. As the royal decree sanctioning these invasions had declared that prisoners should be sold as slaves, one realizes that Don Juan, in having 80 chiefs hanged, did so at considerable pecuniary cost, a most laudable sacrifice on his part when one realizes that in fact it might have been somewhat difficult to prove that each and every one of the 80 was involved in those events at San Marcos so far from their homes.

After Don Juan's forces retired to Alta Verapaz, "Acala remained almost destroyed," as Remesal put it. Unfortunately, we have no specific information on where this Acalan settlement was situated other than behind the rocky island of Lake Miramar. One may suppose it was somewhere in the area between the Chixoy-Salinas and Lacantun rivers, probably not too far west of the Chixoy since they came to San Marcos at short notice for the attack on the Dominican priests.

The Franciscan Antonio Margil and a companion were in the

town later named Dolores some eighteen months before its capture by the Spaniards in 1695. The Indians admitted that their ancestors had slain Frs. Vico and López 140 years earlier, and showed them fragments of the missal and breviary of one of the martyrs and part of the altar cloth and religious ornaments of the church of San Marcos (Villagutierre, bk. 2, ch. 10; Ximénez, 1931–33, bk. 5, ch. 55). Dolores, as we have seen, was in the bend of the Lacantun River almost due north of the Ixil outpost of Chajul, which the Lacandon raided every once in a while (e.g., they captured Tovilla's informant there about 1608; they also fell upon the town in 1664, capturing and sacrificing a small child). They also made occasional forays near Coban, with a particularly bold one in 1678 when they raided the *milpa* lands of the Indians of Coban and captured one boy who was subsequently rescued. From Tovilla's informant we know that they traveled from Dolores to the Nueve Cerros to obtain salt.

I think we must conclude that this whole area, from Los Nueve Cerros perhaps to the Río Azul, was controlled by the sadly diminished descendants of the once powerful eastern Acalan, but that following the terrible vengeance exacted by the Indian cacique Don Juan in 1559, they had moved their towns westward to the lower Lacantun where it flows west to east, certainly by about 1608, perhaps much earlier, and had established themselves in the site later christened Nuestra Señora de Dolores. In other words, the Lacandon of Dolores as seen and partly described by the Spaniards in 1694–96 were the descendants, in culture and by blood, of the Acalan of the Chixoy-Cancuen parallelogram with which the Spaniards from Coban had made contact nearly 150 years earlier. The relics of the martyrdoms at San Marcos prove this.

We have noted the Putun features of Dolores Lacandon; these take on significance when we find that this culture derives from a province known as Acalan, a name already attached to the Putun of Itzamkanac on the Candelaria River. There seems to be a very good case for believing that the people of eastern Acalan were descended from a mixture of invading Putun from the Gulf of Mexico, quite probably from western Acalan (Putun of the province ruled from Itzamkanac), and local Maya of Chol speech. If one may make one more assumption, it seems not improbable that those invading Putun were part of the same succession of waves which reached Altar de Sacrificios and, at a later date, Seibal.

PUTUN INFLUENCES ON THE PASIÓN (LATE CLASSIC PERIOD)

Excavations by Peabody Museum, Harvard University, at Altar de Sacrificios uncovered an occupation, marked by huge quantities of Fine Orange (essentially Y types) and Fine Gray pottery, which overlay all major construction, and the latest dated monument, Stela 15, dated 9.17.0.0.0, A.D. 771 in the Goodman-Martínez-Thompson correlation (Willey and Smith, 1963). This occupation is assigned by those authors to invaders probably of non-Maya origin. It is named the Ximba phase and is equated with the late Classic or immediate post-Classic phase.

In weighing the various factors, the following points are worth bearing in mind:

1. Fine Orange in general and Fine Gray pottery, because of their distribution and lack of tempering material, are thought to have originated at the bottom of the Gulf of Mexico. Indeed, Berlin (1956:115) felt that one variety of Fine Orange Z was made at Jonuta, in the Usumacinta Valley, because of the enormous amount of sherds of that type found there. For Fine Orange Y there is less certainty. It is mainly confined to the Usumacinta drainage and the Petén, not appearing in Yucatan or the Campeche coast (R. E. Smith, 1958:151). A few pieces from the highlands could have been exported from the Usumacinta drainage. The designs and figures on the ware are a mixture of Maya Classic and non-Classic motifs and portraits, the same admixture we have found characteristic of Putun cultures. The figurines are an amalgam with non-Classic Maya features dominant.

Maya Classic-period sites in or on the edge of the Chontalpa seem to show this same blending of Classic and non-Classic features, in which the deformed sloping forehead, prominent nose, drooping lower lip, and receding chin are absent. At Jonuta, the many Fine Orange figurines are a mixture of the two styles (Berlin, 1956). The figure on Monument 1, Jonuta, (Kelemen, 1943, Plate 78*b*) is quite un-Classic Maya in features and clothing, although the accompanying glyphs might have come off a Palenque inscription. Stone being absent at Jonuta, deep in the delta, one concludes that the sculpture was commissioned at Palenque, but depicts the local headman. The stucco reliefs on the tomb of Comalcalco (Blom and La Farge, 1926–27, 1:115–130) are poorly preserved; several are Classic Maya profiles, but the features of Figure 1 are of a non-Classic Maya.

From the above it is most logical to suppose that Fine Orange Y was manufactured by a Putun group, probably, in view of the strong Classic Maya motifs, living in close proximity to Maya Classic centers and, moreover, probably on or near the banks of the Usumacinta sufficiently far inland to be cut off from direct sea transport to Campeche and Yucatan, but not so far as to be well outside the alluvial delta. There are good grounds established by Scholes and Roys (1948) for assigning several of the lower Usumacinta towns, below Tenosique, which belongs to the group, to the Putun. They note that Ciuatecpan, which they locate near the present-day Canizan (Scholes and Roys, 1948: 384), had been conquered by the Acalan Putun not long before the Spanish Conquest, but I think we may deduce that it had earlier been a settlement of some other Putun group. The name means "Palace of the Goddess." As the Putun had a very special cult of the goddess Ix Chel (note the old capital Tixchel, "at the place of Ix Chel," and the great shrine of Ix Chel on Cozumel which they controlled), it is a fair assumption that Ciuatecpan was a shrine of that goddess established, in all probability, by the Putun. Conceivably, its Maya name was something like XChel-ch'una, "temple of Ix Chel."

Reasons for believing that the Ximba occupation of Altar de Sacrificios should be assigned to Putun incursions are these:

1. The Putun were the great traders and travelers of the Maya area, and they were *the* canoemen, as the name of their homeland, Acalan, implies. It is most logical to suppose that Altar de Sacrificios was occupied by groups approaching by river.

2. Altar de Sacrificios stands at the confluence of the Chixoy, trade route to the Alta Verapaz, and the Pasión, waterway to the southeastern Petén and, with a short portage to the Moho or Sarstoon rivers, part of the overland route to the wealth of the Bay of Honduras and the Motagua and Ulua drainages. It was

therefore a strategic center for commerce and invasion, the two main interests of the Putun.

3. The imported wares of the Ximba phase at Altar de Sacrificios almost certainly originated in Putun territory.

4. Fine Orange Y designs are a blending of Classic Maya and Nahuatl features which characterize Putun culture.

5. The Putun, being settled athwart the lower Usumacinta, were nearest neighbors of the Maya adhering to the pure Classic Maya culture.

6. Influences from Campeche, possibly but not certainly attributable to the Acalan Putun, are apparent somewhat earlier at Yaxchilan (Proskouriakoff and Thompson, 1947; Thompson, 1952), perhaps some forty years before the Ximba phase appears at Altar de Sacrificios. The Campeche or Puuc influences at Yaxchilan are most easily recognized in the aberrant method of recording dates by which month sign coefficients corresponding to any given day were always one less than in the standard system. The nearest center from which that practice is reported is Etzna, east-northeast of Champoton. If, as seems possible, the Acalan Putun once extended as far north as Champoton, they might well have transmitted influences from near Etzna to Yaxchilan. The features of late personages on Etzna monuments are not Maya, in contrast to Classic Maya figures on stelae of around 9.13.0.0.0. If the suggestion here advanced is correct, Putun influences slowly extended up the Usumacinta toward Altar de Sacrificios, although Putun or Puuc influences at Yaxchilan were transitory.

7. The territory south of Altar de Sacrificios was, as we have seen, named Acalan or Acala, the same name as that of the homeland of the Putun group around the bottom of the Gulf of Mexico. In colonial times it was occupied by a people whose chiefs, like the Putun, had a mixture of Maya and Nahuat names, placed *ahau* after their chiefs' names, passed their dynastic names from father to son, had their settlements assigned to four quarters (a reasonable inference from the fact that each town had four chiefs), and had as one of their chief gods, Chua, in all probability the same god of merchants called Ek ("black") Chua, for there were other aspects of this god free of the black feature. In view of the trading activities of the invaders of Altar de Sacrificios, the presence

of this god in what one might term New Acalan is very pertinent. One may reasonably infer that the leaders of this New Acalan were descended from our supposed Putun invaders of the Pasión.

8. It is more logical, on general grounds, to suppose that the invaders came from nearby, not originally from Central Mexico as Sabloff and Willey (1967:327) are inclined to believe. The peoples of Central Mexico were not canoemen and to this day generally shun the forest lands of the *tierra caliente* as the devil does holy water. Moreover, none of the imports, so far as is known, derive from Central Mexico. One may also note that the Nahuatl elements of the Chontalpa and neighboring regions is not the Classic speech of Central Mexico, but the variety in which the final *l* is absent (e.g., *ocelot* instead of *ocelotl*) and *u* tends to substitute for *o* (e.g., *tuchit* instead of *tochitl*).

In summary, there is a very strong case, largely on ethnohistorical but partly on archaeological grounds, for attributing the Ximba phase at Altar de Sacrificios to Putun invaders from lower Usumacinta and neighboring regions.

PUTUN OCCUPATION AT SEIBAL (LATE CLASSIC PERIOD)

At Seibal, as is well known, late stelae dated around A.D. 850 display striking non-Classic elements, notably non-Classic Maya features of the ruler(s) portrayed on Stelae 1, 8, 10, 11, and 14, which can hardly be distinguished from those of Putun-Itza notables at Chichen Itza (Plates 1, 2). This is not the place to list all such non-Classic elements, but there is one detail which, in my opinion, is overwhelming evidence that this new dynasty was Putun. At the top of Stela 3 two masked individuals are seated facing each other; above their heads stand two similar glyphs of the Nahuatl day Cipactli (locally Cipacti) (Proskouriakoff, 1950: 153). One has the number seven attached, and the other, number five. Although the identity of the day signs is not open to serious question, the style is not that of Central Mexico or of any of the known codices, so perhaps one may conclude that it is a regionalism, perhaps of the Tabasco coast. It will be recalled that the ruling Putun family of Potonchan, at the mouth of the Grijalva (as well as of one branch of the Usumacinta), was named Cipaque, a corruption of Cipacti; and Cipacti in the forms Atzipac (the *at* is perhaps *at*[*l*] "water"), Cipac, and for women, Cipa, Yscipa, and Yxcipat (with *ix*, the female prefix) is a family name also among the Acalan Putun (Scholes and Roys, 1948: 37n., 482, 483, 488). All names are wretchedly transcribed in the Paxbolon papers. The most reasonable conclusion is that these Cipactli glyphs inform us that the ruling family which established itself at Seibal at the close of the Classic period was named Cipactli (more correctly, the "*l*"–less form, Cipacti), was of Putun speech, and was quite likely a branch of the Cipacti dynasty at Potonchan. Moreover, the Nahuatl of Central Mexico lacked day-name appellatives.

These new rulers of Seibal probably expanded beyond Seibal, for some fifty miles northeast of Seibal across an easily traversed watershed lies the small site of Ucanal. There Stela 4, of the same date as the most "foreign" stelae at Seibal (A.D. 849), has above the standing personage, whose features are partly weathered but appear to be of the same non-Classic type as on the late Seibal stelae, a deity, with darts and spearthrower in his hands and non-Classic features, who emerges from a loop in what must be a celestial serpent. The composition is very reminiscent of the countless sculptures of the Putun-Itza period at Chichen Itza, in which a similarly armed deity peers down from a sun disk. Furthermore, in the accompanying text is a square-framed glyph, surely a name glyph, such as those discussed on Seibal 3. Here the coefficient is twelve or thirteen and inside the square cartouche is a beaked head, reminiscent of the masked figure which is seated opposite a Maya at the bottom of that same Stela 3. Seibal. The most reasonable conclusion is that those Putun invaders did not stop at Seibal, but established themselves also at Ucanal, on the headwaters of the strategic Belize River.

The important point I would make, contrary to the views of Sabloff and Willey (1967), is that these Putun invaders of Seibal and Ucanal were not directly responsible for the end of the ceremonial life of the Classic period. For, as we have seen, the erection of stelae continued under their aegis. Moreover, texts, except for those aberrant name glyphs, continued to be inscribed in the Classic Maya tradition. On the contrary, these invaders kept the old ceremonial ways alive when in many other centers the old order had collapsed.

Such a situation is more easily explained, if I am correct in my view, that power was seized not by a completely alien group from outside the Maya area, but by another Maya group which spoke almost the same language as the local inhabitants and shared in the general Maya cultural heritage.

The new rulers, in turn, were wiped out, probably by the same forces—a proletarian revolt in my belief—as brought other Maya centers of the Central area to an end, for the most part before the Putun invasion. Indeed, revolutionary conditions may well have given these invaders the chance to establish themselves at Seibal and Ucanal and, perhaps, earlier at Altar de Sacrificios.

I deem it a fair assumption that the eastern Acalan, with their clear Putun cultural elements, were the descendants of the makers of that revolt, over whom junior Putun chiefs, perhaps of a status equivalent to the *batabs* (local chiefs) of Yucatan, managed to retain control after the higher nobility and their ways had been wiped out. We may here have an example of the old principle, "If you can't lick 'em, join 'em."

CONCLUDING REMARKS

The Putun (Chontal Maya) are here presented as a virile, expanding group which quite probably developed its aggressive qualities as a result of an earlier injection of Mexican blood and toughness from Nahuat-speaking neighbors in the Chontalpa. The culture and people were hybrid Maya-Nahuat. From a peripheral location with respect to the Maya lowlands as a whole, they expanded in various directions toward the close of the Classic period and more so in the post-Classic period. Their seamanship gave them great mobility, and their pre-eminence in commerce made them acquainted with many parts of the Maya lowlands. Their seamanship and commerce enabled them first to penetrate to the Pasión and beyond to Ucanal, and later(?) enabled them to establish themselves on the east coast of Yucatan, notably at Cozumel Island, Bakhalal, and Chetumal (note in that connection the confirmatory remark of Ciudad Real [1873, 2:468] that

43

in the Province of Uaymil, in eastern Yucatan, stretching as far as Lake Bakhalal, the dialect spoken resembled that of Campeche, that is, Putun, since northern Campeche spoke the prevalent Yucatec dialect, with which Ciudad Real is contrasting that of Uaymil). Finally, those Putun invaders, under the name of Itza, struck out from their east coast bases to seize and hold Chichen Itza and, perhaps then or later, other inland Yucatec centers such as Motul.

It should be borne in mind that the Putun invaders of Seibal and Ucanal brought with them no cult of Kukulcan in the form of ubiquitous feathered serpents. The same is true of the first Itza invasion of Chichen Itza, the *noh emal*, "the great descent," of tradition, if the inner Castillo has been correctly assigned to that occupation of the city. That is understandable if the dates assigned to those invasions are correct, that is, A.D. 850 and A.D. 918, for they are prior to that date (A.D. 987) claimed for Quetzalcoatl-Kukulcan's departure for Nonoualco.

The second wave of Putun Itza to reach Chichen Itza, the *dz'emal*, "the little descent," of tradition, accompanied the arrival of Kukulcan and a small band of followers from Tula in A.D. 987. They brought with them the new religious ideas, symbolism, and architecture of their homeland which, in combination with the local Maya features of architecture, were to find expression in such buildings as the outer Castillo, the very similar High Priest's Grave (with a reasonably sure date of 10.8.10.11.0, 2 Ahau 18 Mol, A.D. 998, falling in a katun 2 Ahau ending in A.D. 1007), the ball court, and the whole Warriors complex. As the High Priest's Grave building was erected over an earlier structure, it is reasonable that the passage of one katun from A.D. 987 would have given ample time for erection of the present Temple of the High Priest's Grave and the present Castillo, for in each case it was merely a matter of building a new outer skin over an already existing mass.

I have wondered whether this second group of Itza who arrived with Kukulcan could have been *yala ah Itza*, "the remainder of the Itza," to whom there are many somewhat obscure references in the Books of Chilam Balam, but, were that so, the colonial scribes who composed the books seem to have confounded them with actors in other events.

The Putun occupation of Seibal and Ucanal did not endure; those ceremonial centers disappeared, along with all others in the Central area, very soon after the new regime took over. Yet with the penetration of the east coast of Yucatan and the conquest of Chichen Itza from the east coast springboard, the Putun Maya established an "Empire," which can be postulated with considerably more certainty than the proposed Teotihuacan and Olmec "Empires." At the same time, the Putun appear never to have loosened their grip on their old territory in southwestern Campeche and extending down the Usumacinta River from Tenosique. The northern boundary of that homeland is hard to define, and doubtlessly ebbed and flowed. I believe it may once have included Champoton within Chakanputun territory.[2]

Quetzalcoatl-Kukulcan is said to have embarked at Champoton on his supposed return to the Mexican mainland. It is logical that he should have left from a port controlled by his allies, or, if the story is a myth, that the fabricators of the legend should have named as the place of embarkation a port which they knew had once been controlled by his Putun friends.

The Putun seemingly retained control of the Bakhalal-Chetumal region during the period of Mayapan domination (A.D. 1200–1480). Apart from Ciudad Real's observation, already cited, that in the province of Uaymil a Campeche-like dialect was spoken, and, of course, the direct statement in the Paxbolon papers that Chetumal paid tribute to the Acalan Putun (p. 78), there is good archaeological support for Putun control of the region. The magnificent murals of Santa Rita, northern British Honduras (Gann, 1900), a site which must have been at or extremely close to ancient Chetumal, show that mixture of Maya and Mexican features which throughout this chapter we have noted as characteristic of Putun culture. Particularly important are portraits of (Ek) Chuah, patron of the Putun merchants, prominent on the murals

---

[2] In connection with that northern boundary one might bear in mind that Pustunich, with its erotic sculpture, might well have been inside Chakanputun, for it lies a trifle under twenty-five miles southeast of Champoton. Accepting Pustunich sculpture as Putun inspired, perforce one must accept as Putun the even more erotic and very un-Maya-looking sculptures of Telantunich (Andrews, 1939; 1943:26–29, 82–85). That site, about seventeen and one-half miles west of Lake Chichan Kanab, lay about halfway between Chakanputun and Putun-controlled Cozumel Island on a logical overland route.

and also on copper disks from the cenote at Chichen Itza which are given a Chetumal provenience on stylistic grounds (Thompson, 1966 a:165–71). This deity, with his Pinocchio or retroussé nose, is prominent also in Codex Fejérváry-Mayer which I believe comes from southern Veracruz or, conceivably, a Nahuat town in the Chontalpa. The internationalism of traders accounts for the "Mixteca-Puebla" influences in these murals.

Portraits of gods from relief figures on the fronts of incense burners, dated A.D. 1350–1500, recovered in Chetumal-Uaymil, are hardly distinguishable from those from northern Tabasco-southwestern Campeche, that is, the Putun homeland. One from Palo Alto (Andrews, 1943, Fig. 28*h*), on the Usumacinta River, a short way below the affluence of the San Pedro Mártir, shows one eye closed in a wink, tongue outthrust to one side, and a ghost of a leering smile. One is reminded on the one hand of the figurine from Alvarado, Veracruz, to which reference has been made (p. 21), with its evil twisted lip and penis in state of erection (Batres, 1908, Plate 48), and on the other of the caustic remarks of the Maya about the erotic practices of their Itza conquerors—"they twist their mouths, they close their eyes." This head from Palo Alto is, I think, evidence of relations with the east coast of Yucatan, but it also serves to show that that erotic cult was still being practiced not long before the Spanish Conquest. As to the Itza who moved from Chichen Itza to Lake Petén, the missionary Avendaño y Loyola (1696:43*r*), who spent some time in their island stronghold, appears to accuse them of widespread homosexuality, but the English translation, alone available to me, does not make it plain whether Avendaño merely quotes common Spanish belief or makes his accusation on his own information. The most one can say is that the Itza of Tayasal appear to have had the same toleration of or pleasure in eroticism as found among other Putun groups.

It is somewhat ironical that the term "New Empire," against which the writer was a front-line fighter for many years, should now be emerging as a reality, although in a very different sense from that which the term once implied.

Because of its aptness I offer no excuse for repeating a comparison I have made elsewhere between Putun expansion between

A.D. 850 and A.D. 1500 and the emergence of Macedonia as a world power in the first half of the fourth century B.C. Both emerging powers were peripheral, geographically and culturally, to the nuclear center; both groups expanded at the expense of the older and more advanced culture; both developed wide empires and in the process themselves absorbed foreign cultural influences, Asiatic in the case of Macedonia, Nahuat and Veracruzan in the case of the Putun; both were militaristic and owed their successes to military innovations, the enlarged phalanx in the case of the Macedonians, the spear-thrower reintroduced by the Putun. The history of Rome in the first centuries of the Christian era supplies another, but less exact, parallel.

Finally, the research summarized in this chapter—be the conclusions reached from them right, half-right, or wrong—has drawn to a small extent on archaeology, but to a far larger extent on the rich and very extensive literature of the Colonial period. Students of the Maya past are extraordinarily lucky to have at hand such a wealth of ethnohistory; the archaeologist neglects it at his peril.

CHAPTER 2

The Maya Central Area
at the Spanish Conquest and Later:
A Problem in Demography

INTRODUCTION

This chapter reproduces the Huxley Memorial Lecture for 1966 of the Royal Anthropological Institute, London, later published in the *Proceedings* of the Royal Anthropological Institute for that year. A few quite minor changes have been made. I am, indeed, most grateful to the Council of the Institute for graciously permitting me to republish the article in the present volume, where it belongs because of a largely ethnohistorical treatment of a matter of archaeological interest.

The purposes of this essay are to refute the widely and too-long-held view that the Maya Central area was largely unpopulated at the time of the Spanish Conquest and had been in that condition for several centuries before, and to show that diseases of Spanish introduction depopulated large parts of the Maya area which were favorable to the spread of malaria and hookworm. At the same time, a parallel is attempted between the situation in the Colonial period and that which may have obtained following the collapse of the ceremonial centers.

Skating over very thin ice, I try to show the post-Classic as a period in which certain areas expanded under the impetus of the aggressive Putun Maya of Tabasco and Campeche whereas in other parts of the central lowlands the people lacked the will to adapt themselves to change and so failed to survive. In that respect this chapter is a continuation of the Putun expansion chronicled in chapter 1.

There is minor duplication of material in chapter 1 and slight contradiction of views representing the four years elapsed between the writing of the Huxley Lecture and chapter 1 of this book. I have allowed such material for the most part to stand on the grounds that one should not change a previous paper except to a very minor extent without changing the title. The archaeologist or ethnohistorian on his ascent of Mount Parnassus often needs to drop back and readjust the steps he has already climbed. Perhaps that is why the top always recedes.

The extent and the causes of depopulation in the Maya Central area after the Spanish Conquest and their bearing on events at the close of the Classic period are the subject of this chapter.

Environment is an important factor, so a brief review of it is called for. The Maya area, like other worthy institutions, is divisible into three parts. These are known as the Northern, Central, and Southern areas or alternatively as the northern and southern lowlands and the highlands. As the southern lowlands contain mountainous areas over 3,000 feet above sea level, and the highlands embrace a strip on the Pacific coast extending over 5,000 square miles with an elevation of less than 300 feet, the first set of terms seems preferable.

The Central area, the subject of the discussion, is for the most part low limestone country not over 700 feet above sea level, with heavy rainfall up to 10 feet per annum in the south, covered with a network of rivers and many extensive swamps. Dense rain forest is found almost everywhere. There are mountains, extending from southern British Honduras into the Republic of Honduras, and not very extensive areas of savanna (Map 1).

There is a gradual transition to a drier climate with accompanying sparser and lower woods as one travels northwestward across the Northern area, with rainfall at the northwestern tip of the peninsula as low as 18 inches per annum, less than a sixth of what it is in the south of the Central area. As a corollary, the tall rain forest becomes low scrub. However, on the eastern side of the Northern area the rainfall is a lot heavier and the forest approximates that of adjacent parts of the Central area. An important point is that the limestone on the western side of the Northern area is very porous with a resulting absence of rivers, lakes, and swamps. In contrast, the eastern half of the Northern area contains a number of lakes and some extensive swamps, although rivers are unknown.

The Southern area is largely mountainous, much of it over 5,000 feet above sea level and with its highest peak rising to 13,800 feet. On the south edge of the highlands, serving as a sort of fence, is a line of extinct volcanoes, from the slopes of which the descent to the Pacific coastal plain is extremely abrupt.

Regional differences in architecture and ceramics, which probably mark the frontiers of ancient provinces, account for the boundary between the Central and Northern areas. The same Maya language, Yucatec, was probably spoken on both sides of the boundary, and, as noted, change in climate and vegetation is gradual.

The division between lowlands and highlands coincides closely with the division between lowland and highland Maya languages and dialects, and also reflects sharp differences in the archaeology of the two regions. Accordingly, the southern boundary of the Central area is reasonably easy to trace. The area around Copan geographically belongs with the highlands, but is assigned to the Central area on archaeological and linguistic grounds. The Chiapan highlands, representing a transitional area, will not be discussed in this chapter.

The view has been widely held that when the great Maya ceremonial centers of the Central area ceased to function at the close of the Classic period, that is about A.D. 900 or shortly thereafter, the whole of the population deserted the region or was wiped out by some unknown catastrophe. It has been further supposed that the great core of the Central area embracing most of the great ceremonial centers, misnamed cities, reverted to forest and remained virtually uninhabited for a millennium until awakened from sleep, like some sleeping beauty of the tropics, by the machetes of chewing-gum gatherers and the kisses of archaeological Prince Charmings.

In the absence of any data indicating a deterioration of climate at the close of the Classic period or the introduction of some dread disease which not only wiped out the population but made it uninhabitable for centuries after, I find it hard to believe that this large area which had once supported a considerable population capable of maintaining those numerous and extensive ceremonial centers could have remained virtually uninhabited for a millennium. In fact, as we shall see, there is evidence that in part it supported a substantial population in the early sixteenth century, with indications that the population was still larger immediately prior to the arrival of the white man.

An alternative explanation of what happened at the close of the Classic period was advanced over a third of a century ago (Thompson, 1931:230). This supposes that high culture came to an end as a result of the overthrow of the small ruling group. Following the expulsion or extermination of that group, the rest of the population, perhaps reduced in numbers by warfare, disease, or disruption of the economic pattern, evolved into small isolated communities under humble leaders without any political or religious cohesion, perhaps a return to Middle Formative status.

Archaeological evidence for a post-Classic occupation of the area with small scale re-use of ceremonial centers by people who were obviously ignorant of the old cults is growing (for brief summaries thereof see Thompson, 1939:236–40; 1954:88–89; Mackie, 1961; W. Coe, 1962:482–87; Willey and Smith, 1963; and Willey, Bullard, et al., 1965:568–69). My purpose, however, is to present information on the population of the area in the Colonial period together with data on decreases which occurred after contact with European culture. Thereby it will be established that there was a considerable decrease in population in various parts of the Central area from which evidence is available, and from that it may be inferred that there were presumably similar decreases in areas from which comparative data are absent. It will be shown that the population was fairly dense in some parts of that area early in the sixteenth century, much less so in others.

NEWLY INTRODUCED DISEASES AND DEPOPULATION

The huge decreases of population among the natives of Middle America which followed the Spanish Conquest are so well known that there is little need to dwell on them. The almost incredible decline in the Indian population of Central Mexico has been studied by, among others, Cook and Simpson (1948), and Borah and Cook (1963). The far more conservative estimates in the former publication show a decline in native population of somewhat over 75 per cent between 1520 and 1600; the decline for the same period is estimated at about 90 per cent in the 1963 report. The authors emphasize that these are estimates, data for accurate counts not being available.

New diseases, introduced by the conquerors, account for much of the decline on the Mexican plateau, but the disturbance and slaughter of the Conquest, the opening of the mines, forcible transfers of population, and often mere lack of will to live on the part of the Indians were other factors.

Diseases of Old World introduction fall into two groups: those which swept through the Indian population, carrying off large numbers, often with long periods between violent outbreaks, and those which were endemic. Among the former, smallpox, measles, and influenza and various pulmonary diseases are most conspicuous, but it is often difficult to identify the various pestilences from brief historical mentions.

Smallpox, as is well known, was introduced into Mexico by a Negro in the forces of Pánfilo de Narváez early in 1520 and spread like wildfire, extinguishing a large part of the population. Native Yucatan histories place the appearance of smallpox in the Maya time period Katun 2 Ahau, which ran from June, 1500, to February, 1520. The scribe, writing long after the event, is correct regarding the year, but about two months out, a very understandable error. Alternatively, the disease reached Yucatan from another locus of infection, perhaps Panama. The historical records of the Cakchiquel Maya of the highlands of Guatemala (Recinos, 1953:115, 143, 145, 156, 158) report plagues which swept off large numbers of the Indians in 1520, 1559–60, 1564, 1588, 1590, and 1601. Of those, the most severe was that of 1520: "It was truly terrible, the number of dead there were in that period . . . great was the stench of dead. The dogs and the vultures devoured the bodies. The mortality was terrible." The symptoms are not clear, but this first outbreak was probably smallpox.

Measles killed over half the Indians of Honduras in the 1530's (Oviedo y Valdés, 1851–55, bk. 31, ch. 6). The Yucatec Maya said tuberculosis, which was rampant among them, had been brought by the Spaniards, calling it Spanish *zob* (Ciudad Real, 1873, 2:469).

The historian Fuentes y Guzmán (1932–33, pt. 1, bk. 14, ch. 3) attributes the great decrease in the Indian population of the Guatemalan highlands immediately after the Spanish Conquest to the introduction of smallpox and measles, which "spread like grass fires wiping out entire towns of innumerable thousands of inhabitants." These diseases, he says, came from Mexico. He adds that when he was a boy of thirteen or fourteen (1656), several of the villages around Antigua were almost wiped out by pestilence, and with his own eyes he saw that there survived only eight or ten Indians, veritable walking skeletons, in each village.

From Tabasco we have a similar story. The author of the *relación* of 1579 (*Relaciones de Yucatán*, 1:350) ascribes the decrease of 90 per cent of the Indian population between the Conquest and 1579 to "the great infirmities and pestilences which there have been throughout the Indies and especially in this province, namely, measles, smallpox, catarrhs, coughs, nasal catarrhs, haemorrhages, bloody stools, and high fevers which customarily break out in this province." Some of the above symptoms are perhaps referable to influenza, believed to have been brought from Europe by the first Spaniards (McBryde, 1947:12); "high fevers" suggest malaria.

Yellow fever seemingly was unknown in the Maya area until the mid-seventeenth century. An entry in the Chilam Balam of Chumayel reads: "1648. Yellow fever occurred and the sickness began." Roys (1933:120), translator of this passage, observes that this was part of the terrible outbreak which originated in Guadeloupe Island that year, spreading from the port of Campeche to Mérida. A contemporary historian, López de Cogolludo (1867–68, bk. 12, ch. 14), remarked that the disease was unknown to the doctors, which supports the view that this was the first outbreak of yellow fever in Yucatan. Scholes and Roys (1948:304) deduce from revised tribute lists that probably half the Indian population of some towns died at that time. Sixteen Franciscans in the Mérida friary died; a terrible percentage, for resident numbers presumably had varied little from the average of twenty friars noted in 1610. The governor and many other men of importance were also victims. Ximénez (1929–31, bk. 4, ch. 79) mentions the great plague of 1647 in Guatemala which carried off many people. This could be an error for 1648, but there was an outbreak of yellow fever in Barbados in 1647, so the disease may have been introduced somewhat earlier. Possibly this Guatemalan outbreak was something different.

Of the endemic diseases, those which most affected and still affect the Maya Central area are malaria, amoebic dysentery, and hookworm. That the first of these is of Old World origin has not been proved beyond reasonable doubt, but it is a widely held view (Shattuck, 1938:45). As to hookworm, the more prevalent *Necator americanus* is generally accepted to have originated in Africa; *Ancylostoma duodenale* is native to the Old World, including Spain. The former very probably, the latter quite possibly, were brought to the New World in post-Columbian times. Hookworm was extremely prevalent in Maya villages of British Honduras until a few years ago; Gann (1925:34), for many years a medical officer in British Honduras, writes that fully 80 per cent of the Indians were affected. As noted below, 94 per cent of the population of the Petén harbor intestinal parasites. Hookworm is an indirect killer; sufferers are so weakened that they have no resistance to malaria, dysentery, and other diseases.

Malaria, dysenteries, and hookworm, because they are endemic and not epidemic, make their appearances in a new land without mention in contemporary sources: tidal waves are news; rising tides are not.

DEPOPULATION IN THE COLONIAL PERIOD

The desertion in the Colonial period of low-lying and partly swampy areas known to have been well populated at the arrival of the white man can most reasonably be attributed to the spread of newly introduced diseases of the kind mentioned in the previous section. This, of course, is not a new idea (see for example Scholes and Roys, 1948:166–67; 324–26).

Let us first review evidence from two widely separated parts of the Maya area outside the Central area. These are respectively the northeastern corner of Yucatan and the Pacific coast of Guatemala and adjacent Mexico and El Salvador.

The northeastern tip of Yucatan has enjoyed a reputation for being unhealthy from colonial into modern times. In fact, it was very largely depopulated from the seventeenth century onward. Scholes and Roys (1948:324) cite the histories of two towns in that region. Chauaca was estimated to have had 3,000 men in 1528; in 1543 there were 600 to 700 citizens; the tax roll of 1549 lists 200 tributaries; by 1579 only twenty families remained, The figures for nearby Sinsimato were: approximately 600 men at the Conquest, 90 tributaries in 1549, and 8 in 1579 (a tributary was an adult man of working age). Both places have long since ceased to exist. This is an area containing much swamp and coastal lagoons (Map 1).

The population of these two towns fell by over 90 per cent in fifty years.

Conil, a port on the coast, was host, doubtless unwillingly, to the conqueror Montejo for two months in 1528. It was said to have held five thousand houses. This may be an exaggeration, but the Spaniards were certainly there long enough to have a good idea of its extent. Possibly, too, these were multiple-family houses. Three thousand adult men should be an ultraconservative figure. The 1549 tax roll gives the number of tributaries as eighty. A drop of over 90 per cent in the population in twenty-one years is indicated. Conil lay in the province of Ecab, of which Roys (1957:146) writes: "We know little about the province of Ecab, because the population decreased very rapidly during the first two decades of the Colonial period. Indeed, the 1582 catalog of churches names only five towns in this area. . . . None of them was large at this time and some were very small." The province of Ecab was certainly mosquito-infested, as the writings of Stephens make clear, and Shattuck (1933:165, 168) reported malaria prevalent.

The rapid depopulation of the northeastern corner contrasts with conditions in the northwestern corner and north of the peninsula. In the latter regions, the Maya, despite great losses from European diseases and from the flight of many into the forests to the south to escape Spanish oppression, survived and finally began to increase in numbers. The reason for the greater salubrity of the western half of Yucatan probably lies in its considerably lower annual rainfall and, above all, in the greater porosity of its limestone beds. Pools and swamps, in which mosquitoes breed, are rare, with the result that malaria, while by no means absent, is not the menace it is in the swamp-tangled lands of the northeast. Support for this theory was unwittingly offered by the traveler Stephens (1843, 1:249–50) who, over a century ago, attributed the malaria at Uxmal to the silting up of the ancient Maya water reservoirs there so that they became swamps. Swamps formed, and mosquitoes, now known to be malaria carriers, bred in them.

The other example of a devastating drop in native population outside the Central area is supplied from the Pacific coast of Guatemala. This had been in part one of the great cacao-producing areas of Middle America. These orchards were on the low coastal strip, with a height of up to seven hundred feet, and on the slopes of the cordillera which drop steeply to them, particularly in what are now the departments of Suchitepequez, Retalhuleu, and Quezaltenango. The coastal strip had supported a dense population in pre-Columbian times, as archaeological remains attest, but after the coming of the Spaniards depopulation was so rapid that there is no information whatsoever on the natives. The *Relación de Zapotitlán y Suchitepéquez*, written in 1579, informs us that there was then only one town on the coastal strip. This was Xicalapa, which had only forty-three tributaries. Its location is now unknown.

On the other hand, the Indian population of the Pacific slope, the piedmont as opposed to the Pacific plain, has continued to maintain itself to the present day. The distribution of malaria seems to explain the contrasting conditions in these adjacent areas. Malaria, until two or three decades ago, was prevalent to a dangerous extent in the lower altitudes. At Cuyotenango (elevation ca. 820 feet) most of the Indians coming down from the highlands to work on the plantations were infected with malaria within two weeks of arrival, and at nearby Retalhuleu city, at the same height, 62 per cent of the deaths were caused by malaria. However, at Moca, not far distant but in the piedmont at an elevation of 3,200 feet, there was almost no malaria, its absence being attributed to the good drainage of the precipitous slope which denied breeding places to mosquitoes (Shattuck, 1938: 107–10).

Shattuck notes that at Mazagua, on the coastal plain of the adjacent department of Escuintla, 65 per cent of the population was treated in a single year for malaria. The percentage of infection was probably considerably higher, for from what I know of the country I would guess that most of the remaining 35 per cent did not bother to report for examination. Yet El Baúl, a large hacienda only thirteen miles distant but set in well-drained land, mostly under sugar cane at an elevation of 1,670 feet, was free of malaria when I dug there in 1942.

On the adjacent coastal area of Mexico, known as Soconusco, depopulation and the abandonment of the cacao orchards similarly took place shortly after the Spanish Conquest. The Aztec tribute list shows Soconusco to have been wealthy and well populated, although towns in the highlands are included. It was one of the greatest sources of cacao for Tenochtitlan, but by 1574 the Indian population of the district had fallen to eighteen hundred, and many properties were ownerless through death (Ponce de León, 1882). Even now, most of the Maya from the plateau who go there to work on coffee plantations develop malaria. Of the Indians of the Sonsonate coastal area of El Salvador, another great producer of cacao, a letter of 1584 (McBryde, 1947: 11) says: "They became very sick because of the hot and humid country. . . . Thus many died and they went on dying because of this new work." The reference is to cacao production.

Thus in northeastern Yucatan and on the whole Pacific coast the natives were wiped out within fifty years of the Spanish Conquest. The present-day prevalence of malaria, as well as dysentery, in those hot swampy lands is good evidence that the invasion of those pestilences led to the depopulation of areas particularly suitable for their proliferation.

DEPOPULATION IN THE CENTRAL AREA

The greater part of the Central area reproduces those conditions under which malaria thrives, and it is therefore reasonable to attribute the large decrease in population there during the Colonial period to that and other newly introduced diseases, such as dysentery and hookworm, which find low-lying and swampy rain forest congenial habitats.

That malaria was widespread throughout the Central area, at least until the last decade, is too well known to need emphasis, but for the record we may note the following observations by medical men. Dr. Rife states that everyone along the middle Usumacinta had malaria, and he speaks of all the laborers at Yaxchilan being infected. Dr. Clark reports malaria common everywhere along the Usumacinta and San Pedro Mártir rivers. The whole department of the Petén is a notorious hotbed of malaria, as is, too, the lower Motagua Valley. At Quirigua, where amoebic dysentery is very prevalent, 47 per cent of all cases treated at the hospital between 1919 and 1931 were malarial, and one must bear in mind that the United Fruit Company was constantly fighting to reduce infection (Shattuck, 1933:198–200; 1938:36, 63, 74). Malaria occurred until recently in many parts of British Honduras, as the writer knows to his cost. Gann (1918:36), speaking of British Honduras, notes, "Practically all Indians suffer from malaria." In the review of population which follows, only contemporary statements on health hazards will be noted; it is assumed that in some parts of all the districts discussed those infections may be expected.

One must also bear in mind that the breakdown of the native economy undoubtedly added to depopulation (Scholes and Roys, 1948:10).

The most detailed and reliable information on population decrease in the Central area is that presented by Scholes and Roys (1948: 159, 323, 328, etc.) for the Putun Maya of Acalan-Tixchel who lived on the Candelaria River in southern Campeche when Cortés passed through their territory on his famous march to Honduras in 1525. They very conservatively estimate the population of the province in that year at 10,000 as an absolute minimum. By 1553 the number had declined to a maximum of 4,000, a shrinkage of 60 per cent in less than thirty years. In 1557 the inhabitants were deported from Itzamkanac and other settlements in the Candelaria basin to Tixchel on the coast, just above the Laguna de Términos, so that they would be more accessible to Spanish authority, both civil and ecclesiastic. By 1561 there remained only 250 tributaries, indicating a total population of about 1,100, a drop of nearly 90 per cent in thirty-six years. As Scholes and Roys note, some of the inhabitants had fled back into the forest rather than remain at Tixchel, but the number who fled is probably offset percentagewise by the authors' purposely conservative estimate of the population in 1525. They list disease, malnutrition, and insufficient housing caused by the forcible removal to Tixchel as causes of the decline. After 1561 there was a rise in population to a peak of around 2,500 in 1639, but the destruction of Tixchel perhaps by buccaneers and then yellow fever finally led to the extinction of the Putun Maya of Campeche.

For the so-called province of Tabasco there is a similar story of decline of the Indian population, in this case of 90 per cent between the Conquest and 1579. The author of the *relación* (*Relaciones de Yucatán*, 1:350) remarked: "This Province of Tabasco has scarcely three thousand Indians. There has been a great decrease since the pacification, for then it had a population of over thirty thousand Indians." The author attributes this decrease to pestilences such as measles, smallpox, catarrhs, dysentery, and fevers as already noted. So much for the western side of the Central area.

On the northeast of the Central area we have a similar tale of decline of the native population in the pre-Columbian province of Chetumal which stretched southward from the eastern shore of Lake Bakhalal (now Bacalar) to New River Lagoon, and possibly to the Belize River. The capital, Chetumal, seems to have stood not far west of the present town of Corozal, in British Honduras, for the Franciscan Fray Fuensalida, who had traversed that territory, says the original site was on a ranch between the mouths of the Hondo and New rivers (López de Cogolludo, 1867–68, bk. 9, ch. 6). It may well have been Santa Rita, where Gann found many specimens which belong to the Mayapan period (Scholes and Roys 1948:83).

Our first information on Chetumal comes from Alonso d' Ávila who invaded the northern part of the province in 1531, lured there by reports of gold. His route was by water from Lake Bacalar, the same as that followed in the next century by Franciscan missionaries proceeding to Tipu. It was a wealthy region producing much honey and cacao, both highly valued in pre-Columbian times. Defeating its ruler, d'Ávila captured masks of gold and turquoise mosaic and some six hundred pesos in gold, the largest haul of gold ever recorded from the peninsula. The town of Chetumal is said to have had two thousand houses, perhaps multiple-family residences which would increase the population considerably. D'Ávila founded a Spanish capital there, naming the ephemeral capital Villa Real, but in a year or so Maya resistance drove him to abandon the settlement. Clearly, the province had been well populated, but its bloody and appallingly cruel conquest by the Pachecos in 1543–45 changed that completely. Of the results of that campaign, Fray Lorenzo de Bienvenida wrote in 1548: "There were towns of five hundred and one thousand houses; now one which has a hundred is large." (Chamberlain, 1948: 103, 235.)

The *visita* list of 1582 (Scholes et al., 1936–38, 2:63) names the once great Chetumal as one of twenty-three villages which shared the services of the single priest at Bacalar; the town of two thousand houses had become a small village. When Fuensalida passed by in 1618, only the memory of the site of that once great town remained. At that date, a scant half dozen small villages lay between Bacalar and New River Lagoon, yet less than a century earlier two hundred warriors had paddled down New River to attack d'Ávila's garrison. Clearly, the reduction in numbers of this province of Chetumal must have been about the same as in the other cases we have examined, that is, in the neighborhood of 90 per cent. A good deal of the land east and south of Lake Bacalar is swampy, but it is highly probable that there were extensive cacao orchards along the Hondo and New rivers, for the province produced large quantities of that bean so highly prized by the Maya and all other peoples of Middle America.

60

North of Lake Bacalar and perhaps subject to Chetumal, although theoretically part of the adjacent province of Uaymil, were the towns of Mazanahua and Yuyumpeten, each said to have been of three thousand houses at the time of d'Ávila's *entrada* (Oviedo y Valdés, 1851–55, bk. 32, ch. 6). This may have been a gross exaggeration as Roys (1957:157) believed, but clearly they were important towns. In the *visita* list of 1582 (Scholes et al., 1936–38, 2:63), they appear among twenty-three villages which were served by the priest of Bacalar and which were "from two to forty leagues by sea, land, and marsh" from Bacalar. This indicates that they were then unimportant villages of not over one hundred houses and probably considerably less. By 1609 "in the town of Bacalar, Spanish settlement, and in its district which covers eighty leagues, there are six small villages with six hundred persons under confessional instruction and only one cura" (Vásquez de Espinosa, 1942: 127). Again, there must have been a decline in population of at least 90 per cent. These two villages, situated in a district of lakes not far west of the great swamp extending from Espíritu Santo Bay to Chetumal Bay, must have been mosquito-ridden; both disappeared, probably before the 1609 report cited above, but in 1641 there was a village on the Tipu (Belize) River with the same unusual name of Mazanahau (López de Cogolludo, 1867–68, bk. 11, ch. 13). It is likely that the handful of families in ancient Mazanahau fled Spanish jurisdiction and gave the name of their old home to the new village on the distant Belize River. Flight beyond Spanish control accounts for a part of the decrease in population, but the apostates generally seemed to have joined groups who had never come under real Spanish authority.

Information on what is now British Honduras south of the old Chetumal province is scant. D'Ávila and his men, on being forced out of Chetumal, made their way southward, in dire want, along the coast of British Honduras. Traveling in native canoes, they made several forays ashore or up rivers in search of food, the brief accounts of which suggest a considerable Indian population (Oviedo y Valdés, 1951–55, bk. 32, ch. 8). Further south, on the banks of what was probably Monkey River, was Campin, from which families were reported to have been settled at Xcoloc on the Golfo Dulce, but because of bad treatment they had fled back to the forest. They spoke a language other than Yucatec (López de Cogolludo, 1867–68, bk. 11, ch. 17); as Mopan differed little from Yucatec, this was probably Manche Chol, a group next to be discussed. Campin was still heathen as late as 1641; it was visited by Fray Joseph Delgado in 1677, but ten years later it was the scene of the murder of two friars, after which it disappears from history.

Annihilation was also the fate of the Manche Chol and related groups who occupied the southeastern corner of the Petén, southern British Honduras, and the Golfo Dulce region west of the mouth of the Motagua River. Cortés passed through this territory in 1525, but by then he was hopelessly lost. He seems to have gone by way of the Maya Mountains of British Honduras, swinging southward to reach the Golfo Dulce's outlet to the sea. He gives the impression that most of this was through uninhabited territory. Probably much of it was; there certainly was a fair population eighty years later, living not in towns but in villages and small settlements scattered through the forest. One suspects that Maya guides carefully steered that band of locusts which was Cortés' army away from larger settlements, or their inhabitants would have faced starvation until the next crop was harvested. The looting by foraging parties of the granaries of settlements of four to ten families would do little to assuage the hunger of an army three thousand strong. So, from the viewpoint of hungry soldiers, it was a poorly populated region.

Following the march by Cortés through their territory, the Manche Chol were left alone in their forest homes until 1603, when Dominican friars, operating from the Alta Verapaz, penetrated their territory and, following the usual pattern of evangelization, concentrated the converted in towns. Like other groups in the Central area, the Manche Chol lacked an advanced political organization with a consequent absence of large towns in their territory. The largest town prior to concentration was Manche, with one hundred houses, but the Manche Chol used multiple-family houses (Remesal, 1932, bk. 11, ch. 19). Twenty-five years later there were 6,000 Indians in the care of the friars. This figure may have included some apostate Maya from Cajabón and other towns, but by no means all Manche-Chol territory had come under control of the Dominicans. One contemporary source estimated the population as high as 30,000; I suggested a figure of 10,000 (Thompson, 1938:593). However, by 1630 the native population must have fallen considerably in line with declines everywhere in Middle America. In 1678 a pestilence killed every child under six and almost all between six and ten in the Manche-Chol town of San Lucas Tzalac and nearby settlements. Deaths, including some adults, numbered over four hundred. Every Indian in the whole region fled to the forest (Ximénez, 1929-31, bk. 5, ch. 35).

Revolts, withdrawals into the forest, fresh reductions, and, finally, the removal of all survivors to new locations in the highlands of Guatemala, notably El Chol and Belén in the Urran Valley, not far south of Rabinal, almost wiped out the Manche Chol. Their former homeland certainly had been far from healthy. The friars complained of plagues of mosquitoes by day and night, and they were continually being replaced because of the unhealthy conditions under which they lived (Ximénez, 1929-31, bk. 5, ch. 46). However, this forceable removal from the rain forest to cold mountain country brought new perils of health and reduced the will to live. The president of the Audiencia sent orders that the Indians were to be clothed and so on, but, as Ximénez (*ibid.*, ch. 85) wrote, "little of this was carried out, for many [Indians] died, although steps were taken to see that they died Catholics." According to Villagutierre y Soto-Mayor (1933, bk. 9, ch. 2), only twenty-one died, the cause of their deaths being fury at being deprived of their plurality of wives. This was in the closing decade of the seventeenth century. Settlement in the Urran Valley would be comparable to a forcible transfer of Sicilians to the remoter highlands of Scotland.

The number of Chol resettled in the highlands was not large. El Chol survives as a small village; in 1770 the Indians—men, women, and children, by then all Spanish speaking—numbered 158, and there were also 102 Spaniards and *ladinos*. There were perhaps as many again in the rest of the Urran Valley (Cortés y Larraz, 1958, 2:33). The rest of the Manche Chol, who had rather clearly been diminishing all through the seventeenth century, ceased to exist, at least as a linguistic group, and the forest settlements reverted to wilderness. Discounting the pitiful handful in the highlands, the Manche Chol had become completely extinct.

The lower Polochic Valley, the area around the Golfo Dulce, now called Lake Izabal, and the lower Motagua Valley were Chol speaking and well populated early in the sixteenth century, as Cortés, who explored the land in 1525, makes clear. Polochic itself greatly impressed him, and Nito, on the southeast bank of the Río Dulce, was a great trading center.

By 1574 the villages around the Polochic and the west side of the Golfo Dulce were reduced to four, containing between them 108 heads of families—exclusive of San Miguel Tucurub, at a slightly greater altitude, which was Pokomchi speaking. The largest was San Andrés Polochic, once "a great town," with forty houses (Viana, Gallego, and Cadena, 1955:28-9). Polochic and the next largest town, Xocolo, survived to 1631. As Ximénez (1929–31, bk. 4, ch. 66) noted, the unhealthiness of that hot, humid climate destroyed them as well as all the other Indians in that country. Remesal (1932, bk. 11, ch. 20) says that the Toqueguas, brought from the coast between Puerto Caballos and Santo Tomás and settled at Amatique and Santo Tomás, "finding themselves outside their natural environment, all died."

Around Naco, on the eastern frontier of Maya territory, the story is the same: a large population when the Spaniards arrived was almost completely wiped out. By 1582 the Indians near Puerto Caballos were reduced to sixty tributaries living in three towns (Contreras Guebara, 1946:16); later they disappeared completely. As noted above, measles carried off over half the population in the 1530's; the constant fighting among the Spaniards must have contributed to depopulation.

The Alta Verapaz lies immediately outside the Central area, but as there are specific figures on its depopulation, let us note them in passing. The Dominicans entered the province in 1544, other Spaniards being purposely excluded. In 1561, when tribute began, there were over 7,000 tributaries; by 1574 that number had fallen to 2,900, a decrease of about 58 per cent in thirteen years. Over 200 tributaries had died earlier that year of a pestilence, perhaps dysentery (Viana, Gallego, and Cadena, 1955).

There remains the interior of the Central area to discuss, where population on the whole was sparser and information on large areas scant.

Tayasal, the island stronghold of the Itza which remained independent until 1697, was visited by Cortés in 1525, but does not seem to have impressed him very much. In 1618 Fray Bartolomé de Fuensalida estimated that there were some two hundred houses on the island (López de Cogolludo, 1867–68, bk. 9, ch. 9). As the Itza had multiple-family houses, this might suggest a population of perhaps 3,000 souls, allowing for huts used as kitchens, and so on. However, that was just the capital; the Itza held much territory on the mainland. Avendaño y Loyola (1696:42r), another Franciscan and a careful observer, was at Tayasal in 1695, and, on the strength of what the Itza ruler and other chiefs told him, he estimated the total population at 24,000 or 25,000. Two years later the Itza were conquered and dispersed.

According to the census of 1778 the whole Petén, of which Itza territory was a small fraction, had only 2,555 inhabitants (Juárros, 1823:497). Included were all whites, mestizos, and other Indian groups (Mopan Maya). A 90 per cent decrease of the Itza is a reasonable estimate. By the mid-nineteenth century the Itza seem to have been confined to three villages, containing perhaps 800 people. Tayasal, renamed Flores, was completely mestizo, and other villages were either inhabited by the Mopan Maya or a mixture of Itza and Mopan, or by Negroes from British Honduras.

The Spanish conquest of the Itza was hardly finished before illness broke out among the conquerors and grew worse with the coming of the rainy season (Villagutierre, 1933, bk. 10, ch. 13). Increase of illness is often noted in connection with the rainy season; the explanation is simple: with the rains, swamps expand, supplying breeding grounds for mosquitoes, malarial or harmless. The region has continued unhealthy to this century. In addition to the prevalence of malaria, dysentery, and other lowland infections, intestinal parasites (which by lowering the victim's resistance are the allies of other diseases) are found in 94 per cent of the population (Shattuck, 1938:70).

Northwest of the Itza and east of the Putun of Itzamkanac were the Cehach who were astride the present frontier between the

Petén and central Campeche. Cortés, who crossed the territory, mentions three towns, all of which were heavily fortified, and speaks of the chiefs of five or six others, "each of whom was independent," and indirectly confirms the general impression of the small population by stating that from the last town in the province there was a five-day march to the Itza border (MacNutt, 1908, 2:269). Indeed, the territory was poor and much of it marshy; d'Ávila gave up his plan to settle there for those reasons. Villa (1962) supposes a total population of only about 7,000, a density of less than five persons per square mile since he estimates the area at some fifteen hundred square miles. Cortés makes it plain that there was no central government; indeed, one town attacked another, and the Cehach were subject to constant aggression from their more powerful and better organized neighbors of Tayasal and Itzamkanac. Cehach territory was almost completely depopulated at the end of the nineteenth century (Maler, 1910:137–52) and probably long before that; apparently most of the few remaining Indians had moved in from elsewhere.

The Chorti, who speak a Chol dialect which substitutes *r* for *l*, extended from Zacapa, in the middle Motagua Valley, east to Copan, south to Chiquimula, and southeast to Esquipulas and further to include lands far beyond Sensenti. The region was thickly populated in 1530, and the Spaniards had a very hard time fighting to conquer first Esquipulas and then Copan. The chief of the province of Copan is said to have put an army into the field which, with warriors from Zacapa and as far distant as Sensenti, numbered 30,000 (Fuentes y Guzmán, 1932–33, pt. 2, bk. 4, chs. 10, 11). This figure is surely exaggerated, but is indicative of a populous region. Subsequent to the Conquest there was, as everywhere, a big drop in numbers, for when Fuentes y Guzmán wrote in 1689, tributaries at Chiquimula, Zacapa, and Esquipulas numbered respectively 542, 286, and 50, and Jocotan had only 120 Indians. He writes of places, populous at the time of the Spanish Conquest, reduced to very small numbers or extinct. However, the Chorti again increased. The 1895 census gave the number speaking Chorti as 20,000, to which Sapper (1904) suggested another 30,000 who spoke only Spanish might be added. Today the numbers are far greater.

The Chorti and Palencano Chol are the only groups in the Central area not brought close to extinction, very probably because their habitats are salubrious. That of the Chorti is mountainous except for the Zacapa-Chiquimula country which is exceptionally arid.

There can be no doubt that at the time of the Conquest the Chorti region was quite populous, but the Chol population in the lower Motagua Valley, a most unhealthy region, was completely wiped out.

Information on the population of the Pasión, Lacantun, and middle Usumacinta drainages is scant and unreliable. West of the Manche Chol and between the Pasión and Chixoy rivers were the Acala (Putun). Spanish writers confused them with the Lacandon, whose allies they were in war. In culture they probably differed little from the Manche Chol and the Lacandon, between which groups they lived. That they spoke Chol can be deduced from their geographical position, from the names of their chiefs (although some had Nahuat names—deriving from alien rulers at Altar de Sacrificios or Seibal?), and from the fact that Fray Domingo de Vico, the apostle to Acala who had previously ministered to the Polochic Chol, preached in their own language on his first contact with them. They appear to have been fairly numerous, for, in the Spanish *entrada* of 1559, 260 were captured (p. 36). Sixty to seventy years later, the group was located farther west, on the upper Lacantun River, where they occupied two towns. One with the Mexican name of Culuacan had more than 140 multiple-family houses; Cagbalan, eight leagues distant, had 300 houses (Map 1). The towns were divided into four quarters, each with its own chief, and were probably spread over a large area with a small ceremonial and secular center in the old Maya pattern (Tovilla, 1960, bk. 2, ch. 8). The fact that the houses were multiple-family structures would indicate a population of perhaps 7,000. Clearly, there was no centralized government.

The big *entradas* of 1695, planned in conjunction with the Spanish attack on Tayasal, brought the Spaniards to Cagbalan (Kak Balam?) which they renamed Dolores. Since 1630 the town had shrunk from an estimated 300 to merely 103 houses. Two of these were for communal purposes; a third, the largest, was the temple and contained many idols (Villagutierre, 1933, bk. 4, ch. 14). Beyond lay two other Lacandon towns, but at a considerable distance, Mop and Peta, with 105 and 117 families respectively. All three seem to have been independent of one another. The region was clearly quite thinly peopled, less so than at the time of the sixteenth century *entradas* but vastly more than at the present day, with the Lacandon reduced to perhaps 150 people. Their culture was simple, that of small farming communities.

Blom and Duby (1955–7, 2:211) state that Dolores was abandoned five years after its capture, by which time half the inhabitants had died of diseases brought by the Spaniards, and the other half had fled back to the forests. In that connection, it is worth noting that the priests, during their extremely short stay in Mop and Peta, "baptized many children, and dying adults." This suggests the pestilence may have spread there also.

The Acala disappeared completely. Ximénez (1929–31, bk. 4, ch. 3), writing about 1720, said that not even a memory of them remained. A number of supposed tribal names from this area are scattered through the literature, but in all probability they are the names of *caciques* of single villages.

The few Lacandon still living between Lake Miramar and the Usumacinta have inherited the culture of the former peoples, but they now speak Yucatec. On the other hand, Lacandon from the forest were settled at Salto de Agua which is Palencano Chol speaking. As noted, Lacandon is a geographical rather than a linguistic designation.

From the forests well to the south of Tenosique, considerable numbers of Chol were brought out and settled in Palenque and nearby towns such as Tila and Tumbala, where they increased considerably. Other Indians were settled at Bachajón and in parts of Ocosingo (Ximénez, 1929–31, bk. 4, ch. 47). The Bachajón speak a dialect of Tzeltal, indicating that a branch of Tzeltal lived in the forest lowlands; those who were settled at Ocosingo, a Tzeltal town, were from Pochutla, a Lacandon island fortress pacified in 1564. The latter were presumably absorbed by the local Tzeltal.

Palencano Chol, the dialect of Chol spoken at Palenque and

neighboring towns, appears to be closer to Putun than it is to Manche Chol, and, indeed, they were geographically closer to the former.

This general region, from which the Palencano Chol had been removed in the sixteenth century, came to be known as the Próspero Kingdom in the seventeenth century. The most important place was Nohaa, on the verge of a lake which is probably the Lake Noha mentioned by Soustelle (1937:3) and which appears as Lake Naha, west of Pelha, on the Blom map (Blom and Duby, 1955–57). Franciscans in 1646 sent a brief mission to Nohaa. The people, a mixture of apostates and heathen, spoke Yucatec, had a church, and used some Christian rites, but they wore their hair long, pierced their ears and noses, and sacrificed humans and dogs (López de Cogolludo, 1867–68, bk. 12, chs. 3–7). Their speech may have derived from an influx of apostates from Cehach territory probably amalgamating with Chol remnants who had escaped the evacuation to Palenque nearly a century before, adopting Lacandon culture with minor European additions, but imposing their language upon them. The Yucatec spoken by the present-day Lacandon who are presumably their descendants differs from that of Yucatan by about the amount one would expect the Cehach to show. Yucatec immigrants to Tenosique similarly imposed their language on the indigenous Putun inhabitants. The Franciscan in charge of the Próspero mission claimed there were more settlements there and in the territory beyond than in Yucatan, and claimed that all spoke Yucatec except the Chol-speaking Locen who lived beyond the Lacandon. The Locen, a group hitherto unmentioned under that name, had seven or eight towns, the largest of which, Locen, had eight hundred houses, a figure I find very difficult to accept. Among the people he mentions are the Itza, Mopan, Cehach, Lacandon, and several with hitherto unreported names. The good friar, who was only in Nohaa a short time and who never traveled further, was passing on a lot of garbled and hear-say reports, but his statement is of value in confirming that this southern part of the Central area was far from depopulated in early colonial times.

Moreover, the Dominican Francisco Morán who knew the eastern part of this territory very well, estimated the population at 100,000 (León Pinelo, 1958, pt. 4). This must be a gross over-estimate and probably includes the Itza, but at least it is yet further confirmation that the whole area was far from uninhabited, even as late as 1635 when he wrote. For the past two centuries, the whole Usumacinta Valley, from Tenosique to the upper Cancuen, has held only a few Lacandon (now about 150) exclusive of very recent immigrants.

North of Cehach territory, around and to the northwest of the great swamp of Bolon Petén, now called Isla Pac, were a dozen villages and towns, mostly comprising refugees from Yucatan, but with some local heathens. Scholes and Roys (1948), in their brilliant study of this region, show that the friars moved the Indians out in 1615, but that fifty years later the region was once more a flourishing center of apostates and other Indians.

Another focus of apostate Maya, with its main and southernmost village at Sacalum, west of Chetumal, has also been studied by Scholes and Roys. These settlement areas have no bearing on the problem of population in the sixteenth century, but they serve to show that there was no obvious obstacle to settlement in such areas and also that the same forces which wiped out local populations early in the Colonial period also wiped out these immigrants at a slightly later date; their villages are unmarked and the areas are once more uninhabited.

There remain for discussion the Maya settlements at Tipu and other places downstream from Tipu on the river of the same name, now the Belize River. Tipu itself almost certainly was located not far from the archaeological site of Benque Viejo, on the bank of the Mopan or on Eastern Branch, which join at El Cayo to form the Belize River.

In theory, Tipu was a Christian village with its church administered by the cura at Bacalar. In fact, it required about a week's journey in both directions to visit it, so the village, which in 1618 comprised one hundred families, was left to its own devices. Enormous numbers of idols were discovered there, more indicative of heathenism than apostasy. Moreover, a *matrícula* of the town, dated 1655 and brought to light by France Scholes, who kindly gave me permission to refer to it, lists men and women with Maya day names, a custom quite unknown in Yucatan at any time. This suggests that Tipu and presumably the other towns or villages on the Belize River should be set apart from the main body of Yucatec culture. Unfortunately, little is known about them.

In the seventeenth century, this region of the upper Belize had a medium population probably swollen by refugees from Yucatan. Each village appears to have been independent and without any defenses. Cacao, vanilla, achiote, and fish and turtles from the river were sources of wealth. Perhaps the market for these products, particularly cacao, was Tayasal, but poor communications probably prevented the area's developing much wealth or population.

These villages disappear from history, but British logwood cutters working on the Belize River in the eighteenth century employed Indians, and three or four Maya villages, although not those mentioned in early sources, survived to modern times. Those Indians working for the cutters and those inhabiting villages such as Yalbac were probably the descendants of the Maya of Tipu culture. There is not a complete disappearance of the old population, but obviously a decrease to a fraction of what there had been earlier.

The data reviewed above make it abundantly clear that for every part of the Central area for which information is available very large decreases in population followed the Spanish Conquest. These amounted to 90 per cent or more according to actual figures or reasonable estimates in the following areas, dates indicating definitely or approximately the time spans involved: Putun of Acalan and Tixchel, 1524–61; Tabasco, 1530?–79; Chetumal province, 1531–82; south Uaymil province, 1531–1609; Manche Chol, 1603–1700; Polochic and Golfo Dulce, 1525–1631; Naco and its coast, 1524–82; Itza of Tayasal province, 1697–1778; Cehach, 1525–1900; Usumacinta, Lacandon, and Pasión drainages, 1625–1900; Isla de Pac and Sacalum regions, 1660–1900; and the upper Belize Valley, 1695–1900. Exceptionally, decrease in the Chorti region, while severe, fell considerably short of 90 per cent, almost certainly because of the healthier terrain. Generalizations in subsequent sections do not apply to the Chorti.

It is clear from the above survey that the belief that the Central area was largely deserted at the arrival of the white man is quite wrong. No doubt it arose because the whole area was almost without permanent habitation by the time modern interest in Maya civilization developed, and much of the information on the position in the sixteenth century which would have corrected that impression was then unavailable or difficult of access.

An estimate of the population of the Central area early in the sixteenth century would not be worth considering. It is clear, however, that it was relatively dense in some parts and that there was a scattering of settlements in the least populated parts. But everywhere stretches of forest with very low population offset parts with greater density. Moreover, population figures from late in the sixteenth century onward have to be considered in light of the fact that throughout Middle America the greatest decrease in the aborigines occurred in the first fifty years of contact with Europeans and was largely due to newly introduced diseases. As these new plagues spread beyond the boundaries of Spanish rule, a high proportion of the natives in unsubdued regions were swept away before the white man penetrated those parts. In short, the longer Spanish entry was delayed, the greater the fall of native population from pre-Columbian levels. A further consequence of the spread of malaria and other lowland diseases was that except for those parts such as Naco and Tabasco provinces, effectively brought under Spanish control during the first decades of the Conquest, the Central area remained largely independent of Spanish rule, defended not so much by the natives as by diseases entrenched in its swamps and lagoons. In fact, in some places, notably the lower Motagua Valley, around the Golfo Dulce, and parts of Chetumal, the pestilences counterattacked and drove out the Spaniards.

LINGUISTIC INFERENCES

As is clear from the above survey, there is quite full information on languages and dialects spoken in the Central area at the time of the Spanish Conquest. Their distribution supplies evidence that the sixteenth-century population of the Central area was descended from people inhabiting that area in the ninth century.

Had the end of the Classic period, about A.D. 900, been marked by the extermination or emigration of the whole population, the subsequent filling of the vacuum would have resulted in a certain geographical dislocation of Maya languages and dialects. There is no such evidence. No Maya highland language seeped into the lowlands, and no Maya lowlands language is spoken also in the highlands, situations which one would expect to find had there been a vacuum in the southern part of the lowlands subsequently filled by other groups moving in. The only possible exception to this statement is the Chorti language prevalent around Copan and Chiquimula in intermediate to high country. This is little more than a dialect of Manche Chol (it substitutes *r* for Chol *l*). If anything, the distribution suggests a penetration from lowlands into highlands, not vice versa, and it appears to have taken place early in Maya history. (p. 101).

That highland groups will move into the lowlands to fill a vacuum is shown by the way Kekchi from Alta Verapaz have pushed north to the Usumacinta and into southern British Honduras in the last century. The Ixil, farther west, are now doing the same thing on a smaller scale, I am informed. Both peoples have been moving into unoccupied country. Lastly, the Bachajon Tzeltal are moving east of Ocosingo, perhaps back into their former territory.

Moreover, the sixteenth-century distribution of Maya lowland languages shows no evidence of irruption or dislocation; there is an uninterrupted transition right across the base of the peninsula from the Putun of the Tabasco plain to Chorti at Copan.

In view of the above linguistic arguments, we can deduce that the peoples of the Central area in the sixteenth century descend from the inhabitants of the area in the tenth century and earlier. It follows that within limits we can name the Maya language or dialect spoken in the various territories administered from each ceremonial center.

EXPANSIONIST VERSUS STATIC GROUPS

The various parts of the Central area at the time of the Spanish Conquest fall into two sharply contrasting categories, and from that arrangement significant deductions may be made. On the one

73

hand there are well-populated areas or provinces, each with a central and authoritarian political organization, and generally wealthy in terms of pre-Columbian values; in contrast to these are those areas in which each town or village is independent with no evidence of any supravillage organization. Towns are smaller than in the first category, normally not exceeding one hundred houses (probably spread over a wide area), and generally a hut of regular house type, although somewhat larger, serves as the temple. Population is considerably less dense and there is little evidence of wealth.

Areas in the first group are:

1. Potonchan and neighboring Tabasco, which was well populated and well organized, for it put an army in the field which numbered 40,000 according to the figure given Cortés (MacNutt, 1908, 1:152). Díaz del Castillo (1908–16, ch. 31) estimated 12,000 men; whatever the figure, a formidable force. Other large towns were subject to the ruler of Potonchan. This was a great trading center, and extensive cacao orchards were a source of much wealth, for cacao beans were the currency of Middle America. Gifts of gold and masks of jade or turquoise mosaicwork, perhaps the most valuable recovered by the Spaniards in the Maya area, testify to the accumulated wealth.

2. Naco, Nito, and the coast from the Chamelecon River to the Río Dulce formed a single economic, but probably not political, unit with a large population. Cortés (MacNutt, 1908, 2:306) writes of four towns, including Naco and Sula, the smallest of which numbered more than two thousand households. Almost nothing is known of the political organization, but mention of broad roads and information on trading quarters, "factories," of Putun merchants indicate well-knit, extensive communities. Wealth again derived from the extensive cacao orchards and the brisk maritime trade funneled through the ports of Naco and Nito (p. 130).

3. Chetumal was an extensive province with a large population. Its capital of the same name was reported to have contained two thousand houses. The ruler, Nachan Can, with the help of his son-in-law, the renegade Spaniard Gonzalo Guerrero, fought d'Ávila to a standstill and finally forced him to flee under humili-

ating conditions to Honduras. He organized fleets of canoes, one of which he sent against the Spaniards in distant Honduras. Chetumal was wealthy for the same reasons as the two areas already reviewed—its cacao plantations and its maritime trade. Very extensive apiaries were another source of wealth, for honey was in much demand in the absence of sugar cane in pre-Columbian America. Chetumal was the only part of the Maya lowlands, apart from Potonchan, to yield an appreciable amount of gold to the Spanish soldiers. This was a product of commerce; there was no native source.

4. Copan province was certainly populous and politically advanced but, for reasons already given, will be omitted from the discussion.

5. The Putun of Acalan-Tixchel had in their capital, Itzamkanac, a place which impressed Cortés, who was already acquainted with the great towns of the Mexican plateau, and it was not until he reached the Polochic that he found anything comparable. The town, said to have contained nine hundred to one thousand houses (perhaps an exaggeration), appears to have been divided into four quarters, a civil and religious administrative arrangement similar to that found, for instance, among the Aztec of Tenochtitlan. There were many temples, although these are not described. The province contained seventy-five "towns," although some must have been tiny. All were controlled by the hereditary chief ruler. The province was reasonably wealthy because of its water-borne commerce and ownership of trading quarters at the bottom of the Bay of Honduras. The seagoing canoes carried produce from the Mexican plateau as well as local specialties, salt from the Campeche coast and slaves.

6. The Itza province of Tayasal was somewhat small but had a fairly dense population. Its ruler was supreme over the twenty (?) districts into which it was organized. The fear in which the Itza were held by their neighbors confirms other evidence of a well-knit political organization. Temples were set on squat pyramids or platforms and were numerous. Religion was not on a village level, for the ruler possessed hieroglyphic books and the computation of time involved the advanced katun system of counting with a cycle of nearly 260 years. On the other hand,

75

there was little wealth. To offset that absence, there is every indication that the Itza were an aggressive, expanding people.

The states ruled from Itzamkanac and Tayasal were clearly of considerably less importance than the first three regions discussed, but in their centralized political organization, and in what one might term their "go-aheadness," they rate assignment to the first category.

In the contrasting category of unorganized, thinly populated regions fall the remaining groups we have discussed, namely, the Manche Chol, the Mopan Maya, the Cehach, the Tipu and Belize River settlements, and the Lacandon-Próspero peoples.

Among these peoples there is no evidence of political grouping above the village level, and, in the case of the Cehach, there was fighting between one town and another. Each village had its chief or chiefs who owed obedience to no one, and in several cases the names which have come down to us of villages and even "tribes" are in fact the names of village chiefs. Towns are small, exceptionally reaching one hundred houses. Specialized temple buildings seem to be absent; instead, as among the present-day Lacandon, a hut of normal residential type, although perhaps a little larger, serves the religious needs of the village. Information on religious practices is scant, but there is a tendency for "idols" to be replaced by incense burners as tangible representations of deities. The lack of idols among the Manche Chol receives comment from various early friars. A regular priesthood seems to be absent, but one can be reasonably certain a village chief had both secular and religious functions and that shamans were ubiquitous. Human sacrifice was sporadic. At least in the case of the Manche Chol, the old Maya count of the days and year-bearers was maintained. There is little evidence of wealth in the hands of the community or the individual.

One is left with the very forceful impression that all these are village cultures which, despite regional variations in essentials, are little different from present-day village cultures throughout the Maya area, from Yucatan to the highlands of Guatemala, and from the Mopan Maya of British Honduras to the Tzotzil of the Chiapan plateau.

The sixteenth century, then, witnessed these two contrasting

76

manifestations of Maya culture side by side in the Central area: thrusting, successful, wealthy, well-populated states alongside thinly populated regions which held only an unorganized scattering of isolated, wealthless villages. Moreover, there is a regional reversal of roles as compared with conditions during the Classic period. The areas of greatest expansion in the sixteenth century, Potonchan, Chetumal, and the northern coast of Guatemala and Honduras, were peripheral to the area of great ceremonial centers in the Classic period; on the other hand, the great expanse of village culture in the sixteenth century was across the base of the Yucatan Peninsula and in the Petén, precisely the region in which Maya architecture, sculpture, and hieroglyphic writing reached their greatest heights during the Classic period.

Fortunately, something is known about these sixteenth-century foci of expansion, enough to suggest one explanation of the above paradox, although whether the correct one I leave to future students to decide.

There is evidence of groups from outside gaining control, or at least influencing the affairs, of all five of these well-organized and aggressive provinces.

Potonchan, like the rest of the Chontalpa region of Tabasco, was a meeting place of Nahuat and Maya culture, and there were Nahuat-speaking villages mingled with those of Putun-Maya speech. The whole province was exposed to Nahuat influence, but it was not merely a question of influence. Scholes and Roys (1948: 37n.) cite evidence that in 1543 the ruler of Potonchan was named Cipaque, and that he had apparently succeeded Acipaque. Cipaque, like other names in the area, derives from a Nahuat day name Cipacti or Cipactli. Scholes and Roys list ten other personal names from the Chontalpa which similarly derive from other Nahuat day names. One must therefore conclude that the ruling family of Potonchan was intrusive from non-Maya stock or had married into Maya ruling families.

With regard to Chetumal, it was stated in a Maya lawsuit of 1618 (Brinton 1882:114–18) that invaders from "the kingdom of Mexico" divided into four groups, one of which erected the sumptuous buildings of Chichen Itza while another established itself at Bakhalal (Bacalar), which was in or on the borders of the province of Chetumal. There are good grounds for identifying these invaders as the Itza whom I believe to have been Putun. A passage in the *relación* of Paxbolon reinforces this identification (Scholes and Roys, 1948:82, 86, 385), for it relates that a certain Putun-Acalan ruler of Itzamkanac exacted tribute from Chetumal, although this was later than the arrival of the four groups. Moreover, murals at Santa Rita (Gann, 1900), quite probably ancient Chetumal, combine Maya and strong south Mexican motifs, and emphasize the merchant god, a chief tutelary of those great traders, the Putun.

The rulers who seized Itzamkanac claimed to have come from Cozumel, seemingly around the latter part of the fourteenth century (Scholes and Roys, 1948:79, 383).

As is well known, the Itza rulers, after their defeat at Chichen Itza, established themselves at Tayasal, probably in the thirteenth century. One may suppose that they imposed their rule on a native population already in the area.

Information on the political organization of the Naco-Nito coastal strip is almost nonexistent; practically the whole teeming population was wiped out before any information could be gathered. Evidence for supposed Nahuatl-speaking villages in the area is tenuous. Nahuatl names for villages in early documents often mean only that names in other languages reached the Spaniards in translation through Nahuatl-speaking auxiliaries. Cortés (MacNutt, 1908, 2:305–306) wrote that he had some of the Nahuatl-speaking chiefs from Mexico and also his interpreter (his mistress, Marina, who spoke Putun and Nahuatl) reassure some natives who had fled Naco of his good intentions.

The captured natives might have been Putun merchants who would also have understood Nahuatl and so might have been more impressed by reassurances which came from the mouths of chiefs in the Valley of Mexico rather than from that of Cortés. Alternatively, they may have been Nahuatl-speaking refugees from a Culhua-Mexica merchants' quarter in the town. There was certainly a Putun merchants' district in Naco, and possibly one from Yucatan.

These foreign merchants, whether they included a Nahuatl-speaking group from the Mexican plateau or not, dominated the trade of the area and must have been a stimulus to local culture. There is even a hint that this area may have been partly controlled by Chetumal; that seems the most obvious deduction to make from the fact that the ruler of Chetumal sent a fleet of fifty war canoes to help in the defense of the region against the Spaniards (Roys, 1943:116); Roys believed that the Chetumal leader had a "factory" in the region.

It is of interest to note that the Putun were in particular associated with these expansionist groups. The Putun controlled Potonchan and Itzamkanac, and their commercial interests along the Naco-Nito strip were extensive. There are, as noted above, grounds for supposing Putun influences at Chetumal. Lastly, the Itza, I believe, were Putun adventurers who had won control of Chichen Itza early in the tenth century (p. 11).

CONCEIVABLE PROTOHISTORIC AND POST-CLASSIC PARALLELS

In this final section, I suggest with some trepidation that the consequences of the overthrow of native Maya rule by the Spaniards may have had precedents in what one might reasonably suppose to have happened had the ruling class been eliminated at the close of the Classic period. Naturally, this approach is highly speculative.

In the sixteenth century, with the destruction of the native ruling class, there was a serious breakdown of the pre-Columbian economic pattern. Articles highly prized in pre-Columbian times (jade, jaguar pelts, obsidian, flint, fine feathers, sting-ray spines, etc.) were no longer traded; trade relations between many communities diminished or ceased and communities became more isolated. Despite a Spanish national government which could, in fact, be very irksome at times, Maya communities frequently became what were, to all intents and purposes, independent entities, in no way politically involved with other towns of the same speech and of the same cultural level and frequently not closely associated with those neighbors in culture, religion, or commerce. This situation obtains to this day in Yucatan, the highlands of Guatemala, and among the Maya communities of the Chiapan plateau. Quiche towns such as Rabinal and Chichicastenango—to take an example at random—are insular communities; they are not fellow members of a Quiche nation.

On the assumption that the elimination of the minority ruling class of priests and nobles accompanied the abandonment in the Central area of the ceremonial centers at the close of the Classic period, a breakdown in the economy leading to widespread isolation of communities may have occurred then as it did in the sixteenth century.

There is little information on the social standing of merchants during the Classic period, but occasional illustrations on polychrome vessels indicate that the top echelon, presumably those who managed long-distance operations, were members of the aristocracy. Accordingly, accepting that the ruling class was eliminated at the close of the Classic period, we must assume that these merchant princes were liquidated at the same time. With their disappearance, the network of long-distance trade routes would fall into disuse. In any case, there may not have been the demand for the luxury products which had traveled along those routes. Village leaders might not have commanded the wealth to pay for such items of international commerce as fine jades and quetzal-feather headdresses. In fact, they may not have wanted them, for revolutionaries lose followers if they ape the ways of those they have dethroned.

On a less luxurious level, most present-day villages in the Central area have their own potters, in contrast to the few centers which distribute pottery in the highlands and Yucatan. Conceivably, this shift reflects the economic breakdown of the Central area a millennium ago. The Lacandon are similarly self-sufficient in many ways.

Furthermore, liquidation of the ruling class would have deprived many artists and craftsmen of their livelihoods. There would have been little or no demand for such products as large sculptures in stone or wood, fine masonry work, and the enormous quantities of stucco needed to renew the acres of floors, steps, platforms, pyramids, and wall surfaces. The call for wooden lintels, sculptured and painted hieroglyphic texts, ceremonial costumes and masks, litters, curtains, and all the elaborate paraphernalia required for temple ceremonies would have largely ceased. With the old ceremonial center, an insatiable customer for such products, replaced by a single thatched hut as village temple, the outlet for the skills of this group would have almost disappeared. That group of the middle class would have moved elsewhere or sunk discontentedly into the ranks of the peasants. In either case, the isolation of the small community increased, and with it its wealth diminished.

Wholesale desertion of the Central area at the close of the Classic period can be ruled out: Willey, Bullard, and others (1965:568) report that of sixty-five mounds examined, no less than sixty-two show a post-Classic occupation, and we have seen that the middle Belize Valley was far from unoccupied centuries later in the Colonial period; San José certainly had an active post-Classic occupation as was noted over a quarter of a century ago (Thompson, 1939:236–40), and there is full evidence of a post-Classic occupation on the outskirts of Tikal. One can conclude that at the close of the Classic period the Maya peasant did not die; he only faded away. The question is how long and how complete was that demise.

The considerable stretches of unoccupied forest, which in so many parts separated settlements at the time of the Spanish Conquest and after, hint that there was some factor, perhaps a pestilence other than those brought later by the Spaniards, which reduced the population considerably in post-Classic times, although one suspects that stretches of forest were by no means unknown at the height of the Classic period.

An important factor may have been a lack of will to live after the old cultural pattern of life based on the ceremonial center ended.

It seems possible that when the rulers were no more and the ceremonial centers were reverting to forest, the peasant's relief at being free of that never-ending service to gods and their representatives on earth may not have long endured. It may have been replaced by a loss of purpose, of lack of interest in living, and of regret for the past; for with obligations to the ceremonial center and its rulers went privileges and a sense of participation. Pageantry, color, beauty, bustling markets, security against the enmities of gods and neighboring peoples, and rewards for service had gone; the world had shrunk to a village very much on its own.

The haphazard dragging of stelae around abandoned ceremonial centers and the resetting, upside down, of pieces of sculpture are pathetic acts which may reflect this loss of purpose and security, but there could be no return to the past. Such attitudes with their accompanying disquiets might well have led to a marked decrease in numbers.

That the lack of will to live is an important factor in declining population was certainly true of the Mexican plateau after the Spanish Conquest, and we have seen that something similar happened to the Manche Chol forcibly removed from their old habitat and resettled in the Guatemalan highlands. Gann (1918:36) has an interesting comment on this lack of will to live: "Indian men and women of all ages and classes, when attacked by any serious malady, are found to be lacking in vitality and stamina; they relinquish hope, and relax their grip on life very easily, seeming to hold it lightly and as not worth a fight to retain. An elderly man or woman will sometimes take to the hammock without apparent physical symptoms of disease beyond the anaemia and splenitis from which nearly all suffer, and merely announce . . . 'I am going to die.' They refuse to eat, drink, or talk, wrap themselves in a sheet from head to foot, and finally do succumb in a very short time apparently from sheer lack of vitality and absence of desire to continue living." Gann was a medical officer in British Honduras for many years.

Starr (1908:312–13) reports the case of a Yucatec Maya who decided to die after dreaming he was going to do so. Apparently in good health, he made his will, took to his hammock, and, refusing to eat, drink, or speak, died in six days. According to Starr's informant, "These Maya often die for spite or because they have made up their minds to do so."

My colleague Isabel Kelly has called my attention to a sixteenth century report from Colima, western Mexico (Lebrón de Quiñones, 1951:13–14), that in many towns the Indians took steps that women should not conceive. If a woman did conceive, an abortion was arranged, for, the Indians said, "they did not wish to see their children in the captivity and servility in which they were."

To suggest that a lack of desire to live was a factor in the decline of Maya post-Conquest population, even if associated with other adverse factors such as new pestilences, may sound far-fetched, but in that connection the fate of the Santa Cruz de Bravo Maya of Quintana Roo in recent years is worth consideration. They have decreased to an enormous extent in the past seventy or eighty years for no obvious reason. An explanation may be that once the need to fight to preserve their entity ceased they seemed to lose their spirit. Perhaps as a consequence they have shrunk to a shadow of their former strength. Once cultural arteriosclerosis sets in, there may be no recovery. Yet the introduction of soccer has given some primitive communities in disintegration a fresh interest in life and saved them from extinction.

Despite the post-Classic decline, forces were at work which would set Maya culture, or at least parts of it, on a new course. Aggressive new groups came on the scene and with fresh energy established new dynasties over new and expanding provinces, and no doubt hastened the decline in static areas by drawing off people attracted by the opportunities an expansionist policy offered. As we have seen, the dominating force in this resurgence appears to have been the Putun Maya. Conquest and the acquisition of wealth by trade or conquest seems to have been the compulsive factor.

The speculative ideas in this final section are advanced in the hope that they may stimulate archaeologists to elicit the data from which more securely founded conclusions may be drawn. Small sites of the post-Classic period have scarcely been touched. It is true that they are not easily found, but, excavated in sufficient numbers, they should supply facts to replace theories.

CHAPTER 3

The Eastern Boundary
of the Maya Area:
Placements and Displacements

It is hardly necessary to say that a prerequisite for an understanding of Maya history is a firm grasp of the extent of Maya territory. For the solution of that problem two sources are available: archaeology and colonial documents. The one may inform us of conditions perhaps at the height of the Classic period; the other enlightens us on boundaries at the arrival of the Spaniards. The two sets of data can, with caution, be integrated, for, so far as the area under discussion is concerned, there is reasonable agreement between them. Investigation of the Maya eastern frontier has suffered from a poor interpretation of the archaeological remains and a failure to make full use of documentary sources.

So far as archaeology is concerned, there has been an unfortunate tendency to deduce a Maya occupation from the scant artifacts of definite Maya workmanship and from the far more numerous Maya-influenced pieces found over much of western Honduras and El Salvador. The one lot can equally well be ascribed to trade, the other to influences from a neighbor with attractive decorative styles.

In the Ulua-Yojoa area of western and central Honduras, polychrome pottery of local manufacture shows a combination of numerous Maya motifs with locally developed decorative elements. For instance, Maya hieroglyphs, so highly conventionalized that they are meaningless and clearly serving only as decoration—the same broken-down glyph may be repeated around the whole circumference of a vessel—are common on pottery of that area. To accept them as indicative of a Maya occupation is no more logical than to suppose that the huge quantities of china with the willow-ware pattern distributed all over the United Kingdom and United States indicate a Chinese occupation of those countries. Nor, for that matter, can one deduce a Mediterranean invasion of the United States from the number of cities named Athens, Troy, Memphis, Ithaca, and so on.

Archaeologists, too, have tended to assign to the Maya cultural features in that area which, to the best of our knowledge, were common to many peoples of Central America. For instance, it has been claimed that groupings of mounds on all sides of a square or rectangular court are indicative of Maya occupation. Were that so, the Maya empire must have stretched from the United States to Panama or beyond. In seeking evidence of Maya occupation, one must use only details believed to be specifically Maya.

So far as dependence on historical documents is concerned—and they, of course, are far more dependable as evidence of the limits of Maya expansion at the time of the Spanish Conquest—research in the past has suffered from the fact that those who have examined such sources have been archaeologists whose acquaintance with that field was not as profound as it might have been. That was partly because those students, as archaeologists, were operating outside their primary field of interest, and partly because, again as archaeologists, they were unconsciously inclined to set up postulates based on archaeology and to seek confirmation of them in documentary evidence. Furthermore, sources then unknown are now available to the student.

Let us accordingly make a fresh survey of the problem from the standpoint of the ethnohistorian by integrating the rather limited archaeological data into the far fuller information in colonial documents.

Somewhat rashly I propose to carry the matter a stage farther and indulge in some speculation on possible historical developments during the Classic period. Archaeologists are uncommonly frightened of the effects of speculation on their reputations, but in our field, without benefit of experimental laboratory, it is only by exposing oneself as the target of a coconut shy that one can stimulate others to make the county fair a success.

Linguistic maps vary in marking the eastern boundary of the Maya area (map 3).

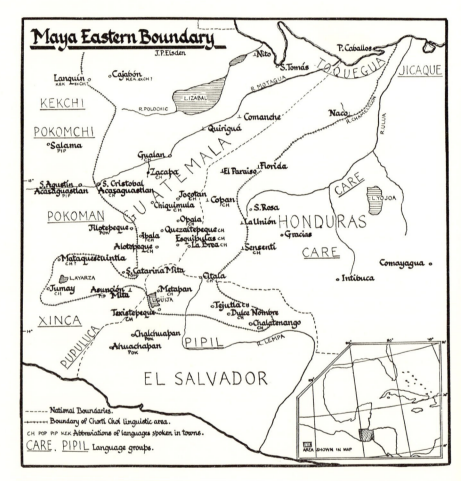

Map 3.—The Eastern Boundary of the Maya Area and Chorti Expansion. *(Drawn by J. P. Elsden.)*

Thomas and Swanton (1911) start the eastern limit of the Chorti, easternmost Maya group, immediately east of the mouth of the Motagua River with the non-Maya Jicaque beyond, astride the Chamelecon and Ulua rivers. The boundary curves to include within Chorti territory the lower Chamelecon. Then, about due south of Puerto Barrios, the direction swings to the south-southwest to include Santa Bárbara in the Maya area, terminating against the territory of the Mexican-speaking Pipil on the Sampul River a little southeast of Ocotepeque. From there the boundary passes west-northwest to near Quezaltepeque where Chorti, Pokoman Maya, and Pipil areas join. Thence it bears south-southwest to about halfway between Asunción Mita and Jutiapa, where Pokoman, Pipil, and Xinca meet and Pupuluca just fails to join the rally. Xinca and Pupuluca are non-Maya groups of uncertain linguistic affiliations who form small, weak enclaves.

Lehmann (1920) draws his boundary from about midway between the mouths of the Motagua and Chamelecon rivers in a southwesterly direction to a point between Santa Bárbara and Santa Rosa, somewhat closer to the former. From there he takes it west of south to a point a little west of the city of Intibuca. Thence it follows a course a little north of west to the northern shore of Lake Güija, where Chorti, Pokoman Maya, and Pipil meet. Thereby the whole of the Honduran department of Gracias is assigned to the Chorti, but the strip between the southern boundary of the Chorti and the Lempa River is about evenly divided between the Lenca, a non-Maya group dominant in much of central Honduras and almost certainly in El Salvador west of the lower reaches of the Lempa, and the Pipil to the west of them.

Lothrop (1939), in a somewhat controversial presentation, discussed below, considerably enlarges the Maya area. His boundary, beginning a little east of the mouth of the Ulua River, swings south-southwest to the northern tip of Lake Yojoa. Thence the line curves to an apex a little east of Gracias. The curve continues south-southeast to where the Lempa River turns sharply southward, following that river southward to its mouth on the Pacific. Thereby the whole of El Salvador west of the Lempa is (Pokoman) Maya territory. It should be noted that Lothrop says that his boundary marks "the maximum expansion of the Maya to the south and east without regard to period, as indicated by both archaeological and linguistic evidence." In fact, his maximum expansion fell long before the Spaniards came. The other map shows the boundary as it was thought to have been in A.D. 1520. As we shall see, Lothrop's reasoning was not up to his usual high standards of scholarship.

Johnson (1940) accepts Lothrop's boundaries as far south as the Lempa, but, adhering to conditions as they were at the Spanish Conquest, assigns western El Salvador to the Pipil except for those centers Lothrop had supposed to have been Pokoman at that date.

Longyear (1947), in a thoughtful and cogent contribution to the problem, published two maps, one showing the Maya eastern frontier as he supposed it to have been toward the close of the Classic period (ca. A.D. 850) and the other as he believed it to have been at the time of the Spanish Conquest. In the earlier period he has the frontier running from the approximate position of Puerto Barrios south to cross the Chamelecon at Los Higos. Thence it travels in a flat curve with its apex slightly east of La Unión and Sensenti to the point where the Lempa River turns south, and thence southward following the course of that river to the Pacific. That is to say, he moves the boundary considerably to the west of Lothrop's line in the northern half, but agrees with Lothrop from Sensenti south to the mouth of the Lempa. The Lenca are neighbors of the Maya for the whole length of the frontier.

Longyear's A.D. 1500 map has the northern half unchanged except that the Jicaque have taken over as neighbors of the Maya from a point west of the north end of Lake Yojoa to the Atlantic. For the southern third, the boundary between Maya and Pipil runs eastward from the north shore of Lake Güija to the Lempa, and follows that river to shortly west of its turn south. That is to say, the whole area south of the Lempa has ceased to be Maya except for a couple of outposts of Maya at Chalchuapa and San Salvador, as indicated by Lothrop.

Longyear, writing as an archaeologist, makes the point that the appearance of occasional pieces of Maya polychrome pottery is no proof that the sites in which they occur were necessarily Maya speaking. He sees no evidence that Ulua-Yojoa polychrome pottery is Maya, nor that such seemingly unspecialized features as the layout of small courts can serve to identify a linguistic group. I am in agreement with all three points he makes.

In the discussion which follows I shall endeavor to reconstruct the boundary as it was around A.D. 1500 on the basis of a closer examination of linguistic references in colonial documents. Archaeology will be used to indicate an earlier Maya occupation of a site for which there is sixteenth-century testimony. That archaeological evidence will be confined to occurrences of corbelled vaulting, Maya-style ball-court ornaments, and (once) dressed stone.

There are reliable source materials to establish the starting point of the Maya eastern boundary. Remesal (1932, bk. 11, ch. 20) states that the Toquegua lived between Santo Tomás, near present-day Puerto Barrios, and Punta Caballos, a little west of the mouth of the Chamelecon. Ximénez (1929–31, bk. 4, ch. 5) repeats the above, adding that the Toquegua were Chol (he does not distinguish between Chol and Chorti). The Toquegua had been settled at Amatique where Mercedarians from their convent at Santo Tomás evangelized them (Samayoa, 1957:38). In a lucky aside, Ximénez (bk. 5, ch. 23) indirectly confirms his previous statement, telling of a certain Fray Juan de Apresa who returned to Guatemala City from administering the sacraments in Amatique and the Castillo del Golfo Dulce, "bringing with him a grammar of the Chol language, and as the Father had to go to Chiapas, he gave the grammar to Friar José Delgado . . . so that he might study the language . . . and in a short time he knew it by heart." Indeed, shortly thereafter he surprised some Chol on a visit to Guatemala by talking to them in their own language. Clearly, then, the Toquegua spoke Manche Chol. Furthermore, some Manche Chol brought from the forests were settled at Amatique (Villagutierre, 1933, bk. 6, ch. 11). We may reasonably conclude that these reduced Chol were settled among Indians of their own speech to hasten their absorption into Hispano–Christian culture. That is, the Toquegua would be their bellwethers. Chol-speaking Toquegua, accordingly, once occupied the coast to Puerto Caballos. This is confirmed by John Galindo's inclusion of Omoa in his "Chorti Empire."[1]

What of beyond? In a memorandum of 1751 to the Spanish crown on coastal fortifications, Diez de Navarro (1946:59) states that the coast "from Punta Astillas, which is by Puerto Caballos, to Triunfo de la Cruz is Xicaque territory although they inhabit it only when they come to catch turtles." This is an eighteenth-century source, whereas the population of coastal Honduras was largely wiped out soon after the Spanish Conquest.

Doris Stone (1941:14–15) quotes two important documents of 1533. The first, a memorial of Alonso López to the Council of the Indies, states: "From the Ulua River to the Cupilco [*sic*] Zaqualco River is all one tongue and all trade with one another and are held to be one . . . and all the Indians of those parts say that these are their boundaries and that beyond the Cupilco Zaqualco River the language is that of New Spain, and in the same way beyond the Ulua the language is another." The second statement is almost a paraphrase of this.

The Copilco, in fact, enters the Gulf of Mexico just east of Comalcalco, westernmost Maya site except the newly discovered López Mateos, and certainly marks the western frontier of Putun (Chontal Maya) speech, as well as of the Maya at the Spanish Conquest.

However, in setting the eastern boundary at the Ulua, the statement disagrees slightly with that of Diez de Navarro. The mouth of the Ulua lies only twelve and one-half miles east of Punta

[1] John Galindo (in Morley, 1920:595, 603), the Dublin-born English "enthusiast"—a title, in the eighteenth-century meaning of the word, Ian Graham (1963) most felicitously accords him—took a prominent part in the siege and capture of Omoa. One may suppose that his inclusion of the town or district in his "Chorti Empire" derived from local information. He assigns to the Chorti domain equated with distribution of that language the following places: Cuaginiquilapa, Los Esclavos (department?), Quezaltepeque, San Jacinto, Santa Elena, San Estéban, San Juan Ermita (or del Río), Jocotan, Camotan, Chimalapa, Zacapa, San Pablo, Chiquimula, and Esquipulas in Guatemala; Texis (tepeque), Dulce Nombre, Metapan, Tejutla, and Citala in El Salvador; Copan, Omoa, the mines of San Andrés, Sensenti, Ocotepeque, Tipalpa, and La Brea in Honduras. To the El Salvador list must be added Tachaluya, for Galindo reports a tradition that Camotan was founded by Chorti immigrants from that town.

Nearly all the places he mentions are known to be, or to have been, Chorti speaking (Cortés y Larraz assigns Chimalapa to the Algüilac tongue), so there is justification for accepting other towns in his list (e.g., Ocotepeque, Dulce Nombre, and Metapan) whose assignment to the Chorti lacks corroboration.

Astillas, Diez de Navarro's terminal point of Maya occupation, and a bend of the river is only six miles east.

The Putun (Chontal Maya) at the base of the Gulf of Mexico are known to have had trading posts on the coast of Honduras including Naco on a small tributary of the Chamelecon. To keep trade with Naco open, control of the mouth and lower reaches of the Chamelecon was essential. Accordingly, one may guess that the Sula area was occupied by Xicaque, with Chol-Toquegua on the coast as far as the Chamelecon mouth and perhaps a sprinkling of Nahuatl, as Stone believes (some may have been traders at Naco), but the whole probably under the political control of a recently established Putun-Maya minority. This last point is surely borne out by the expedition of fifty war canoes sent in 1536 by Chetumal, probably Putun controlled, to aid Ulua against the Spaniards (Chamberlain, 1953:53, 57). Surely Maya would have sent an expedition only to aid those of their blood or, conceivably but less probably, to defend their trade posts in the area. It is true that "Copilco to Ulua, one language, one nation" was part of Montejo's propaganda when he hoped to be allotted control of all that area including Yucatan, but that may have been one of those rare occasions when propaganda is also the truth.

It might with reason be supposed that Maya domination of the Chamelecon dated only from Putun expansion at the close of the Classic period and later, and started, like European expansion in Africa and Asia, with trading posts, the "factories" of the eighteenth century. The local population having remained non-Maya, the Spaniards would have made their first contacts with the "traveled" ruling Maya group and would have assumed the whole area to have been Maya speaking. With the Maya minority wiped out by disease, deportation, and war, known to have almost eliminated the Indians of coastal Honduras, the Jicaque survivors would have absorbed the few remaining Maya.

Accepting the above, the northern Sula plain to the Chamelecon had a Maya minority ruling over non-Maya peoples at the time of the Conquest, and that domination probably extended to the lower Ulua. Thence the frontier of the Maya, but now Chorti, probably followed the lower Chamelecon from near Los Higos, a Classic-period Maya site, to the headwaters of the Río Amarillo and from there in an obtuse curve with blunted apex a little east of Copan to La Unión and southward to the Sensenti Valley. La Unión, or Talqueselapa as it is also called, lying some twenty-two miles southeast of Copan, is another Classic-period Maya site. Here is a ball court with macaw heads which, until some three decades ago, were still set in its walls. Strömsvik (1952:199) noted their strong similarity to those in the ball court at Copan and called attention to the Copan-style dressed stone. There can be no question that this was surely a Chorti-Maya site, a view with which Stone (1957: 118–19) concurs: "The first site that can be definitely classed as related to the Copan Maya."

E. G. Squier (1855:385) remarked that "the Chorti dialect was spoken between Gracias and the frontier of El Salvador in the Valley of Sensenti." Beyond informing us that Chorti was spoken in that valley, it is difficult to gather what exactly that sentence means. Gracias certainly was not Chorti territory.[2]

Stone (*op. cit.*:117) discusses the Sensenti Valley, and illustrates a stone carving to my eyes definitely Maya and not out of place in Copan. She calls attention to the beautiful worked stone, again suggestive of Copan. Here, then, there is both archaeological and linguistic evidence for the northward extension of the boundary at least to La Unión, and perhaps to the neighborhood of Santa Rosa de Copan.

Galindo (*loc. cit.*) includes both Sensenti and Ocotepeque in his "Chorti Empire." This is the only source for assigning the latter to the Chorti, but it is acceptable, for Ocotepeque, as we shall see, lies between two Chorti concentrations.

[2] Gracias and the surrounding country as far as the town of Intibuca were Care speaking, according to a seventeenth-century report by the Mercedarians who evangelized them (Samayoa, 1957:40). Care was also the speech of the old *curato* of Tencoa along the upper Ulua, including Santa Bárbara and Ilama, and of the *curato* of Cururu. The Mercedarians distinguished Care from Lenca, but places they assign to the Care are sources of Lenca vocabularies in Lehmann (1920). There is sad confusion in this matter of Lenca, but it is likely Care and Poton are distinct dialects of Lenca. Herrera informs us the two groups were enemies, but Lempira united them against the Spaniards. Normally Indian alliances were between those of a single language, which tends to support that Care and Poton were closely related. The suggestion that the Poton were Maya is surely quite untenable, as, too, must be the statement that the north coast as far as Trujillo was Maya. The last probably rests on a misunderstanding by Columbus of the ports of call of the Maya trading canoe he encountered off the Bay Islands. From it he seized a man as informant, but since they could converse only by signs, the error could easily have arisen.

Almost thirty miles due south of Sensenti within El Salvador lies Chalatenango, which, as Lothrop notes (1939:46), is assigned to the Chorti in an eighteenth-century document. Another eighteenth-century source (Cortés y Larraz, 1958:208–10) supplies two links between what formerly had seemed a lone outpost of Chorti speech at Chalatenango and the Sensenti Chorti. The information which the Archbishop, in the course of a visitation to his diocese (1769–70), supplies is extremely important, for he reported that the towns of Tejutla, seventeen miles west-northwest of Chalatenango, and Sitala (Citala), twelve and one-half miles north-northwest of Tejutla, were Chorti-speaking. The last is just on the El Salvador side of the border with the Honduras department of Ocotepeque which we have seen was also Chorti, according to Galindo. The latter writer includes Dulce Nombre in the same vicinity in his "Chorti Empire." He also states that the Chorti of Camotan had moved there from Tachaluya, in El Salvador, a village I have not managed to locate.

That is not all. Galindo also includes in his Chorti domains Metapan, northeast of Lake Güija, and Texis(tepeque), immediately south of the same lake. Cortés y Larraz, who is careful with his linguistic data, writes that the maternal tongue of the parish of Quezaltepeque, south-southeast of Zacapa, was Chorti. That huge parish extended from Sulay, south of Copan, as far south as the Concepción Valley and Alotepeque, the last only eleven miles north-northeast of Lake Güija, the assumption being that Chorti stretched that far. Chorti, then, were living north, northeast, northwest, and south of that large body of water, contrary to all former assumptions.

More startling is Cortés y Larraz' (1958, 1:54) statement that the villages of Jumay and Mataquescuintla in the parish of Los Esclavos also spoke Chorti; Alonso Crespo (1935:14), writing in 1710, assigns Jumay to the Xinca. The local cura, presumably the source of the Chorti attribution, had been only two months in the parish, but his curate, whom he must have consulted, had been there eight years. Moreover, Galindo assigns (the department of?) Los Esclavos and the town of Cuajiniquilapa to his "Chorti Empire." In view of that confirmation of the Archbishop's statement, we must accept Jumay and Mataquescuintla, as well as Cuajiniquilapa, as Chorti, and assign a zone northwest and southwest of Lake Ayarza to that people. It is abundantly clear that the Chorti occupied a far more extensive area in the southeastern part of the Maya area than was formerly supposed, and Pokoman territory was smaller.

At Asunción Mita, Mexican speaking according to the Archbishop who gives the speech of nearby Santa Catalina as Pokoman, there is evidence pointing to a former Chorti occupation, for here are lowland-style vaulted buildings with stone laid in mud, as at Copan, as well as a ball court with macaw-head ornaments or markers, as at Copan and La Unión, although of cruder workmanship. García de Palacio reports that the Pipil, Chontal, and Indians of other nations went there to sacrifice, the widespread custom of repairing to abandoned ceremonial centers. In all probability the term Chontal was locally applied to the Chorti, who, although dislodged from Asunción Mita, remained in the vicinity (Metapan was less than nineteen miles west).

In short, the area west of a line from Sensenti to Chalatenango as far as Los Esclavos clearly was Chorti with enclaves of Pipil, Pokoman, and Xinca in the southwest corner.

To define more clearly the extent of Chorti territory in colonial times, let us turn to the middle Motagua. Cortés y Larraz (1958, 1:54, 264, 280, 283) wrote that the Chorti extended downstream from Zacapa to Gualan and upstream to San Cristóbal Acasaguastlan, but surrounding settlements, already specified as Usumatan and Chimalapa, spoke Alagüilac although Galindo has Chimalapa as part of his Chorti domain. As Alagüilac (final -*ac* plausibly Chol or Chorti *ac*, "tongue") became extinct not later than three or four decades after Galindo wrote, and possibly much earlier, it is highly probable that it was supplanted by Chorti, long dominant in the surrounding territory, thereby reconciling the contradictory statements. Brinton (1887), seemingly confused over the two Acasaguastlans (San Agustín was Mexican speaking), supposed Alagüilac to have been a local name for Mexican; it was probably something quite different, perhaps that of the ancient people who terminated place names in *agua* (see below).

Reverting to the Maya boundary, this had been traced as far as the Chorti town of Texistepeque south of Lake Güija. South again of that there was a medley of Pipil, Xinca, and Pokoman, with the first dominant. The Pokoman held two, perhaps three towns: Chalchuapa, Ahuachapan, and perhaps Atiquisaya. In the extreme south, Pipil and the nebulous Pupuluca stood one on each side of the El Salvador–Guatemala border. Nearly all El Salvador south and west of the Lempa River was Pipil except for the Chorti settlements noted around Lake Guija, an enclave of "Chontal" near the great bend of the Lempa, to be discussed, and the Pokoman towns just inside the border of El Salvador, listed above.

As previously noted, Lothrup (1939) advanced the theory that all that territory from Guatemala to the lower Lempa River, although overwhelmingly Pipil speaking at the Spanish Conquest, was once Pokoman. His linguistic arguments were:

1. Chalchuapa and Ahuachapan, Pokoman Maya at the Spanish Conquest, represent islands left when Pokoman was submerged.

2. García de Palacio, in his *relación* of 1576, said of the town of Iztepeque, north of the volcano of San Vicente and only a few miles west of the Lempa River: "From the said place, although it is in the same province, there begins another language of Indians whom they call Chontals." Lothrop had developed a far from convincing argument that the Chontal mentioned by Palacio as living around Mita were Pokoman, and, on the strength of the above sentence, concluded that the Chontal of Iztepeque were also Pokoman Maya.

3. Some Achi reported by Ciudad Real as living in the city of San Salvador in 1586 were another Pokoman group which survived the Pipil flood.

Lothrop's first point is perfectly acceptable but of little importance, for those two Pokoman towns are only a few miles over the border from Guatemala.

With regard to the citation on which he bases his second point, surely that can only mean that from that place eastward, the direction in which García de Palacio's survey is pointed, there is spoken another language of the Indians they, the Pipil, call Chontal. In other words, Palacio, having previously mentioned the Chontal around Mita who spoke one language, is informing us that there, almost on the boundary of San Miguel, is another group whom they, the Pipil, also call Chontal. Palacio seemingly had recognized that *chontal* merely meant "foreigners," and here was a second group the Pipil called foreigners, but they spoke yet another language. Quite apart from the fact that the passage will not bear the construction Lothrop placed upon it, logically, as those Chontal of Iztepeque continued eastward beyond the Lempa, Pokoman must have been widely spoken there. For that there is not a tittle of evidence; Lenca was the dominant tongue in western San Miguel, beyond the Lempa, where it was known as Poton. Iztepeque was almost certainly a trans-Lempa outpost of Lenca. For purposes of linguistic identification, "Chontal" is as useless as our word "foreign."

Lothrop's second point was that the Achi in the city of San Salvador were Pokoman. His argument rested on three lines of reasoning: that Ciudad Real applied Achi to Guatemalan tongues in general, including Pokoman; that Palacio omits Pokoman from his list of Guatemalan languages and therefore meant it to be included under Achi; and that Fuentes y Guzmán says Achi was spoken in the Sacatepequez Valley which was Pokoman in speech. It follows, therefore, Lothrop said, that Achi equals Pokoman.

Nevertheless, there is massive evidence that *achi* was a term applied to the cognate Maya languages Cakchiquel (or Guatemalteca), Quiche (or Utatlatleca), and Zutuhil, as Ciudad Real (1873, 1:383) specifically states, and to no other tongue unless it be a dialect of one of those. Ciudad Real omits Pokoman from his list of Guatemalan languages because, as he carefully points out, he is giving only the tongues spoken within the Franciscan province of Guatemala (The Most Holy Name of Jesus). All twenty-five towns which he lists as Achi speaking were Quiche, Cakchiquel, or Zutuhil. When he passes through Petapa, a Pokoman-speaking town, he notes that the language of that town was much like Achi and even had some Yucatec words. He does not list the language as one spoken in his province for the simple reason that the Pokoman towns were under Dominican ministration. Ciudad Real came from Yucatan, was a brilliant student of Yucatec, and was extremely interested in Indian languages. Accordingly, when he remarks that there were a few Achi-speaking Indians at San Salvador, we can be sure that that is precisely what he means, and that those Achi belonged to one of those three closely related linguistic groups. As to Lothrop's argument that Palacio mentions Achi but omits Pokoman from his list of Guatemalan languages, and so by Achi he means Pokoman, one may note that Palacio also omits from his list of Guatemalan languages Quiche, Zutuhil, Jacalteca, Chuh, and Xinca, any one of which could be equated with Achi by that same argument.

Finally, we examine Lothrop's citation of Fuentes y Guzmán's statement that Achi was spoken in the valley of Sacatepequez, which in fact was Pokoman speaking. One might note that the passage is not from the pen of that discursive and somewhat unreliable writer, but is an editorial note by Justo Zaragoza, no doubt a most worthy gentleman but one who lived in the late nineteenth century and, I believe, never set foot in Guatemala. Moreover, Sacatepequez is predominantly Cakchiquel, that is, Achi, not Pokoman.

We can be sure that Ciudad Real's statement can only mean that those Maya in San Salvador were Zutuhil, Cakchiquel, or Quiche.

A more reasonable explanation for the presence of those few Achi at San Salvador is that they were settled there by Alvarado when he founded the town in 1526 on his return from his first expedition to Honduras. It was common practice to settle Mexican allies close to newly founded Spanish towns—note such settlements at Almolonga, outside the first capital of Guatemala, and at Ciudad Real, chief settlement of Chiapas. Had Alvarado followed that pattern at San Salvador, presumably he would have settled Achi Indians there in preference to his Mexican auxiliaries who would be less dependable in the event of an uprising because they spoke the same language as the natives around the city; the Achi spoke a foreign language, and so were more likely to side with the Spaniards. Alvarado definitely had Achi-speaking Maya with him on his 1536 expedition to Honduras (Chamberlain, 1953:88), and very probably he took Achi Indians with him on the earlier, 1526, expedition, for he is known to have had Zutuhil auxiliaries at that time (Recinos, 1953:125).

I know of no direct evidence that Achi-speaking Indians were settled at San Salvador—precious little is known of the foundation of the city—but such a procedure is the most plausible explanation of the presence there of that small group (a similar explanation

97

probably accounts for the presence of a Mexican-speaking colony at Comayagua, another early Spanish administrative center). In no case could those Achi-speaking settlers have been Pokoman.

Lothrop's Pokoman occupation of western El Salvador, in fact, rests on two Pokoman-speaking towns about nine miles over the border from Guatemala. Archaeologically, there is nothing in present information which indicates a Maya occupation of the country. Moreover, it is now known that Pipil influences reached the Pacific Coast far earlier than was believed to have been the case when Lothrop postulated a late Pipil invasion obliterating an earlier, Classic-period, Pokoman occupation.

The keys to the southern end of the eastern boundary of the Maya group are, I think, the relations between Chorti, Pokoman, Pipil, and an unidentified group.

As is well known, the Mexican auxiliaries who participated in the Spanish Conquest passed on to the Spaniards Nahuatl names for the most important towns in the conquered territories, and that was particularly true of Guatemala. However, in contrast to the important towns such as Huehuetenango, Quezaltenango, Totonicapan, Utatlan, Atitlan, and others, smaller settlements in the central highlands largely retained their Maya names, as a glance at a good map makes clear. That, however, is not true of the eastern strip of Guatemala and adjacent western Honduras, for in Chorti-occupied territory there are remarkably few Maya place names.

Aside from towns rechristened with Nahuatl names and those given Spanish names, there are many which bear non-Maya designations, some of which incorporate syllables found in place names across Honduras in areas to which we can be reasonably sure the Maya never penetrated. Most important of these are words incorporating the di-syllable *agua* or *ahua* somtimes reduced to *gua* or *ua*. The distribution of this group (a fuller coverage would undoubtedly add to the number) is as follows:

In eastern Guatemala and western Honduras, approximately the area of the Chorti at the time of the Conquest, are Toquegua Indians, Motagua and Managua rivers; and the sites of Tigua north of Camotan, Tigua east of Paraiso, Chanmagua or Chaumagua, Jagua, Pasasagua, Anchagua, and Cocuyagua.

In central Honduras, approximately between 86° 50' and 88° 10', that is to say, east of Chorti territory, are the rivers Jacagua, Jalagua, Chilistagua, Comayagua, Sasagua, Chasnigua, and perhaps Ulua; and the sites of Silisgualagua, Manzaragua, Masahua, Mulacagua, Tircagua, Chumbagua, Chapulistagua, Xagua, Xelegua, Eraxagua, Moncagua, Teconalistagua, Laxigua, Talgua, Colomoncagua, Tiscagua, Apacilagua, Conchagua, as well as Masaguara, Sicaguara, Yaguacire, and Yamaguare.

In El Salvador we find Comasahua, Atepammasagua, Quixnagua, Masahua, and Moncagua, as well as Aguasarca and Guahtajigua.

One may also note other examples in territory even farther east and southeast, such as Nicaragua, Managua, and even Veragua.

I have been unable to associate this di-syllabic element with any living language. It surely has nothing to do with Spanish *agua*, nor in most cases can it be regarded as a Nahuatl termination. The only conclusion I see is that it was an ending used by some group (conceivably allied to Misquito-Sumo-Ulva-Matagalpa) which preceded the arrival of the Chorti in the territory they held in the sixteenth century and the appearance of the Lenca or other linguistic stock, notably the Jicaque, in central Honduras. It appears not to occur in other parts of the Maya area, although there is a Jalpatagua, southwest of Jutiapa, in Xinca territory.

If one assumes that the *agua* people of eastern Guatemala were displaced, the invaders presumably were a lowland Maya group because the vaulted structures at Asunción Mita, as noted, are close to the Copan tradition; the highland Maya made almost no use of the corbelled vault except for tombs, and then only on the peripheries of the lowland area. Similarly, the concentration of vaulted chambers in the San Agustín Acasaguastlan part of the middle Motagua presumably derive from the Maya lowlands. One can, therefore, logically assume that the Chorti dwellers in the vicinity of those two ceremonial centers in colonial days descended from invading lowlanders of the same speech who had established themselves there during or before the Classic period. The Pipil had in turn occupied San Agustín and probably Asunción Mita, but the Chorti remained close to both sites. In view of the numerous towns they occupied in the vicinity of Asunción Mita and to the north-

east, the Chorti are surely the Chontal mentioned by García de
Palacio as neighbors of the Pipil and other groups near Mita, and
as occupying the portion of the province lying in the direction of
Gracias á Dios. There is no evidence that the only other candidates
for that name, the Lenca, were established near Mita.

If, as seems most probable, the architecture of Asunción Mita
and Acasaguastlan is referable to the Chorti, those sites were not
far short of high-water marks of the Chorti tide. As to a lowland
origin, Chorti, to all intents and purposes, is merely a dialect of
Manche Chol, as Gates (1920:605–10) noted, different from it
mainly in the substitution of *r* for *l*. Gates also cites the most important statement in Palacio's *relación*—that in ancient times
people from Yucatan had conquered the provinces of Ayajal
(Aycal?, a name for the Mopan Maya), Lacandon, Verapaz,
Chiquimula, and Copan, and that it was certain that the Apay
language which is spoken here is current and understood in Yucatan and the aforesaid provinces. Certainly Chorti (Pay? The
language of the Ah Pay?) was never spoken in Yucatan, but the
closely related Manche Chol was current in Lacandon and parts
of the Verapaz, notably in towns such as Cajabon and Lanquin,
which were later overrun by the Kekchi, as well as on the Polochic
side. If by Yucatan we are to understand the base of the peninsula
of that name—and the Indians who handed down this tradition can
have had only the vaguest idea of the location of Yucatan, a geographical term unknown in pre-Columbian times—this old tradition probably relates to a movement of the Chorti part of the Chol
out of the southeastern Petén and adjacent areas of the lowlands
into the highlands.

Such a movement out of the lowlands, one imagines, might have
displaced, directly or by indirect pressure, the people whose place
names or river names often contained *agua* or *gua* from the whole
area south of the Motagua from its mouth to San Cristóbal Acasaguastlan and eastward to the mouth of the Chamelecon, to Copan
and southward to La Unión, to the Sensenti Valley, and thence
to northwestern El Salvador.

Our postulated thrust up the Motagua and south almost to Lake
Güija conceivably could have sundered the Pipil around San
Agustín Acasaguastlan, Guastatoya, Tocoy, the Sanarate Valley,

and Salama from their brethren around Asunción Mita and the Pacific slopes of Guatemala and El Salvador. The splitting of Pokomchi from Pokoman could have occurred at the same time, but might have resulted from earlier Pipil incursions. In the absence of all evidence, I rather favor the latter theory.

Events in history are seldom as simple and clear-cut as in theoretical reconstruction. Doubtlessly, the above speculations are grossly oversimplified. The splitting of the Pipil and Pokoman areas may have been widely separated in time and cause. Furthermore, we know that there was a sort of Pokoman backlash in the form of Pokoman movement out of El Salvador to Ayampuc (Ximénez, 1929–31, bk. 1, ch. 26) due to overcrowding and apparently not long before the Spanish Conquest.

On the assumption that there was such an invasion of Chorti, it must have occurred not later than early Classic times, for there are Maya sculptures from Copan and Quirigua which can be dated with reasonable certainty to the late fifth century A.D. Stela 24, Copan, carries an Initial Series of 9.2.10.0.0 (Morley, 1920:78–83), but may have been dedicated at A.D. 495, ten years later. Stela U, Quirigua (Morley, 1937–38, 4:89–94), I think was dedicated at the same time, although Morley tentatively dated it about two centuries later (the *cauac* element at A8a and the pinched-top Ahau of B5a are both of early type, so I would suppose the defective Initial Series was about contemporaneous with the erection of the stela), perhaps also at A.D. 495. Our postulated Chorti invasion therefore must antedate the closing decade of the fifth century A.D.

It is now recognized that the Pipil were established in Guatemala by early Classic times, and in that connection I would again call attention to the definite sculpture of Cotzumalhuapan style known as Altar V at Quirigua and representation in sculpture of non-Maya folk at Copan (Thompson, 1948:29–30). Both would support the thesis of a Chorti invasion of non-Maya territory in or before the Classic period. It is by no means certain that in the fifth century the Chorti had become differentiated from the Chol to the extent of substituting *r* for *l*. As is well-known, there are traces of an *r* in modern Lacandon and in seventeenth-century Manche Chol. I would suggest that thought be given to the possibility that the western frontier of South American influence or occupation in the sixteenth century (Stone, 1959) may have stood farther west in the opening centuries of our era. Lothrop (1921) advanced that view but extended the boundary to the Isthmus of Tehuantepec nearly a half century ago. Conceivably, the *agua* folk might explain resemblances in the earliest pottery in Honduras and Chiapas.

The greater part of this chapter is based on early written sources of unquestionable reliability. In contrast, the concluding section is highly speculative and should be treated as such.

The demolition of the hypothetical Pokoman occupation of El Salvador, except for two towns just across the Guatemalan border, clears the ground. In its place, we can now speak of a Chorti thrust on a broadish front from the Atlantic lowlands right across the highlands along both sides of Guatemala's eastern border, not only in force into El Salvador, north and west of the Lempa River to Lake Güija, but also, it would appear, on the Guatemalan side to south of Lake Ayarza.

Those lowlanders, whose forebears may have lived around Lake Izabal, came almost within sight of the Pacific, doing considerably better in that respect than "stout Cortez" of the poem. Perhaps Galindo, the "enthusiast," was not too imaginative in writing of a "Chorti Empire."

CHAPTER 4

Tobacco Among the Maya
and Their Neighbors

INTRODUCTION

Scant jottings of mine on "the weed" appeared over two decades ago as "Some Uses of Tobacco Among the Maya" in the mimeographed *Notes on Middle American Archaeology and Ethnology*, No. 61, Carnegie Institution of Washington, 1946. I have tried to improve the mixture by blending with it more gleanings, particularly data from Central Mexico, which parallel or expand Maya usages. Emphasis has now shifted to present tobacco, as seen through native eyes, with corresponding stress on the spiritual role played by the plant. Although this chapter is triple the length of the mimeographed article, complete coverage of the non-Maya field is not attempted, for that would duplicate the fine study by Muriel Porter (1948) which appeared not long after the mimeographed paper.

An important purpose in recasting and expanding this material is to examine the transformation in cultural values which an element suffers when taken over by an alien and self-designated superior culture. Tobacco, like cacao, on being annexed by the Spaniards and other Europeans, was wrenched from its setting of religious ceremony, and its medicinal values were ignored. It survives in its new cultural setting only as a pleasure.

Fig. 1—Panels at Palenque. These two figures stand on each side of the entrance to the sanctuary of the Temple of the Cross, Palenque. The chief at left is plastered with symbols of Itzam Na—headdress, back ornament, collar, ornament dangling from waist, and

water giver in hand. The old man at right, impersonator of the jaguar god of number seven, smokes his cigar or perhaps tubular pipe. *(After A. P. Maudslay.)*

In mitigation, there is a new development of tobacco in Europe as an insecticide, presumably a case of independent invention; the Old World gardener or scientist who first propounded the efficacy of tobacco juice against aphids can hardly have known that for perhaps two millenia the Maya had used tobacco juice as a sovereign cure for beef worm.

ARCHAEOLOGICAL MATERIAL

Archaeological evidence for Maya use of tobacco is scant. The great slab which stood on the right of the entrance to the sanctuary of the Temple of the Cross, Palenque, provides the best evidence of smoking during the Classic period. An impersonator of an aged god, with huge Roman nose, outjutting chin, and hollow cheeks to indicate the loss of most of his teeth, is shown in profile with jaguar skin hanging from his shoulder and jaguar ears peeping out above his earplug (Fig. 1*b*). He is smoking what appears to be a tapering cigar with three bands on it but which may have a reed wrapping, or just possibly the whole object represents a tubular pipe. A double volute presumably indicates the smoke. The whole could represent a ceremony analogous to the blowing of smoke to the four world directions by North American Indians. The personage may be the jaguar god of number seven (p. 292), conceivably God L.

On page 79*b* of Codex Madrid is painted a compressed 260-day sacred almanac divided into five parts of 52 days apiece. Each of these has three subdivisions presided over respectively by the gods of rain, death, and maize. Each god lies on his back on the ground (identified by the *cab*, "earth," symbol) and has in his mouth what seems to be a cigar. These resemble the cigar on the Palenque relief, tubular but tapering somewhat to the mouth end, and with a black band or rim at the opposite end. Just above the tip of each cigar is a cascade of black dots, pretty clearly indicating smoke or sparks (Plate 4*c*).

Pages 86*b*–87*b* of the same codex illustrate another 260-day sacred almanac, and the three gods presiding over its subdivisions are again smoking tapering cigars (?), but here the gods are squatting on their haunches. Red and black dots before the cigars clearly stand for smoke and sparks or glow. God D is similarly enjoying a smoke on the adjacent page 88*b*.

A complex design on the inner rim of a late Classic tripod plate from Uaxactun (R. E. Smith, 1955, Fig. 2g) includes a seated man with what looks like a long white cigarette in his mouth. A double volute at the end of the cigarette is a crude parallel to the large one on the Palenque relief. The smoker is again an aged man with a large, rather Roman nose and very prominent chin, which may well be significant. The white of the cigarette probably indicates that the tobacco was enclosed in reed or corn husk, practices known to have been common at a later date.

A beautiful pottery pipe—just possibly an incense burner—was found under a colonnade floor of the Temple of the Warriors at Chichen Itza. This is not Maya but of a recognizable type manufactured in Michoacan, western Mexico, and dates to about A.D. 1150. With its length (1 foot, 9 inches) and its fragility, this imported piece can hardly have been in daily use. It was probably a pipe; the narrow bore argues against a heat vent to prevent breakage in baking. The same type turns up at Tula, and, as the Temple of the Warriors was a complex devoted to the Mexican warrior cult, its users probably were not Maya of Yucatan.

Apart from this import, excavation in the Maya area has produced nothing positively identifiable as a pottery or stone pipe. That is certainly true of Uaxactun, Piedras Negras, Barton Ramie, San José, and Mayapan. Two unslipped fragments of pottery tubes were found at Tazumal, El Salvador (S. Boggs in Longyear, 1944:68, a citation I owe to Muriel Porter). This site is on the Maya southeastern frontier (p. 95), where foreign influences may have impinged, but the fragments could as well have come from brazier handles which are usually hollow.

Elbow pipes turn up in central and western Mexico in large numbers, but none apparently are earlier than the end of the Classic period, circa A.D. 900 (Porter, 1948). An elbow pipe said to have come from Palenque (Douglass, 1899) must be viewed with deepest suspicion.

TOBACCO IN COLONIAL AND MODERN TIMES

Early Spanish accounts of smoking among the Maya are not very informative.

Juan Díaz, chaplain of the Grijalva expedition of 1518, a precursor of Cortés, reported that on the Island of Cozumel the Maya presented Grijalva and some of his men with some *cañas* ("reeds" or "canes") about a palm long which gave off a delicate odor on being burned. *Caña* is a term early chroniclers generally employ to describe the aromatic cigars used by the Mexicans.

Bishop Landa, our prime source on Maya culture at the coming of the Spaniards, refers only once to smoking. This is in connection with a puberty rite for boys and girls. At one point in the ceremony the priest's assistants gave the boys smoke (*humazo*) to swallow (*chupar*). The early Spaniards, with little knowledge of smoking, had difficulty in describing the process. One may conjecture that Landa wished to say that each boy was given a few puffs at a cigar.

Cigars are mentioned in the Popol Vuh, the sacred book of the Quiche Maya. The two heroes, as part of the ordeals they must face, are required to pass a night in the cave of darkness and to keep their cigars and pine torches alight all night. The young men extinguish their cigars, putting fireflies on the ends to deceive their enemies, the people of the underworld, that they are still alight. In the morning they relight their cigars and emerge triumphant. In a present-day Quiche folk story, Christ faced the same ordeal when He was in prison and solved it in the same manner. A similar idea must have been current in Yucatan. Candidates for chieftainship in Yucatan had to answer certain riddles, the questions and answers being preserved in the Chilam Balam of Chumayel (Roys, 1933:97). One riddle reads: " 'Son, bring me the firefly of the night. Its odor shall pass to the north and to the west.' . . . What he asks for is a smoking tube filled with tobacco." As Roys notes, these riddles were designed to elicit information about whether a candidate had a sufficient fund of the esoteric knowledge necessary for his future office. A good grasp of Maya tradition and myth was clearly a required subject.

A description of a raid in 1685 on some Yucatec Maya who

were engaged in a little backsliding into paganism mentions that at the scene of the ceremony, in a milpa, were found some cigars still alight and resting on a sort of hoop of vines. They were larger than those usually made, were of tobacco, and were wrapped in corn husk. (Uchmany de De la Peña, 1967).

A few years later the Spaniards captured the Lacandon Chol stronghold which they renamed Dolores (p. 27). In the abandoned huts they found cigars of tobacco wrapped in leaves of the nance tree (*Malpighia glabra*) according to the source on which García de Pelaez drew, but of curiously painted pottery according to Villagutierre y Soto-Mayor (1933, bk. 5, ch. 6). The latter suggests tubular pipes, but the wrapping in leaves of some other plant is more in the Maya tradition so I favor the García de Pelaez version.

In the Guatemalan highlands, leaves of the guayaba-fruit tree (*Psidium guajava*) were used for wrapping cigars, according to the local author Fuentes y Guzmán. Still other leaves are mentioned as wrappings in an account of cigar manufacture in the *Registro Yucateco* (1:349–50) for 1845. This article, signed *"Un Curioso,"* is entitled *"Cocom"* which, in turn, is the name of an unidentified tuberous plant with yellow leaves. These tubers were cut in narrow strips which were carbonized on a very hot griddle. The material was pulverized and placed in a gourd or vessel. *Atole de camote* (sweet potato and corn gruel) and a little honey were added so that the whole formed a thick paste. The cigar maker then took leaves of the zapote (*Achras zapota*) or, were he a resident of Chichanha, allspice (*Pimenta officinalis*) and split them lengthwise. Each half-leaf was next rolled on small spindle-shaped stick about the thickness of a turkey quill, and tied with henequen thread. The surface was then coated with the *cocom* paste, except about an inch at the thinner end which was left uncoated to serve as a mouthpiece. After the whole had dried in the sun, the stick was pulled out and regular cigar tobacco was inserted in its place. The end was doubled over to prevent the tobacco from spilling, and the cigar was ready for enjoyment.

The Franciscan Fray Margil reported that the Lacandon Chol caciques of Dolores held a feast called *hicsion* or "cigar feast." The people were employed twenty days making these cigars. Special offerings to the idols followed, and then each family gave its cacique a small bundle of cigars to signify that he was their recognized lord (Tozzer, 1913). Present-day Lacandon make bundles, nearly two feet long and tightly wound with cord, of their home-grown tobacco (Blom and Duby, 1955–57, 1:148–51).

POWDERED TOBACCO AND LIME

Powdered tobacco, equivalent to our snuff although never sniffed, mixed with lime, was and still is chewed by Indians over much of Middle America. The habit was found among highland and lowland Maya.

The author of the *Descripción de San Bartolomé* (para. 26), writing in 1588, remarks that the Zutuhil Maya, immediately south of Lake Atitlan, kept a quid of pulverized strong tobacco mixed with a little lime in the mouth. The mixture was thought to give strength and quiet thirst whether at home or traveling. It was carried in a small gourd. These same Indians also smoked tobacco in little tubes (*canutillos*).

The Tzeltal Maya of Chiapas chew powdered green tobacco mixed with lime and chile. The mixture is dipped from a long, tapering gourd with a little sticklike spatula; it strengthens the teeth and enables one to withstand the fatigues of the road (Starr, 1900–1901, 2:71). Starr adds that the mixture was called *mai*, a general term for tobacco in several Maya languages and dialects. The Motul dictionary defines it as tobacco powder made by rubbing the leaves between the fingers; in Kekchi Maya the word is applied to the leaf. It has been suggested that the homonym *mai*, "twenty," originated from the custom of tying tobacco leaves in bundles of twenty. The Motul dictionary lists *bux* with the meaning of "gourd for holding powdered tobacco," so we may conclude that the custom also existed among the Yucatec Maya.

The habit of chewing tobacco and lime is prevalent also among the Tzotzil as a schoolmaster at Zinacantan informed me some twenty-five years ago; it formerly existed among the Jacalteca Maya (La Farge and Byers, 1931:123). It was also found among peoples immediately west of the Maya area in the ancient province of Coatzacoalcos. Stuck against the gums, it alleviated hunger and thirst (Suero de Cangas y Quiñones, 1928). The distribution of the trait continued to the northwest, for Starr wrote that the Mazatec universally carried powdered green tobacco leaves in little gourds fastened to the girdle or some part of the clothing. It was thought to relieve fatigue when traveling and was employed in witchcraft as noted below. Starr (1900–1901, 1:78) fails to mention lime as part of the formula, but as he opined that the Tzeltal mixture with lime, quoted above, was the same as the Mazatec *piciete*, it is pretty clear that he did not doubt that the Mazatec also used lime.

Pomar (1891, answer 26), writing of Texcoco, says the peasants but not the nobility, used ground dry tobacco mixed with a little lime, putting in the mouth between lips and gums about as much as would go in a walnut. This they did before going to work or to sleep to alleviate the effects of hard work, to take away aches, and to induce sleep. A few Totonac are said to chew tobacco at the present time, but the practice was not observed (Kelly and Palerm, 1952:176).

Sahagún writes in the Spanish version (1938, bk. 10. ch. 26): "He who sells *piciete* (tobacco) first grinds the leaves, mixing them with a little lime, and thus mixed, he rubs it very thoroughly between his hands.... Put in the mouth, it makes one's head giddy, it intoxicates one; it also helps to digest what has been eaten, and takes away tiredness." The Nahuatl version fails to mention lime.

The same author (1950–69, bk. 8, ch. 18), describing initiation rites of a ruler, recounts how he was dressed as a priest for a penitential ceremony: "They had him put on a green sleeveless jacket. And they had him carry on his back his tobacco gourd with green tassels." Green was the color of the ruler in this ceremony; his assistants wore black tunics and carried black tobacco gourds with black tassels. Indeed, the tobacco gourd was the insigne of the Aztec priest. Seler (1904:146–47), discussing this, succinctly remarked: "Tobacco played precisely the same part among the priests and medicine men of ancient Mexico as it has from the remotest times down to the present day among the various tribes of North and South America."

The creation deities, who also functioned as priests and diviners, cast maize seed on a mat in a well-known scene of divination in

Codex Borbonicus, an Aztec book. In that role, tobacco gourds are prominently displayed on their backs. The tobacco gourd was as much a badge of paid-up membership of the Union of Clerics as a stole or a dog collar are symbols in our society. As we shall see, it was also the insigne of women doctors.

In the many descriptions of powdered tobacco, there is usually uncertainty whether lime was also present. Strictly, *piciete* was the term for powdered tobacco, *tenexiete* was tobacco with lime, and *iyetl* was the leaf.

The easternmost extension of ground tobacco and lime of which I know is among the Jicaque of north central Honduras. Anguiano (1908: 395), writing in 1798, relates that the Jicaque chewed green tobacco and lime, the latter obtained from the small freshwater shells called *hutes* over much of Middle America; they did this to protect themselves from being infected with malaria through contacts with Europeans.

It is quite likely that tobacco and lime chewing of Middle America is a transmutation of the Andean habit of chewing coca leaves with lime. In both areas the mixture, or the lime alone, is stored in narrow-necked gourds and dipped by means of a spatula. The coca and lime trait once extended as far north as Nicaragua (Oviedo y Valdés, 1851–55, bk. 6, ch. 20). Thence it is but a metaphorical step to Jicaque territory.

The lime, of course, reacts chemically on coca and tobacco.

TOBACCO AS AN OFFERING

Tobacco was pleasing to the gods and it had magical powers.

The first tobacco harvested by the Lacandon is offered to the gods as cigars. Each is lighted in the new fire or with the aid of a crystal to concentrate the sun's rays. It is momentarily held in front of the mouth of a sacred jar, and then is leaned against the mouth of the god whose head is in relief on the side of the incense burner and who is the recipient of the offering (Tozzer, 1907: 142–43).

The lighted cigars in cornhusk wrappings, mentioned as part of a ceremony in 1685, have disappeared from present-day milpa ceremonies in Yucatan, but the tradition still lingers that the Chacs, the rain gods, are heavy smokers, and comets are said to be the glowing cigars they throw away (Tozzer, 1907:158). Surely Tozzer means meteors; the rarely seen and nearly stationary comets would not indicate that the Chacs were heavy smokers. Another reference to the Chacs speaks of the owner's great cigar and of lightning and thunder when he lit it (p. 171).

One may conjecture that behind this association of the Chacs with cigars is the ancient world-wide magic law—or better, lore—that like produces like. The Maya burned rubber and black powder so that the clouds of black smoke would attract rain-filled black clouds. The Lacandon offerings of cigars is another example of this magical process. One may therefore suppose that the smoke of the Chacs' cigars aided them in forming black clouds.

A most impressive ceremony at the Tzeltal Maya town of Oxchuc attends the transfer at New Year from one *calpul* (sort of clan) to another of a greatly venerated book called "Our Master." At the climax of the rites, which last thirteen days, the book is placed on a table with thirteen candles, thirteen rosaries, thirteen calabashes of lime mixed with tobacco, and thirteen vessels of *atole* (maize gruel). The revered book is a notebook containing regulations set down in Spanish in 1674 (Redfield and Villa, 1939: 114). The mixture of paganism—the reiterated number thirteen, the atole, and the gourds or calabashes of lime and tobacco—and Christianity—candles and rosaries—is typical of present-day Maya religion. Perhaps these ceremonies echo others once held in honor of a hieroglyphic book.

References to offerings of tobacco to the deities in Central Mexico are numerous. Many have been harvested by Muriel Porter in her paper already cited. I shall accordingly limit my coverage to two items.

The Tlaxcalans offered to Camaxtli, the regional variation of Mixcoatl, god of hunting, a peculiar collection of cut paper, thorns, cockleburs, and *piciete*, that is, tobacco (Muñoz Camargo, 1892:62).

In the Aztec festival to the war god Huitzilopochtli, held on the day 1 Tecpatl ("flint knife"), the offerings included capes of blue, red, yellow, white, and green feathers and flowers of all colors; and "they burned [tubes of] tobacco only in bundles. First they bound them about the middle. As they burned them, they filled [the area] before [the image with smoke]. It was as if the smoke arose, spread a cloud, extended, came to settle, and lay billowing" (Sahagún, 1950–69, bk. 4, ch. 21). What a sight it must have been: those bright-hued capes, the massed flowers. Moctezuma was present in all his glory, and his chiefs strutted around like a flock of popinjays to rival the spread-out capes. Note the vivid description of the cigar smoke couched in poetry, because it was the smoke that was the offering, not the cigars themselves. The Spanish paraphrase informs us that the "smoke canes" or "smoke reeds" were in bundles of twenty, but the imagery of the clouds of smoke is wanting. The abbreviated account in Spanish lacks the rich word picture and metaphor of the original Nahuatl version; it is but a plucked peacock.

SMOKING FOR PLEASURE

References to smoking as a social grace, as well as to its inclusion with food and drink as a ceremonial gift to be consumed by the recipients, are many. Often these were on important private occasions, such as gifts to a young man's future parents-in-law, baptismal parties, and so on; they could also be on "state" occasions.

Sahagún (1950–69, bk. 9, ch. 7) describes in Nahuatl the ritual on the occasion of a banquet given by a wealthy merchant on some appropriate day in the 260-day sacred almanac. Smoking took place before food was served:

The tobacco server to perform his task, bore the tobacco [tube] in his right hand; thus he held it; there where it was sealed off; not by the tube. And he went bearing the bowl for the tobacco tubes in his left hand. First he offered one the tobacco tube. He said: "My beloved noble, here is thy cane of tobacco." Then [the guest] took it up; he placed it between his fingers to smoke it. This denoted the spearthrower or the spear; war equipment; valor. And the bowl for tobacco tubes stood for the shield, wherefore he bore it in his left hand. He went holding it only by the rim, to carry it. He laid it before perhaps the commanding general or the general; perhaps the *atempanecatl* [a kind of officer, of the general staff?], all the lords, and the eagle warrior guides, or the noblemen: indeed, all were invited.

This description seems to make it clear that the tubes of tobacco were not the pottery elbow pipes which are so plentiful in post-Classic archaeological deposits. The tobacco server clearly was the person mentioned as one of those slain to accompany his master to the next world (p. 122). His functions and rank were surely as defined as those of the cupbearer, food taster, or butler in western mediaeval society.

Possibly the allusions to war have some connection with the fact that offerings of tubes of tobacco were particularly associated with Huitzilopochtli, god of war, and with Ciuacoatl, who had a war-like aspect, for she was patroness of women who died in childbirth and who, because of their pains and because they produced new life, were regarded also as warriors.

We have a glimpse in this account of the extraordinary richness of the ritual and symbolism attached to tobacco even in secular settings. Why a tobacco tube should symbolize a spear-thrower is beyond our comprehension, but the aside makes us sorrowfully aware of how much of the allusive imagery of the past escapes us.

TOBACCO IN DIVINATION

The prominent tobacco gourds on the backs of creation gods engaged in divination has been noted. Chorti Maya of eastern Guatemala rub the saliva of tobacco they have chewed on the right leg in order to question the spirit *sahurin* who dwells in the calf of that leg. The spirit twitches the muscles of the calf to give an affirmative answer; no movement is a negative reply (Wisdom, 1940:344).

However, it was as an inducement to trance conditions that tobacco appears to have functioned more often in divination. Here, I suspect that the lime increased the tobacco's effect on the individual. The Guatemalan writer Fuentes y Guzmán (1932–33, pt. 1, bk. 12, ch. 3) has this to say of the divinatory aspects: "They also worshiped and attributed deity to the herb they call *piciet*, which is tobacco, concerning which they had superstitions. Smoking it and becoming intoxicated with it, they invoked the demon to learn of future events and to consult on the requests and petitions of others with which they had been charged."

The Tlaxcalans employed a most uncommon method to divine whether a god would grant a request. "They placed very finely ground tobacco, which was highly prized, in some large vases on the altars and benches of the temple among other offerings. Those of the tobacco they watched with particular care for, if there were to be any miracle, it would be seen there rather than in any other place. Thus it was that when the priests arrived to see other [*sic,* these?] vases, they found in them tracks or footprints of some creature, and particularly and most often, claw prints of eagles. This was an occasion of great public rejoicing." The author (Muñoz Camargo, 1892, bk. 1, ch. 20) adds that this tobacco was highly efficacious against many illnesses.

PERSONIFICATION OF TOBACCO

In the discussion of the medicinal properties of tobacco, superficially the plant appears to function as does any medicine bought at a drugstore. That it is much more than that, a sentient being in fact, is apparent. For instance, it is reverently addressed in several incantations recorded by Ruíz de Alarcón (1900) in Nahuatl and Spanish translation as "nine times pounded, nine times beaten or rubbed." It also possesses active powers, and, as appears below, was regarded as a god.

Guiteras' (1961:209, 217, 235, 264) Tzotzil Maya informant told her tobacco was an *anhel,* a term used to describe the rain and mountain deity and protector of mankind, because it takes care of our bodies. He added: "There are people who chew *moi* [ground tobacco, cf. Yucatec *mai* and Larrainzar Tzotzil *mui*] every day from the time they get up in the morning because the little gourd bottle containing it is kept at the head of their beds, the way others will smoke cigarettes. On hearing thunder, people will bring out their *moi* and keep it in their cheek and in that way it will not thunder too loudly. When we die the *pilico* (*moi*) defends us." On other occasions, he added, ground tobacco protects people from being killed by the lightning *anhel,* and is a cure for the harm caused by black magic; rubbed on the forehead, back of the neck, and the inside of elbow and knee joints, it protects one from being seized by the dead.

This power to protect from death, a task clearly beyond an inert substance, is brought out by Holland (1963:97, 129) in his study of the Tzotzil of Larrainzar (formerly San Andrés Istacostoc). If a person anoints in time his face, breast, and wrists with well-ground tobacco, the death gods, particularly Pucuh, cannot come near him because of their aversion to tobacco. A similar tradition is preserved in a story of how Citsil Bac, "Noisy Bones," another death god, stripped off his flesh and wandered off as a skeleton. A man chanced upon the piled-up flesh and, suspecting it pertained to one of the malignant gods, urinated on it and threw on powdered tobacco. When Citsil Bac returned, he was unable to re-clothe himself in his flesh because of what the man had done. Strangely, tobacco seems to play no other part in Tzotzil life; it is not named as an inert cure for any illness.

The quotation from Fuentes y Guzmán already given, "They also worshiped and attributed deity to the herb they call *piciet*," extends the deification of tobacco to the highland Maya of Guatemala. In Yucatan, the assignment of world directional colors to tobacco hints at a similar belief. There is mention in a cure in Ritual of the Bacabs (Roys, 1965:28) that asthma, subject of the treatment, drinks for four days the juice of the red tobacco, the white tobacco, and the black tobacco, whereby it is banished from the sick person. In another incantation (*ibid.*:52) there is reference to a certain Ix Muk-yah-kutz, "Lady Strengthener of the Tobacco." Could she by chance personify the lime added to powdered tobacco?

Mendieta (1870, bk. 2, ch. 19, a reference I owe to Muriel Porter) has a passage confirming the divinity of tobacco among the Nahua of Central Mexico: "Others say that some regard a herb which they call *picietl* and the Spaniards tobacco as the body of a goddess they name Ciuacoatl. And for this reason as it is to a certain degree medicinal, it must be regarded as suspect and a source of danger seeing that it takes away the judgement of him who takes it, making him foolish and wild."

Ciuacoatl, "Snake Woman," also known as Quilaztli and under the titles Our Mother and Princess, was the Aztec goddess of pregnancy, childbirth, and the sweat bath. She was also a war goddess because women in childbirth were regarded as warriors—they underwent dangers breeding fighters for the nation—a sort of forerunner of the ideas of Hitlerism. As we shall see, tobacco is in some way connected with war. Accordingly, it is not unreasonable that a war goddess should have her body made of that plant.

MEDICINAL USES OF TOBACCO

In the eyes of Middle America's Indians, tobacco came near to being a panacea for all ills of the flesh.

In his study of Yucatec ethnobotany, Roys (1931:259) lists the use of tobacco as a remedy for such a wide range of complaints as asthma, chills, fevers, convulsions, sore eyes, bowel complaints, nervous disorders, skin diseases, urinary infections, and bites and stings. To these Ritual of the Bacabs (Roys, 1965), a Yucatec Maya book of incantations for diseases, adds fever, eruptions, *nicte* seizure, snake pulsation (tape worm?), worm in the tooth, ailments of the placenta, and, as previously noted, asthma.

For Central Mexico, Ruíz de Alarcón (1900) lists tobacco in the treatment of scorpion bite, needle jabs, ringworm and similar skin ailments, earache and jawbone ache (both treated with tobacco powder and lime), toothache (as supplement to copal), and in childbirth. To this list Sahagún adds headaches, boils, cysts or tumors on head or neck, snake bite, coughs and catarrh.

The use of powdered tobacco and lime as a remedy for tiredness and aching muscles has already been cited for several regions; equally widespread is the use of tobacco for bites and stings. In addition to mentions of this use immediately above for Yucatan and Central Mexico, the Mam Maya use an infusion of tobacco for snake bites (Valladares, 1957:120) and the Zutuhil Maya, according to the source already cited, applied tobacco juice to the bites of snakes and other animals and insects, covering the juice with a tobacco leaf. Similarly, the Yucatec Maya of Socotz and the Mopan Maya of San Antonio, both in British Honduras, cover the hole of a beef worm (*colmoyote*) with tobacco juice, over which is laid a leaf of the same plant. In a few minutes the beef worm raises his head to the edge of the hole and can be readily squeezed out. I have had that treatment myself.

The medicinal value of tobacco is to be seen in the fact that a gourd of tobacco was the badge of office of women practitioners of medicine and midwifery. In the great festival of the mother goddess Toci, those women engaged in certain skirmishes in her honor. All wore tobacco gourds attached to a girdle at the waist (Sahagún, 1950–69, bk. 2, ch. 30).

The Chorti Maya practice a peculiar spitting technique which is standard treatment for curing and warding off the evil eye and strong blood, especially in children. The cure calls for the use of rue, sage, artemesia, and, most important of all, tobacco. Partially smoked tobacco is particularly efficacious; Indian women pick up cigars and cigarette butts in the towns and sell them to the curers.

> The curer chews one or several of these plants and spits his saliva all over the body of the patient, blowing or spraying it with a hissing sound through his teeth. The patient is spit on from head to foot, especially on the face, and in serious cases the curer spits the form of a cross on the body, running from the head to the crotch, and from shoulder to shoulder. This is usually done four times and is repeated after eight days [a week in Spanish counting] if the patient does not improve. Spitting is often done in connection with seizing [a special treatment], the two together, especially if repeated four times over a period of 32 days [four weeks?], being said to be extremely curative (Wisdom, 1940:349).

Curers who specialize in this treatment are called *ah huht* or *ah t'uhp*, both Chorti terms denoting the action with the masculine *ah*, *nomen actoris*, prefix. This spraying treatment does not seem to have been reported of other Maya groups, but Chinantec medicine men of Oaxaca, who make little or no use of tobacco in ceremony or cures, spray patients with mouthfuls of water from a well which has been the recipient of certain offerings (Weitlaner and Castro, 1954: 186). Conceivably, the rite derives from Roman Catholic teaching of Christ's healing of the blind.

Clearly, it was generally accepted that tobacco was an intoxicant. This applied also to non-humans, as Sahagún (1950–69, bk. 11, ch. 5) makes clear in his account of the capture of a rattlesnake.

In order to prevent its attack a man "wraps up fine tobacco in paper; he throws it at [the serpent] or else he fills small jars; to throw small jars at it so that the small jars suddenly burst, and the fine tobacco suddenly scatters. Thus [the serpent] stretches out enfeebled. Then he puts on the end of a stick a paper, a rag well provided with fine tobacco; he inserts it in its mouth, so that it then does nothing more. He then captures it, he kills it." This Lucky Strike technique is somewhat involved unless the chief purpose is to catch the rattler alive.

The Indian view of tobacco as a stimulant or intoxicant is brought out in an observation of Thomas Gage (1958:225) on the making of *chicha*, fermented sugar-cane syrup, by highland Maya, presumably Pokoman, among whom he dwelt in the seventeenth century. They include in the brew the roots and leaves of tobacco and roots of other plants "which grow there and which they know to be strong in operation. Nay, to my knowledge, in some places they have put in a live toad, and closed up the jar for a fortnight or a month, till all they have put in be thoroughly steeped, the toad consumed and the drink well strengthened." That is, indeed, a tale of uncommonly strong waters; the witches' cauldron of *Macbeth* contained only a leg of a frog.

TOBACCO AS A TALISMAN

Landa's description of the puberity rite (p. 108) clearly implies that the tobacco smoke served as a charm or as a sacred act to ward off evil. The same idea is more explicit in the custom of the Mazatec of northern Oaxaca that a shaman starts to rub the forearm of a pregnant woman with ground tobacco and lime a month before parturition to make her invulnerable to witchcraft. This procedure appears to continue until the child is born (Villa, 1955: 114). Their neighbors, the Chinantec, also used tobacco to ward off witchcraft.

The Tzotzil view that tobacco shields one from the evil beings of the underworld and from death has already received comment. Among Yucatec uses of tobacco was included that of preventing certain seizures. As these are primarily mental disorders, tobacco probably functioned in such cures as a magical rather than as a therapeutic substance.

Tobacco also serves as a vehicle of black magic. Until recently a witch doctor in the Pokoman town of Jilotepeque used the method of inserting a hair or something else pertaining to the victim in the tobacco of a cigarette he rolled. This cigarette was given to a close friend of the intended sufferer to give in turn to the victim to smoke. Neither was aware of its dangerous content. On smoking the treated tobacco, the victim would fall ill or might die (Gillin, 1951:116). It is not clear whether the tobacco was merely a cover for the magic or increased its potency.

TOBACCO AND WAR

The *Relación de Michoacán* has a peculiar reference to war discussed by Seler (1902–23, 3:114) and cited by Muriel Porter. It occurs in an account of a feast given by the ruler of Michoacan immediately before a declaration of war. The priest, apparently impersonating the god of fire, burned at midnight a number of balls of tobacco, pronouncing at the same time the names of certain deities. Later, two men were dispatched to place two balls of tobacco, two blood-stained arrows, and some eagle feathers in enemy territory, in the house of the enemy chief, or in the enemy's city or chief temple. "This indicated an act of witchcraft as well as a declaration of war." The symbolism of the arrows and the eagle feathers, as insignia of the military orders of Jaguars and Eagles, is obvious; the significance of the tobacco is less certain.

Nevertheless, the importance of tobacco in the rites in honor of Huitzilopochtli, Aztec god of war (p. 113), and the belief that the body of Ciuacoatl, a patroness of war, was made of tobacco supply additional evidence that tobacco somehow has bellicose associations.

TOBACCO WITH BURIALS

I know of only two reports of tobacco in connection with burials, and in neither case does the presence of tobacco appear particularly significant. Villagutierre y Soto-Mayor (1933, bk. 5, ch. 6) reports that the Lacandon Chol of Dolores customarily placed on men's graves male possessions, and on women's graves objects having to do with women. The male property listed comprised *puquietes*, a term for tubes of tobacco, and small stools which men normally carried around with them.

Las Casas (1909, ch. 228) writes at length on the elaborate funerals of rulers of Michoacan. With the ruler were slain a great number of his attendants so that they could continue to serve him in the next world. Among them was the man who handled the perfumes or tubes (*cañutos*) of sweet smells. *Cañuto* usually describes tobacco containers, apparently the reed tubes in which tobacco was smoked. However, so many slaves, each with his special occupation, are mentioned that there is no emphasis on smoking.

In the preceding chapter Las Casas tells of the ceremonial cremation of a chief of Mexico, presumably Aztec or of some related group. There is no mention of tobacco at the cremation, but at ceremonies held at each anniversary of his demise birds, butterflies, and rabbits were sacrificed, and much food, flowers, incense, and intoxicants were placed before the image, and also "some tubes or canes which they call *acayyetl*, which are canes two palms long full of a certain odorous substance, the smoke of which they take into their mouths and which they say is healthy for the head." *Acayietl* is precisely a cane (*acatl*) of tobacco (*yietl*).

Again, I do not believe this offering of cigars or canes of tobacco is significant. It is better regarded as a course in the soup-to-nuts meal of the deceased.

SUMMATION

This review makes clear the extent to which the taking of tobacco in every form permeated Indian life in ancient Middle America. The attitude of noble, priest, and commoner was imbued at times with something approaching mysticism, as when tobacco was personified or even deified or when it was accepted as an ally fighting beside man to overcome fatigue or pain or to ward off so many of the ills of human flesh. There is deep beauty there which we, in our materialistic world, bombarded with advertising on television and in print of some young man lighting a girl's cigarette as a prelude to conquest, are unable to share or even to perceive. The relationship is that of compline to a blast of the Beatles and their sad imitators.

CHAPTER 5

Trade Relations Between
Maya Highlands
and
Lowlands

INTRODUCTION

This chapter was originally a contribution to a symposium *"Semejanzas y diferencias entre las culturas de las tierras altas y bajas del área maya"* ("Similarities and differences between the cultures of the highlands and lowlands of the Maya area"), held during the Thirtieth International Congress of Americanists in Mexico City, 1962. My old friend and colleague Alberto Ruz took pity on this waif, too lengthy to be published in the *Proceedings* of the congress, and found a home for it in the pages of *Estudios de Cultura Maya* (Volume 4). I am much obliged to Dr. Ruz for surrendering his rights over the orphan he had succored and permitting me to re-adopt it in this book. I have made some small additions to the published text and have given it a short introduction.

"Man shall not live by bread alone," but *alone* is the key word. Cultures can indulge their taste for the arts to the extent that there is supporting wealth accumulated by the labor of their peasants, the products of their artists, and the ability to find export markets for surpluses. It is well, therefore, to glance at the Maya as a man of business able to organize and maintain a network of trade routes. We may note that in addition to the large two-way trade in raw materials, the lowland Maya developed a wide market for his artistic products, exporting brocaded textiles from Yucatan, painted pottery, carved jades, and beautifully worked flint from other parts of the lowlands. Maya art clearly gave wide satisfaction to connoisseurs centuries before museums with a corner labeled Primitive Art found it fashionable to display a belated interest in its products; there were plenty of Maya predecessors of Lorenzo the Magnificent.

The division between highlands and lowlands is approximately the boundary between the Central and Southern areas of Map 1. This line was drawn to separate from the highlands Maya of the lowland linguistic group—Yucatec (in the Northern area, spilling over into the Central area), Putun, Palencano and Manche Chol, Mopan, Chorti, Tojolabal, Tzeltal, and Tzotzil—which share certain cultural elements, namely, stelae and altars with lowland hieroglyphic texts, buildings with corbelled vaulting, and fine polychrome pottery. However, it is not always easy to separate sheep from goats on ethnic and cultural grounds, as drawers of boundaries have learned to their cost since the first sessions of the Treaty of Versailles witnessed the deplorable spectacle of Woodrow Wilson setting the ethnic cat among the pigeons between uplift sermons to his assumedly baser colleagues.

The incursions of the Chorti into the highlands (ch. 3) brought lowlanders and their culture into mountain country, with the result that Copan, for instance, a typical lowland ceremonial center, stands two thousand feet above sea level and is surrounded by far higher mountains, and San Agustín Acasaguastlan, at about fifteen hundred feet, is similarly situated. The deeper incursion of the Chorti to lakes Güija and Ayarza creates fresh problems. Compromise is essential. Accordingly, I include Copan in the lowlands, but assign the southern territory under Chorti control to the highlands. As Copan is geologically highland, one must bear in mind that some highland exports found in the lowlands may, in fact, have come from Copan and its vicinity. Moreover, the Maya Mountains of British Honduras form an enclave within lowland territory and cannot be excluded from it.

There are also geological reasons for including the Chiapan plateau, inhabited by the Tzeltal, Tzotzil, and Tojolabal, with the highlands; it is really neither one thing nor the other. Linguistically it is lowland, and in its area are stelae with lowland texts (but sites are not numerous), as well as buildings (as opposed to tombs) with corbelled vaulting. Neither, it is true, occurs in Tzotzil territory, but one can hardly assign the Tzeltal to lowland culture and, at the same time, the Tzotzil, their linguistic and cultural first cousins, to highland culture. The great ceremonial center of Tonina stands at over three thousand feet; its forty-six sculptured monuments are part of the lowland tradition, but their marked local style argues against a Classic-period invasion from the north. Chinkultic, at five thousand feet, is also a lowland site in architecture and sculpture. Assignment of the northeastern Chiapas plateau is largely irrelevant here, for Chiapas plays little part in the discussion which follows.

I have moved the southern boundary of the Central area slightly southward to include the middle Chixoy, the ancient name of which was Dz'ununteilha, "Hummingbird Tree Water." The identity of the makers of the magnificent polychrome pottery and the many beautiful pottery figurines from Chama and other sites in the middle Chixoy drainage is unknown. The polychrome wares are certainly local, but they are definitely in the lowland tradition, stylistically and iconographically. The considerable use of true glyphs including sequent day signs reinforces this conclusion. In fact, the stela with glyphs at Salinas de los Nueve Cerros, mentioned above, shows a lowland occupation, presumably Chol, less than twenty-five miles north of Chama. Moreover, San Marcos, perhaps west of Chisec, was Chol-Acala territory in the sixteenth century (p. 33). That would place that people even closer to Chama.

Dieseldorff (1909) also concluded that the area north of Coban was once Chol territory, assigning also those figurines to that people. He notes a number of place names in that area which are not Kekchi. Indeed, one place name, Boloneb, is the lowland day name 9 Eb.

There seems, then, full justification for including that middle Chixoy drainage in the lowlands.

PAST AND PRESENT TRADE ROUTES

Water. The most dramatic case of prehispanic trade was that which Columbus and his sailors witnessed on their fourth voyage when they chanced upon a large trading canoe near the Bay Islands. The story is too well known to need repeating in detail. The cargo consisted, according to Las Casas (1877, bk. 2, ch. 20), of cotton mantles, huipils (sleeveless blouses), and loin cloths, all with multi-color designs, *macanas* (wooden swords with pieces of flint glued into slots down each side), little copper axes, bells, large quantities of cacao beans, plates (*patenas*), and crucibles (*crisoles*) to melt the copper. Peter Martyr (Dec. 3, ch. 4) adds razors and knives of latten (*read* "copper") and hatchets of a sharp bright yellow stone with wooden handles. Unfortunately, there is no direct information regarding whence the canoe came and whither it was bound. The copper implements point to a cargo from Central Mexico, but fine textiles were an export of Yucatan to Honduras, suggesting that they had been picked up there in transit. I know of no hatchets of bright yellow stone. If they were of yellow flint, an origin in the Peninsula of Yucatan is indicated. The cacao beans present a problem. They would not be taken to the north coasts of Guatemala or Honduras, a case of coals to Newcastle. However, if the canoe had traded on the way along the coast of British Honduras, its owners might have obtained cacao there for what they sold, for the Belize and other valleys to the south produced large quantities of cacao, and Chetumal Bay was an outlet for cacao of the Río Hondo. The copper in that case would have been for the bottom of the Gulf of Honduras and the cacao would have been disposed of in Yucatan on the return voyage.

On the whole, it seems most probable that the vessel had come around the Peninsula of Yucatan, perhaps from the great trade center of Xicalango, with the bottom of the Gulf of Honduras as its terminus. If that is correct, it indicates a long voyage with active trading at many ports en route. One may guess that merchants and crew were Putun (Chontal Maya), the Phoenicians of Middle America.

The canoe, as long as a galley, eight feet wide, and with cabin amidships, carried upwards of twenty-five men as well as women and children. Clearly, commerce by sea was on a large and well-organized scale.

It is highly significant that Cortés, telling of interviews on routes with men of Xicalango and Tabasco (home of the Putun), writes: "Some who had been in those parts described to me most of the villages *on the coast* [italics of J.E.S.T.] as far as the residence of Pedrarias Dávila" (MacNutt, 1908, 2:231). The territory of that swashbuckler was ill defined, although officially it was Panama. We can only conclude from what Cortés writes that there was sea trade between the bottom of the Gulf of Mexico and at least present-day Costa Rica, if not with Panama (to obtain gold?).

There is no lack of confirmation of this east coast trade route. Herrera (Dec. 4, bk. 8, ch. 3) states that the people of Yucatan were especially prominent in trade with Honduras, bringing mantles, feathers, and other things and returning with cacao. Honduras was famed for its feathers, but Yucatan raised muscovy ducks, probably unknown in Honduras, so the feathers may have been of ducks. Again, the *Relación de Tekanto* (*Relaciones de Yucatán*, 1:125) states that cotton mantles, wax, honey, and salt were exported to Mexico, Honduras, and other parts. According to the *Relación de Motul* (*ibid.*:87) cacao was brought from Tabasco and Honduras. Trade was so active that Yucatecan merchants stationed factors in Honduras to handle their interests (Scholes and Roys, 1948:84).

That this sea route down the east coast of the peninsula was very busy is shown by indirect evidence. Cacao and feathers, being very valuable and, in the case of the latter, of light weight, could also have been sent by land, but it is probable that large and not very valuable products would have been sent by water wherever feasible. Granite metates (corn grinders) have been reported from San José, Uaxactun, Tikal (where they are particularly abundant), and Mayapan. The nearest source known to me is the Pine Ridge and Maya Mountains area of British Honduras. To the first three places they were presumably taken by river and overland, but in the case of Mayapan one must conclude that they went down the Belize River and thence northward to a port in Yucatan near Mayapan. Similarly, the large number of tripod metates of lava at Lubaantun (huge numbers of fragments were found) must surely have traveled by sea and the Río Grande from the highlands, for there are no lava deposits in the Peninsula of Yucatan. Those of lava found at the lowland sites may have gone by either west coast or east coast routes, depending on accessibility. Those that reached Tikal and Uaxactun, for example, presumably traveled up the east coast and the Belize River.

The need for shipment by water is obvious when one realizes that the load of a present-day highland Maya *cargador* comprises two metates and six *manos* (mullers for grinding corn) (McBryde, 1947:73); it would clearly be uneconomic to have porters carry them from the highlands to Uaxactun or Mayapan. Flints, for the same reason, must have been shipped by water, and, as we have just seen, there is a probability they were in the canoe Columbus met off the Bay Islands.

Salt also traveled the east coast route. The Manche Chol vocabulary has an entry that *xoxom* is coarse salt. "They bring it from Cozumel." There were important salt works all along the north coast of Yucatan and on the nearby Mujeres Island, but none on Cozumel, so Cozumel was probably the point of transshipment, thence perhaps via Nito near the mouth of the Río Dulce, and then up the Sarstoon River. The fact that it came from Cozumel, apparently long after the Conquest, suggests that that ancient native route survived into Colonial times. Cozumel did pay a small salt tribute (Roys, 1957:155), but one may suppose that this was gathered elsewhere by natives of the island.

Ascension Bay also contributed to the coastal traffic, for the lords of Chichen Itza embarked there on trading journeys to Honduras for cacao and plumage (Ciudad Real, 1873, 2:408).

Chetumal must have had a considerable interest in this east coast trade, for the province sent fifty war canoes to help defend its commercial interests on the Ulua River from the Spaniards (Scholes and Roys, 1948:317), and cacao was shipped up the Río Hondo to Ucum and thence overland to the Xiu towns at the foot of the Puuc Hills, a distance of 147 miles by air (Roys, 1943:52). Vessels of Yucatecan slateware at San José (Thompson, 1939:150) probably came by sea to Chetumal and thence up the New River at the very close of the Classic period and in the early post-Classic period. Vessels of the same ware, sherds of which occur at Uaxactun in both early and late Classic deposits (R. E. Smith, 1955:35), may have come the same route or by the Hondo or Belize rivers. The famed marble vessels of the Ulua, fragments of which occur in late deposits at both the above sites, presumably came by sea and thence by one of the three rivers mentioned.

Many of the accounts of trade with Honduras almost certainly refer also to the small coastal strip of northern Guatemala through which must have passed a great part of the trade between the highlands and lowlands, for the west coast route involved much more travel by land. Nito, at the mouth of the Río Dulce and close to the present-day port of Livingston, was a most important entrepôt, visited by Cortés. Here a special quarter of the town was reserved for the Putun merchants of Acalan, under the command of a brother of the ruler (Cortés, 1908, 2:264). Through it passed the commerce which funneled through Lake Izabal and the great volume from the highlands which followed the Motagua Valley route. Nito was certainly in Chol territory, as probably was Naco, the great commercial center for the Ulua Valley. This is not on the Ulua River, but on a small tributary of the Chamelecon River, the lower reaches of which flow almost parallel to the Ulua and a few miles to the west.

Trade by sea along the west coast must have been equally brisk, for the imports from most of Mexico also passed through the Chontalpa territory which stretched across the deltas of the Grijalva and Usumacinta rivers to the north shore of the Laguna de Términos. Scholes and Roys (1948) have covered this commerce in detail, and it remains only to summarize their findings with a few additions.

Landa (1941:5) refers obliquely to that water traffic in noting the signs placed on trees to mark the route through the maze of waterways which crisscross the deltas between "Tabasco and Yucatan." As these would not have been needed by local watermen, they must have been for the benefit of trading canoes, for there were few other travelers and no Thomas Cook in pre-Columbian America. Pilgrims are mentioned, but Scholes and Roys (1948:33–34) make the very reasonable inference that pilgrims from distant points were in fact merchants who stopped to pay their respects at a shrine.

One of the greatest trade centers in ancient America was Xicalango, to which Aztec-Culhua merchants came. It was probably Putun, but with a quarter occupied by Mexican soldier-merchants (Ruz, 1944:11; Scholes and Roys, 1948:35–36). I would suppose that Xicalango was a great entrepôt, and all traffic north and east of it was in Putun hands. Apparently it stood at the north end of the south arm of the Laguna de Términos. Ruz, in minor excavations, found evidence of a Formative occupation, much material of the period of Toltec domination of Chichen Itza, and, on the surface, *incensarios* decorated with spikes and thumb marks (Ruz, 1945:68). The last is perhaps equatable with early Mayapan. Ruz suggests that erosion may have carried Xicalango beneath the sea.

Cimatan, on the Grijalva, was a Nahuat town on the land route of merchants from the Valley of Mexico and probably was a depot for merchandise brought down the Grijalva from Chiapas (Scholes and Roys, 1948:32). Potonchan, at the mouth of the same river, presumably controlled the water route down that river and thence by the coastal route to the Peninsula of Yucatan. Gage (1958:148) mentions the commerce of the Zoque territory with Yucatan down the Grijalva to Puerto Real which stood at the south end of the north arm of Laguna de Términos and is listed as a port of call of canoes proceeding from Jonuta, on the Usumacinta, to Yucatan (*Relaciones de Yucatán*, 1:347).

The *encomendero* of Cozumel (*Relaciones de Yucatán*, 2:54) states that pilgrims used to come to the great shrine of Cozumel from Tabasco, Xicalango, Champoton, and Campeche. Acceptance of the inference of Scholes and Roys that these pilgrims were in fact merchants points to sea trade around the peninsula. The copper tools in the trading canoe encountered by Columbus confirm this, for they were certainly not exports from Yucatan, but must have been brought from Central Mexico.

A tripod metate of volcanic stone in the Museum of the American Indian, Heye Foundation, reportedly found at Quirigua, has a lizard in relief on the underside, the head forming one leg. The same type of metate, also of volcanic stone but with the head of a feline (?) forming one leg, was found in the Jalapa region of Veracruz (Strebel, 1885–89, pt. 2, Plate 14). These pieces suggest sea trade round the Peninsula of Yucatan, with exportation presumably from Veracruz. A flat variant type with a monkey in relief on the underside, also attributed to Quirigua, is in Peabody Museum, Harvard.

We may also infer considerable trade around the peninsula from the fact that informants from Chontalpa told Cortés of the total disruption of the trade of Nito (Cortés wrongly writes Asunción Bay) due to Spanish depredations there (MacNutt, 1908, 2:160). For heavy goods a sea route was so much easier than by river, with the long portage from the Pasión to the Sarstoon, that one can assume that the merchants of Chontalpa did not make Cozumel their final port but continued to Nito. Lighter material may have gone by river, and doubtless much trade derived from buying and selling along the river route.

It has been assumed that Cortés followed the overland trade route of the Acalan merchants from Acalan to Nito, but I think the existence of such a through route is questionable. By the end of October Cortés' intentions to make for that region were known to the Putun merchants, yet the people along his route were apparently quite unaware of his march until he was upon them. It was the height of the dry season when travel was easiest and, although trade was disorganized because of Spanish occupation of Nito, it is most unlikely that news of his advance should not have reached the Itza at Tayasal—they knew nothing about it six months later when Cortés arrived—had Itza territory been on the merchants' route. Trouble at Nito would not affect trade with the Itza. Cortés did meet Acalan merchants, but they were returning from a journey to the neighboring Cehach. Furthermore, Canek, the Itza ruler, advised Cortés to proceed from there to Nito by sea (i.e., down the Belize River and then southward along the coast). This would indicate his route of commerce and argues even more strongly against a land route from Itzamkanac, the Acalan capital.

There is one last point. Between Tayasal and Nito, Cortés came upon an Acalan trader, one of a group which had taken refuge there (Azuzulin) when Nito fell into Spanish hands. The trader lamented that the trade was completely disrupted. One might suppose that under those conditions he and his friends would have gone back to Acalan were there a regular trade route thither. Can it be that the Acalan ruler sent Cortés via Itza country not solely because it was the most direct route, but because it was one which his countrymen did not use since it passed through the land of his enemies? At least the Cehach were enemies of the warlike Itza (Scholes and Roys, 1948:462) and friends of the Putun, so an Acalan-Itza enmity is plausible. If the Itza were enemies of the Acalan ruler, he was probably quite happy to send that swarm of Spanish locusts to their capital. Moreover, no merchants' route would have traversed the terrible mountainous country (the Maya Mountains of British Honduras, one supposes) Cortés describes between Tayasal and the Golfo Dulce. Cortés was provided with guides. One must conclude that the guides were equally lost for the simple reason there was no through overland route, as Canek's advice to Cortés indicates; travelers headed for the limits of canoe navigation on the Belize, Mojo, or Sarstoon rivers.

The need to present the view that travel by a circuitous water route was probably chosen by coastal peoples before a shorter land route is the justification for this somewhat lengthy digression.

The transport of salt must have contributed greatly to traffic. The *Relación de Uexutla* (*Papeles de Nueva España*, ser. 2, 6: 190) states that salt was then (1580) brought from Campeche by sea to the port of Amoyoc, fifteen leagues distant. Huejutla is in the northeastern corner of Hidalgo. This could have been a post-Conquest development, but I feel it more likely, in view of the unimportance in Spanish commerce of Amoyoc, that it was a colonial continuation of an early trade route. Traffic in feathers and gold ceased, but salt was an essential. The salt of Campeche came from farther up the coast in the province of Ah Canul (Roys, 1957:15).

The Putun of Acalan exchanged salt for the products of the Cehach in the interior of the peninsula. Scholes and Roys (1948: 59) note that this probably came from the same Ah Canul salt beds, and was brought down the coast and then up the Candelaria River. Cortés (1908, 2:263) is the earliest source for the information that the Acalan carried on a considerable trade by water also with Xicalango and Tabasco.

Products which Sahagún (1950–61, bk. 9, ch. 4) lists as being taken by Aztec-Culhua merchants to Cimatan and Xicalango, such as objects of gold, obsidian ear plugs and points, obsidian knives with leather handles, rabbit fur, and medicinal herbs, were undoubtedly carried thence by sea to all parts of the lowlands by the Putun. The landlocked Aztec Culhua had little experience on the sea, and it is significant that Sahagún's informants, who went to great lengths to glorify the merchant class, give Xicalango as the terminal of their route.

A sea route for commerce from Tehuantepec and points beyond to the province of Soconusco and thence, one may suppose, to Guatemala, existed; the canoes traversing the coastal lagoons sheltered from the sea by long spits of land (Ponce de León, 1882: 425). By this route probably were carried the huipils of Teotitlan del Camino to Soconusco and Suchitepequez for cacao (*Papeles de Nueva España*, ser. 2, 4:215), and this was presumably the route followed by merchants who were still going from Cholula to Soconusco and Guatemala at the time Durán (1880, ch. 84) wrote (1580).

Land routes. I have pointed out that the Putun traders who dominated the commerce of the peninsula almost surely went by land only when they could not go by water. Indeed, it is reasonably certain that Acalan is a corruption of a Nahuatl word *acaltlan*, "place of the canoes." The *t* in fact drops out in some Nahuatl dialects and we find the *lan* termination in some place names, as in Yoalan and Cempoalan.

References to terrestrial trade routes between highlands and lowlands at the time of the Spanish Conquest are scant or nonexistent, probably because the Spaniards were not interested in those based on products which they did not value highly. Material on such trade in colonial or modern times is very unsatisfactory, probably because of the general collapse of the native organization. What there is points to trade by individuals or small groups of merchants.

It is probable that the Manche Chol of southeastern Petén and adjacent British Honduras made trading visits in the seventeenth and eighteenth centuries to Cajabon in the Alta Verapaz, for they seem to have had the custom of arriving there for the feast of the Nativity of the Blessed Virgin, who was the patron of the town. At least we have accounts of such visits in the years 1596 and 1697 (Remesal, 1932, bk. 11, ch. 18; Villagutierre, 1933, bk. 9, ch. 2). As is well known, such festivals are everywhere occasions also for commerce. Similarly, the Indians of Cajabon "always used to enter and trade with them" (the Chols) (Ximénez, 1929, bk. 5, ch. 38). Gates, in his introduction to the Manche-Chol vocabulary, has noted that one Manche-Chol word for huipil is *pot*, the Kekchi term, which would indicate the nature of the trade. We are also told that salt was much desired by the Manche Chol perhaps because of disruption of the Cozumel trade. Cacao seems to have been the principal item the Manche Chol offered in return, for on one occasion they left bundles of cacao in trees near Cajabon to indicate they wished to make contact, and, one can infer, barter cacao for the products of Cajabon (Remesal, 1932, bk. 11, ch. 18).

Alta Verapaz trade with the former Manche-Chol territory continues to this day, or at least until recently, and the same commodities are exchanged, Kekchi traders bringing huipils and mats to sell in Aguacate, San Pedro Colombia, and other Kekchi-speaking villages in southern British Honduras, taking home cacao. Whether they also trade with the Mopan villages I do not know.

The Kekchi now get their salt from the beds on the middle Chixoy near Salinas de los Nueve Cerros (Termer, 1957:78), but this was outside Kekchi territory at the time of the Conquest. Perhaps one may suppose that originally their salt came thence by trade, but when the land was abandoned they went there to help themselves. The Lacandon did the same thing, for about 1630 they sent 140 men to extract salt from an unnamed locality which, from the account, is surely these same salt beds in the Chixoy Valley (Tovilla, 1960, bk. 2, chs. 8, 9).

The Ixil, who are great traders, at the turn of the century had routes extending from Coban in the east to Chiapas in the west and to the lowlands of Tabasco. In the last place they sold garlic as well as onions perhaps from Solola or Panajachel, and passion fruit (*Passiflora*), eaten raw, seeds and all, and much enjoyed by Indians, which they obtained in Alta Verapaz. They brought back cacao (Sapper, 1897:305).

Tobacco from the Copan Valley travels to the Motagua Valley and thence is carried to many parts of the highlands. Zacapa is an outlet for Chorti traders who carry there the products of Jocotan and Olopa. They share this commerce with Pokoman traders (Wisdom, 1940:201–202).

There is, as is well known, an enormous amount of trading by land routes throughout the highlands, but this does not now concern us except to emphasize the highlander as one who travels on foot (some use now of horses and mules), and therefore is unlikely to have been engaged in trade by water with the lowlands.

MERCHANTS AND THEIR DEALINGS

Accounts, unfortunately not detailed, have survived of the merchant class among the Putun and the Yucatec Maya, but there are no such descriptions for the highlands. That may be accidental, but it is more probable that it is because long-distance travel, perhaps at times into hostile territory, calls for larger and more organized bodies than does land travel over shorter routes. As we have seen, water travel was in all probability in the hands of the Putun and, to a less extent, the Yucatec.

Of the social status of the merchant class among the two groups in the fifteenth century there can be no doubts. The quarter of Nito occupied by the Acalan traders was governed by the brother of the Acalan ruler, Paxbolon (MacNutt, 1908, 2:264). At the time of the overthrow of Mayapan, about A.D. 1450, one son escaped the massacre of the ruling Cocom family because he was away in the Ulua Valley on a trading trip (Landa, 1941:39). We also learn that the lords of Chichen Itza traded with the same area through the port of Ascensión Bay, but whether they themselves went or sent their underlings is not clear. At least we have evidence that members of the nobility were not above active participation in commerce. Yucatec merchants, like those of Mexico, had certain gods in special veneration. Among these was Ek Chuah (Landa, 1941:107), a god intimately connected with cacao and, therefore, particularly close to the merchants who used cacao as their chief currency and transported it in huge quantities (p. 306).

A mirror back found in Yucatan (R. H. Thompson, 1962) shows two merchants or porters with packs on their backs. In one case a bird is above the man's pack, a feature of representations of merchants in codices from eastern Mexico. The appearance of this bird is confirmatory evidence of the close association in ritual and religion between the two areas.

It is quite probable that the famous Ratinlixul vase (Gordon and Mason, 1925–43, pt. 3, Plates 1, 2) depicts merchants on a journey. The chief personage, in a litter, holds a fan, symbol of the merchant class, and behind him is a porter with a heavy load. There follow three individuals with elaborate headdresses holding what may well be ceremonial staves, also badges of merchants and of great ritualistic importance among Aztec merchants. The staves are partly covered with plaited straw or leather and at the top are painted with circles (made with rubber?). The tops have U-shaped nicks. They do not closely resemble the merchant staves Sahagún illustrates or those depicted in codices, but there seems to be no standard form and we are dealing with great geographical and temporal spans. Dr. Satterthwaite has suggested to me that they represent paddles, but the elaborate headdresses of their bearers hardly indicate paddlers, nor would one expect plaited coverings or painted designs on paddles. Moreover, paddles are not normally carried on land; they are usually kept hidden near the canoes. On the other hand, as Dr. Satterthwaite remarks, paddles on the Usumacinta have nicked ends to prevent slippage on rocks when used as poles. He also makes the point that paddlers are either three or five in number, the odd man being in the stern. Whether these objects are paddles or staves, the scene in all probability represents a trading trip.

There is one other feature which supports this identification. This is the only life scene on pottery of which I know in which a dog is shown. Moreover, the dog is extremely prominent. Landa remarks that in the month Muan the owners of cacao plantations made a feast to Ek Chuah, Chac, and Hobnil, sacrificing a dog with markings of the color of cacao. Ek Chuah was the principal god of Yucatec merchants, who were, of course, vitally associated with cacao. It is, therefore, not unreasonable to assume that such specially marked dogs were intimately connected with merchants and their specialized rituals. The dog in the Ratinlixul scene has a very prominent black patch on his back, so he may well be the dog associated with the cacao ritual and thereby with merchants.

The matter is of some importance, for if this scene does, indeed, represent merchants on a trading expedition, it supplies evidence that the paraphernalia of the merchant class—the fan and perhaps the staves—were fully developed in the Classic period, and that merchants were persons of importance then as later, as the gorgeous quetzal feather and the litter demonstrate.

Beyond occasional references to the existence of markets in both highlands and lowlands, early sources have very little information on their nature. We can suppose that every fair-sized town had a market, and, in earlier times, markets were a feature of every important ceremonial center. Presumably they did not differ, except in importance, essentially from the great markets of Central Mexico, notably that of Tlatelolco, about which there is ample information. The present-day markets of the Guatemala highlands probably mirror the general picture and bustle of old times, but the pagan ceremonial which was once an important feature has gone. On the other hand, the holding of a great market to coincide with a religious festival or the situation of markets at important religious shrines, such as Esquipulas, probably reflects pre-Columbian practice, as well as European custom. Perhaps the Nebaj vase (Joyce, 1914, Plate 24) illustrates a merchant showing his goods to a chief. For further information on markets and their relation to distant commerce, see Cardós de Méndez (1959) and Chapman (1959); for modern markets in Guatemala see McBryde (1947).

The principal currency throughout the area was the cacao bean. Thompson (1956) has dealt at length with cacao as a currency and its fluctuations in terms of the peso in colonial times. Cacao survived as a currency in remoter parts until the mid-nineteenth century. Other forms of currency—copper celts, red shells (probably from *Spondylus*), shell beads, stone axes, feathers, and possibly stone beads—are listed by early writers, but they were probably used more as barter, having values in direct terms of cacao, just as miners used gold dust as currency in the western United States because it had a fixed value in dollars.

TRADE GOODS

Indian markets in present-day Central America are vibrant with life and redolent with strange odors, which no report can convey. In an attempt to bring a slight reminder of that atmosphere I have included two or three items—live iguanas, for instance—which cannot have been of much commercial importance. And what of the edible ants, enjoyed by the Indians of the Lempa Valley, which were for sale in markets of El Salvador late in the sixteenth century?

At the same time, I have not gone deeply into some categories, notably pottery, which are well known or highly complex. They require either a few lines or ten thousand words.

Jade. This, the most valued of all Maya products, is very scarce or does not occur in the Yucatan Peninsula. Foshag (1955:11), in listing seven varieties of jade found in archaeological collections from Middle America, notes the intimate association of jade *in situ* with serpentine deposits and points out that normally they have an enveloping skin of albite in process of conversion into jade. He observes that where there are deposits of serpentine, there is a good possibility of finding jade and lists the following known deposits: the Sierra de las Minas north of the middle Motagua, with an outlying spur south of San Agustín Acasaguastlan, the Sierra de Santa Cruz northwest of Lake Izabal, the Sierra de Chuacus in northern El Quiche north of the Río Negro and extending into adjacent Baja Verapaz, and a small area north of Huehuetenango. More recently, jade has actually been found *in situ* near Manzanal in the Sierra de las Minas (Foshag and Leslie, 1955), and boulders and detritus of jade have been found nearby and farther up the Motagua Valley. Small deposits of serpentine are situated, according to Sapper, near Chimalapa, in southern Chiapas, close to the Guatemala border.

Of these areas—and it must be remembered that except for the middle Motagua jade has not actually been found; the rest are only potential sources—only the Sierra de Santa Cruz and perhaps the northeastern end of the Sierra de las Minas are in lowland territory. Whether there is jade in these two areas and whether the Manche Chol who inhabited the area (they were called Toqueguas there but were of Chol speech) worked it if it exists there are uncertainties. Pusilha and Lubaantun, which were in Chol territory at the time of the Spanish Conquest, have not shown much evidence of jade wealth, and the same is true of Quirigua, which lies in territory probably occupied by the Chol in the sixteenth century. On the other hand, the insignificant sites of Pomona, Kendall, Camp 6, and the not very important Mountain Cow, to the east and west of the Maya Mountains in British Honduras, have yielded some very fine worked jades in the course of quite minor excavations. One is led to speculate whether there could be jade in that range.

Herbert T. Grant, of Belize, and R. S. Sears, of the Phillips Petroleum Company, have called my attention to a rare pamphlet by the geologist C. H. Wilson (1886) giving the results of a survey of the Monkey River, which originates in the Maya Mountains and flows through the south of the Stann Creek district. His published notes contain the following significant entries:

> Monkey River, Trio Branch. Mile 43¼ (from mouth) "North Bend" crossing the river heads north. Block of hard, green rock, apparently from the serpentine bed above, with specks of grey sulphide, millerite?
>
> West Fork. Mile 47¾. Black slates disappear, replaced by massive green rock, serpentine?
>
> Mile 48½. Green banded rock resembling serpentine, occupying channel for ¼ mile to mouth of a branch heading south. Falls a little way up branch, over ledge of massive felsite: boulders of a flinty green rock resembling nephrite.

Unfortunately, Wilson died shortly after his trip, and I have been unable to locate his collection which was sent to England for exhibition at the Colonial and Indian Exhibition. Here however, we have good grounds for supposing that serpentine occurs in the Maya Mountains, and a reasonable possibility that there are also jade deposits there.

A fragmentary small flat metate of serpentine was found at San José. (Thompson, 1939:173). This is a rare but widely distributed type which Kidder believed to have had some special use. So far as I know, this is the only example of serpentine, and it is without supports. It is slight confirmation of probable serpentine deposits in the Maya Mountains, for granite metates, presumably from the Maya Mountain region, are common at San José.

The Maya Mountains appear to be a continuation of the Sierra de las Minas, where jade deposits exist, so deposits there would not be startling. The matter is, of course, far from settled but does suggest a possible lowland source for jade.

All in all, it is probable that the lowlanders, except perhaps those of Copan, received all or most of their jade in trade with the highlanders, for whom it must have been an extremely lucrative exchange.

There is evidence, particularly in the hieroglyphic texts engraved on them, that the lowlanders worked jades after receiving them; there are texts which definitely originated in Piedras Negras and Palenque. Jade boulders have been found in Seibal in caches, but one can assume that others were worked.

There seems to have been a certain re-export of jade from the lowlands after it had been carved. The famous Nebaj jade (Smith and Kidder, 1951, Fig. 59*b*) is a case in point. The Gann jade, now in the British Museum, is said to have been found at Teotihuacan, but there is some doubt about that. I was informed a number of years ago that the piece was given no locality when it was first offered for sale. A fine jade with part of a lowland Maya ceremonial bar, now in the Museo Nacional, has Tarango, Distrito Federal, as its provenience.

Albite, which occurs around jade and has, in non-technical terms, not gone the whole way to become jade, is found sparingly at a few lowland sites and in all probability came from the same sources as the jades.

Worked lava. Metates and manos of lava and other stone of volcanic origin are found throughout the Petén and can safely be regarded as having originated in the volcanic areas of the highlands (here considering Copan as geologically a highland site, for the local andesite was the source of its stone). Certain unusual tripod metates with animal head in relief at one end and made of volcanic stone occur sporadically in the lowlands (e.g., Jacinto Creek and Santa Ana, British Honduras, and a fine example in a Tulum fresco). Eventually, their distribution should reveal interesting trade patterns. They are finer than those found at Zaculeu and other highland sites. As noted above, metates from near Quirigua appear to have come from Veracruz.

Of interest are the small, flat metates found both in the highlands and lowlands, which Kidder (in Wauchope, 1948: 160) discusses, making the cogent suggestion that they had some special function. Can it have been to grind chile pepper? They are often of sandstone or schist, but one from Chichen Itza (Strömsvik, 1931, Fig. 11) and another from Mayapan (Smith and Ruppert, 1956, Fig. 9r) are of volcanic stone and presumably derive from the highlands. As already noted, metates and manos, being very heavy but not particularly valuable, almost certainly were sent by canoe wherever possible.

Volcanic ash (tuff) is very widely used as temper in pottery-making throughout the lowlands because it can stand higher firing temperatures than calcite. The possibility of wind-blown and water-borne deposits in the Petén and Yucatan must be considered.[1]

We are probably safe in supposing that much volcanic ash was imported, but some may have come from local deposits. That volcanic ash was prized is, I think, established by the fact that at San José and Benque Viejo almost all unslipped culinary ware lacked tuff temper, and the same is probably true of the neighboring sites in the Petén and British Honduras.

Specular hematite was used rather sparingly in the lowlands but frequently in parts of the highlands as the basis of an easily recognizable red paint. It commonly forms, Miss Shepard tells me, as a sublimate around volcanoes. It is particularly common in the "Copador" pottery of western Honduras and contiguous parts of Guatemala and El Salvador, notably at Copan. It is also common at La Victoria, El Baúl and other Pacific coast sites, and in the middle Motagua, but occurs sparingly at Kaminaljuyu. In the lowlands it has been reported from Uaxactun, Tikal, San José, and Benque Viejo. In Yucatan the only probable examples reported by

[1] Miss Anna Shepard informs me that she discussed this with oil geologists who had worked in the Petén. Some thought deposits possible, others were doubtful. In his survey notes, Wilson (1886) notes along the Río Trio "ledges of blue diorite or whinstone with intermixed ashy layers [and] channel occupied, wherever seen by ashy volcanics and porphyry." No geologist has visited the area to amplify these brief notes. Vulcanologists told Miss Shepard that ash could be carried that far, but the prevailing winds are in the wrong direction. Some ash temper, Miss Shepard adds, is too coarse to have been carried by the wind, but she found some ash temper impregnated with calcite, which, she suggests, could best be explained as coming from deposits in the local limestone. Pumice stone from highland tributaries is said to be carried by the Usumacinta.

Brainerd (1958) are on Fine Orange ware, not a local ware but almost surely originating near the bottom of the Bay of Campeche. For that reason the specular hematite paint might have been traded from farther west, not from the highlands. This paint was not found in Quintana Roo by Sanders (1960). Dr. Rands informs me it occurs but very rarely at Palenque and Piedras Negras.

Miss Shepard has pointed out that two examples found at San José were calcite tempered, good evidence that the paint ingredient, not the complete pots, was imported, as I had then supposed (Shepard in Kidder, Jennings, and Shook, 1946:271).

Crystalline hematite occurs at several Petén sites, notably Uaxactun, Tikal, Piedras Negras, and San José. Miss Shepard says that first one would have to be quite sure of the identification. She rules out lowland limestone as a source, but feels uncertain whether the Maya Mountains might not have been a source.

Cinnabar, found in volcanic areas, occurs in many lowland sites. The Maya were fond of covering their jades and their dead with it.

Obsidian is universal at lowland sites, and cores are frequent, indicating that many of the finished products came from lowland workshops, but there are no lowland deposits. There are extensive beds around La Jolla about twelve miles northeast of Guatemala City, and enormous deposits around the volcano of Ixtepeque, about six miles north of Asunción Mita and so perhaps controlled at one time by the Chorti. Blom reported obsidian beds north of Coban, close to the Central area, but I have not seen this confirmed, and I know of no volcanoes thereabouts. If there are deposits north of Coban, some supplies may have gone thence by the Chixoy River to sites of the upper Usumacinta drainage. It is generally accepted that green obsidian came from Central Mexico. Strangely, in view of the links of the Usumacinta delta with Yucatan at the time of the Conquest, it is extremely scarce at Mayapan.

Small polished celts of diorite and other igneous rocks superficially resembling diorite, but for the most part unidentified, appear rather sparsely in most lowland sites. The materials of which they are made and the fact that they are nowhere common suggest that they are imports, some of which presumably originated in the Guatemalan highlands. Occasionally these celts are of greenstone, perhaps in some cases jade. Occasionally long celts, obviously imports, occur as at Mountain Cow (Thompson, 1931, Plate 33).

Pottery. Full information on the movement of pottery depends on more extensive studies of the constituent clays and their tempers. For instance, nothing definite is known about where the cylindrical vessels of the early Classic period found at Kaminaljuyu and in the Petén were made or decorated. By and large the highlands did not produce much pottery sufficiently attractive to overcome the disadvantage of high cost of transportation to the lowlands. A ware with the novelty of an unusual surface finish which had a wide appeal was the well-known plumbate which was traded far and wide. It almost certainly originated on the Pacific slope near the Guatemala-Mexico border. Some early (San Juan) plumbate was exported toward the close of the Classic period (a piece is reported at Palenque by Ruz), but the great expansion in pieces exported and distances covered was in the post-Classic period; this great commerce ceased about A.D. 1200. The route plumbate followed to the Peninsula of Yucatan is not easy to guess, but across the plateau of Chiapas and then down the Grijalva River is a possibility, and that route would have also served Veracruz with the coastal or sea route to Tehuantepec as an alternative.

Thin Orange ware, so widely distributed in early Classic times from its supposed center of manufacture in what is today the state of Puebla, appears both at Kaminaljuyu and in the Petén. Its distant range was doubtlessly due to its light weight which made it an attractive novelty to customers and at the same time, by reducing transportation costs, kept the price competitive.

A late pre-Classic tomb at Tikal yielded vessels of the Usulutan complex, that is, they are decorated almost certainly in a negative painting (resist) technique with designs of wavy parallel lines drawn with an applicator of up to five "brushes" so that intervals between lines do not vary. This novelty appealed to the Maya, and vessels thus decorated were widely traded (they are very numerous in early tombs at Kaminaljuyu). They are believed to have originated in Usulutan, El Salvador, but with probably more than one center of manufacture and, later, local imitators.

The record for long-distance trade in pottery is perhaps held by the pottery pipe found beneath a floor in the Temple of the Warriors complex at Chichen Itza (Morris, Charlot, and Morris, 1931, Plate 21), which probably originated in northern Michoacan, some 950 miles by direct overland route, much farther by road and coastal canoe (Porter, 1948, Table 1). Miss Porter supposed this came from Tula, but the Michoacan type is closer.

Shells. A number of shells from the Pacific have been reported from lowland sites. They are:

> *Arca pacifica* (Uaxactun)
> *Cerithium adustum* Kiener (Tikal)
> *Chama echinata* Broderio (Tikal. Numerous)
> *Crucibulum spinosa* (Piedras Negras)
> *Lambidium tubercolosa morum* (San José)
> *Morum tuberculatum* (Piedras Negras)
> *Oliva porphyria* (Copan, Quirigua, Tikal. Represented on
>   stelae)
> *Oliva spicata* (Copan)
> *Pecten subnodosus* (Uaxactun and Tikal)
> *Spondylus crassisquama* (various lowland sites).

Worked shell. Ekholm (1961) has established that the so-called horse-collar shell pendants which have been reported from various sites in Middle America are, in fact, cut from *Patella mexicana*, a native of the Pacific. The irregular shape of the sections makes the identification of examples reasonably certain. They occur at Uaxactun, San José (shaped as a snake), and probably Holmul (Merwin and Vaillant, Fig. 28*b*).

Shellfish dye. One can reasonably suppose that the purple dye obtained from *Purpura patula* on the Pacific coast (Nuttall, 1909) was traded to the lowlands in pre-Columbian times.

Quetzal feathers. The chief habitats of the quetzal are the cloudy, damp ranges of Alta Verapaz, Honduras, and Chiapas preferably five thousand to ten thousand feet high. According to a sixteenth-century source quoted by McBryde (1947:72) ten thousand feathers were obtained annually in the Alta Verapaz alone. This figure seems excessive since each bird yielded only three or four long (tail) feathers. Tovilla (1960, bk. 1, ch. 23) tells us that trapping rights at the special places where the quetzal were caught when they came to drink were inherited. In view of the great value of the commodity, control of the trapping areas must have been a source of huge wealth.

Agricultural products. Trade in foodstuffs must have been largely from lowlands to highlands, but no doubt at times, when crops failed in the lowlands, maize and other produce were attracted by famine prices. It is possible that maguey products were shipped from the highlands. *Ocote* (pitch pine)—the sticks were much used for outdoor illumination—is more plentiful in the highlands than in parts of the lowlands, notably much of the Usumacinta drainage, to which sticks may have been shipped, but the central Petén probably drew on supplies from the Pine Ridge land of British Honduras and the savanna lands south of Lake Petén.

LOWLAND EXPORTS

Worked flint. Points and knives delicately worked with secondary pressure flaking are quite rare in the Maya highlands and on the Pacific slope. The two principal reports on the work at Kaminaljuyu (Kidder, Jennings, and Shook, 1946; Shook and Kidder, 1953) list between them exactly one piece of worked flint, an eccentric flint which, most surprisingly, was in a Formative deposit; Nebaj yielded one flint implement, an extremely fine point; Zacualpa produced two pieces of worked flint, one of which was a small white arrowhead (?), an almost exact duplicate of a type found at Chichen Itza. Zaculeu, on the other hand, produced eighteen points of flint, but of no standard type. All the main shapes—leaf-shaped, triangular, tapering stemmed, and expanding stemmed—are represented. Most of them come from burials or caches, suggesting that they were valued.

Blom found flint deposits which had been worked near Moxviquil, above San Cristóbal Las Casas, Chiapas. I examined points from there in his museum. They were of crude workmanship and seemed to resemble those from Zaculeu, but I did not have Zaculeu illustrations at hand. The two sites are not too far apart and stand on an ancient route, so the flints excavated at Zaculeu may well have come from Moxviquil beds.

At Tajumulco, excavations produced no flint implements, but

there were six complete or fragmentary projectile points of chalcedony, including one small point with expanding stem. El Baúl yielded a rich votive cache comprising thirty-six leaf-shaped points or knives of flint, two fine eccentric flints, and two obsidian points or knives with straight sides. Apart from that haul, only one flint point was found. La Victoria, on the Pacific coast, yielded no flint and precious little pressure-flaked obsidian.

Eccentric is a term applied to flints, as well as obsidians, worked into all sorts of curious shapes—crescents, rings, Maltese crosses, and sinuous forms shading into surrealist designs with projecting knobs and curls added apparently at the will of the flint knapper; a few are fairly realistic portraits of men, dogs, scorpions, members of the cat family, and snakes. They could have served no useful purpose, but are usually found in groups of nine in offertory caches beneath stelae and buildings. They occur in large numbers in the eastern half of the Central area, but the very few found in Yucatan and the western part of the Central area are probably imports. Palenque, for example, has not yielded a single eccentric flint. Probably they were never made in the highlands.

The two eccentric flints of the trident type found at El Baúl are almost unquestionably imports from the lowlands. Precisely similar pieces have not been reported from lowland sites, to the best of my knowledge, but they are represented in sculpture and paintings of the late Classic period (Thompson, 1948:40). A poorer version comes from Piedras Negras (W. Coe, 1959, Fig. 6n), and one with the same grip but with only one prong is in the Museum in Campeche labeled as from Jaina, but perhaps from the Usumacinta Valley since it was previously in a private museum at Carmen.

Eccentric flints in the Guatemalan highlands are scarce. Apart from those two at El Baúl and the one at Kaminaljuyu, I know of only two others. One, said to be from Chimaltenango, is in the Museum of the American Indian, Heye Foundation; the other, over thirty centimeters long, was found at Salcaja and is in the Robles collection, Quezaltenango. There is a large (about forty centimeters long) obsidian eccentric, shaped like a Stillson wrench, in the National Museum, Mexico, and labeled as from Guerrero. A three-pronged eccentric flint, but without provenience, is in the

Museum at Tuxtla Gutiérrez; it probably came from the Usumacinta drainage. A large eccentric flint of horseshoe shape found at Naco (Lunardi, 1946) is of interest as probable evidence that the trade was by sea and that Naco was an important port even in the Classic period.

In view of the distribution of flint implements and the great concentration of eccentric flints in the Petén and adjacent British Honduras, it is fair to assume that the eccentrics were imports from the lowlands. I think it is also a reasonable assumption that some, at least, of the better flint points or knives were exported from lowlands to highlands. Almost all those in the El Baúl cache are almost indistinguishable from examples from lowland caches in shape, ripple, pressure flaking, and preference for those of sepia color.

The only chipped implement found at Nebaj is of honey-colored stone, about twenty centimeters long, and described as "one of the finest pieces of pressure flaking ever found in Mesoamerica" (Smith and Kidder, 1951:51). One can reasonably suppose it to have been imported. The shape is a little unusual, but I think this can be explained as perhaps the work of an individual or a center of flint knapping not yet identified but in the lowland Maya tradition.

The only flint excavated at Guaytan, a part of San Agustín Acasaguastlan, was a beautiful knife or point in a pottery cache box. Kidder and Smith (1943:164) note, "Seven knives of the same stone, of identical workmanship, and of similar shape were found at Quirigua cached under Zoomorph B (Strömsvik, 1941, Fig. 30); five in a cache at San José (Thompson, 1939, Plate 26)." Here again we are almost certainly dealing with exports from the lowlands. The leaf-shaped, stemless blades from Zaculeu, particularly the longest (Woodbury and Trik, 1953, Fig. 121*c*), look like lowland work as does the damaged point of brown chert in their Figure 125. The stemmed point from Zacualpa (Wauchope, 1948, Plate 24*k*) is both aberrant in shape and of too good workmanship to be of local manufacture.

The material is described in the caption as chert but in the text as an almost opaque gray stone with a glassy luster, perhaps not obsidian. A lowland home seems a reasonable guess.

It is worth bearing in mind that obsidian and glass are generally considered easier to work than flint and related stones. The highland Maya seem to have normally shown little skill in working obsidian, so it is unlikely that they would be capable of far more proficient work in less tractable substances.

Worked obsidian. In view of what has just been said of the rather poor workmanship in obsidian in most parts of the highlands, one wonders whether the finest pieces may not have been fashioned elsewhere. There is evidence for this: the eight finest pieces of worked obsidian at Kaminaljuyu are of the green variety believed not to be native to Guatemala. As it is unlikely that those of that variety would be far better worked than the regular gray-black obsidian, if they all came out of a local worshop, one may reasonably conclude that those of green obsidian were imported fully worked. The excellent workmanship of the green obsidian knife points at Uaxactun and fragments at Zaculeu reinforce this conclusion. David Pendergast writes me that eccentrics of green obsidian were found in 1969 at Altun Ha, British Honduras. Eccentric obsidians do occur at Teotihuacan, northeast of Mexico City and close to green obsidian deposits, but they are smallish. It would seem far more likely that those of Altun Ha were imported as raw material and fashioned by local craftsmen.

It is not therefore an unreasonable guess, on present evidence (there are immense deposits near Pachuca, north of Mexico City) that green obsidian was worked in the Maya lowlands and then exported to the highlands, and it seems possible that Maya lowlanders, who certainly worked obsidian received as cores from the highlands, re-exported some of their best products. The leaf-shaped obsidian point from Zacualpa noted by Kidder as aberrant (Wauchope, 1948, Plate 23g) may have been worked in the lowlands. The two obsidian points in the El Baúl cache are of superior workmanship and were with presumed flint imports from the lowlands. Here, too, one suspects lowland workmanship. A few years will show this speculation to be fact or fancy.

Salt is heavy. At the present time the Pacific coast or the salt flats at Sacapulas are the principal sources of salt for the highland Maya of Guatemala. We have seen that salt collected off the northeastern corner of Yucatan was shipped from Cozumel to

Chol territory in southeastern Petén and adjacent British Honduras. It is reasonable to suppose that salt may also have been carried from Cozumel to Nito and thence up the Motagua or across Lake Izabal to nearby highland communities. Apparently, the Indians prefer ocean salt to the purer salt of Sacapulas (McBryde, 1947:58), and it is possible that the lowland traders could sell their salt more cheaply in the middle or upper Motagua Valley than could those who brought supplies overland from the Pacific coast, for some trading canoes were of very considerable size. Moreover, it is probable that Pacific coast supplies were at times cut off, for part of the coastal strip was in non-Maya hands. An overland trade in salt from Nueve Cerros (p. 29), on a short tributary of the middle Chixoy, to the Verapaz almost certainly existed. The middle Chixoy is now in Kekchi hands, but that northward eruption of the Kekchi is a posthispanic development. In prehispanic times, lowland Maya surely controlled the salt beds on the middle Chixoy (there is a stela with glyphs at Nueve Cerros).

Lime from the Golfo Dulce area or southern British Honduras probably was shipped to contiguous highland areas.

Pottery. Fine polychrome pottery which turns up sporadically in the highlands and is not referable to the polychrome wares of the Verapaz and the middle Motagua may be presumed to represent imports from the lowlands. The superb polychrome vase at Zaculeu (Woodbury and Trik, Fig. 265s) is an example, and the glyphic sherd marked *o* in the same figure is another piece almost surely of lowland origin.

A tetrapod bowl of the so-called proto-Classic horizon with a fish painted on its floor from a tomb at Tzicuay, El Quiche, (Smith and Kidder, 1951, Fig. 75k, l) is practically a duplicate of a vessel from a *chultun* burial at Mountain Cow (Thompson, 1931, Plate 42). Shape and colors are precisely the same, but the fish painted on the floor is treated a little differently. There can be little doubt that the vessel was taken to Tzicuay from the lowlands. One may suppose that a number of basal-flanged bowls of the Tzakol period passed from the Petén to the highlands.

Fine Orange vessels with carved or molded scenes and often with a band of glyphs at the top occur sporadically through the highlands. Their center of manufacture is still unknown, but doubtlessly lay in the western Maya lowlands and so presumably reached the highlands via Chiapas. Copan Carved Brown ware, with its beautiful glyphic texts, also found its way to the highlands doubtlessly through the middle Motagua Valley. Indeed, the ware is known at San Agustín Acasaguastlan.

Because of the glyphs and the figures they carry, one may reasonably suppose that the pottery stands which turn up in the Alta Verapaz (Dieseldorff, 1926–33, Vol. 1, Figs. 18, 19) derive from the middle Pasión, although they have not yet been found in that poorly known area so far as I know. Presumably they or the molds for making them were shipped down the Chixoy River.

These few examples suffice to illustrate what must have been an active trade in time and space of lowland pottery to the highlands.

Shells. Trade in Atlantic shells to the highlands probably did not equal that of Pacific shells to the lowlands, but in the case of one shell the quantity traded must have been very large. Atlantic shells in highland sites are these:

> *Marginella apicina*, which is extremely abundant. Several score have been reported from Kaminaljuyu, and the excavations at San Agustín Acasaguastlan brought to light "about 1,000." It was probably represented at Nebaj and is also common at lowland sites (Uaxactun. San José, Copan).
> *Dolium galea.* One at Kaminaljuyu.
> *Cassis tuberosa.* One at Kaminaljuyu.
> *Turbinella ovoidea.* One at Kaminaljuyu.
> *Fasciolaria papillosa.* One at Zaculeu.
> *Murex pomum.* Identification not certain. Kaminaljuyu.

Shark teeth. Borhegyi (1961) has pointed out that fifty-four perforated shark teeth found at Nebaj are from cub shark, a species found only in the Atlantic.

Slaves. Bishop Landa states that slaves were sent from Yucatan to Ulua and Tabasco in exchange for cacao. It is uncertain whether some of these slaves reached the highlands, but it is at least probable. The Putun of Acalan also had a hand in the slave trade.

Pelts. Jaguars and other animals whose skins were valued were not common, one may suppose, in the highlands, and the demand for their pelts, particularly that of the jaguar as a symbol of rank, must have been met largely by imports from the lowlands. Jaws of jaguars were in the most important tombs at Kaminaljuyu and at Nebaj, and of unidentified members of the cat family at Zaculeu.

Plumage. Although the Yucatan Peninsula does not shelter the quetzal, it is the home of many birds, such as toucans, humming-birds, herons, parrots, trogons, and so on, the plumage of which must have been exported to the highlands. Moreover, there were in Yucatan "two or three kinds of ducks of the country bred for their feathers" (*Relaciones de Yucatán*, 1:86), and from other sources (Torquemada, bk. 3, ch. 41) we know that plumage was exported from Yucatan to the bottom of the Bay of Honduras, most logically with the highlands as ultimate destination, for Honduras was famed for its plumage. Macaws were bred on the Bay Islands and exported to the mainland (*Relaciones de Yucatán*, 1:391).

Iguanas, much prized as food and for their medicinal properties, presumably were shipped alive to the highlands, as at the present time.

Tortoiseshell. Working of tortoiseshell was an important industry in Campeche in Colonial times, and continues on a reduced scale to this day. Exports to the highlands in pre-Columbian times are at least a possibility.

Honey and wax. Yucatan, particularly the province of Chetumal, produced large quantities of honey. Oviedo y Valdés (1851-55, bk. 32, ch. 6) has left a lengthy description of apiculture in Chetumal.

At that one place there were two or three thousand hives of the log type, still in use among the Maya of Yucatan. Cozumel, too, was a great center of apiculture (Martyr, 1612, Dec. 4, ch. 3). As noted, there are various references to the export of honey and wax from Yucatan. I know of no mention of apiculture in the highlands of Guatemala on a large scale in pre-Columbian times. The present-day Kekchi sometimes bring hives of wild bees to their homes, but there is hardly an industry. The rarity of bee-keeping among the present-day Maya highlanders may be due to the replacement of honey by sugar, but the higher regions are almost too cold for the domesticated stingless bee of ancient America, so I suspect that the lack of notices on pre-Columbian apiculture in the highlands reflects actual conditions. Accordingly, it is logical to suppose that a good share of the export from Yucatan found its way to the highlands, and, who knows, perhaps a pre-Columbian predecessor of that delectable (?) drink *xtabentun* was part of the cargo.

Wax candles almost surely were unknown in pre-Columbian America, but wax was of ceremonial importance and had many uses. If the assumption that hives were scarce in the highlands is correct, wax was probably brought from Yucatan.

Vegetal products undoubtedly passed in large quantities from the lowlands to the highlands. That trade unfortunately is not mirrored in archaeology, nor did it arouse the curiosity of colonial writers; we can infer its nature and range only from present-day conditions much affected by the introduction of Old World crops and domestic animals. Below is a selection of such products.

Cotton textiles are the exception to what has just been said. The fine brocaded textiles of Yucatan were famed all over Middle America, being one of the most important items of tribute paid in early Colonial times. Landa (1941:94) says they were exported to Ulua and Tabasco; the best description is that given in Las Casas' (1877, bk. 2, ch. 20) account of the cargo of the canoe Columbus encountered in the Bay Islands: "Many cotton mantles, much decorated with diverse colors and designs, and short sleeveless shirts, also colored and with designs, and loin clothes which the men use of the same colors and designs." Incidentally, the statement concerning "cloaks calling them *Zuyen*," which Blom (1932:533) attributes to Las Casas or Oviedo y Valdés, has no value, for it originated with López de Cogolludo (bk. 1, ch. 1), who wrote nearly two centuries after this encounter.

Oviedo y Valdés (1851–55, bk. 32, ch. 8) also mentions canoes laden with cloth and other merchandise passing from Yucatan to Ulua, as does Torquemada (1713, bk. 3, ch. 41). Finally, the *Relación de Tekanto y Tepacan* (*Relaciones de Yucatán*, 1:125) speaks of cotton mantles, wax, honey, and salt traded to Mexico, Honduras, and other parts.

Rabbit fur was brought to Yucatan from Central Mexico—the Mixteca according to one source—was embroidered or, more probably, brocaded on textiles, and some of these in turn seem to have been re-exported. Feathers were also woven into cotton goods, particularly loin cloths. Much of this trade in cotton goods seems to have been in return for cacao from the coastal strip from the Ulua to Lake Izabal, but some surely got to the highlands. The export of wax and mantles from Yucatan to Central Mexico continued into Colonial times under Spanish auspices, for Zurita (1891, ch. 16), writing about 1570, mentions the trade as still active. Teotitlan del Camino, in northern Oaxaca, traded huipils to Guatemala, notably Suchitepequez, for cacao (*Papeles de Nueva España*, ser. 2, 4:215) so perhaps the producers of chocolate wealth could command the finest textile products of Middle America.

Tobacco was probably imported from the lowlands as today. Much tobacco is now grown in the vicinity of Copan, but this seems to be a fairly recent development. Tobacco had an important outlet as a medicine.

Maize. At the present time, the Guatemalan highlands are not self-supporting, and much of their maize is obtained from the Pacific coast. In pre-Columbian times the inhabitants of the Pacific coast cultivated much cacao and other tropical produce, and so perhaps had little surplus maize. Moreover, hostilities may often have cut off supplies. It is, therefore, reasonable to suppose that maize was brought from the Atlantic lowlands, particularly in early summer, for lowland maize ripens before that of the highlands.

Cacao. With strategic entrepôts near the mouths of the Motagua and Dulce on the east and others in the Usumacinta and Grijalva deltas, the Putun were in a position to share the highland market with the producers of the Pacific coastal slope. Cacao is still cultivated in Tabasco, notably between Villahermosa and Teapa, and it is still grown by the Mopan Maya of southern British Honduras. The cacao plantations in Tabasco were of immense importance in the sixteenth century, and large orchards lay along the Belize River and the parts of northern British Honduras comprised in the state of Chetumal. Such areas must have exported both to Yucatan, too dry, and the highlands, too high, for these money-producing orchards.

Vanilla. Some of this lowland crop may have been sent to the highlands. It is reported as cultivated in the Belize Valley in colonial times, and it also grows wild in the Petén.

Rubber. There was probably some export to the highlands.

Mamey, chicozapote, and nance plums are still taken from the Pacific slopes to the highlands. It is likely that the Maya lowlands shared in the traffic in pre-Spanish times.

Copal. Groves of copal trees (*Protium copal*) were noted in Yucatan at the time of the Spanish Conquest, and the tree grows wild in the lowlands. This resin is superior to other varieties of native incense and doubtlessly was shipped to the highlands, presumably in maize-husk containers as still used by the Maya, but no copal is now imported from the Central area.

Palm products. The Zutuhil Maya of Atitlan send young men to the Pacific lowlands to fetch spathes of cohune buds—three to four feet long—which are used in the Easter ceremonies. The sheaths open to display and then scatter their thousands of sweet-smelling blossoms (McDougall, 1955:64).

From cohune palm leaves are made *suyacales*, the rain cloaks still widely used in Middle America and surely in use in pre-Columbian days, although some claim they were introduced from Japan during the Colonial period. Cohune leaves are also used by the highlanders to make fire fans, and no doubt highlanders living near stands of cohune might follow the lowland custom of using their leaves for thatching, but obviously sufficient cohune leaves to thatch a hut could not be carried long distances. McBryde (1947:146) writes of the sale in the highlands of swathes of the *pacaya*, a lowland palm, which are much enjoyed for their slightly bitter taste. The same is true of the hearts of the cabbage palm (*Sabal mexicana*), which also have a slightly bitter taste and are much relished by the lowland Maya. They are now eaten widely as a Good Friday dish, but there is no reason to suppose that their consumption was not general long before the Spanish Conquest. All of these palm products may well have been shipped up the Motagua and Lake Izabal routes in earlier times.

Chile. Dried chile is still brought in large quantities from the Pacific coast. Imports from the Atlantic lowlands may also be assumed.

Vegetal dyes. One may confidently assume that logwood and brazilwood dyes were exported from the lowlands to the high-lands in pre-Columbian days.

Annatto. Cortés listed this as a product in which Acalan traders dealt. It was used to a large extent for staining the body and for giving flavor and color to food. The tree produces in abundance without any attention. Accordingly, annatto should have been able to undersell other red pigments when durability was not a factor.

Bark cloth. References to clothing of bark cloth are, I believe, confined to the lowlands, but it is probable that there was some use of it by commoners, both for clothing and for combined *manta*-blankets. Bark cloth was also used for making paper and, to judge by present-day practice in Mexico, for sorcery. Far and away the greatest use of paper in ancient Mexico, and probably also throughout the Maya area, was for sacrificial purposes, either by itself or splattered with rubber or copal. Bark cloth was made principally from trees of the *Ficus* genus, notably *Ficus cotinifolia.* One doubts that the productions from local stands in the high-lands would have met the demand; large-scale imports from the lowlands seem likely.

Other agricultural produce, such as beans and huisquil (*sechium edule*), and perhaps some henequen products may have found their way to the highlands. It is not certain that the pineapple was known in the Maya lowlands in pre-Columbian times. At least there appears to be no Maya name for the plant.

SOME GENERAL CONSIDERATIONS

With our present knowledge of geological conditions, it is not easy for even an expert to rule out one area or the other. Miss Shepard suggests that in the case of beryl, amazonite, and mica the Maya Mountains cannot be excluded as a source. For that reason and also because they are not common, they are not brought into the discussion.

Turquoise, I think, was not mined in any part of the Maya area. Quiche and Cakchiquel dictionaries give *xit* as "some precious stones like turquoise." The word appears to be a corruption of the Nahuatl *xiuitl*, "turquoise," and leads one to suppose that the highland Maya, on obtaining turquoise from Nahuatl-speaking traders, adopted the foreign name for it. Turquoise, never common in the Maya area, appears more frequently in Yucatan than in the Guatemalan highlands, a situation understandable if the turquoise came from Veracruz.

Amber was produced in central Chiapas, and the trade was controlled by the Chol, Tzotzil, Chiapanec, and Zoque. Blom (1959) has discussed the matter. There was a brisk export of this amber to Mexico. In Yucatan, Landa tells us, the men used nose rods of amber stone which must have come from Chiapas. Among the Chol Lacandon, some women wore amber disks the size of a silver *real* linked together or linked to the septum of the nose (Villagutierre, 1933, bk. 5, ch. 6—the passage can be read in either sense). Amber artifacts are very rare in Maya sites, but they have been found in Oaxaca and Veracruz, and the Cempoallan and Aztec merchants used nose plugs of that material.

Metal is not listed above. It is doubtful that any metal was sent from the highlands to the lowlands, although, as is well known, gold from Panama reached Chichen Itza, an exceedingly long journey, surely made by sea.

I have not attempted to place items of trade in archaeological periods, for subsequent excavations will greatly amplify our knowledge. There is no doubt that trade was extensive at all periods.

Yet one must realize the limitations of spade archaeology. Let me illustrate this with an example from the Old World. In mediaeval times, the great wealth of East Anglia and much of eastern England derived from its export of wool to northwestern Europe. Exports of wool built those magnificent churches in Decorated or Perpendicular Gothic style which grace almost every town and village. Yet I do not believe that excavation could produce evidence of the source of the local wealth. Nowadays, sheep in East Anglia are not much commoner than Indians in Manhattan; it is now the cereal-producing part of Britain. It is true that there are a few examples of Flemish art in East Anglian churches, but they are, in fact, Victorian acquisitions. Any such pieces installed in mediaeval times would have been chopped down by Puritans.

157

With written sources absent, that tale would stay untold. So, vital twists in Maya growth may likewise go untraced.

I have tried to underline my belief that wherever possible those great merchants, the Putun, carried their goods in canoes, in contrast to the highlander who perforce had to travel on foot. Conditions may have been different at an earlier period, but even during the Classic period one gets an impression of much commerce radiating from the Usumacinta-Grijalva delta. On the other hand, Palenque seems to have had little commerce with Petén sites—note, for instance, lack of eccentric flints and rarity of fine polychrome pottery. In contrast, there is an explanation for the great quantities of imported Fine Orange and Fine Gray pottery at Altar de Sacrificios (p. 38).

In reviewing the above, one is struck by the rarity of manufactured products among highland exports. These are largely confined to lava metates and manos, the working of which was far from intricate. On the other hand, lowland exports, although they included many raw materials, embraced many artistic and skillfully worked products such as worked jade and flint, polychrome pottery, and finely woven textiles. This confirms the general archaeological picture that in the arts the lowlanders were streets ahead of their highland cousins.

The picture we piece together of commerce at the moment of Spanish irruption is one of great and widespread activity. Yet the archaeological evidence shows Mayapan apparently more isolated than were earlier Maya sites. The period of Mayapan's ascendancy is known to have been one of cultural decline, and in the few decades between the fall of Mayapan (ca. A.D. 1460) and the arrival of the Spaniards, the cultural collapse was accentuated. Yet this complex traffic garlanded the whole Peninsula of Yucatan in those last years of autochthonous culture. If this was the trough of cultural depression, how must things have been when the Maya were riding the wave of prosperity—or can it be that the Putun, those Argonauts of the western Caribbean, were the spearhead of a Maya cultural revival through their search for *Theobroma*—and how truly and poetically it is the food of the gods—that New World equivalent of the golden fleece?

CHAPTER 6

Lowland Maya Religion:
Worship

To understand a people one must comprehend that people's religion. "Understanding is the beginning of wisdom."

GENERAL CONSIDERATIONS

Although the religion and rites of the lowland Maya are the subjects of chapters 6–8, some reference will be made to highland Maya practices to amplify aspects of the discussion. The bulk of the material comes from Yucatan, information from there being far fuller than from other parts of the lowlands, except for what is available from studies of the present-day Yucatec-speaking Lacandon of Chiapas.

Our knowledge of lowland religion derives from six sources. The earliest but least reliable of these is represented by the archaeological monuments and murals of the Classic period with supporting material from post-Classic sites, but the great bulk of the latter, coming from Chichen Itza, must be handled with caution, because much of it is marked by strong influences from outside the Maya area.

The three surviving hieroglyphic books—codices Dresden, Madrid, and Paris (named for the cities where they now repose)

159

—form the second source. They deal almost exclusively with religious practices, but many parts of them are still not wholly understood. They date from about A.D. 1250 (Dresden) to perhaps A.D. 1450 (Madrid), but show very little alien (Mexican) influence. Codex Dresden is a new edition of a lost original which surely was written during the Classic period.

The third source comprises documents written by Yucatec Maya, in European script, in the Colonial period. The most important of these are the so-called Books of Chilam Balam. Compiled by Maya antiquaries desirous of preserving the traditions of their people, they contain a wealth of detail on Maya religion. The material is drawn from ancient recitations, dramatic performances, and songs which, in turn, had been expanded, in many cases, from short key texts in hieroglyphs. Much of this comprises ancient prophecies which contain a mixture of history and religion. Through ignorance, the writers made errors in the historical reconstructions and garbled passages with obsolete phrases, but the material is invaluable. The most informative of the Books of Chilam Balam, in order of importance, are those of Chumayel, Tizimin, Mani, and Kaua. Chilam Balam derives from the name of a famous prophet (*chilan*) called jaguar (*balam*); the other names are of the towns in which they were once kept.

Ritual of the Bacabs, another colonial document, contains a number of cures with invocations of deities. Unfortunately, the material is wrapped in symbolism, much of which is beyond the comprehension of present-day Maya and modern scholar alike. The only parallel which comes to mind is the Book of Revelation. Many plants, birds, and insects, all clothed in symbolism and allusions to lost mythology, are important features. This was translated by the great Maya scholar, Ralph Roys (1965), but even in translation the incantations are very hard to comprehend.

The fourth source is the most important contribution made by Spanish writers of the early Colonial period. The outstanding writer is Diego de Landa, third bishop of Yucatan, who came to Yucatan in 1549 as one of the early Franciscan missionaries when Maya culture still flourished. His *Relación de las cosas de Yucatán* was composed in 1566 while he was in Spain (1563–73), but internal evidence makes it clear that much of the material was gathered as early as 1551. It is a small encyclopedia of Maya religion and ethnology.

Documents on inquisitorial proceedings against Indian relapses into paganism, instituted by Landa in 1562 (Scholes and Adams, 1938), further illuminate the subject, as do many other colonial writings.

Modern ethnological investigations of lowland and highland communities, which have amassed a vast amount of data on Maya religion, form the fifth source. Comparative data on the religious practices and beliefs of non-Maya neighbors are the final and a most helpful source, because all peoples of Middle America inherited their fundamental beliefs from those current before Maya culture had emerged as a separate entity.

I believe the Maya to be deeply religious. That is true, above all, of the Maya of the Guatemalan highlands and Chiapas. There, communities have remained isolated—at least until the past three decades—from modern life. One may perhaps be permitted the generalization that the less exposed a Maya community is to the outside world, the stronger are its religious attitudes.

Allowance must obviously be made for the fact that our sources cover a span of two thousand years of Maya religion, and in that time change must have taken place. Nevertheless, the same principal Maya deities can be recognized in sculpture, painting, and hieroglyphic texts of the Classic period as in sixteenth-century Yucatan, which encourages the belief that religious shifts were not great.

One can not easily measure the religious fervor of a people, but, as a straw in the wind, note that La Farge and Byers (1931:146) calculate that during the four hundred days of a Jacalteca prayer-maker's term of office he was called on for upwards of two hundred days of intensive prayer, which required rising or staying up till late at night and being on hand again shortly before dawn. This is no mean manifestation of religious susceptibility.

In present-day Yucatan, religion plays a less dominant role in the life of the community and the individual. There are, I think, two historical reasons for this. The Maya in Yucatan were tied for three centuries to the haciendas, with a consequent loosening of community and religious life, particularly of those elements of pagan origin. In contrast, the haciendas' Catholic chapels exerted strong Christian influence. On top of that, much of the old paganism centered on agricultural rites, and the Maya on the haciendas were for the most part landless.

The second historical reason, as I see it, arises from the consequences of the downfall, in 1911, of President Portfirio Díaz. That was followed in Yucatan by an upsurge of extreme socialism coupled with distribution of land to the Maya, break-up of the haciendas, and the liberation of the peones working on them from something akin to serfdom. The Maya welcomed the new order with unbounded enthusiasm but were met with a militant antireligious campaign which, because it was linked to the gratifying liberation, left a decided mark on Maya preoccupation with religion. This took the form of apathy rather than opposition to religion. Indeed, Ralph Roys told me of how a "cultural mission" which went to the village of Numkini in those troublesome times to smash the statues in the church and wreck its interior was badly beaten up by the villagers. This action perhaps exemplifies Maya moderation in all things; they wanted no extremes. The religious fervor which is still very evident among the independent Maya of Quintana Roo shows that the lessening interest in religion in Yucatan has nothing to do with racial character.

That same tendency to religious indifference is noticeable also in Maya villages in central British Honduras. There, the reason perhaps lies in the growth of the chicle industry which drew men away from their villages, loosening the ties of community life and the old ways. It is not apparent in Mopan-Maya villages in southern British Honduras, from which chicle bleeding has never drawn recruits. Likewise, the extremely isolated Lacandon of the Chiapan forests have held fast to the old rituals, at least until the last decade saw the population almost wiped out.

Present-day religion of the Yucatec Maya is an amalgam of the old paganism and the externals of Christianity, for the Maya has adopted an unconscious eclecticism in this. He has taken to his heart the saints of the Roman Catholic church, but has very little interest in the founder of Christianity; the crucifixion means almost nothing to him, whereas the cross plays a very large part in his religious practices.

At the same time, several of the most important deities of the old pantheon have completely disappeared; the present-day Maya has no knowledge at all of such leading gods as Itzam Na, Kukulcan, and Ek Chuah; and the sun god and moon goddess live only in tales, save only in Chiapas where the sun god survives as a rather unimportant deity. It is the gods of the soil and the protectors of the village who are enshrined in the heart of the Maya peasant.

A state religion, if I may use that grandiose adjective, has given way to a village folk religion. This shift can be explained by the disappearance of the old priesthood and the collapse of a centralized and autocratic rule. This took place in two stages, the first of which was marked by the collapse of the ceremonial centers—the so-called cities—of the Central area at the close of the Classic period; the second by the coming of the Spaniards.

I suspect that the "state" religion of the ceremonial center had little appeal for the Maya peasant, whose interest lay in the simple agricultural ceremonies of his own small outlying community. In the ceremonial center, the high priest carried out his rites on top of a high pyramid, remote from the crowds gathered far below in the court. Much of the ritual, there is reason to believe, took place inside the temples where there was room for only a handful of priests or chiefs; congregational participation must have been almost nil, and, for all we know to the contrary, attendance may have been obligatory. A peasant forced to attend ceremonies, often in honor of gods in whom he had no interest, when he would have preferred to be about his own business in his milpa, may have taken a dim view of state religion if calls on him to be present were too frequent.

With the collapse of the ceremonial centers and, as I believe, the massacre or expulsion of nobles and priests, the peasant would have happily devoted himself to the propitiation of his own gods of the soil, of the hunt, and of the village under village prayermakers—a purely folk religion.

The old order, in transformed shape, continued in northern Yucatan, but there the same fate overtook it six centuries later with the institution of Spanish rule. The high priests were liquidated—not in blood, but by taking the sons of nobles and priests from their surroundings and educating them in the white man's ways—but the village prayermaker, the *hmen*, continued unmolested. Many of the outward forms of Christianity were willingly adopted by the Maya; within two decades of the Conquest they had taken over such Christian ideas as candles and had even added crucifixion to their sacrificial repertoire.

This shift from state to folk religion accounts for the disappearance of favorite deities of the old hierarchy, such as those mentioned. The villager had little interest in feathered serpents, celestial dragons, and personifications of the planet Venus; and although "God the Father, God the Son, and God the Holy Ghost" are normally invoked at the close of Maya prayers, the concept of the Trinity is meaningless to him and the second and third Persons of no real importance. That partakes of theology remote from peasant religion.

In the newly evolved religion there is a distinct, although to the Maya hardly perceptible, division of functions between the two groups. The old pagan gods of the soil and of nature rule the forests and fields in which the Maya labors; the Christian saints preside over village affairs with the assistance of the pagan gods who, seated at its four entrances, protect the village from "any terror by night [and] the arrow that flieth by day."

The saint to whom the village church is dedicated became the patron of that community. Saint Anthony is asked to find lost objects, and the Virgin Mary merges with the moon goddess, who was very far from being a virgin, and takes over some of her functions, notably that of protectress against certain diseases. Even the Chacs, the beloved rain gods, are mounted on horses—the Chacs are multicolored and four in number as are the horses of the Four Horsemen of the Apocalypse. Yet efforts by the clergy to foster San Isidro as patron of agriculture met with resounding failure.

Nonetheless, the important members of the new pantheon are the old pagan gods of the rain and the soil—at least for the men. Women, whose life is in the village, are more interested in the Christian saints. A man's life is bound up with his crops; his is an unremitting struggle against encroaching forest, drought, insect plagues, and the incursions of birds and animals—above all, the destructive raccoon. In that unceasing war he needs supernatural allies, and for them he turns to the old gods. Yet he considers that side of his religion to be an integral part of Christianity; he regards himself as a true and orthodox Catholic.

The Maya believes wholeheartedly in animatism, that is, that all creation is both alive and active. Trees, rocks, and plants are animate beings who aid or oppose him. The earth and the crops are living beings whom he must propitiate. When he cuts down the forest to make his milpa, he apologizes to the earth for "disfiguring" its face; when he kills a deer, he excuses the act on the grounds of his need. La Farge and Byers tell how the Jacalteca Maya of a remote corner of the Guatemalan highlands, when they needed to cut down a large tree to make a village cross, sent a prayermaker to a stand of high trees to ask a tree to volunteer to serve that purpose. One agreed, and, on being asked how high she wished to be, replied that she would indicate this by breaking at the appropriate height when she fell. This she did, the smaller piece being given the honor of serving as the crosspiece.

The Tzotzil Maya believe that when forest is felled, some of the fallen trees go to heaven to complain. The Quiche Maya of Chichicastenango hold that the maize is frightened of earthquakes and call to the maize during an earthquake to reassure it. In the same town, it is thought that if yellow and white ears of corn are left lying together in the patio they will copulate. The Tzotzil Maya say that only fools dig their nails into maize to see whether it is ripe because that hurts the maize as it would us.

Guiteras, source for the last observation, has perhaps the most charming example of animatism: makers of musical instruments pray while working that their handicraft be perfect, and the instruments are given a little liquor to make them happy. One wonders what happens when "The Dead March" is the tune.

One could cite instance after instance of similar beliefs. Naturally, they affect Maya prayer and ritual.

MAGIC

Magic is said to be the contrary of religion in that with magic man, provided he follows the ritual without error, can compel the action he wants; but in religion, man petitions the gods and hopes they will accede to his wishes.

Imitative magic, in which action against one object or being will similarly affect something related to it or sharing with it some feature such as appearance or name, is common all over Middle America. A good example of this is the Maya *hetzmek*, "hold in arms," ceremony performed when a boy is four months or a girl three months old. The implements the children will use when grown up—machete, axe, cooking and (formerly) weaving implements—are placed in their hands according to their sex, and they are guided in the actions of using them. Thereby they will grow up proficient in their adult occupations, milpa and household work, respectively. Four is the age chosen for the boys because four are the "sides" of every milpa; three for the girls because as women they will spend their lives stooping over the three stones which form the hearth.

Various forms of magic occur in British Honduras. For example, in order that a girl grow up a good tortilla maker, one should rub her hands with a *uo* frog, for its stomach is known to be full of dough of new maize; so that she will develop upright breasts, those should be rubbed with a hummingbird's nest. A hunter will become more successful if on a Friday he eats tortillas in which have been baked some ants of the kind called *chacmool zinic*, "jaguar ants," so called because their red and black markings resemble spots on a jaguar skin. Here clearly, eating jaguar ants gives one the prowess of the jaguar which preys on all game.

A charming, if pungent, example of such magical acts, of which there are scores, comes from the Chamula Tzotzil (Pozas, 1947: 193). One should get a regular wife-beater to sow one's chile so the crop will be piquant; a crop sown by a man kind to his wife will lack bite.

In the religious context, perhaps the most important example of "like produces like" is the widely held belief that the black smoke of copal or rubber attracts the black rain clouds, and it is probably for that reason rubber plays such an important part in Tlaloc rites and paraphernalia. The croaking of the *uo*-frog boys and the brandishing by the impersonator of the chief Chac of his lightning stick in the *ch'achac* ceremony (p. 261) summons the rain. The Yucatan Maya, like the European mariner, whistles up the winds as he runs from place to place setting fire to forest felled to make his milpa. Both are rare examples of magic being worked on the gods.

The Yucatan ceremony of driving out evil as a purificatory rite by hurrying with contaminated articles to a secret place outside the town is another magical formula set in a religious context.

Sorcery, as such, is outside the scope of this chapter, but I would emphasize the tremendous importance in Middle America of nagualism, the belief that everyone has an alter ego in animal form. If a man's nagual is shot, say, in the leg, a similar wound will appear on the owner's leg (see also p. 317).

PRIESTS AND PRAYERMAKERS

In pre-Spanish Yucatan there were several grades of priesthood. The land, including northern Campeche, was divided into fifteen independent provinces, each ruled by a head chief called the *halach uinic*, "true man," whose might was such that no man was permitted to speak to him face to face; a cloth was held before his face.

The *halach uinic* was also an ex officio high priest. Such a dual function was not confined to Yucatan. Among the Chol Lacandon, not conquered by the Spaniards until 1695, the same situation obtained (Tozzer, 1913). A like arrangement prevailed among the Aztec; Montezuma was not only the civil and military leader but also a high priest. This duality is brought out by the Motul dictionary's definition "*halach uinic*: bishop, *oidor* [justice of the supreme court], governor, provincial of [a religious order], or commissary; it is a name for these dignitaries and others of the same kind." His position was hereditary. The Prince Archbishops of Salzburg supply an interesting parallel, although the succession officially was never from father to son, but Archbishop Makarios hardly qualifies. Moreover, one can be sure that the Maya, had they the habit, would have raised their eyebrows at his peculiar headdress which hardly sorts with iridescent quetzal plumage.

Next in rank was the high priest known as *ahau can mai*, "Rattlesnake-tobacco" or "rattlesnake-deer," or *Ah kin mai* (*ah kin* means "priest"). Roys (1943:78) says that the name Mai was that of the family which supplied the high priests of Mayapan, which was sacked and abandoned some eighty years before the Spanish Conquest; I do not know the source for his statement. Mai is an extremely common Maya patronymic, and I know of no evidence specifically connecting it with Mayapan. I would conjecture that it was the title of the high priest of each province and perhaps derives from the fact that a gourd of powdered tobacco (*mai*) was the badge of a priest in much of Middle America (p. 112).

The high priest's main functions were to teach hieroglyphic writing, calendric computations, rituals, divination, and the art of prophecy to candidates for the priesthood and appoint them to office. He officiated at only the most important functions. He was succeeded by a son or near relative. The regular priesthood was recruited from the sons of priests and second sons of nobles.

The high priest's relation to the *halach uinic* is not clear. The Aztec had a dual organization: the civil and military leader, such as Montezuma, shared authority with the high priest known as Ciuacoatl, "Snake Woman," which was also the name of a goddess (p. 117). The matter is not clear, but it would seem that although the rule was dual, the civil leader had somewhat higher rank—*primus inter pares*. I suppose that the same arrangement held in Yucatan, and, in theory but not in practice, the high priest was equal in rank to the *halach uinic*. Note a possible tenuous connection; the goddess Ciuacoatl, whose name the Aztec high priest bore, was reputed to have a body of tobacco (p. 117), and, as noted, the name *mai* of the Yucatec high priest can mean "powdered tobacco."

Regular priests were called *ah kin*. This can signify "he of the sun," but I am inclined to derive the name from *kin*, "divination" (*tzac kin*, a sort of spell; *kinyah* or *kintah*, "to prognosticate"). The two probably have a single derivation, for *kin* also means "day," and most prognostications were based on examination of the luck of the days. The *ah kin* was a member of the regular clergy, functioning as a parish priest in a town and taking the lead at its ceremonies.

These priests, in turn, could be specialists. One who normally presided over human sacrifices was called *ah nakom*; those outstanding in prophecy were known as *chilan* (*n* becomes *m* before *b*, hence Chilam Balam), but they appear also to have undertaken other duties of a priest. Their prophesying is described on p. 186.

There is plenty of evidence that the chiefs of towns, called *batab*, "axe wielder," like their superior, the *halach uinic*, combined religious with civil functions. Reports on the Inquisitorial proceedings of 1562 mention several *batabs* who sacrificed children.

There were also, Landa informs us, old men—elders of the kirk, so to speak—who played minor parts in ceremonies. They were called *chacs* (also the name of the rain gods), and undertook such duties as holding down sacrificial victims. Four of them usually co-operated in a ceremony. For instance, in the puberty ceremony (p. 108) they stood at the four corners of the roped-in area in which the rites were performed. However, boys hold the arms and legs of the victim in a scene on a gold disk recovered from the sacred cenote at Chichen Itza and clearly of local manufacture.

The minor priests or prayermakers who also practice cures and make divinations in present-day Yucatan are known as *hmen* (*ah men*), "performer or doer." They take charge of all community rites in connection with the fields and forest. With the disappearance at the Spanish Conquest of the superior clergy, they alone survived, because of their humble rank, as religious leaders of villages. In the Guatemalan highlands the shaman or prayermaker functions in a rather similar way except that the *hmen* is an individual, a self-employed professional, whereas the highland prayermaker is, so to speak, a member of a clerical guild.

There was also an order of "vestal virgins," who lived under a "mother superior" in a building alongside the temples. Their duties included tending the sacred fires in the temples. Death by arrows was their punishment for loss of chastity. There was a tradition that the building at Uxmal known as the Nunnery was their abode, but I much doubt that. Among the decorative elements of the façade are naked men with prominent genitals, a very rare feature in Maya art and hardly what one would expect on a building to house dedicated virgins.

I cannot leave the subject of the Maya priesthood without mention of a Maya cult and its high priest which flourished (?) from 1933 to 1941. The high priest had the slightly un-Maya name of Harold D. Emerson, and his temple was located in the ceremonial center of Brooklyn, New York, hard by Ebbets Field. Ahau Can Mai Harold edited for the Maya temple a periodical, *The Mayan, Devoted to Spiritual Enlightenment and Scientific Religion.*

The Mayan, as I recollect, was a queer hodgepodge of astrology, divination with Maya day names, admonitions to eat spinach and do "Maya" setting-up exercises, and a section on the Maya calendar, not that used during the Classic period or any of those still current in remote villages of Guatemala but something *sui generis*, but there, Brooklyn has always followed its own line. My memory of the divination section is hazy, so perhaps I am at fault in supposing that "4 Caban. Buy General Motors; unload Middle West Utilities" was the sort of advice the days had for us.

Yet Brooklyn should be proud of Halach Uinic Emerson; with more than a touch of Concordian transcendentalism he made of the Maya religion a scientific one, rendering the incompatible compatible.

MAN'S RELATION TO THE GODS

Essentially, Maya religion is a matter of a contract between man and his gods. The gods help man in his work and provide him with his food; in return they expect payment, and much of the time that payment should be made in advance.

There are countless stories in Maya folklore which bring home to the listener the need for payment for benefits received. Very much to the point is an incident in a story of the Mam, the mountain god of the Kekchi, told to me in southern British Honduras forty years ago (Thompson, 1930:140). A hunter cursed the Mam because he could find no game even when he hunted on his friend's hunting land where there was always something to be shot. The Mam, summoning the hunter to his home, asked him why he had hunted game on land where he had no rights and why he had cursed him. The man answered that he had gone there because his friend always found game on that land. The Mam agreed that that was true, "but your friend buys his animals from me. Look." He then showed the man a mass of copal weighing perhaps one hundred pounds.

When my old informant Juan Cocom moved to Socotz, in British Honduras, from the Petén, he knew nothing of making offerings in his milpa. His maize grew to a certain height but no higher. It rained all around, but no rain fell on Cocom's milpa. One night he dreamed he came home through a downpour of rain. Entering his hut, he saw a naked man lying in his hammock. Cocom remarked to the man how hard it was raining and how wet he was. "Yes, it is raining," replied the man, "but not on your milpa. The lords of the milpas have sent flames to keep the rain off yours. Lord Chac does the work, after God, and he must eat, but you have given him nothing to express your gratitude and assuage his hunger."

Cocom awoke frightened; he could eat nothing for two days. He consulted a *hmen* who advised him to have a *primicia* (offering of food, *balche* mead, and copal) in the milpa with a *hmen* in charge. Cocom complied, rain fell, and he had a fine crop.

Brinton (1870:173) tells a didactic story, obtained near Tihosuco a century ago, of a Maya who had failed to make his milpa offering. Visiting his milpa when the maize was beginning to ripen, he saw a tall man (the Chacs were reputed to be giants) rapidly gathering and throwing the ripening ears into a basket over his shoulder. The stranger told him, "I am here gathering that which I sent." Resting from his work, he drew out an immense cigar and struck a light with flint and steel. The sparks were flashes of lightning and his blows were thunderclaps. The man fell senseless to the ground. When he came to, hail had destroyed his crop, and he himself caught a fever which nearly cost him his life.

Nevertheless, I think the Maya attitude is not just one of sharp bargaining for a good crop or a fat wild hog. Gillin (1951:12) and his assistants, in the course of casual conversation, asked sixty-one men of the Pokoman-Maya village of Jilotepeque what each would do if someone gave him fifty dollars out of the blue. Most said that they would first buy candles to burn in church as a thank offering. Here, the planned gift did not form one side of a bargain; the candles would have been a genuine expression of thankfulness.

Maya prayer is directed to material ends; I cannot imagine a Maya praying for ability to resist temptation, to love his neighbors better, or for deeper insight into the ways of God or of his gods. There is no concept of goodness in his religion, which demanded a bloody, not a contrite, heart.

PREPARATION FOR CEREMONIES

In the rites leading up to an important ceremony, there seems to have been little difference, except in scale, between those followed in the village and those performed in the ceremonial center. One must bear in mind that data on the former largely come from modern ethnological observation and must allow for the disappearance of rites—human sacrifice for instance—suppressed by the friars and colonial governments, whereas material on "state" religion derives largely from eyewitness accounts of four centuries ago and from sculptured or painted records.

There are two prerequisites to all ceremonies, large or small, past or present: continence and fasting; and to these a third, confession, is commonly added, but this is common today only in the Guatemalan highland communities. Failure to maintain continence endangered both the ceremony and the guilty person. For that reason, participants in a ceremony had and still have the custom of sleeping apart from their wives on such occasions.

Periods of continence and fasting were normally reckoned in Maya twenty-day months or in the highly important thirteen-day "week" and its multiples. Las Casas reports of the Maya of Guatemala—he almost certainly had in mind those of the Alta Verapaz—that they were accustomed to separate from their wives and take up residence in special men's houses near the temples for 60, 80, or 100 days before some great festival (he writes 60, 8, and 100 days, but obviously 8 is a slip for 80). Those are three, four, or five "months" before the event. During that period, the men fasted, did not bathe, blackened their faces with pine-torch soot, and drew blood continually from their bodies. Landa tells us—and no doubt the interdiction was general—that one must not even think of women on such occasions.

Among the Zutuhil Maya, a specially chosen member of the nobility was selected to learn the will of the gods, that is, to prophesy. He first fasted for 260 days, the length of the sacred almanac of thirteen "months." It is not so stated, but this was surely also a period of continence.

The fast before throwing victims into the cenote at Chichen Itza lasted sixty days, during which participants were not permitted to raise their eyes to look at their wives or the women who brought them their scanty food. Continence and fasting before New Year ceremonies in Yucatan lasted from thirteen days to three "months," depending on the individual and his office; continence and fasting for forty days still precedes participation in the *volador* ceremony in the Quiche town of Joyabaj as well as in ceremonies of the Kekchi Maya in the sacred cave of Pecmo, Alta Verapaz. Similar abstinences for one month (five days before and sixteen days after, but note the Spanish system of counting days at both ends, so the period is really twenty days) are observed by some Kekchi at sowing; among the Mopan Maya the period is a few days before and about fifteen days after.

Fasting and continence for thirteen days precedes the Tzeltal ceremony of the transfer of the sacred book (p. 113), before certain Kekchi pilgrimages to caves on mountaintops, before sowing by the Kekchi of Cajabon (they are probably Manche Chol who changed to the Kekchi language), before sowing and harvesting by the Mam Maya, before and after sowing by the Chorti, and before and after the puberty rite in Yucatan in the sixteenth century.[1]

The period of continence could be less. There was a five-day vigil in the temple of Cit Chac Coh before his feast, and the Maya of Quintana Roo still observe a nine-day period of continence. Often the length of abstention is not specified.

[1] Sources for fasting and continence: Las Casas, 1908:177; Pérez Martínez, 1938:121, 174, 182, 202; *Descripción de San Bartolomé*; *Relaciones de Yucatán*, 1900, 2:25; Termer, 1957:236; Sapper, 1901:259; Thompson, 1930:49; Redfield and Villa, 1939:114; Goubaud, 1949:35; Cerda Silva, 1940; Sapper, 1897:283; Wisdom, 1940:441; Villa, 1945: 138–39; Lincoln, 1942:119; Recinos, 1950:226.

Fasting varied in severity. Landa gives one the impression it was mainly a matter of abstaining from salt, chile, and meat. Yet during the unlucky five days at year's end, the whole Ixil (highland Maya) community eats only a little meat with chile sauce on a very small piece of tortilla. In the long fasts described by Las Casas, participants ate only dry maize grains and fruit. A passage in the Popol Vuh, sacred book of the Quiche, reads: "Nine men fasted and another nine men made sacrifices and burned incense [or] thirteen men fasted and another thirteen made sacrifices and burned incense before the god Tohil. . . . They nourished themselves only with *zapote*, *matasano*, and *jocote* fruit. They did not eat any tortillas . . . neither had they women to sleep with. . . . They were in the house of god."

In ancient times, the body was painted black during periods of fasting. That is reported by Las Casas in the cited passage, referring probably to the Alta Verapaz, and the same was true in Yucatan (soot was used according to Landa; black paint according to the *Relaciones de Yucatán*, 1900, 1:157). Black was the paint color of unmarried men rather generally in the lowlands; why it should have represented penance is not clear.

Landa informs us that during the five dangerous days which were a prologue to the new year the whole population abstained from washing, combing their hair, and delousing themselves. That old custom, probably once widespread, still survives, for Kanhobal-Maya prayermakers of the northwestern highlands of Guatemala refrain from washing over long periods. It was said that they washed neither themselves nor their clothes during their entire period of office, but that proved to be an exaggeration (La Farge, 1947:133).

There is evidence from two sources that before important ceremonies, priests and novices withdrew from the community and took up residence in the ceremonial centers.

Landa tells us that before the great festival in honor of Kukulcan, priests and lords remained in the Temple of Kukulcan for five days and nights without returning to their homes. They did the same in the temple of a god called Cit Chac Coh, "Father Red Puma," and one may suppose that they did the same before all major festivals. Similarly for the long fasting and continence pe-

174

riods described by Las Casas, "all had to sleep, not in their homes, but in houses which for the time of the penance were near the temples." These, presumably, were men's houses within the ceremonial centers.

Public confession, a form of purification, was general before participation in a ceremony and when a person was seriously ill. The custom survives to the present day, for instance among the Ixil Maya during the five unlucky days. Among the present-day Jacalteca, it is accepted that quarreling, anger, uproar, or drunkenness will nullify the good to come from a ceremony being performed or about to be performed. Failure to observe continence before a ceremony is regarded as dangerous to the individual and the community throughout the Maya area.

It is clear that one must be in the right state in body and mind before approaching the gods. In view of the emphasis on continence, it is worth noting that in some areas, at least, the Maya regarded sexual intercourse as sin. The Tzotzil of San Pedro Chenalho, according to Guiteras' informant, definitely have that opinion: "No one sins until he marries." "A man has not sinned until he has known a woman." "With the sexual act, man's and woman's *ch'ule* ["soul"] leaves the body." In Yucatec *coo* means both "madness" and "(unusual?) sexual excitement"; *coil* (-*il* is merely a relationship suffix) is "adultery."

SACRIFICES

The general Yucatec term for sacrifice was *p'a chi*, "to open the mouth," presumably referable to the common practice of smearing blood or the victim's heart on the idol's mouth.

Sacrifice took many forms: offering one's own blood or that of human or animal victims, or sacrificing produce and other material we classify as inanimate.

Drawing blood from various parts of one's own body was an extremely common act of penance and sacrifice throughout the Maya area and certainly goes far back in time, for it is represented on lintels, stelae, pottery, and almost certainly murals of the Classic period, as well as in Codex Madrid, on late pottery figurines, and on a mural at Iximche, capital of the Cakchiquel.

Commonly, blood was drawn from the tongue, ears, fleshy parts of the arm, and penis—more rarely from nose and legs—and was allowed to fall on sheets of bark paper or gathered in dishes and offered to the gods.

Blood was commonly drawn with the sting of a sting ray. Landa tells us that these were customarily buried with a priest as a mark of his office, more or less as chalice and paten were buried with a mediaeval priest in western Europe. In fact, they are frequently recovered from burials; in Tikal alone, finds, including imitations in bone, run into hundreds. A few are incised with small glyphs, an indication of their ceremonial importance. Obsidian blades also served this purpose, and through the bored holes were inserted grasses or cords, sometimes set with thorns. This is the instrument used in the penitential scene on a lintel from Yaxchilan frequently reproduced, the cord being passed through or touching the tongue. Landa describes a ceremony in which several men in line passed a cord through holes pierced in the penis, and that ceremony is depicted in the Madrid codex. Drawing blood from the tongue is almost certainly illustrated on the murals of the Classic site of Bonampak.

Human sacrifice was prevalent, and there is archaeological evidence that the custom goes back to the Formative period before Maya culture was completely differentiated from that of their neighbors. A sculptural detail on a stela of the Classic period at Piedras Negras shows a person stretched over a stone for removal of the heart. The blood spurting from the incision is represented by feathers, probably those of the quetzal, for quetzal feathers symbolized something precious, a definition applied to human blood. Murals at Chichen Itza of the post-Classic period, as well as a gold disk dredged from the sacred cenote, show the ceremony of removing the heart. The victim's arms and legs are held by two or four assistants, the Chacs according to Landa. This seems to have been the commonest method employed (Plate 5b). Archaeological work has brought to light the sacrificial stones over which the victim was stretched.

Removal of the heart from a victim tied to a stake or upright frame was also common. The auto-de-fé in Yucatan in 1562, inquiring into lapses into paganism, brought to light several such sacrifices. In one case, a youth of eighteen, brightly dressed and decked with masses of flowers, was tied to a stake and his heart removed. The most horrible of such sacrifices was the fate of a little girl who, while tied to a stake, was beaten to death with blows on her breast from a branch of the thorny ceiba tree called *pochote* (*Ceiba aesculifolia*; in Yucatec, *piim*). The allied *Ceiba pentandra*, the *yaxche* of the Maya, was very sacred; its trunk has nodular projections lacking the thorny quality of the *piim*. Accordingly, it is possible that the thorny ceiba was employed in this rite to bring about more speedy death and to insure that blood, so important in such rites, flowed freely, but at the same time to make associations with the sacred *yaxche*. There is no information whether that victim's heart was torn out, but it is probable. In another case, the victim was spread-eagled on a ladder.

Christian influence is apparent in one sacrifice before the auto-de-fé. Two small girls were tied to crosses, whereupon the priest said, "Let these girls die upon the cross, as Jesus Christ died, He who they say was our lord, although we do not know that He was." Thereupon men lowered the cross, untied the children, tore out their hearts, and threw the bodies into a cenote.

Binding the victim to a stake and removing the heart were rites also practiced along the middle Usumacinta, the so-called territory of El Próspero.

Similar was the fate of the Franciscan friar Juan Henríquez and a Captain Francisco de Mirones, who, with a force of Spaniards, mestizos, and Indians, were attacked at mass in a small village in southern Quintana Roo while attempting to penetrate to Itza territory. The whole party was caught unarmed in the church and was massacred. The priest and the captain were each tied to a mainpost of the little pole-and-thatch church, and their hearts were wrenched out. The aggressors were mainly Christian Maya who had lapsed into paganism. That was in 1623; despite eighty years of Christianity, the old rite and the technique of heart removal had not been forgotten.

The same rite was followed by the independent Itza of Tayasal. The Dominican friars Cristóbal de Prado and Jacinto de Vargas fell into the hands of the Itza in 1696, less than a year before the downfall of that last Maya stronghold. Tied hand and foot to an

X-shaped wooden frame, like the Apostle Saint Andrew, they were raised, presumably to a vertical position, whereupon the Itza high priest opened their breasts and removed their hearts. I cite these sacrifices of friars and military men because, in our frailty, the enormity of such actions is more apparent if men of our own skin are the victims.

A graffito on a building at Tikal shows spear (later arrow) sacrifice, a rite also prevalent among the Yucatec and Cakchiquel Maya. As described by Landa, the victim, stripped naked, was painted blue, a color associated with sacrifice. After dancing with him, the participants in the ceremony tied the victim to a stake. Dancing, they circled around him, and each man, as he came into position, fired an arrow at the victim's heart, previously marked in white. Pollaiuolo's *Martyrdom of Saint Sebastian* in the National Gallery, London, is tranquil compared with that wild, sadistic dancing of the Maya around their victim. The sexual element in such sacrifices was recognized by the Maya; the chief priest first hit the victim in his private parts.

Beheading was clearly practiced at Chichen Itza. A Toltec-style relief in the ball court shows a victorious ball-game player holding up the victim's head while blood is represented by snakes fanning out from the decapitated body. Decapitation has a long history in Middle America; it is shown on a Formative period sculpture at Izapa, on the Pacific coast of Soconusco close to the Guatemalan border. Stela 21 shows blood, in the form of (quetzal?) feathers, flowing from a headless body. The decapitated man has his right hand gloved, indicating that he was a defeated ball-game player. The victor, severed head in hand, stands over him. On the murals of the Classic period site of Bonampak, the head of a victim rests on leaves; in the Dresden codex (p. 34*a*), a head of the maize god is the focus of attention in ceremonies involving various musicians (Plate 5*a*). The head was probably that of an impersonator of the god, for victims often represented the deities to whom they were sacrificed.

Skulls, often with cervical vertebrae and frequently enclosed in pairs of dishes placed lip to lip, turn up in many Classic-period sites and presumably belonged to persons sacrificed at dedicatory rites. The custom continued into later times; at the join of platform with stairway of the Caracol, Chichen Itza, were fourteen skulls, some with cervical vertebrae, arranged in four rows. A few other bones were present. The whole suggests a dedicatory sacrifice when the stairway was added. Two decapitated skulls, together with fragmentary iron pyrite disks and pieces of jade, were inside the *tzompantli*, "skull platform," at Chichen Itza, where the skulls of victims were supposed to have been displayed as the reliefs around the platform indicate.

Recently, no less than forty-eight decapitated skulls, complete with cervical vertebrae, were found at Iximche, ancient capital of the Cakchiquel Maya. Some were in groups of four or five, but others occupied individual holes in the plaza floor. Most were accompanied by obsidian knives. In connection with these archaeological finds, it is well to bear in mind that decapitation at times followed removal of the heart. Commonly, heads were placed on poles. That was a usual practice among the Itza of Tayasal. The Aztec built regular skull racks, like palisades, on which the skulls were "threaded."

In Yucatan, the victim was sometimes bound and hurled from a height onto rocks below, or a dog could substitute for the person. Removal of the heart usually concluded this form of sacrifice too. In the Popol Vuh, the heroes bound and hurled to the ground their enemy Cabracan. Afterwards, they buried the body. It is a fair conjecture that this was a ritual sacrifice.

The barbarous custom of flaying the victim, with the priest then donning the skin, was known in Yucatan. In Mexico and elsewhere, this rite was associated with a god of vegetation called Xipe and with certain earth goddesses. In the first case, the flaying followed a mock fight in which the victim defended himself with a wooden "sword" having clumps of down instead of a cutting edge against warriors dressed in jaguar skins or in the guise of eagles, the uniforms of the members of those orders. Extraction of the heart followed. There is no evidence for this gladiatorial fight in Yucatan, but in the Guatemalan highlands the Quiche and Zutuhil Maya continued to perform a dance mimicking that fight long after the Spanish Conquest, and it is extremely probable that in pre-Spanish times the flaying rite concluded the ceremony. There is some evidence for a Xipe cult in the Classic period, and incense burners recovered at the late site of Mayapan carry in relief effigies of Xipe impersonators wearing the victim's skin over their own.

There is a single reference to a form of sacrifice called in Yucatec *pech'ni*, "squash the nose," which is described as to bruise the nose and afterward slay the person.

On the famous murals of Bonampak, of the late Classic period, blood drips to the ground from the fingers of prisoners brought before the victorious ruler presumably for sacrifice. Nothing similar has been encountered in other archaeological sites or in the literature.

Finally, offerings to bodies of water must be mentioned. This was the work of a rain-seeking cult. In many parts of the Maya area, oblations were made to lakes; many offerings have been recovered from lakes Amatitlan and Petén and are still made to lakes by the present-day Tzotzil of Chenalho, but there in honor of the moon goddess. Lakes being unknown in western Yucatan, cenotes, above all the famous sacred cenote at Chichen Itza, were recipients of offerings.

At Chichen Itza, the victims, most frequently children, were thrown in still living or with their hearts already torn out. Adults and adolescents thrown in alive were expected to converse with the Chacs, the rain gods at the bottom of the pool. If still alive at midday, the person was drawn out and gave the message the rain gods had entrusted to him or her, but as the victim struck the water with tremendous force, having been hurled from the edge of the cenote some sixty feet above, it is unlikely that many survived. Moreover, the victim may have been bound. The Maya desired seemliness in their ceremonies; a victim paddling around in the water for several hours nowise enhanced the dignity of the rite. Survival under such conditions would, indeed, have been little short of miraculous, and the Maya were interested in miracles. Hunac Ceel, conqueror of Chichen Itza, volunteered to be thrown in, survived the ordeal, and was rewarded by election as chief ruler of Chichen Itza, evidence of the rarity of survival and hinting that that resolute man may have had a trick up his sleeve.

Normally, the victim co-operated with the sacrificers, for he or she was guaranteed a place in heaven; but one old Indian, recalling times long passed, told of an uncommonly pert hussy who roundly declared that if she were thrown in, she'd be damned if she would ask the gods for a good maize crop or anything else. Another victim was sought.

Rain gods throughout Central America had a predilection for children—hence the many sacrificed. As did their cousins the Tlalocs, rain gods of the peoples of Central Mexico, the Maya rain gods probably liked all things small. In the sixteenth month, Coming of the Rains, the Aztec made small images of the mountains which were intimately associated with the Tlalocs, they laid very small tamales on tiny plates, they offered corn mush in tiny bowls and a very little cacao in small gourd vessels, and small boys were the singers at this feast. Miniature vessels of that nature have been found at Teotihuacan and elsewhere. At Kaminaljuyu, Guatemala, nine miniature metates and manos (mullers with which corn was ground on the metates) together with nine miniature "mushroom stones" were in a cache (Borhegyi, 1961), although without any evidence of pluvial associations. In the recently discovered shrine of the rain gods of Balankanche, on the outskirts of Chichen Itza, large numbers of miniature metates, manos, and pottery vessels formed part of the offerings. However, the presence of many incense burners with features not of the Maya Chacs but of their cousins, the Mexican Tlalocs, suggests that this was a shrine of the Mexicans, as, indeed, the Carbon—14 dating confirms. However, enough has been said to demonstrate the fondness of the rain gods for everything on a small scale, whether humans or utensils.

We return now to more general considerations of human sacrifice among the Maya. It was customary to smear the hearts and blood of the victims on the face of the idol which received the sacrifice, surely with the idea that the deity fed on the offering (placing a lighted cigar in the mouth of the god depicted on a pottery censer by the modern Lacandon [p. 112] supplies a modern parallel). The belief was widespread in Middle America that the deities needed thus to be strengthened. That was particularly true of the sun god who, having acquired skeletal characteristics during his journey each night through the underworld from west to east, needed to be clothed with flesh when he emerged each dawn into the upper world. Sometimes the victim's heart was burned, or blood was scattered to the four world directions. The sacrificial knife was called the hand of god.

Clearly, human sacrifice was practiced by the Maya throughout their history, but surely not on the scale reached by the Aztec. Immediate sacrifice of prisoners captured in battle was a Maya practice (p. 35); the murals of Bonampak confirm that more formal sacrifice some time after capture was also customary. Pending sacrifice, prisoners were kept in cages and fattened up or were bound and placed in a sort of corral. One Christian Maya managed to escape from a corral of that kind on the island of Tayasal and got clean away, but such escapes must have been very rare.

Almost every living thing and many inanimate objects were offered in sacrifice.

Archaeological work has revealed offertory caches containing the bones of jaguars (in one case partly painted red), opossums, shrews, manatees, parrots, quail, pygmy owls, species of finch, various species of fish including porcupine fish, and turtles (carapace). The range must have been much greater, for those sacrificed in most rites would not be interred. Colonial and modern sources add to this list dogs, deer, turkeys, wild hogs, iguanas, squirrels, pumas, crocodiles or alligators, feathers, and insects, the first three being commonest.

Offerings of vegetal origin comprised copal incense—of which large quantities have been found in excavations—resin, rubber, cacao, maize in every conceivable form, corn husks, squash seeds (a great Maya delicacy), annatto (a red coloring from the fruit of *Bixa orellana,* much used in coloring cacao and stews and, formerly, the human body, particularly as a war paint), flowers, pine boughs and needles (often smeared with turkey blood), and branches or the bark of *habin* (*Ichthyomethia communis*), the leaves of which are used to this day as aspergilla or scoops in milpa rites and its branches as arches to shelter altars from the sun. A common offering was the mead called *balche,* made of fermented honey to which is added the bark of the *balche* tree (*Lonchocarpus longistylus*). This was the favorite Maya tipple and had strong religious associations. Despite strong Maya protests, the early Spaniards tried to prohibit it. Chi, an educated Maya who helped some of the Spaniards with their answers to a questionnaire on Yucatan from the royal government in Spain, inserted a vigorous complaint about the ill-health of the Maya resulting from that prohibition in about a dozen of the replies. As these were sent in from all over Yucatan, the bureaucrats must have received the impression that the Maya were dying in droves from lack of that purgative. The prohibition became a dead letter, and that essential element of Maya ritual is still a most important feature of milpa rites.

Other offerings were honey, wax, *zuhuy ha* ("virgin" water collected from distant cenotes and cave drippings and so free from contamination), pottery vessels, blue pigment, textiles, jade or turquoise mosaic plaques and objects of jade, flint, obsidian, shell and bone, pieces of coral, pumice, stalagmites, and iron pyrite mirrors. To those must be added the many objects of gold and copper and pieces of carved wood (spear throwers, idols, lip plugs, etc.) recovered from the sacred cenote at Chichen Itza.

As the author of Ecclesiasticus has it: "In the handywork of their craft is their prayer."

One must keep in mind that these offerings fall into two categories. Wealthy gifts, notably the contents of offertory caches beneath stelae and buildings, were a feature of the "state religion" of ceremonial centers. The village communities make—and in ancient times surely made—offerings consonant with their humbler status: produce and game at village shrines, in particular at the heaps of stones at the four "entrances" to the village, and at temporary family altars—slats supported by four posts beneath a sort of bower of *habin* leaves—in their milpas. The two provinces of religion flourished side by side, but, with the eradication of the hierarchical sphere at the coming of the Spaniards, only the peasant cults have survived.

Cave worship, a highly important factor in ancient Middle America, was a third focus of Maya religious life. Many vestiges, both of offerings and of religious architecture (altars, shrines, and stairways), occur in caves, and pilgrimages to certain caves continue to this day in areas to which European influences have not penetrated in strength. Caves were used for worship of rain and earth gods, and in many, incense burners are found in considerable quantities. Sometimes, too, they served as depositories of human remains. A notable use of caves in the Yucatan Peninsula was as a source for "virgin" water used in ceremonies, for water, like all participants and utensils used in ritual, had to be uncontaminated. Water dripping from the roofs of caves was about as uncontaminated as could be found anywhere. Accordingly, in dripping caves—and they are very numerous in limestone country —scores of pottery and sometimes stone vessels were placed below stalactites to collect the drips, particularly under those farthest from the entrance where the danger of contamination by the approach of women was least likely. Consequently, immense quantities of sherds of pottery jars often strew the floors of the remotest chambers of labyrinthic caves, where, because of complete darkness and difficult and sometimes dangerous access, one can be sure no one ever lived. In such caves, sherds of incense burners or of polychrome pottery are seldom, if ever, found.

Caves, then, were adjuncts of both ceremonial center and peasant religion.

RITUAL PURITY

Mention above of the need for "virgin" water (*zuhuy ha*) in rites emphasizes a cardinal requirement in carrying out any ceremony: the need for ritual purity. That, of course, was the purpose of continence and fasting before rites; confession similarly cleansed the body of sin. Children were sacrificed not only to the Chacs, who craved them, but also in large numbers in other ceremonies, and I have little doubt that was because they were virgin, *zuhuy*. Virgin dogs were also sacrificed, and the dishes in which the human heart was placed were called *zuhuy* plates, which surely means they had not previously been used. Before many ceremonies, *zuhuy kak*, "virgin fire," was kindled, and the temple was purified before a ceremony. As among many people, the Maya regarded women as contaminated (the view that menstruation is ritually impure is world-wide). Normally, they were not allowed to attend ceremonies, and, as noted above, water which had been touched by a woman was no longer *zuhuy*. The vestal virgins attended the fires, and we have a record of a ceremony being cancelled because a drummer made a mistake in the rhythm, thereby contaminating the ceremony. *Balche* was important in ritual because it was a purge.

HALLUCINATORY DRUGS IN PROPHECY AND DIVINATION

Ritual purity is one way of bringing oneself in touch with the gods; the elation of alcohol—to this day Maya shamans will not undertake a ceremony without drinking *balche*—is another; and narcotics are yet another approach.

The Indians of continental Mexico used various drugs in divination and curing ceremonies, the most important being toxic mushrooms; peyote, the term for certain cactus buttons and the stimulant of a cult which swept through the Indians of the United States; and *ololiuhqui*, the seeds of more than one variety of morning-glory.

The highland Maya almost certainly used toxic mushrooms, for large stone representations of mushrooms are fairly plentiful in archaeological sites in the highlands of Guatemala from Formative times onward. They also occur in Chiapas and Tabasco. For the Maya lowlands I know of only one example. That was found at Morales, British Honduras (a stone fragment from a cave near Mayapan might be the top of a stone mushroom, but equally well part of a pounder).

Colonial sources on the lowland Maya, including several books on remedial plants, have not a word about toxic plants, but it is hard to believe that the lowland Maya had nothing of that sort in view of the widespread use of toxic aids in other parts of Middle America.

Two parallel passages in the Books of Chilam Balam of Tizimin and Mani deal with prophecy seemingly induced by some drug. I have combined the passages and offer below a translation. This partly follows an unpublished version of one source by Ralph Roys, who, however, is not responsible for the hobgoblin identification. After telling how various priests and prophets assembled to receive the prophecy, the passage continues:

> Then they gathered at the house of Ah Nacom Balam, the *chilan* ["prophet"]. Then was the message above the house

of the *chilan*; then was the interpreting of the words of counsel given to them. Then was given to them the hidden message, but they did not understand it because of the reciting of the speech by the *chilan* because he is mouth to the ground. He does not move, he does not rise from where he is, within the small room, within the house, as long as the hobgoblin speaks above the rafters [?] of the house because he was crossways above the rafters [?] of the house.

Then will begin the declaring to the priests assembled in the house of the *chilan* of the message which came to them. They did not know who was speaking to them. Then they said "True god, great Snake Father." Those were their words. Then they turned their faces down to the earth. Then they heard the message as they lay face down, listening, of that Chilam Balam, the great priest.

I conjecture that this passage describes the *chilan* in a trance, lying face down without movement and talking in a way which the listeners could not comprehend, after taking some narcotic. He was seeking the prophecy for the katun, most important of all Maya prophecies. The word for hobgoblin is *maax*, Yucatec for the spider monkey, but also applied to hobgoblins.

The Maya were not alone in believing that messages were transmitted through hobgoblins. The Mixe Indians of Oaxaca say that two hobgoblins, male and female, give the mushroom eater a message or divination as he lies in a trance. On two stone reliefs from Santa Lucia Cotzumalhuapa, a non-Maya site on the Pacific slope of Guatemala, hobgoblins—one in the form of a death figure, the other a creature half-human, half-deer—are talking to an individual reclining on the ground.

There may be representations in Codex Dresden of the reception of the prophecy. Two scenes of a divinatory almanac show a god or, as I think, a priest impersonating a god striding toward a temple or hut. In one picture, a small figure whose glyph shows him to be dead, unconscious, or asleep (closed eye) sits in the house or temple. In the other house or temple is placed the sign for evil which elsewhere serves also as the head of a manikin figure. The scenes closely parallel those in Mexican codices. Although one cannot be certain, there is a good chance that these scenes show the *chilan* going to receive the prophecy.

IDOLS

At the Spanish Conquest, the Maya of Yucatan had immense numbers of idols, most of them probably effigy incense burners which were both receptacles for burning copal and gods in their own right, as among the Lacandon of today.

The situation in the lowlands during the Classic period may have been different. Several of the *Relaciones de Yucatán*, but probably all derived from a single source, state that Kukulcan (and the Putun?) introduced idolatry in Yucatan when he came to Chichen Itza. Some support is to be found for this in the report of those "hounds of the Lord," Frs. Esguerra and Cipriano, at the close of the sixteenth century, that the Manche Chol had no idols, worshiping mountains and sources of rivers presumably like the Tzultacah cult of their neighbors (p. 272; Remesal, bk. 11, ch. 19). There is also a statement (López de Cogolludo, 1867–68, bk. 12, ch. 7) that in the Próspero area of the lower middle Usumacinta, only priests had idols.

Certainly, idols and effigy incense burners excavated at lowland sites of the Classic period are few compared with the huge numbers found in protohistoric sites in Yucatan. Yet they do exist, and the well-known lintel of Yaxchilan showing an individual offering blood to a serpent with the head of a god in its mouth is complete proof of idolatry, although this may have been confined to priests and nobles. What are presumably jade idols also turn up in graves of important persons. There is no information whether the many representations of deities in stone and stucco on façades and roof combs of buildings, stairways, and so forth were accorded worship. Effigy incense burners, notably those of Palenque, can be very ornate.

Excavation at Mayapan confirmed the statement on the growth of idolatry in Yucatan. The site yielded immense quantities of fragments of effigy incense burners as well as a considerable number of stone idols, among which figures of turtles, beings associated with rain, predominate. The former were mass-produced, the various parts—hands, feet, arms, legs, faces, and ornaments—being cast in molds and then assembled. Small details in appliqué identified different gods. The addition, after firing, of many colors

187

over a lime wash failed to distract attention from the uncommonly low standards of design and workmanship. All date from around A.D. 1300 to 1450, when the site was abandoned.

Excavation of one colonnade building produced over 38,000 sherds of these effigy censers. Excluding deposits beneath the building, they formed from 55 to 99.8 per cent (in one huge lot of 17,915 sherds) of the sherd totals. The Temple of Kukulcan produced 8,067 effigy-censer fragments, over 88 per cent of the total of all sherds. It is true that this type of pottery, being soft-baked, breaks into many pieces, but the number is truly astonishing, and large quantities were at every excavation including that of private houses, particularly in the room which served as an oratory. Increase of family worship accounts in part for the huge output. In contrast, excavation at Uaxactun, of the earlier Classic period, produced about half a dozen effigy incense burners, but decorated with animals, and three squat, open-based vessels with features of probable gods on the sides, which could be regarded as effigy incense burners.

Idolatry continued rampant in Yucatan after the Spanish Conquest, as the Mani proceedings against relapses into paganism make clear. One man had sixty idols inherited from his father; other testimony concerns up to one hundred clay idols in a cave, from one and one-half to two spans (twelve to seventeen inches) high. These they prayed to for rain, good crops, and deer. One estimate of the number of idols collected was one hundred thousand; another, one million. Even allowing for gross exaggeration, the number was clearly enormous.

A somewhat later report of 1583 describes briefly 1,160 *cizines* (Cizin, the Maya death god, used by the Spaniards to describe devils, that is, pagan gods). Some were as large as a child of three to five years. Some wore on their heads animal devices, miters, and tiaras; others were figures of lions, jaguars, and dogs (Scholes and Adams, 1938; Scholes, Roys, and Adams, 1945:178).

Idols not destroyed in such Spanish campaigns against paganism were often hidden in caves, but since the Maya now fear such things, believing that they are malignant and wander around at night, they usually smash any they find, so not many have survived.

On the east coast of Yucatan, the situation is somewhat different. There, several large idols escaped destruction, doubtlessly because practically the whole native population was wiped out by disease soon after the Spanish Conquest (p. 55) and few friars penetrated the area.

Gann (1927:131–32) was shown a remarkable idol, about eighteen inches high and still *in situ*, seated on a small dais within a very small building on the outskirts of Tulum. The upper part is of pottery with a lime wash, the lower half of cement. It has a headdress from which flaps fall over the ears, necklace, earplugs, loin cloth, and sandals, as well as lateral projecting wings such as one finds on effigy incense burners extending from head to waist. A fair amount of color—red, green, blue, yellow, and plum— remains. In front were a small incense burner, three broken turtles of stucco, and a large obsidian knife, all of which had undoubtedly been there since the last pilgrim came to the shrine four centuries ago.

Gann also illustrates another larger, seated idol from a nearby site. It is of stucco. He also mentions a third, in the round, just over four feet high.

There is a description (López de Cogolludo, bk. 4, ch. 9) of the famous idol of Ix Chel once on Cozumel Island, a magnet for pilgrims from near and far. It was a large pottery figure attached to the shrine wall with mortar. Behind was something like a sacristy with a small hidden door opening into the back of the idol, and from there the priests answered petitions to the idol. "The unhappy dupes believed the idol spoke to them and so venerated it more than the others, sacrificing to it birds, dogs, their own blood, and even men." Folk memory is very much more important than is generally realized,[2] so perhaps the talking cross of the revolted Maya of eastern Yucatan, with a hidden man to pronounce the oracles, was a nineteenth-century case of folk memory.

[2] Two examples are: The site of the magnificent underground shrine of the Tlalocs on the outskirts of Chichen Itza, sealed off 1,000 years ago and rediscovered a few years ago, has been known to generations of Maya as Balankanche, "hidden seat" (p. 270). In the village of Hadstock, two miles from my home, a tradition still exists that there was once a monastery on the north side of the village. Documentary evidence recently brought to light suggests that there was such a monastery, sacked by the Danes about A.D. 1000.

As to materials, archaeology and colonial sources inform us of idols of jade and greenstone, variegated stone, rubber, and copal, in addition to those of pottery. I know of no reference to idols of obsidian or of ground corn or other food products, although one can be reasonably confident that the latter existed because they were so common on the Mexican plateau. Eyes and mouth were sometimes inlaid with shell or mother-of-pearl. The cenote at Chichen Itza has yielded wooden torsos with detached arms and legs.

If, as seems probable, two mosaic pieces—one in Rome, the other in Copenhagen—represent Maya merchant gods (Thompson, 1966a:169), we can add that kind of idol to our list.

Stelae are worshiped now, but whether they were during the Classic period is debatable, although objects buried beneath and before them show that they were holy. Whether ornaments engraved with gods' features had a religious significance is similarly uncertain, although that is possible since jade idols were buried with important persons.

Landa has left an account of the dangers, and rites to ward them off, involved in making wooden idols:

> One of the things which this poor people considered most arduous and troublesome was to make wooden idols, and this they called to make gods. And so they had appointed a special period to make them, and this was the month Mol or another if the priest told them it sufficed. Those who wished to make [have made] them, first consulted the priest, and taking his advice [presumably on a lucky day to start], went to the craftsmen of that trade. And they say that the craftsmen always excused themselves, for they feared that they or someone in their house would die or that faintings would overcome them. Once they had accepted, the Chacs [assistant priests, not the rain gods] whom they also chose for this task, the priest and the craftsman began their fast. While they were fasting, the owner of the idols went himself or sent people to the forest for the wood, which was always cedar [Maya *kuche*, "divine wood," used for religious purposes]. When the wood arrived, they made a small hut of straw, fenced in, and in it they put it together with a pottery jar in which to place the idols and keep them there covered

over while they were being made. They placed in [the hut] incense to burn to four demons called Acantun which they placed at the four points of the compass. They put in the implements with which to cut themselves or draw blood from the ears and the tools to carve the black gods. And with these preparations [completed], the Chacs, the priest and the craftsman shut themselves in the little hut and commenced their work of gods, frequently cutting their ears and with the blood anointing the gods and burning incense to them. Thus they kept at the task until they finished, the owner of the idols giving them their food and necessities. And they must not sleep with their wives, not even in thought, nor was anyone allowed to come to the place where they were.

The carving of idols is illustrated on Codex Madrid, pages 95 to 99 and 101, and the cutting of the cedar trees, one of which carries the *ku* or *kul* sign, indicating that it is a cedar, on page 98a. Clearly, the work was very dangerous, as the creation of gods by man must always be. The Lacandon have important rites at the making and consecrating of new effigy incense burners; the old ones are deposited beneath a cliff (Tozzer, 1907).

PRAYERS

At the very outset of the Conquest (1518), the chaplain of the Grijalva expedition reported that while some Spaniards were in a temple on Cozumel Island, an old man with toes cut off entered with three others who remained guarding the door. "He censed the idols with some sweet-smelling perfumes which seemed to be liquid amber [surely copal] reciting in a loud voice almost that of a tenor a song, and from what we could make out we believe that he was calling on those idols."

The Maya prayed squatting on their haunches, perhaps seated cross-legged, and standing; kneeling seems to have been introduced with Christianity and is still not widely followed except in contexts with moderate to strong Christian influence.

Such pre-Christian prayers as have been recorded are very short, and one suspects that only the gist was set down. One such addressed to Itzam Na ran: "Great lord of the sky who art placed in the clouds and the sky give us a good year of maize [or whatever the sacrifice was for]." One Indian examined said he prayed for a deer to be given him; he did not pray for a good harvest, for he was a hunter.

Las Casas (1909, ch. 178), describing a human sacrifice in Guatemala, almost certainly in the Alta Verapaz, writes that the chief ruler and other lords led or dragged forward by the hair the prisoners to be sacrificed, and the chief ruler went saying in a loud voice, with the other lords joining in and all the people adding their voices, the following prayer: "Lord god remember us who are thine, give us health, give us children and prosperity so that thy people may increase and may serve thee. Give us rain and good weather to support us so that we may live. Hear our petitions; receive our prayers. Help us against our enemies. Give us leisure and time for recreation."

The following prayer occurs in the Popol Vuh (Recinos, 1950:226):

Oh. Thou beauty of the day! Thou, Huracan; thou, heart of heaven and earth! Thou, giver of riches and giver of the daughters and the sons! Turn toward us your power and your riches; grant life and growth unto my sons and vassals; let those who must maintain and nourish thee multiply and increase; those who invoke thee on the roads, in the fields, on the banks of the rivers, in the ravines, under the trees, under the vines.

Give them daughters and sons. Let them not meet disgrace nor misfortune, let not the deceiver come behind or before them. Let them not fall, let them not be wounded, let them not fornicate, nor be condemned by justice. Let them not fall on the descent or on the ascent of the road. Let them not encounter obstacles back of them or before them, nor anything which strikes them. Grant them good roads, beautiful, level roads. Let them not have misfortune nor disgrace, through thy fault, through thy sorceries.

Grant a good life to those who must give thee sustenance and place food in this mouth, in thy presence, to thee, heart of heaven, heart of earth, bundle of majesty. And thou, Tohil; thou Avilix; thou Hacavitz, arch of the sky, surface of the earth, the four corners, the four cardinal points. Let there be but peace and tranquility in thy mouth, in thy presence, oh god.

There is poetic imagery in this prayer. The passage about the roads has a pleasant parallel in an old Gaelic blessing "May the roads rise with you and the wind be always at your back."

A Lacandon prayer for the welfare of a son was collected by Tozzer (1907:175):

Guard my son, my father, let any evil cease, let fever cease. Do not injure him by letting evil trample him under foot. Do not injure him by letting fever trample him under foot. Do not injure him by letting a serpent bite my son. Do not injure him by sending death. He is playing, my son. When he is grown up he will give you an offering of *posol*, he will give you an offering of copal. When he is grown up he will give you an offering of tortillas. When he is grown up he will give you an offering of bark-cloth fillets. When he is grown up he will sacrifice to you.

Brasseur de Bourbourg heard a milpa prayer within a metaphorical stone's throw of the ancient Maya capital of Mayapan over a century ago. The transcription is not perfect. I attempt below a new translation, but readily admit that this also falls far short of perfection:

O lord [sun] high in the east, at the four corners of the sky, at the four corners of the earth. Now my prayer travels [falls, in Maya] to each of the four ends of the earth, in the name of God the Father, God the Son, and God the Holy Ghost. To the rising of the clouds in the east, to the ascension to the middle of the heaven, the majesty, to the thirteen layers of clouds in the east, the yellow Chac [rain god of the south], set in order, the lords of the companions, all the inhabitants, he of the tables placed in order for the holy steeped *balche* drink. And the holy reverential lover for the revered lords, the guardians of the milpa that they may bring the holy offering to the holy great God the Father, God the Son, and God the Holy Ghost. I offer his virgin harvest corn together with my holy reverence. You are going to reward me resoundingly every moment. I beseech you that you send down on me your benediction with all your heart, that you give to me your holy love, that you make me deserving of your well-founded and virgin gift. This is necessary [?] in order that I may make my offering into the hands of God the Father, God the Son, and God the Holy Ghost.

Note the use of the term *virgin* to which we have referred under Ritual Purity. Mention of the sun is not in the prayer, but is given by Brasseur de Bourbourg surely on the basis of what his informant told him. The mention of a single Chac is unusual; generally all four Chacs and their corresponding colors are given, and if one only is cited, it would be the red Chac of the east, the most important.

Finally, a prayer (slightly amended) before felling to clear a milpa in southern British Honduras is given (Thompson, 1930:45):

O god, my father, my mother, lord of the hills and valleys, spirit of the forest treat me well. I am about to do as has always been done. Now I am about to make my offering to you that you may know that I am molesting your heart. Suffer it. I am going to dirty you [destroy your beauty], I am going to work you in order that I may live. Suffer no animal to pursue me, suffer not the snake, or scorpion, or wasp to bite me. Do not allow a [falling] tree to hit me, nor axe or machete to cut me. With all my heart I am going to work you.

The above constitute a fair sample of Maya prayers except, perhaps, that the gods of the four world directions and colors receive scant mention. It will be observed that the petitions are for material, not spiritual, benefit.

Wounds from axe or machete are far commoner than snake bite, yet protection from the latter is besought in prayers recited in widely separated parts. Perhaps the greater rarity of prayer for safety from axe and machete lies in the fact that steel tools are of relatively recent introduction. Formulae for prayer are traditional; four centuries ago snake bites were probably more feared than injury from stone tools.

COSMOLOGICAL NOTIONS

Maya creation myths are summarized in chapter 9. As to our

Plate 1.—Portrait of a Ruler

The features of this determined individual are totally at variance with the Classic Maya style of beauty. The portrait is almost certainly that of a leader of the Putun Maya group which gained control of Seibal a few years before this face was carved on Stela 10, Seibal, A.D. 849. *(Photograph by Ian Graham.)*

Plate 2.—Usurper at Seibal

The personage lacks the soft features characteristic of Maya art of
the central lowlands, although the sculptor gave him a Maya mouth.
He is clearly one of the invaders, but, being Maya, he uses Maya symbolism, notably the Itzam headdress. Part of Stela 14. No surviving
date; probably mid-ninth century. *(Photograph by Ian Graham.)*

Plate 3.—A Sea Coast Village and Merchants

Doorways at the sides of hut fronts (above) are not of Yucatec type, evidence that the village of this landscape was not in Yucatan although the mural is at Chichen Itza. Note that four of the unpleasant people in the interview (below) carry fans, evidence that they are merchants. Attendant on the extreme right has hand on shoulder, standard gesture denoting peace or submission. Chama, Alta Verapaz.

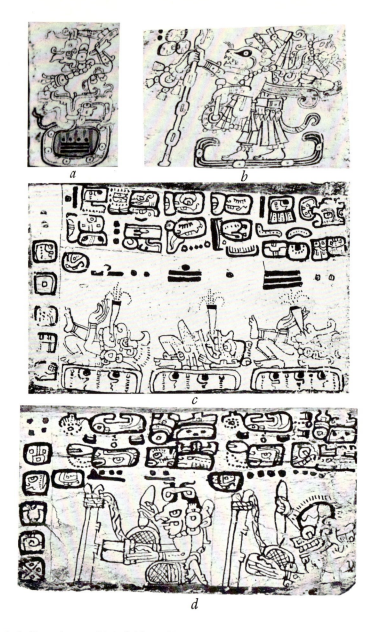

Plate 4.—Gods in Dresden and Madrid Codices

a: Chac in jaws of a serpent whose coiled body forms water container (rain
storage). Codex Dresden 33 *b*. *b*: Bacab disguised as opossum carries in
the maize god, one of the rulers of incoming year. Codex Dresden, 27.
c: Smokers' almanac. Itzam Na, death god, and maize god lie on ground (note
caban-earth "query" sign. Codex Madrid 79*b*. *d*: Old Goddess O, Ix
Chebel Yax, and death goddess weaving. Above heads is skein of cotton affix
above Men, Worker, glyph—that is, weaver—preceded by portrait
glyph of old goddess on left, of death goddess on right. Codex Madrid, 102*d*.

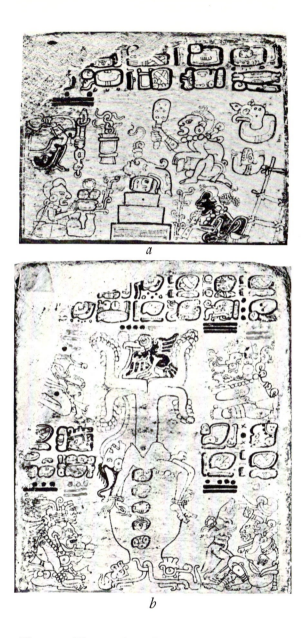

a

b

Plate 5.—Human Sacrifice

a: The head of an impersonator of the maize god on an earth sign resting
in turn on an altar? Musicians play two types of drums, rattle, and
flute. Offerings are of maize, including turkey tamales, iguana (?), and
copal. *b*: Sacrificial victim with hands and feet tied. From wound for
removal of the heart a tree rises. A vulture on it has plucked out one
of the victim's eyes. Gods, clockwise from top right, are Bolon
Dz'acab, an evil aspect of the Chicchan god, the maize god,
and the death god (badly damaged). Codex Dresden, 34*a* and 3*a*.

Plate 6.—Bolon Dz'acab *(top)*

Bolon Dz'acab, a manifestation of Itzam Na and perhaps another name for
Itzam Na Kauil, is set in the center of a quadruple *bil*, vegetal growth,
element. The design is very close to the *bil* hieroglyphic affix; the grains here
show the derivation of the design from sprouting maize. Relief on four stones,
west court, Copan. *(After A. P. Maudslay. Courtesy British Museum.)*

Plate 7.—Itzam Na Façade *(bottom)*

Partly restored model of building in Chenes style at Hochob, Campeche. The
façade is a huge face of Itzam Na with open mouth set with teeth in upper
and lower (the sill) jaws, forming the entrance to Iguana House. Restoration
of the roof comb is conjectural. *(Courtesy Brooklyn Museum.)*

Plate 8.—Portraits of Gods in Codex Dresden

a-c: Chacs perched on world directional trees or striding. *d*: Death god.
e: Old red goddess Ix Chebel Yax pouring rain earthward from an inverted
jar. *f*: God D, personified Itzam Na. *g*: The maize god. *h*: The Chicchan
deity, here in feminine form. *i*: God K, Bolon Dz'acab. Codex Dresden,
12a, b, 15c, 31c, 33a, 43b.

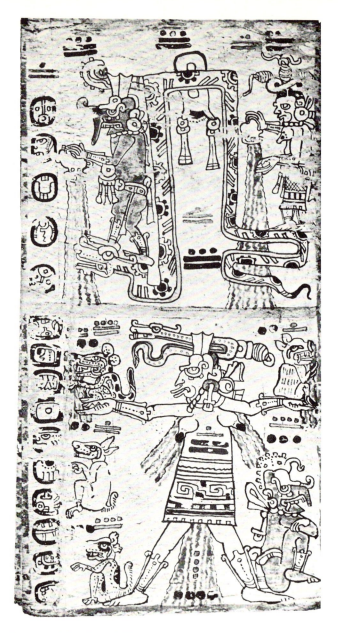

Plate 9.—Chacs and Ix Chebel Yax

Above, a Chac, standing on the head of serpent, and Goddess O, Ix
Chebel Yax (note spindles with spun cotton in the headdress),
pour rain water earthward from inverted jars. Below, a goddess,
perhaps a Chac's wife (but note the snake headdress such as usually
worn by Ix Chebel Yax). Rain pours down from her armpits and
from between her legs. Note peccary, deer, dog *(pek)* and
jaguar, probably signifying different rains. Codex Madrid, 30.

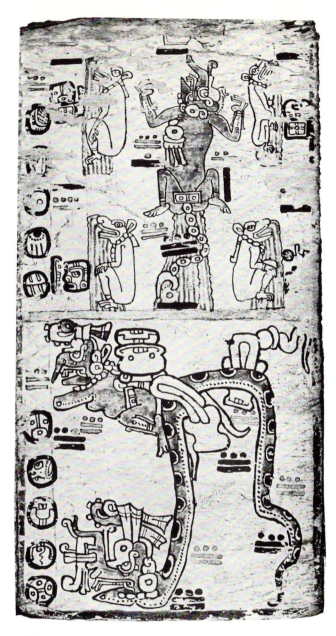

Plate 10.—Chacs and Frogs

Above, water pours earthward from the anus of a Chac, a probable reference to the Maya expression for falling rain, *kaxal ha*. The root *kax* is that of the term "to defecate." Four frogs, servants and musicians of the Chacs, spout more rain earthward. Before each stands a directional glyph, clockwise from top left, east, west, south, north. Below, a Chac with a dish of maize on his back sits on a snake with head of God K. Codex Madrid, 31.

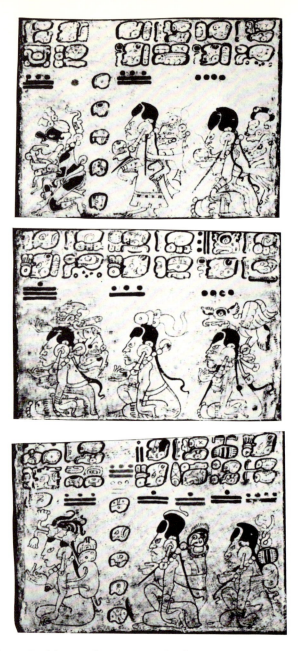

Plate 11.—Moon Goddess and Merchant God

All pictures represent Acna Ix Chel, the moon goddess, except the portrait, top left corner, of God M, Ek Chuah, god of merchants, with his Pinocchio nose and projecting lower lip. His glyph, above, is the merchant's pack against a black ground. The moon goddess carries man's fate *(cuch)* as a load on her back *(cuch)* or the disease she sends *(koch)* as a weight on her shoulders *(koch)*. Maya punning. Codex Dresden, 16*b*, 18*b*, 19*c*.

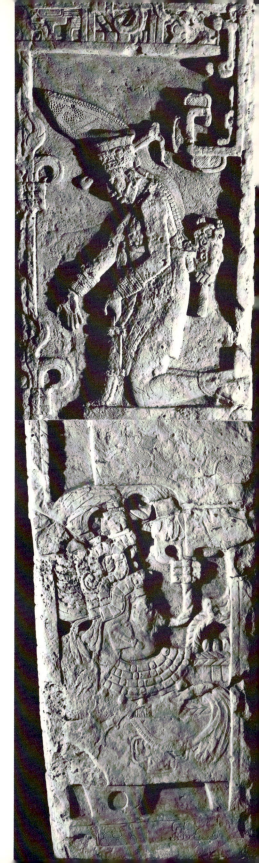

Plate 12.—Maize and Earth

A ruler personifying the maize god, or the god himself (note the ear of corn in the headdress). From his open hand, maize seed (not visible in illustration) falls on the earth god below. Faint traces on the latter's face suggest the query-mark design, Maya earth symbol, a distinguishing characteristic of the earth god, Buluc Ch'abtan. Stela 40, Piedras Negras. *(Courtesy University Museum, Philadelphia.)*

Plate 13.—The Maize God

This magnificent portrait once adorned the façade of a temple at
Copan. The top of the maize foliage has broken off. Note the *bil*,
"vegetal growth," element projecting behind earplug. *(Courtesy British Museum.)*

a

b

c

d

Plate 14.—Designs on Pottery and Mural

a: Personification of the earth from whose stomach emerges a two-headed serpent. Bacabs and vegetation left and right. Mexican period, Ball Court, Chichen Itza. *b*: Fish deity, detail on vase from Caracol, British Honduras. *(Courtesy Museum of Archaeology and Ethnology, Cambridge University.)* *c*: Maize god impersonator making a wooden mask. Carved vase, Copan. *d*: Death god on vase. *(Courtesy Museum of Primitive Art, N.Y.)*

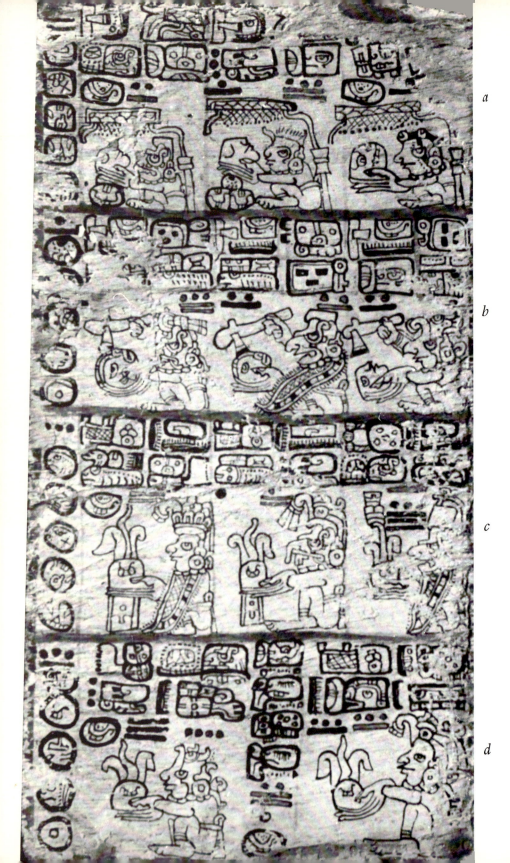

a

b

c

d

Plate 16.–Pyramid 1, Tikal *(above)*

The peasant conciliated his gods with simple offerings of food and copal in forest clearing or thatched hut; the hierarchy demanded towering pyramids with stone temples atop. Were those stupendous building programs which never ceased only to the glory of the gods? It is as well Maya culture preceded the Wright brothers; a Chac's-eye view of even Tikal is not overly impressive. Had the peasants been in a position to share it, the ruling class might have gone much earlier. *(Courtesy University Museum, Philadelphia.)*

Plate 15.–A Page of Codex Madrid *(left)*

Strips *a* and *b*: Making idols or masks of gods. *a*: Left to right; Gods D, R (Buluc Ch'abtan), and Q (evil god, probably of sacrifice). *b*: Left to right; Chac, Itzam Na, and maize god. Strips *c* and *d*: Gods hold plants growing from *ik*, "life," sign. *c*: Left to right; unidentified god, Chac, Itzam Na. *d*: Left to right, maize god and unidentified god. Codex Madrid, 97.

Plate 17.—Head of the Maize God

This detail from a mask at the base of Stela 1, Bonampak, is a most sympathetic portrait of the beloved maize god. Note the tapering forehead reminiscent of an ear of maize. The head emerges from maize foliage, not visible in the detail, which sprouts from the temples of a representation of Itzam Cab Ain, the earth manifestation of Itzam Na. (*Photograph by Raul Pavon Abreu.*)

world, it was regarded as a flat square block with skies above and underworlds beneath.

At the four points of the compass or at the angles between stood the four Bacabs (p. 276) who, with upraised hands, supported the skies. In the view of the Tzotzil Maya there were also four gods who supported the earth on their shoulders; I have not found that view shared by any other Maya group, but one or two early Classic period reliefs may represent that concept, and reliefs at Chichen Itza appear to show Bacabs in the underworld (Plate 14*a*).

There were thirteen "layers" of heaven and nine of the underworld. Although the Maya spoke of the thirteen *taz* ("layers") of the heavens, *taz* covering such things as blankets spread out one above the other, in fact, the thirteen celestial layers were arranged as six steps ascending from the eastern horizon to the seventh, the zenith, whence six more steps led down to the western horizon. Similarly, four more steps led down from the western horizon to the nadir of the underworld, whence four more steps ascended to the eastern horizon. Thus there were really only seven celestial and five infernal layers. The sun followed this sort of stepped rhomboid on his daily journey across the sky and his nightly traverse of the underworld to return to the point of departure each dawn. There is some inconclusive evidence that the Maya divided the day into thirteen "hours" and the night into nine "hours," corresponding to the numbers of steps or layers.

Countering this severely geometric structure, a giant ceiba tree, the sacred tree of the Maya, the *yaxche*, "first" or "green" tree, stands in the exact center of the earth. Its roots penetrate the underworld; its trunk and branches pierce the various layers of the skies. Some Maya groups hold that by its roots their ancestors ascended into the world, and by its trunk and branches the dead climb to the highest sky.

There is antagonism between the sky and the underworld, and struggles occur between the Thirteen Gods and the Nine Gods (p. 281) which personify those abstracts. The sky, its powers, and its personifications stand for goodness and light which inspire confidence and right doing; the underworld, with its associations with death, upholds the powers of evil to whom belongs darkness, a cloak for fearful beings which then issue forth to harm man.

At the same time, there exists in Maya thought a sexual drama: the sky is male, the earth female, and their intercourse mystically brings life to the world. Similarly, light is male and darkness, female. The day 4 Ahau, day of the sun god, is creation (in Maya thought, darkness preceded creation); the day 1 Ahau, Venus at heliacal rising, emerging from the underworld, represents darkness. In the creation story of the Quiche in the Popol Vuh, the people anxiously wait in darkness for the rising of the morning star, harbinger of the light to come to the world.

Apparently, although again the evidence is not as good as it might be, the creator deity lives in the highest (seventh) heaven; the death god in the lowest (fifth) underworld.

The heavens were also thought of as a celestial iguana dragon, sometimes two-headed and at times given the cleft hoofs and antlers of a deer. Apparently, there were four such beings called Itzam, "Iguana," which formed the four walls and roof of Itzam Na, "Iguana House," within which is set our world (p. 214). In addition, trees were set at the four sides of the world. They have color associations and are of importance in the creation story. World directional trees are found in Mexican codices, and in the Maya Dresden codex, Chacs are shown seated on world directional trees with corresponding colors, and special birds of correct colors perch on trees or Itzam Na (Figs. 2, 3, 4a, d).

East is always the most important direction, and ancient Maya maps (normally circular) seem usually to have had east at the top. The idea of a fifth direction, apparently assigned the color green, is present in Maya thinking. This could be either at the zenith or below the ground, depending on whether celestial or terrestrial matters were under consideration. For example, one group of Chacs enthroned on their directional trees are followed by a fifth Chac seated in a sort of cave or underground chamber with the glyphic label *yolcab*, "in the heart of the earth" (Codex Dresden, 29a–30a). Directional trees are of this world, so the center is a spot below the center of the world; had the subject been one of celestial inhabitants, the fifth direction would have been the zenith.

CHAPTER 7

Lowland Maya Religion:
The Major Gods

Inclusion of the principal Maya deities in one chapter and relegation of the remainder to a sort of Cave of Adullam in the next
accords more closely with the rules of book composition than
with Maya religious ideas. Other arrangements have other de-
fects, for religious beliefs and attitudes, as well as the gods about
whom they cluster, are fluid; our containers for them are apt to
turn into colanders.

Admission to the category of major gods has been influenced
by what rites happened to survive extinction of the Maya priesthood and spread of Christianity. For instance, the moon goddess'
present popularity owes much to her identification with the Virgin Mary. Even artistic considerations or personal pride may
have indirectly advanced the candidacy of some god. An example
is the jaguar which symbolized leadership and courage and which,
with his attributes, shared a simplicity of design which surely
appealed to artists. Both factors might partly account for the
popularity of the jaguar god in Maya Classic art, making awry our
assessments of the importance of Maya gods.

CHARACTERISTICS OF MAYA GODS

In considering the nature of Maya gods, we may first rid our-selves of certain misconceptions by noting that in our field the term *pantheon* should not be taken in its strictly Greek sense. The idea of a general assembly of gods finds no place in Maya theology, and the visions of the behavior of the very carnal gods of Greece and Rome that the word conjures up would have been rated by the Maya as conduct totally unbecoming divine beings. As we have seen, commerce with the gods required of a Maya petitioner a condition of ritual cleanliness and freedom from sexual preoc-cupation; the Hellenic idea that the gods had constant love affairs with mortal flesh and from time to time entered into homosexual relationships would have been abhorrent to him. Nor can one conceive of the Maya paralleling our western coinage of the adjec-tive *jovial* from what they would have regarded as an undignified failing of Jove. The Maya moon goddess, it is true, was a wanton before she took up her celestial duties prior to her deification, but it seems natural to make a deity of—*inter alia*—sexual relations in man's or woman's image. More properly, Maya deities were im-personal. For the most part, their only marked human vice was a desire for recognition in the form of frequent offerings, and I suspect that the idea behind that concept was the wish to inculcate gratitude in the community.

Below, in a slightly expanded version from an earlier publica-tion, are listed what strike me as the outstanding characteristics of Maya gods, features which they share in large part with the gods of neighboring peoples of Middle America.

1. Few gods are in human form; most show a blending of human and animal features. For instance, the rain gods and the earth deities reveal details which in large part derive from repre-sentations of snakes and crocodiles, fantastically elaborated and often merged with elements drawn from other members of the animal kingdom. The Chicchan god of number nine, for instance, borrows both snake (temple markings) and jaguar (whiskers and spots on chin) features. Yet animal-derived gods can appear in purely human form; the creator aspect of Itzam Na, for example.

2. There is a quadruplicity of gods, each of the four assigned

to a different world direction and world color, yet at times mystically regarded as a single being in a way reminiscent of the doctrine of the Trinity (amplified in discussion of the Chacs below).

3. The gods had a duality of aspect. Gods could be both benevolent and malevolent. In art this is shown by adding death symbols to the usual appearance of a god. This duality extended to age, for in some cases there are both youthful and aged aspects of a god, and both apparently share the same basic functions. There is also sex duality. For instance, the Chacs are normally masculine, but one is occasionally shown as female. Possibly we are dealing with the wife of a Chac, but there is little evidence that in the Chacs' heaven there was marrying or giving in marriage. In features and attributes, female counterparts are indistinguishable from the males. Sex duality is particularly developed among the Chorti Maya.

4. The gods were indiscriminately marshaled in large categories so that a god could belong to two diametrically opposed groups. The sun god, for instance, was primarily a sky god, but because he passed at night through the underworld on his eastward journey from point of sunset to point of sunrise he became one of the nine lords of the night and underworld. Similarly, the god of merchants, for reasons unknown, was patron of one of the lunar groupings.

5. There is overwhelming importance of the numerous gods connected with all time periods, and deification of days and other time periods.

6. Inconsistencies and duplication of functions arise from the imposition of alien concepts by the hierarchy on the simpler structure of nature gods worshiped by peasant communities. An example is the usurpation by the god(s) of the planet Venus of the patronage of game and its hunters at the cost of the proletariat's gods of the chase.

7. The gods had the ability to merge with alien deities, as the moon goddess with the Virgin Mary; the sun god, to a lesser extent, with Jesus; and the Chacs with archangels and saints of the Roman Catholic church.

8. A cult deifying clan ancestors seems to have proliferated in

the post-Classic period. It appears to have been important also in the Classic period but received a strong impetus with the rise of militarism near the close of that era.

9. Inanimate objects were endowed with indwelling spirits which sometimes achieved the rank of deities.

10. Animals were worshiped; the jaguar is an example.

11. A divine social order patterned on a mundane one developed, with minor gods as messengers and servants and a chief of a group of four deities as their leader.

12. A single god may have had various manifestations with accompanying distinctive names. This gives the impression that Maya gods were more numerous than they were in fact (250 names and titles of lowland gods are in the index).

13. There is some evidence for something approaching monotheism among the ruling class during the Classic period, worship being directed to Itzam Na, "Iguana House," a group of deities who formed the frame containing the earth, and who, by being both sky and earth, gave man his sustenance produced from correct watering of the soil.

CREATION GODS

Information on creation deities is far fuller from the Mexican plateau than from the Maya area and is helpful in assessing data from the latter region. In Nahuatl mythology, there is a divine pair, male and female, perhaps personifications of the male and female principle, who are the original creators. Of their various names, Ome Tecutli, "Two Lord," and Ome Ciuatl, "Two Woman," are the commonest. In Mexican codices they are frequently shown behind a sort of cloth drop with heads and shoulders visible above and legs below, and in postures which have generally been taken to represent the sexual act. Myths are confused, but they seem to have given birth to, or created, other gods who later assisted in the creation of the world. They lived in the topmost (thirteenth) heaven, and ruled over the day Cipactli, first of the twenty days, the alligator or crocodile on whose back the world rested.

This same concept of a divine pair who created the world with the assistance of other gods to whom they had probably given birth was, one may conjecture, generally held in the Maya area. It is most clearly set forth in the account of the creation in the Popol Vuh, the sacred book of the Quiche Maya of the Guatemalan highlands. The primeval pair in the Popol Vuh bear, among other names, E Quaholom, "Begetter of Children," and E Alom, "Conceiver of Children." In most Maya languages the term used for a child depends on whether one is speaking of it as offspring of father or of mother. Here, the presence of both terms indicates that the creation deities are male and female. As creators of the world, their names are followed by others, and it is not clear whether some of these are additional titles of the original pair or names of distinct gods. However, among them figures Gukumatz, whose name is the Quiche translation of Quetzalcoatl, "Feathered Serpent." In Nahuatl myths of the creation, Quetzalcoatl is said to have been a son of Ome Tecutli and Ome Ciuatl and to have played a large part in the creation. Whether the Quiche followed the Nahuatl tradition and accepted Gukumatz as a son of the primeval pair who assisted in the creation is not clear, although it seems probable, but the wording of the passage in the Popol Vuh rather suggests that Gukumatz and Tepeu are other names for the creation pair, a view which Recinos (1950:78) accepts. One must bear in mind that the Popol Vuh, although deriving from ancient oral tradition, was reduced to writing long enough after the Spanish Conquest for the Quiche author to have acquired a thorough mastery of European writing and for the original campaign to suppress all pagan tradition to have lost impetus. In that half-century or more, little confusions concerning those obscure titles and relationships could have arisen. Certainly that was what happened with regard to Nahuatl mythology. All in all, I think that before the impact of Christianity was felt, Gukumatz was held to be a separate individual and probably, like Quetzalcoatl, the son of the original spouses. Other names of the original couple are Tzacol and Bitol, "Creator" and "Maker," again paired names.

A similar belief in a creator, father-mother couple appears to have existed among the Tzotzil of Chenalho (Guiteras, 1961:292). They were known collectively as Totilme'il, "Father-Mother," and Guiteras regards them as a single deity, the ancestor. He (they) existed when the world began and only gods lived on earth. He helped the deserving and punished the wicked. He destroyed various evil apparitions which preyed on man, and waged constant war on evil powers and all the enemies of man. His nagual (p. 167) is the hummingbird, with whose help he vanquishes his enemies.

However, the Tzotzil situation is complicated by two other gods. One is Ohoroxtotil, "God Almighty," the father of the sun. He made the world livable for man by destroying the jaguars which once infested it. The other is Manohel-Tohel, man's creator and maker, who led man out of the caves and provided him with a body and a soul. Perhaps these three were once a single personage, for a god who destroyed evil creatures and all enemies of man might just as well have included jaguars in his cleanup. According to Holland (1963:113), Totilme'iletik, who must be the same personage, is a collective name for the ancestral deities. Ancestor deities unconnected with any lineage suggest to me creation gods. Chul Tatic Chitez Vanegh (Uinic), "Holy Father, Creator of Man," was a Tzeltal creator (p. 322).

In Lacandon belief, the various gods descend from the mating of the red and white *plumeria* flowers (in English, frangipani). These were well-established symbols of sex activity, licit and illicit, a fact which supports the idea of a male and female pair who gave birth to the gods. The actual creator of the world was his son Hachacyum, "Our Very Lord," also called Nohochacyum, "Our Great Lord," who was assisted by his wife and three other deities, two of whom were his brothers (p. 344). This is according to the information of Baer and Baer (1952) and Tozzer (1907). Bruce (1967), however, says that Kacoch was the remote creator and he created the water-lily flower from which are descended the other gods, a plausible alternative (p. 220). According to Tozzer, Cacoch *(sic)* was a somewhat unimportant god who carried the offerings to Nochacyum, a sort of messenger; Baer and Baer, who also call him Cacoch, say that he was a brother of Hachacyum and therefore a son of the *plumerias*. Hachacyum sacrifices to him, but he, in turn, sacrifices to the god in the next highest heaven. Lacandon culture is now in the last stages of disintegration, so in any conflict between early and late investigators, one is more inclined to trust the earlier ones, particularly when, as in this case, they are in substantial agreement. I think Bruce's informant was harking back to another tradition—association of the water lily with the earth-lizard crocodile who was also involved in creation. Both Tozzer and the Baers assign that role to the *plumeria*, which is in accord with the sexual implications of the *plumeria* in colonial Yucatan. Moreover, certain characteristics of the *plumeria* shrub recall rather obviously the act of generation.

All in all, I feel that there can be little question that the *plumerias* were the Lacandon ancestral pair (they probably had other names), but as in the myths of other cultures, they were assisted by their sons in the creation of the world.

The ancestral gods of the Jacalteca and of the Kanhobal of Santa Eulalia (p. 316) were, I suspect, creation gods. The former, who existed while the world was still dark, are called Old Father and Old Mother, *old* being a term of respect, but they also bear calendar day names, 9 Kana' and 9 Imux, equivalents of Yucatec 9 Lamat and 9 Imix (La Farge and Byers, 1931:114).

The Cakchiquel Maya recognized the same father-mother pair who similarly appear to have been the authors of creation, but data are meager.

Turning now to Yucatan, it is necessary to be a shade digressive to emulate creation gods and bring order out of chaos.

There is an entry in the Motul dictionary, composed about A.D. 1590 by the Maya scholar Ciudad Real, which reads: "Hunab Ku: Only live and true god. He was the greatest of the gods of Yucatan. He had no image because, they said that being incorporeal, he could not be pictured."

The late Maya scholar Ralph Roys wrote me a dozen years ago: "I suggest very tentatively that Hunab Ku was an early post-Conquest invention, although there may [earlier] have been some vague idea of an all-powerful god who was not portrayed." Certainly Maya paganism was affected by Christianity at an early date; candles had become part of Maya ritual within two decades of the Spanish Conquest. The idea of an only living god could easily have been taken over from Christianity in a mutated form, or the friars may have misunderstood the meaning of *hunab*, which does not convey the same idea as the Christian concept of

God. The notion of a single creator god is out of keeping with the prevalent Middle American concept of a pair of creators who populate the world by sexual intercourse. Moreover, just as a wifeless Maya is a bit of an oddity—despised if he is young, pitied if he is old—so a Maya god without a wife to make his tortillas and weave his clothes would hardly have won much respect from his worshipers. I agree with Roys that Hunab Ku comes to us distorted by the biblical views of friars, but I don't believe he was their invention.

The Vienna dictionary, the date of which is unknown, has an entry in almost the same words as that in the Motul dictionary: "Principal god which these Indians of this land had, from whom they said all things proceeded and who was incorporeal, and for that reason they made no image of him: Colup u Uich Kin." The sequent entry is : "God which they said was of this: Hun Itzamna. Yaxcocahmut." The wording is clumsy, but can be read in no other way.

Other sources quoted on page 210 definitely state that Itzam Na was the creator, and one calls him Hunab Itzam Na, thereby confirming that Hunab (Ku) and Itzam Na were one and the same.

However, López de Cogolludo (1867–68, bk. 4, ch. 6), who wrote about 1650 when the old hierarchic concepts had disappeared and whose material is all secondhand, remarks: "The Indians of Yucatan believe that there was an only live and true God who, they said was the greatest of the gods, and that he had no form, nor could one picture him as he was incorporeal. They called him Hunab Ku, as will be found in his [*sic*] great dictionary which begins with our Spanish. From him they said that all things proceeded, and as he was incorporeal, they did not worship him with [the aid of] any idol, nor did they have one of him (as is said elsewhere) and [they said] that he had a son whom they called Hun Itzamna or Yaxcocahmut."

In wording, all three sources are almost the same. It will be noted that the first half of López de Cogolludo's statement comes from the Motul dictionary, the second half from the Vienna dictionary, almost word for word. He merely adds that the first statement came from the Spanish-Maya part of the great dictionary (he erred; it is from the Maya-Spanish part) and that Hun Itzam Na was the son of Hunab Ku. I think we must accept this as an error on his part; he was not really interested in Maya religion.

Hun inserted before Itzam Na has about the same meaning— "one" or "unique"—as *hunab* and is a rare addition; it reminds us of the form Hunab Itzam Na given in the *Relaciones de Yucatán* (p. 210). The only possible deduction I can make is that Hunab Itzam Na was the creator and that he was also known as Hunab Ku, Yaxcocahmut, and Colop u Uich Kin; the functional name Ah Ch'ab, "Creator," is also given in the Vienna dictionary.

Colop u Uich Kin, "Tears out Sun's (or Day's) Eye or Face," appears with some frequency in the Ritual of the Bacabs, in which Colop is sometimes written Kolop, "Wounder," and may be preceded by the titles Chac Ahau, "Red Lord," or Kin Chac Ahau, "Sun Red Lord." Sometimes the name is joined to Colop u Uich Akab, "Tears out Night's Eye or Face." He is said to live in the midst of the sky, and his night variant lives in Metnal, land of the dead. He is creator of several diseases, subjects of the incantations.

The god's peculiar name might indicate that he was thought to cause eclipses by attacking the sun, but I am inclined to think it refers to the creator's having brought several creations of the world to abrupt and destructive ends. In the Nahuatl myth, each such creation was called a sun (p. 332); "Tears out Sun's Face" accordingly might mean "Destroyer of (Past) Creations." This, however, is pure speculation.

Itzam Na, as we shall see, was the most important of Maya deities, to whom, at least in the eyes of the hierarchy, mankind owed its creation, preservation, and not a few of the blessings of this life. Although Itzam Na, "Iguana House," was primarily of reptilian configuration, in his role as creator he seems to have been depicted in human form, the early chroniclers notwithstanding, and was, I believe, the aged God D of the codices (Figs. 4c, 8f, 15a, b; p. 228).

I feel reasonably confident that he and his wife appear in the center of the "world" in the role of the creation pair on Codex Madrid, 75–76. *Ik*, "Life," glyphs stand before both of them, and an *itzam* is before the goddess (her clothing suggests a god, but her hair color and arrangement leave no doubt of her sex).

That he did conform to the pattern of Middle American creators in having a female counterpart is clear from what follows.

THE CREATOR'S SPOUSE: IX CHEBEL YAX

Caesar's wife had to be above suspicion; alas! even the marriage lines of Itzam Na's wife are blotted. I refer to the personified form of Itzam Na as creator, God D; in his iguana form he appears to have had a mate, the earth iguana, and iguanas perhaps attach less importance to such formalities.

Las Casas' (1909, ch. 123) early informant in Campeche, couching his sketch of Maya religion in terms of Christian doctrine, equates Itzam Na with God the Father, Bacab with God the Son, and names the virgin goddess Chibirias (Ix Chebel Yax) as the latter's mother, that is to say, barring complications, as the wife of Itzam Na, identified as the creator.

López de Cogolludo (1867–68, bk. 4, ch. 8) writes that she was goddess of painting and brocading. Indeed, *chebel* signifies "related to paint brush." In Ritual of the Bacabs (Roys, 1965:55) a goddess called Ix Hun Tah Dz'ib and Ix Hun Tah Nok is named. I differ from Roys in translating those names which I take to mean "Lady Unique Owner of the Paint Brush" and "Lady Unique Owner of Cloth." The incantation states that she had a red paint brush (*cheb*) with which she had painted the red earth (a common soil in Yucatan), the red leaves of various trees, the red (barked) gumbolimbo tree, and the red (crested) woodpecker. Clearly, she is the same as Ix Chebel Yax, and her activities are those of a creation goddess.

There is little doubt that she is the old red goddess (O) of the codices, whose glyph includes a hank of cotton or cloth and which may have the red affix prefixed. In Codex Madrid she is weaving, and her glyph is usually the head of an old woman with *zac* prefix (Plate 4*d*). *Zac* is "white," but here must stand for *zac*, root of *zacal*, "to weave." Once this head is followed by Goddess O's regular name glyph with hank of cotton or cloth affixed, confirmation that she is Ix Chebel Yax and also goddess of weaving.

Goddess O shares old age with God D, and their features are quite alike. Moreover, in her red aspect she sends rain like Itzam

Na (Plates 8*e*, 9). On Codex Dresden page 74 she helps him, here in iguana (Itzam) form, flood the world. Probably a vague memory of her survives in the legend of the sun (p. 355). His grandmother is XKitza, not far different from XItzam, "Lady Iguana." She had sharp claws, a prominent feature of Goddess O, and her husband was a monster, a tapir according to some.

López de Cogolludo, in the passage cited, throws a wrench in the machinery, saying that Ix Azal Uoh (surely a garbling of Ix Zacal Nok), inventress of weaving, was the wife of Kinich Ahau, "the greatest of all the gods." Formerly, I (1939*a*) accepted this and correlated this goddess with the moon, wife of Kinich Ahau, the sun god; I am now certain that he confused Kinich Ahau (Itzam Na) with Itzam Na himself, just as, in the same paragraph, he credits Itzam Na instead of Kinich Ahau with the introduction of writing, and as he erred in saying Itzam Na was the son of Hunab Ku (p. 204). Kinich Ahau was merely the sun god and, as such, an aspect of Itzam Na; it was Itzam Na, not he, who was the greatest of all gods.

Ix Zacal Nok, in the corrected form—and how easily *uoh* could be misread for *nok*—"Lady Cloth Weaver," is merely a variant on Ix Hun Tah Nok, noted above. Ix Chebel Yax, accordingly, was goddess of painting, brocading, and weaving and equates with Goddess O of the codices.

Colel Cab, "Mistress of the Earth," mentioned in the creation story in the Chilam Balam of Chumayel, is probably another of her titles.

Ix Chebel Yax is said by Las Casas' informant to have been the daughter of Ix Chel (written Hischen), whom he equates with Saint Anne. This is clearly wrong; Ix Chel was the wife of the sun god.

Finally, there is the elusive XKan Le Ox, "Lady Yellow Ramón Leaf" (*ramón* is the breadnut tree, *Brosimum alicastrum*; the fruit is a standby in times of famine). Her name is coupled with that of Itzam Na in a prayer discussed in an early source; the Lacandon (Bruce, 1967) say she is the wife of the creator Hachacyum and creatress of Lacandon women and all female things; López de Cogolludo, in the cited passage, calls her mother of the other gods; in a prayer to the Chacs of over 150 years ago, she replaces the Chac of the south. Since Goddess O is a rain deity and appears with the Chacs in Codex Dresden, XKan Le Ox is probably her name in her rain-sending aspect.

She is clearly the wife of the creator, hers yet another name for Ix Chebel Yax, and as such she shares Itzam Na's conjugal bed, although the more modest Maya do not follow the Nahuatl custom of depicting the creation pair in bed together.

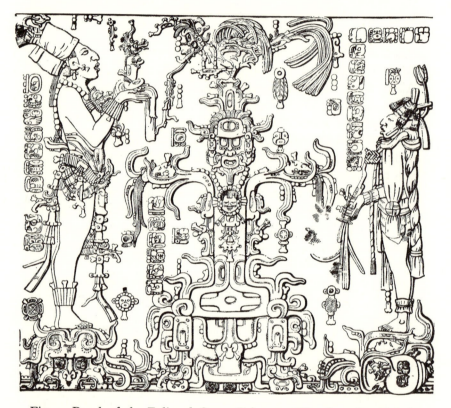

Fig. 2—Panel of the Foliated Cross, Palenque. The "tree," which is really a maize plant, grows from the head of the earth manifestation of Itzam Na, Itzam Cab, Kauil, or Bolon Dz'acab. Note *bil* elements protruding from the head. Heads of the maize god, complete with corn tassels, are set amid the maize foliage of the "tree" and in the maize plant emerging from the shell at bottom right. The priests offer figures of Itzam Na to the tree. Compare with Figure 3. *(After A. P. Maudslay.)*

208

It is in keeping with Maya ideas that this goddess should have at least six names (others probably have not survived) which reflect her sundry activities.

ITZAM NA: IGUANA HOUSE

The greatest god of the Yucatec Maya, but in some respects

Fig. 3—Panel of the Cross, Palenque. This tree is of the same general type as that of Figure 2, but the maize vegetation is lacking. Possibly that depended on the associated world direction—east and north are favorable, west and south unfavorable to maize. Yet the head from which the tree grows has symbols of vegetation. The planetary band to which the head is attached reminds us that the earth aspect of Itzam Na, although merely the floor, is an integral part of Iguana House. (*After A. P. Maudslay.*)

the most puzzling, is Itzam Na. As we shall see, he came near to incorporating most of the other major gods in his person as various of his aspects.

The author of the *Relación de Valladolid and Tiquinbalon* (*Relaciones de Yucatán*, 2:161) states that the Indians of the latter town (and presumably all others in Yucatan), before the introduction of idolatry, worshiped a single god named Hunab Izamana (Itzam Na). Hunab, "Unique," was a name applied to the creator.

Las Casas' (1909, ch. 123) informant from Campeche said that Itzam Na (it is printed Izona) was God the Father, maker of men and all things.

Two consecutive entries in the Vienna dictionary read: "Principal god [*idolo*] which these Indians of this land had, from whom they said all things proceeded, and who was incorporeal, and for that reason they made no image of him: Colop u Uich Kin." "God [*idolo*] which they said was of this [*que decían ser de este*]: Hun Itzamna: Yaxcocahmut." The last sentence must refer to the previous entry, so we deduce that in one of his aspects Itzam Na was the creator, as the name Hunab Itzam Na suggests, and that Colop u Uich Kin was a name for that aspect. However, the author of the dictionary erred in saying that no image was made of him.

There are various other aspects of Itzam Na: Itzam Na Kauil, "Itzam Na Bountiful Harvest"; Itzam Na T'ul, "Itzam Na Rabbit (rains)," an evil aspect; Itzam Na Kinich Ahau (Landa writes the name Kinich Ahau Itzam Na), "Itzam Na Sun-face Lord (the sun)"; Itzam Na Kabul, "Itzam Na Producer with his Hands" (probably here, "Creator"); Itzam Cab or Itzam Cab Ain, "Itzam Earth" or "Itzam Earth Crocodile." I believe I can also show that Bolon Dz'acab was another of his names. Strangely, this all-important god was of reptile origin.

There is good evidence that Itzam Na dwelt in the sky and sent rain to mankind, in that respect duplicating the work of the Chacs, the regular rain gods. The reason for this overlapping of functions is that Itzam Na was primarily a god of the hierarchy, whereas Chacs were cherished by the peasants. In confirmation, one may note that Itzam Na is completely absent from present-day peasant rites in Yucatan. Evidence that Itzam Na sent rains follows.

The badly garbled opening sentence of a prayer to Itzam Na (*Relaciones de Yucatán*, 2:183–84) can be restored as: *Cit Ah Tepale ninmi* (?) *caan yamte muyalyam ti caan*, "Father Lord Ruler (?), the sky, in the midst of the clouds, in the midst of the sky." The ceremony was to plead for good crops, which naturally depended on good rains.

The Chilam Balam of Tizimin, page 7 (Roys, 1949: 172), has this entry: "Drought. So there will be praying to Hunab Ku." But Hunab Ku is merely another name for Itzam Na (p. 205).

An early writer, Lizana (1893:4), wrote of Itzamat Ul, a garbled version of Itzam Na T'ul, an aspect of Itzam Na, that he said of himself, "I am the dew and sustenance [*substancia*] of the sky and of the clouds," and that his title meant "He who receives and possesses the grace or dew or sustenance of the sky." *Itz*, here translated by those terms, is defined in the Motul dictionary as "milk," "tear," "sweat," "resin or gum of trees and shrubs," "candle wax," and "rust." The idea seems to be of a liquid excreted drop by drop. It is really a pun—and how the Maya loved them—on the first syllable of Itzam Na's name, reminding us that from his home in the clouds he sent rain (his tears). Tears are common magic for rain in the New World. For instance, children to be sacrificed by the Aztec to bring rain were made to weep so that their tears would attract the rain—like produces like.

In the auto-de-fé of 1562 (Scholes and Adams, 1938, 2:334) there is an account of the sacrifice of a dog to Itzam Na, Ix Ku (goddess), the Bacabs, and the Chacs for the health of the chief and for rains.

In the month Mac, Landa writes, old men interceded with the Chacs and Itzam Na. One rite called for daubing the bottom step of a structure with fresh mud from a well (cenote) and the other steps with blue unguent. Mud from the cenote was obviously a like-attracts-like magic to bring water, and blue was the special color of rain gods. López Medel (Tozzer, 1940:223) writes of a large crocodile which emerged to receive the cenote sacrifices at Chichen Itza, evidence that cult was also directed to Itzam Na.

Itzam Na in his Itzam Na T'ul aspect could withhold good rains. Two passages in the Chilam Balam of Chumayel (Roys, 1933:154, 157) read: "There are rains of little profit, rains from a rabbit [*t'ul*] sky . . . rains from a vulture sky" and "rain from a rabbit [*t'ul*] sky during the evil katun." In the Chilam Balam of Tizimin (p. 1) there is a reference to T'ul Chacs who seemingly produce little or useless rain. On page 4 of the same book, Ix Kan Itzam T'ul, "Yellow Itzam T'ul," is linked to terrible drought. He is, accordingly, the evil side of Itzam Na; Itzam Na Kauil was his bountiful side.

Itzam Na means "Iguana House." Itzam is defined in the Vienna dictionary as "*lagartos* like iguanas of land and water." *Lagarto* can mean anything from lizard to crocodile (our alligator is from Spanish *el lagarto*), but lizard is usually *lagartija*. Moreover, the Itzam in Codex Dresden, pages 4b–5b and 74, are surely iguanas, not that it matters much whether the god was iguana or lizard. Sometimes Ix or X is prefixed to the god's name as in Ix Kan Itzam T'ul cited in the previous paragraph and Ix Hun Itzam Na mentioned in Ritual of the Bacabs (MS:150). *Ix* or *x* is the female prefix, but quite commonly it is prefixed to the names of insects, reptiles, and birds. The *toloc* lizard is often called *xtoloc*; *xbebech*, *xmemech*, and *xp'icune* are names of other lizards. Accordingly, I conclude that *ix* or *x* is sometimes prefixed to Itzam Na precisely because as an iguana he belongs in that category.

Thirty years ago I (Thompson, 1939a:152–61) tentatively identified Itzam Na with the celestial monsters, so common in Maya art, which are part crocodile, lizard, or snake and may even have deer features (antlers or cleft hoofs). At that time the Vienna dictionary was undiscovered. Now that we have its entry defining *itzam* as "iguana," the case for that identification is immeasurably strengthened.

In fact, there are four Itzam Na, for Chant Eight of Ritual of the Bacabs names four, each correctly assigned a world color and direction—the red Itzam Na to the east, the white to the north, the black to the west, and the yellow to the south. Chant Thirty-eight of the same book invokes Itzam Kan, who is associated likewise with the correct sequence of colors and directions. The four Itzam Kan repeat four times, and there is a final invocation of Red

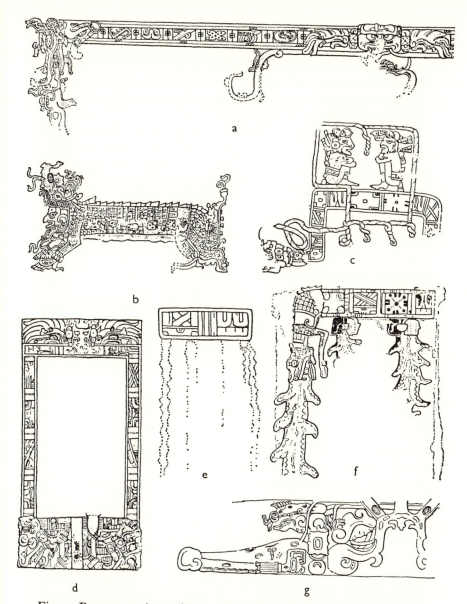

Fig. 4—Representations of Itzam Na. *a*: Left half of a two-headed It-zam Na with planetary glyphs on the body and a superimposed world directional bird. The rear head (not shown) is inverted with death symbols. Stucco, Palenque Palace. *b*: Codex Dresden, 4*b*–5*b*. *c*: Bacab and another god seated in rope enclosure on part of an Itzam with planetary glyphs. Codex Paris, 22. *d*: Itzam Na frames a seated ruler, Stela 25, Piedras Negras. Rear head is inverted with death symbols. *e*: Rain falling from a segment of Itzam Na. Codex Dresden, 39. *f*: Water pouring from Itzam Na. Codex Dresden, 74. *g*: Part of head and front leg of Itzam Cab with fish and water-lily motif. Note the claw. Palenque, Temple of the Cross. (*a, g, after A. P. Maudslay;* *d, after H. J. Spinden.*)

Itzam Kan. How *kan* is to be translated here is not clear (*kan* is an egg-bearing iguana in Cakchiquel), but in every case the direction is behind the east, north, west, or south sky; confirmation of the celestial nature of Itzam Na.

These celestial monsters often bear planetary symbols on their bodies (Figs. 4*a*, *c-f*, 5*a*, *e*), evidence that the monster both inhabited and represented the heavens. Features vary, but bodies are often easily recognizable as those of iguanas or crocodiles (Figs. 4*b*, *f*); others have snake bodies or markings (Figs. 4*c*, 5*b*, *d*) and commonly there is a head at each end (Figs. 4*a* [other head not shown], *d*, 5*a*, *b* [other heads not shown], *d*, *f*). Water cascades from one (Fig. 4*f*) in what is clearly a flood; sometimes rain falls from short sections of planetary bands which in a *pars pro toto* abbreviation stand for the complete reptile (Fig. 4*e*).

The Chilam Balam of Chumayel, page 73, mentions Itzam Na Itzam Tzab. *Tzab* is the rattles of the rattlesnake and also the Pleiades. If Barrera Vásquez (1948:106) has correctly identified Itzam Na's title of Yaxcocahmut as a constellation—he makes the important point that *ek* in the alternative form, Ekcocahmut, means "star"—Itzam Na was presumably identified with the Pleiades and conjecturally other constellations, a not unreasonable supposition in view of the god's residence in the sky and his planetary decoration.

As to the *na* part of Itzam Na's name, I believe it is to be interpreted in the ordinary sense of "house." I surmise, although the evidence is not as strong as I would wish, that the Maya conceived the world to be set within a house, the roof and walls of which were formed by four giant iguanas, upright but with their heads downward, each with its own world direction and color. For instance, Chac (Red) Itzam Na would have been the eastern side of the sky perhaps from zenith to horizon, that is, from apex of roof to floor. No doubt confusion arose about whether a single Itzam represented the whole vault (as we would say) or house of heaven, or whether there were four. Itzam, then, was the name of the creatures themselves. Itzam Na is often two-headed. That, I take it, is because one is viewing, so to speak, a section drawing of the whole "house" of Itzam with an Itzam forming each wall and the corresponding part of the vault of heaven. Their tails, meeting at the zenith, are eliminated to produce a two-headed being.

Supporting evidence for this belief is supplied by those Maya temples with façades sculptured to represent the faces of celestial monsters; the doorway, often set with teeth, representing the creature's mouth (Plate 7). The occasional presence of planetary symbols in the façade (Adivino, Uxmal) confirms the identification. Other evidence is supplied by the Itzam beings who form a frame in which a ruler on his throne is set (Fig. 4*d*). The matter is discussed at greater length below. At this point, suffice it to say that the Itzam who form the *na* of the world appear to continue their courses to form the floor of the house, which normally is the surface of the earth, and are then called Itzam Cab or Itzam Cab Ain, "Iguana Earth" or "Iguana Earth Crocodile." As to the four Itzam, the sides of the Itzam Na, Mexican iconography provides a parallel: four earth or sky monsters, each with a pair of saurian legs and crocodile heads, occupy the four quarters of Codex Borgia, page 72, to which are assigned the groups of days associated with each. In a parallel passage in Codex Vatican B, conventionalized serpents are similarly disposed.

Gann (1900:680–81) found at Santa Rita, northern British Honduras, a cache comprising an urn, two flint points, and ten pottery figures of late, crude workmanship. Of the last, pairs representing, respectively, a lizard-like monster with front legs and human head in its jaws and a jaguar sitting upright were set around the urn at the four cardinal points; a fifth lizard creature, like the others, and a sixth, with a head at front and rear, one of which had a human head in its jaws, were on top of the urn. This last was more saurian in appearance than the rest. Jaguars (*balam*) stand on the four sides of a Maya village to protect it (p. 291), and may have functioned similarly on a world basis. It is likely that the lizard creatures fulfilled similar roles in relation to the four world directions. Those on top, together with the spears and urn, complete the sacred tally of thirteen. Conceivably, they represent the zenith. The arrangement suggests the four Itzam were placed at the four sides to represent the walls of Itzam Na, with those above as its roof and perhaps its floor.

With regard to the directional aspect of Itzam Na, in the prophecy in the Chilam Balam of Tizimin for the year 8 Kan, drought is foretold, and in that connection there is mention of Ix Kan Itzam T'ul. *Kan* is yellow and is associated with the south, a region of death and misfortune. It will be remembered that in discussing the reconstructed Itzam Na T'ul, it was noted that *t'ul*, "rabbit," rains were of little profit. Here, then, the Yellow Itzam of the south, land of misfortune and death, sends rains of such little value that drought will ensue. The Itzam house, with its different colored "walls," reminds one of those rooms with contrasting wallpapers popular a few years ago.

However, the Itzam Na concept does not merely embrace four Itzam forming the roof and walls of the world, for the Itzam, when they touch the horizon, turn to form the floor of the house in which our world is set, thus completing the rectangle of Iguana House. Most important, the Itzam take on fresh functions when they exchange their celestial locations for the floor of the world house. Whereas the Itzam in their celestial aspect are senders of rain to earth, in their terrestrial aspect they are the soil in which all vegetation has its being, and now they receive that rain which formerly they dispensed from on high.

The various names of Itzam Na relate to this duality. Thus Itzam Na, Itzam Tzab, and probably Yaxcocahmut refer to the celestial aspect of Itzam Na; Itzam Cab or Itzam Cab Ain, "Iguana Earth" or "Iguana Earth Cayman," are names of Itzam Na as an earth deity, the floor of Itzam Na. I feel confident that Bolon Dz'acab is another name for this terrestrial aspect of Iguana House. Itzam Na Kauil, "Iguana House Bountiful Harvest," could refer to both aspects for both the rain of the celestial and the soil of the terrestrial iguana god are essential for a good harvest.

Before examining further the terrestrial aspect, let us see what the colonial sources and archaeology can tell us.

First, it is apparent that there is confusion between two conflicting traditions: one that the earth rested on the back of a crocodile or cayman and the other that the surface of the earth was the continuation of this iguana house.

On the Mexican plateau, the belief was widely held that the earth rested on the back of a crocodile which, in turn, floated in a huge lake or sea. Representations of these saurian earth monsters are common in Mexican art. In Codex Borgia, page 27, maize plants complete with ears of corn—almost a field of them—grow from the creature's back. Sometimes a human skull rests in the monster's open jaws (Codex Borgia: 3), and at times the nostrils of the beast are stopped with tubular plugs.

The Huaxtec, that detached Maya group in and around northern Veracruz, share that belief in an earth crocodile, but she is female and is fertilized by celestial beings, small gods of rain, thunder, and lightning (Stresser-Péan, 1952).

Maya colonial documents contain no direct statement about the earth's resting on the back of a crocodile or alligator or cayman (the Maya do not distinguish between them so far as I know—the crocodile is scarcer; his habitat is inland. All are called *ain*). However, there are two indirect statements which are good evidence that the belief widespread in Central Mexico of the earth on the back of a crocodile was shared by the lowland Maya. A statement in the *Relación de Mérida* (*Relaciones de Yucatán*, 1:51) reads: "They also had knowledge . . . of the flood and that the world must come to an end with fire, and to show this they made a ceremony and painted a *lagarto* [iguana or crocodile] which signified the flood and the earth, and on it they placed a great mound of fire wood, and set fire to it." The author goes on to describe briefly the fire-walking rite. The Spaniards use *lagarto* loosely; the reference could be to crocodile or iguana.

An entry in the Motul dictionary reads "*Tan cucul a*: a bottomless thing without floor; also, hell [*el infierno*], an ancient word." *Tan cucula* literally means "in the midst of the waves," for the *h* of *ha*, "water," frequently drops out when the word is attached to another. Since hell is a Christian concept, I think *infierno* must be taken here in its literal meaning, the lower region. Indeed, an underground chamber, such as that holding mill machinery, is called *infierno* in Spanish.

Finally, we have the statement by Lizana that the Maya worshiped the crocodile. The first statement informs us that the lizard-crocodile represents the earth; the second that there was a great sea below the earth; the third that the crocodile was worshiped (there is much confusion between crocodile and lizard, probably because of shifts in cosmological ideas). Taken together, they are good evidence for the crocodile-floating-in-a-pond concept; archaeology dissipates any lingering doubts.

Lizana's observation that the crocodile was worshiped is confirmed by references to Itzam Cab, "Iguana Earth," and Itzam Cab Ain, "Iguana Earth Crocodile," as a deity in the Chilam Balam of Tizimin and Ritual of the Bacabs. In both books, he is also called Chac Mumul Ain, "Great Miry Crocodile." In the Chilam Balam of Chumayel, the name is written Itzam Kab Ain, which means "Iguana with Crocodile Legs," but this is probably a miscopying, perhaps a *lapsus calami*, or even a variant of the name, for the parallel passage in the Chilam Balam of Tizimin has, correctly, Itzam Cab Ain.

We must try to separate the sometimes inseparable—Itzam Na, the celestial manifestation of the Itzam, and Itzam Cab Ain, its terrestrial manifestation. This has been a source of much confusion in iconographic interpretation made worse by the artistic license of Maya sculptors and painters, whose productions would drive any zoologist round the bend. We can shed only crocodile tears for him, since those non-zoological appurtenances are what interest us, disquieting though their confusion be.

In the monumental art of the Classic period, there is a constant blending of the sky and earth aspects of Itzam Na, and that is surely done to call attention to the fact that the two are not separable. Itzam Cab, as the surface of the earth, has the regular attributes of earth and underworld, such as vegetation and death symbols, but these are combined with other signs referable to the sky. Thus, in the magnificent sculpture of the Panel of the Foliated Cross, Palenque (Fig. 2), the head of Itzam Cab, adorned with innumerable symbols of vegetation, is attached to the conventionalized body of an iguana decorated with signs representing sun, moon, and planets. This surely is to underline the great concept that Itzam Cab is merely the floor of a far greater entity, Itzam Na, "Iguana House," in effect, the Maya universe.

Palenque reiterates this doctrine in designs in stucco on four pillars. Itzam Na, its body completely covered with planetary symbols, forms a frame within which the ceremony is depicted (Fig. 6). The one head—at the bottom—is that of the Earth Itzam.

This could be taken further and an Itzam's planet-decorated body used as a frame without a vestige of a head.

As has been noted—but it is an important point so I have no hesitation in recurring to it—there appear to be two traditions in Maya thought with regard to the earth monster. One is that the surface of the earth is an isolated crocodile floating in a huge pond; the other, just discussed, is that the earth, as the floor of Itzam Na, is part and parcel of the great iguanas which reach from the zenith to the horizon and thence turn to form the surface of the earth.

Let us first review archaeological evidence on the saurian personification of the earth.

Each balustrade of the stairway of the north temple of the great ball court at Chichen Itza is carved with a tree of abundance, on the flowers and fruits of which birds and butterflies feed (Marquina, 1951:865). The roots of each tree grip the long-volute-nosed head of some reptile clearly representing the earth from which each tree grows. On Codex Dresden, page 67*b*, Chac is seated on a tree which rises from the head of a long-nosed god without a lower jaw. The tree is not as clear as it might be, but a branch with blossoms is visible behind Chac's shoulder and the glyph "on the *yaxche* (the ceiba tree)," which stands above, puts the identification beyond question. On Codex Madrid, page 96*a*, a tree rises from two heads of Chacs occiput to occiput.

The same concept occurs at Palenque where the trees of the Tablets of the Cross, the Foliated Cross, and the sarcophagus slab rise in each case from a grotesque non-human head with death symbols, such as fleshless jaws and symbols of the underworld, but are decorated with vegetal motifs (Figs. 2, 3).

This concept of an earth monster as the earth on which vegetation grows is not confined to the Maya area; Codex Borgia, perhaps from southeastern Mexico, has on page 27, as already noted, a regular field of maize plants growing on the back of a Cipactli crocodile. Another of many representations of trees which terminate in the head of a crocodile is in Codex Laud, page 38*b*, and flowers grow from the head of another on page 32 of the same codex.

Treatment of Maya earth monsters ranges from the purely naturalistic to near surrealism. The best example of naturalism in portraiture is the crocodile stretched across the top of Altar T, Copan, and dangling down on three sides (Maudslay, 1889–1902, 1, Plate 95), but even here mythology creeps in, for the three paws (the fourth is destroyed) are human hands. Water lilies are attached to each "wrist." Fish nibble at two of them and play around the third. The water lily (*nab*) is a frequent symbol of water in lakes and ponds and may be confined to the primeval lake beneath the earth. *Kaknab* is the Maya term for the sea; jaguars commonly are decorated with water lilies, I have supposed because they are beings of the underworld.

Imix, first of the Maya twenty days, equivalent of the crocodile Cipactli of the Nahuatl calendar, appears to derive from conventionalized water lilies. It is a sign for water and for abundance, but has also connections with the earth, like Cipactli, for the Quiche associate Imox, their form of the day Imix, which is Mox in Pokomchi with M'ox, their earth god (Thompson, 1950:89, 117). To close the circle, the Maya earth monsters are often decorated with water lilies (Figs. 1*a*, headdress; 4*g*) and may have the Imix sign on their foreheads (Figs. 7*m, n*).

In the more conventionalized representations of the earth monster and the rear head of the two-headed creature which represents the same thing, particularly in those shown full face, the following characteristics may be noted:

1. Very commonly fleshless jawbones, symbols of death and, by extension, the underworld realm of the death god, replace normal jaws (Figs. 3, 5*b, f*).

Fig. 5.—More Examples of Itzam Na. *a*: Front head of Itzam Na. Note Venus glyphs, scales on leg. Temple 22, Copan. *b*: Rear head of Itzam Na. Original was twisted to look up, here is shown horizontal. Note maize vegetation, bared jawbone, and remains of beard below. Temple IV, detail of lintel, Tikal. *c*: Pottery vessel. Note antlers and the face in the mouth. Santa Rita, British Honduras. *d*: Two-headed Itzam Na, body closer to a snake than an iguana. Palace, House E, Palenque. *e*: Ceremonial bar in the form of Itzam with planetary symbols. Stela 10, Seibal. *f*: Naturalistic Itzam Na. Altar D, Copan. (*a, b, f, after Maudslay; c, after Elliott Smith; d, after Seler.*)

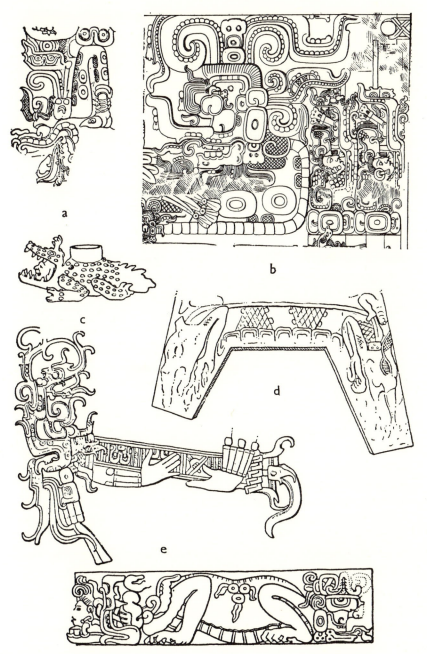

a

b

c

d

e

f

2. The lower jaw may be entirely eliminated, as is customary in representations of Cipactli (Figs. 4g, 7m).

3. The large eyes are square with rounded corners or almost round, a Maya convention for deities of animal origin (Figs. 2, 3).

4. Bone-shaped stoppers may be inserted in the nostrils (p. 297) (Fig. 1b before waist and behind buttocks).

5. Ear pendants hanging from earplugs are shaped as bones, again symbols of death and the underworld (Fig. 5b, f).

6. The Maya had trouble in depicting the long snout of the crocodile full view; it appears as a sort of elongated blob (Figs. 2, 3). In profile it is usually similar to the pendulous nose of the long-nosed god, but more horizontal and often turning up at the end (Fig. 7).

7. A *kin* ("sun") glyph is very often set in the forehead. This may be replaced by a Kan cross (Figs. 2, 3).

8. As noted, an Imix sign may occupy this position or, very rarely, an *ik tau*, sign of life, from which plants sometimes grow (Codex Madrid 97d–98d) (Plate 15).

9. Often, fairly naturalistic representations of maize or the *bil* sign (growth affix, p. 226) project from both sides of the head at about temple level (Figs. 2, 3, 7a, m, r). These maize plants and the maize plants growing out of the head (below) convinced Lizardi (1956) that this deity is in fact a maize god.

10. On top of the head is usually a tripartite sign of uncertain meaning. One element is the Saint Andrew's crossbands with extraneous decoration, either vegetal or bone plugs; the middle element looks like a large leaf bulging out at the base, but what it represents is unknown; the third element is a shell, symbol of the underworld, sometimes with little bone plugs attached (Fig. 3).

11. The same Saint Andrew's crossbands may cover the eye (Figs. 4g, 5f).

12. Sometimes a conventionalized maize plant or tree rises from the head (Figs. 2, 3; p. 219).

13. Water symbols may occur on the body. These are often the pawnbroker three-ball arrangement which has sometimes been interpreted as representing clouds, as in the *cauac* sign (Figs. 4g, 5f).

14. Planetary bands may extend on both sides of the head, forming the creature's body (Fig. 3).

15. A beard, deriving from corn silk (?), often hangs from the lower jaw, if present (Fig. 5*b*).

Of the above characteristics, some are definitely connected with the earth or the underworld (Nos. 1, 2, 5, 8, 9, 10 [in part], and 12); others have celestial associations (7, 10 [in part], 11, 13 (?) and 14). It should be remarked that the sun glyph (7) does not carry elements to convert it into the night sun in the underworld,

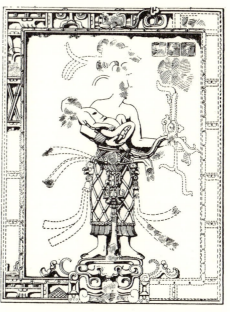

Fig. 6.—Itzam Na as Frame. Frame completely encloses figure within the *na*, "house." One of four scenes on pillars, Temple of Inscriptions, Palenque. (*After Maudslay.*)

notably crosshatching, the convention for representing black in sculpture. Both the Kan cross (7) and the crossbands (10, 11) are commonly found in planetary bands, and the latter are often infixed in the sky sign.

For further light on this mixture of celestial and terrestrial symbols, let us glance at celestial iguanas which seemingly represent the roof and walls of Itzam Na, that is to say, ones which are not completely horizontal but turn down at the end as though to represent the walls of the iguana house. Generally, the front head is that of a lizard without extraneous embellishments except that water may fall from the open mouth. The rear head is often upside down and is the head of the earth monster with many of the elements listed above as those of Itzam Cab.

In the case of Stela 25, Piedras Negras (Fig. 4*d*), the heads form part of the floor of the lizard house, and again, the rear head is upside down and has a bared jawbone, shells, the tripartite element (10), and, apparently, the sun sign on the forehead, but details are not too easily made out because of weathering. The rear heads of the comparable iguana houses of Stelae 11 and 14 at the same site are likewise upside down, with the seated ruler within the house, but in the somewhat similar arrangement on Stela I, Quirigua, the heads face outward and do not form a floor, nor is the rear one upside down.

Although one purpose of the above discussion of attributes is to hammer home the point that celestial and terrestrial elements of Itzam Na are intermingled precisely because they are parts of one undivided body or edifice, the main reason is to present arguments for accepting God K as a manifestation of Itzam Na, particularly in his vegetal aspect.

In the codices, God K is easily recognized by his long, branching nose which without much doubt derives from a pair of unfolding leaves, presumably of a maize plant, resembling those which sprout from Itzam Cab's head and which equate with the *bil*, "growth," affix (Catalog No. 130). Apart from the resemblance in shape, God K's curviform nose often has infixed the little oval with interior parallel lines and two circlets on the exterior which is the mark of the maize god and his glyph (Plate 8*i*). In one instance, God K's head is that of a snake on which sits a Chac with a bowl of maize on his back (Plate 10).

In the codical glyph of God K, this branching nose is absent. Instead, there projects from the forehead a circular or wedge-shaped element from which, in turn, issues a double flame-like motif. This is the key to the god's identification.

The glyph of God K in the codices is clearly the same as the glyph of the long-nosed god (Fig. 7) corresponding to the innumerable profile portraits of Itzam Na on the monuments, such as almost every personage depicted on a Classic period relief wears

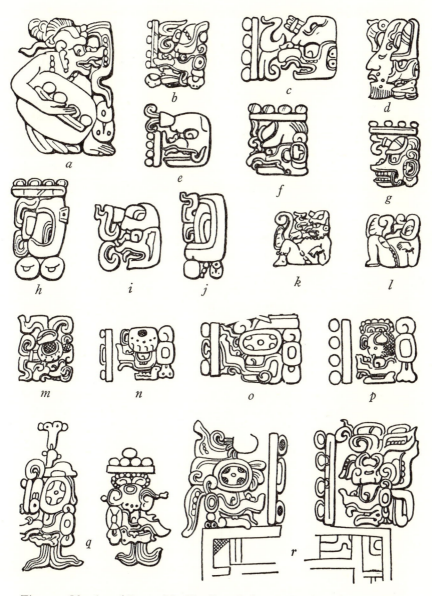

Fig. 7.—Glyphs of Itzam Na Kauil or Bolon Dz'acab. *a-h, p-r*: With number nine. *n, o, q, r*: Perhaps Uuc ti Cab, "Seven Earth." *h, j, l*: Symbolic forms with vegetation sprouting from hollow. *a-i, m-p, r*: Copan. *j*: Quirigua. *k, l, q*: Palenque. *(After Maudslay and Spinden.)*

as headdress or bears as manikin scepter or holds out right side
up or upside down with water pouring from it, and which, again,
usually combine celestial and terrestrial attributes (e.g., Fig. 1
left, inverted, with *kin* [celestial] and jawbone [terrestrial] or
Fig. 3 left with sky sign and no lower jaw [terrestrial]).

An inspection of glyphs of this god (Fig. 7) show that, apart
from the long, reptile nose, the chief characteristic is the foliage
emerging from the forehead. In some cases, this definitely takes
the form of the *bil* (vegetal ornament) and may have maize grains
(Fig. 7*a*, *m*). The overwhelming importance of this attribute is
shown by the fact that the symbolic form of the god's glyph is
precisely this vegetation element emerging from the hollow in the
god's forehead (Fig. 7*h*, *j*, *l*). As previously noted, it is highly
probable that this hollow represents either the seed or the soil or
both from which the vegetation grows, emphasizing the vegetal
nature of the god. As further evidence of this, the full portrait
glyph of this god shows him on his back with knees, shoulders,
and head raised (Fig. 7*k*, *l*) a posture seemingly reserved for earth
deities or personages from whom trees grow, both in Mexican
and Maya art.

An examination of some of the glyphic forms of the Classic
period makes clear why the foliage element emerges from the
hollow of the god's forehead on the monuments and in the codical
glyph of God K, but is merged with the nose of God K in the
codices. The vegetal element may be detached from the forehead
and appear as a separate motif before the god's face (Fig. 7*c*, *i*),
and from there it is but a short step to merging it with the nose as
in portraits of God K (Plate 8*i*).

The emphasis on vegetation makes me inclined to see in these
glyphs portraits, not of Itzam Cab—because death symbols are very
scarce and in the case of God K absent—but of Itzam Na Kauil,
"Iguana House Bountiful Harvest," the vegetal aspect of Itzam
Na, but I think this manifestation of the all-pervasive iguana god
had yet another name, to wit, Bolon Dz'acab.

Bolon Dz'acab, literally, "Nine or Many Generations," is defined in the Motul dictionary as "*cosa perpetua*," which might be
freely translated as "eternal" or "everlasting," a reasonable title
for a supreme god of the heavens and the earth.

226

Landa writes that Bolon Dz'acab was regent of one of the four groups of years, namely, of years beginning with a day Kan and assigned to the east. They were very good years, which for the Maya meant years of good crops. In the New Year pages of Codex Dresden, which has a different set of year bearers and a different sequence from those Landa describes, God K is patron of the first group of years, also assigned to the east, and in an arrangement which corresponds reasonably well with the Landa series. There are, accordingly, good grounds for identifying God K with Bolon Dz'acab. For the above reason and because glyphs of the Classic period corresponding to God K often have the number nine (*bolon*; it means also "many" or "innumerable") attached (Fig. 7*a–g*), Seler many years ago paired God K with Bolon Dz'acab and identified him with the rear head of the earth monster, seeing him as a water god. My view that he is a manifestation of Itzam Na as a deity of vegetation is not far removed; as I have reiterated, celestial and terrestrial aspects of Itzam Na are purposely mingled. In any case, identification of God K with Bolon Dz'acab, has, I think, been generally accepted by students.

Bolon Dz'acab plays an obscure part in the creation story of the Chilam Balam of Chumayel (Roys, 1933:99, 104, 105). There occurs the sentence "Three years was the time when he said he did not come to create Bolon Dz'acab as the god in hell." The other appearance of the god is in the struggle between the Thirteen Gods and the Nine Gods quoted on p. 281. This, again, is not easily understood, but it definitely shows Bolon Dz'acab as closely associated with growing crops, perhaps, above all, their seeds, and it is in accord with the hint in the first quotation that he was a god of the earth, but certainly it is in agreement with the view expressed above that he represents the vegetal aspect of Itzam Na, and, of course, by vegetal are meant food crops, in particular, maize. Once he sits at the center of a quadrupled *bil* element (Plate 6).

The link between Itzam glyphs with coefficients of nine and Bolon Dz'acab on the surface seems strong (but note that in the codices neither God K nor his glyph carries the number nine), but I cannot convince myself that the association of nine with Itzam Cab and the pairing of 9 Itzam Cab with 7 Itzam Cab (Fig.

7*n–r*) may not involve something quite different—perhaps with the Bolon ti Ku (p. 281). Suffice it that the personage with seven before his face—he is clearly an aspect of Itzam Cab or Itzam Cab Ain—might be Ah Uuc ti Cab, "Lord Seven Earth," mentioned in Ritual of the Bacabs, or conceivably Ah Uuc Cheknal, cited in a passage in the Chilam Balam of Chumayel (p. 339). The number seven does seem to be associated with the earth. The paired god with nine normally has Glyph 629 in his headdress (see also head beneath left figure of Figure 3).

Let us now turn to the relationship of Itzam Na with Schellhas' God D of the codices. That deity, as pictured on monuments and in the codices, is aged with a large eye which is round or a round-cornered square (generally indicative of an animal origin) and with a loop under it, a large Roman nose, a mouth which is toothless or with a single molar in the corner (sign of age), a prominent chin, and often with the area around the lips and chin and also the forehead painted yellow. Frequently, there dangles before the god's face a creature which has been identified as a centipede; its face, resembling the upper part of the *akbal*, "night," glyph, almost touches the god's hair. No obvious connection between God D and a centipede is known (Plates 4*c*, 8*f*, 15*a*, *b*).

Reasons for seeing God D as an aspect of Itzam Na are:

1. Landa gives the names of the patrons of the four sets of years as Bolon Dz'acab, Kinich Ahau, Itzam Na, and Uac Mitun Ahau, a death god; the sequence in the Dresden codex, pages 25 to 28, runs God K, whom we have seen is almost surely Bolon Dz'acab, Kinich Ahau, God D, and a death god. As three gods in each group not only pair, but are in the same sequence, Itzam Na and God D remain odd men out, each in the third position. It is a reasonable assumption that they are the equivalent one of another, or, more probably, that God D is yet another aspect of Itzam Na.

2. We have seen that Itzam Na was regarded not only as the creator, but as the chief god in Yucatan. We also know that he was an important deity in other parts of the Maya area. He should therefore occupy a prominent position in the codices. Gods C and D are the only important gods in the codices not satisfactorily identified. For sundry reasons God C does not seem eligible, so

we are left with God D as a pair for Itzam Na. The Chicchan god, the only other possibility, is surely too young to be a creator god and chief god of the Maya pantheon.

3. In a prayer previously cited, Itzam Na is addressed as Ah Tepal, "Ruler." The titular glyph of God D is *ahaulil*, "rulership."

4. God D's head may be set in the mouth of an Itzam (Fig. 4*b*). Such a placement apparently indicates that the god in question is an aspect of Itzam Na. For example, Kinich Ahau's head is often placed in the mouth of Itzam Na, but as his full title, Itzam Na Kinich Ahau, demonstrates, he is an aspect of the iguana god.

God D has no apparent connection with rain, so he probably does not primarily represent the rain-sending Itzam. Rather, in view of his age and the fact that Itzam Na is equated with God the Father and is a recognized creation god (p. 206), we are justified in regarding God D as primarily the creator and anthropomorphic aspect of Itzam Na.

Mention should also be made of Amaite Kauil or Amaite Ku (*ku* is "god"). *Amai* in Yucatec means "corner," but "flute" or "whistle" or the wood of which they are made in various Choloid and Maya-Chiapan languages. However, "cornered" (with participial-*te*) reminds us of the four sides of Itzam Na and the four corners of the world at which gods were set, and which, of course, corresponded to the corners of Iguana House. Amaite Kauil was the countenance or patron of katuns I Ahau and 8 Ahau and so must have been extremely important. Roys was inclined to identify him and Amaite Ku with Itzam Na Kauil, a view with which I entirely concur.

Itzam Na was also a god of medicine. He was invoked, together with Ix Chel and others, at the feast of doctors and sorcerers in Zip. Also, Lizana tells us, he was able to cure the sick and even bring the dead to life. People came from all over the land to his shrine, and for that reason he was known as Kabul, "Maker with his hands," but I suspect the name was applied to him in his role of creator; it seems to be the equivalent of Bitol, "Maker," title of the Quiche creator.

Lastly, before we can leave this all-pervading deity, we must review the documentary evidence that Itzam Na, in his earth aspect of Itzam Cab, functioned also as a fire god.

In an incantation for cooling water on the fire in Ritual of the Bacabs (Roys, 1965:49–50), the hearthstones are called the head of Itzam Cab; the sticks of firewood, his thighs; the blazing fire, his tongue; and the pot on the fire, his liver.

Pib is the pit oven in which the Maya bake food, usually for ceremonial occasions, but at times in secular cooking. A pit is dug and a wood fire lit on the floor, and over this are placed stones. When the fire burns out, the food, wrapped in banana or *platanillo* leaves, is placed over the raked stones and ashes and the pit closed with earth on top. The food cooks with the retained heat.

There is an incantation in Ritual of the Bacabs (MS:183) for opening the *pib*, that is, removing the earth, the closing words of which are: "Open your mouth, Itzam. Lo it is broken apart." Roys supposed, correctly one can be sure, that Cab after Itzam had been accidentally omitted. Here Itzam Cab may have been addressed as an earth god, as a god of fire, or, most probably, as both.

In an incantation for the placenta in the same book (MS:177) occur the words: "When I cast it [presumably the placenta] in the bowels of Itzam Cab." As Roys notes, it is still the custom in Yucatan to bury the placenta under the hearth. Among the closely related Maya of Socotz, British Honduras, it is placed on the hearth, and a fire is lit over it. The bowels of Itzam Cab are therefore either the hearth or the ground beneath the hearth. The ceremony takes on more meaning when it is remembered that the earth symbolizes creation (pp. 294–96).

Archaeological evidence confirms the above identification; the head of Itzam Cab, with jawbone or without lower jaw, may wear the fire glyph (563) as his headdress (Glyph 1035), indicative of his connection with fire.

There is also supporting data from the Mexican plateau, where Xiuhtecutli, the fire god, may be addressed as Tlalxictentican, "He who is at the Edge of the Navel of the Earth." He is also called Tlalxicco Onoc, "He who is Stretched Out in the Place of the Navel of the Earth." Ayamictlan, perhaps "He who is Among the Clouds of the Land of the Dead," is another of his names (I am indebted to Charles Dibble for help in translating these Nahuatl terms). Moreover, it is Xiuhtecutli who is at the center of

Fig. 8.–Ruler with Mani-
kin Scepter. Typically a
snake replacing one leg
serves as handle of the
scepter. Note the foliage
from the forehead and
fish nibbling at water lily
motif in the headdress.
Stela 7, Machaquila.
(*After Ian Graham.*)

page 1 of Codex Fejérváry-Mayer, and from whom grow the four world directional trees.

These Mexican links between fire and earth gods confirm the evidence that Itzam Cab was also a deity of fire. For the Maya, whose territory sheltered more than one active volcano, a residence of the fire god beneath the surface of the earth is logical.

Maya art of the Classic period is seldom free of representations of Itzam Na in one or another of his manifestations. This is partly a reflection of the overwhelming importance of the god, but, I think, much of it is the outcome of efforts of members of the ruling class to identify themselves with this supreme power.

Thus, rulers had themselves portrayed seated in niches set in the roof and walls of Itzam Na, and here, I think, we are faced with some inflated notion of grandeur; the ruler is proclaiming himself as something like king of kings, ruler of the world, regent on earth of the great Itzam Na—a sort of divine right of kings which would have turned James I green with envy.

Such representations are rare; it is rather the surfeit of attributes to an extent far beyond the point of monotony which I have in mind—headdresses laden with masks of Itzam Na one above another, the so-called manikin scepters, the ceremonial bars, the Itzam heads, right way up or upside down, from which flow streams of water, all of which the ruler or priest wears or holds, surely to make patent his affinity with the omnipresent and all-powerful iguana god.

Clearly, those Maya rulers would exalt their fame by clothing themselves in the finery of their maker. There is nothing original in this. In many parts of the Old World the same custom obtained; indeed, there is no need to cross the ocean for a parallel—Aztec rulers donned the clothes of tribal gods.

It is not surprising that Maya rulers should thus wish to identify themselves with Itzam Na. He pervaded all aspects of life. He was the creator to whom all men owed their very existence; mankind—in fact, all creation—depended on his caprice as giver of the two essential requisites of life: rains at the right time and fertile soils. He controlled the lesser beings who moved across the skies or dwelt on or in the earth. He gave life, but he could take it away and then, if he so willed, restore it again, even to the dead. As the house which sheltered the world, he was protector of all.

His many names are consonant with his multiple activities. To the student they are confusing and seem endless, but there is nothing unusual in such an arrangement. Other Maya deities bore sundry names to cover diverse activities, and the same is true of Aztec deities. *A Smaller Classical Dictionary* lists for Jupiter, who, like Itzam Na, started off as lord of heaven, no less than seventeen names referring to his many activities, and hints that there were others.

The conception of Itzam Na is, indeed, a majestic one. One realizes why the Maya rulers came at one time to consider him the only great god, for it rather looks as though the Maya of the Classic period had developed the cult of Itzam Na into something close to monotheism, with all other beings, such as sun and moon, probably the Chacs, and so on, as Itzam Na's servants or his manifestations, expressed by setting their heads in his open jaws. We find the god retaining his iguana form, but also developing two anthropomorphic manifestations, Gods D and K. Perhaps such ideas were too abstract to appeal to the Maya peasant, for, as we have seen, the cult of Itzam Na completely disappeared with the collapse of the old ruling class following the Spanish Conquest.

With the end of the Classic period, the fragile cult of postulated near-monotheism was overcome. It was still remembered six centuries later as a golden age before "idolatry" was introduced (p. 187).

The children of Israel found difficulty in adhering to monotheism notwithstanding the fulminations of their prophets; perhaps there was always greater difficulty in persuading the Maya peasant to abandon his down-to-earth Chacs for the monotheistic abstractions of the Itzam Na cult, but after the collapse of the old order and the end of the ceremonial centers there may have been no Maya prophets around to destroy the peasants' golden calves and altars to "Baal" and "Moloch."

SUN GOD AND MOON GODDESS

Because of the intimate relationship between sun and moon,

they will be discussed first as a pair and then as separate personages. Both are prominent on the monuments of the Classic period and in the hieroglyphic books, yet neither receives much attention from present-day Maya largely, I think, because both pagan personages have been merged to varying degrees with Jesus and the Virgin Mary, respectively, identification of the moon with the Virgin Mary being far stronger. Vestiges of the couple's former importance are found everywhere in myth and obsolescent rite.

Belief that the sun is husband of the moon is, or was, held by the Yucatec, Mopan, Lacandon, Chorti, Kekchi, and Cakchiquel. Chief dissenters from this view are the author of the Popol Vuh and the Maya of Chiapas.

The Popol Vuh, sacred book of the Quiche, after recounting the adventures on earth of the twin-brother heroes, concludes with the information that they ascended to the sky to become, respectively, sun and moon. Because of their names I suspect the identifications. One was called Xbalanque, (the prefixed X- indicates diminutive according to Recinos), but Balamque is the title of the sun god among the Kekchi, from whom the Quiche seem to have borrowed parts of the myth, and means "Jaguar-sun"; the other was Hunahpu, a day name corresponding to Ahau in Yucatec. Ahau was the day of the sun and Ahpu means "Hunter with Blowgun." In the Kekchi myth, the sun was a hunter and was closely linked with his blowgun. Accordingly, both twins were called sun in the Popol Vuh version. Apart from the fact that in no other source is the moon regarded as masculine, the present-day Quiche of Chichicastenango, the original home of the Popol Vuh, look upon the moon as feminine and call her Grandmother, whereas they refer to the sun as Grandfather. Alternatively, moon and sun are known as Mother and Father (Schultze-Jena, 1946: 29; Bunzel, 1952:266).

In Tzotzil-Maya belief, the sun is son of the moon who is equated with the Virgin Mary—they even recite the Hail Mary to her! His father was Saint Joseph. Clearly, Christian influences have made a strong impact on old pagan belief. Indeed, Jesus and the sun are partly merged and partly confused with one another. On the other hand, the Tzotzil retain the names Holy Father and Holy Mother for sun and moon respectively, from which one may conjecture that formerly they, too, accepted the general Maya pattern of sun and moon as spouses, as indeed do their neighbors, the Tzeltal Maya.

Many incidents of sun's and moon's life on earth before they took up their celestial duties are given at length in chapter 9 (pp. 355–68). The exploits of sun as a hunter, his taking the form of a hummingbird to woo moon, their flight and uncommonly tempestuous married life, and her elopement with the king vulture have entertained generation after generation of young Maya.

Popular explanations for eclipses, solar and lunar, vary considerably. Among the Maya of the Peninsula of Yucatan, as well as among the Tzeltal and Kanhobal Maya, it is widely held that eclipses are caused by marital quarrels between sun and moon; sun is taking it out on his wife for her wanton ways when they lived on earth or because she is a talebearer. The Palencano Chol and some Yucatec believe that lunar eclipses are caused by a jaguar, a variety of ant called *xulab* in Yucatec, or by certain demons. Everywhere it is customary to make much noise to distract the attention of the aggressor and save the attacked moon or sun. The people beat drums and tin cans, fire off guns and rockets, and hurt dogs to make them howl. The writer Fuentes y Guzmán tells how, about 1665, the Pokoman Maya of Mixco tried to kill the local priest because he sought to stop a "ceremony" during a lunar eclipse. The Indians beat drums, planks, pieces of iron, hoes and iron gratings, and shouted and wept, declaring that they wanted to help the moon.

A common Maya belief is that the moon is less bright than the sun because the sun plucked out one of her eyes when people complained that they could not sleep since it was as bright by night as by day. Others say she lost one eye in a fight with the sun.

THE SUN GOD

Principal names for the sun or sun god in the Maya area are: *kin*, "sun" or "day" (Yucatec, Mopan, Putun, Palencano and Manche Chol, and Chorti); Ah Kin, "He of the Sun" (Chorti); Kinich Ahau, "Sun-face" or "Sun-eye Lord" (Yucatec); *kih* (Quiche, Cakchiquel, Zutuhil, and Pokoman); *ki* (*kih?*) and

Kitix (*tix* signifies god, Ixil); Balanke, "Jaguar-sun," and *sac ke*, "bright" or "white sun" (Kekchi); *kih sac*, "bright" or "white sun" (Cakchiquel); *kak* or *kakal*, "fire" or "fiery" (Tzeltal, Tzotzil, Tojolabal, and Chicomucelteca); Hun Kak, "Unique Fire" (Lacandon); *ku* (Chuh); and *tzaiic* or *tz'aic* (Jacalteca). Since highland final *h* corresponds to final lowland *n*, *kin* and *kih* are the same, and *ke* presumably is a variation; one may say that *kin-kih* and *kak* or *kakal*, "fire" or "fiery," cover the whole Maya area with minor aberrations.

Certain titles of respect survive: Our Father or Grandfather (Palencano, Quiche, and Jacalteca); Our Lord (Kekchi, Cakchiquel, and Lacandon [Ciyum, contraction of Cit Yum?]); and Holy Father (Tzotzil and Tzeltal). No doubt many titles along those lines are now lost. A Tzotzil name, Nichimsat, "Eyes of God," is reminiscent of Yucatec Kinich Ahau.

No Maya group appears to have subscribed to the view that the sun was a creator god; information is scanty, but such as exists on the matter has the sun as the son of, or created by, some other deity.

The sun god is represented in the art of the Classic period as aged with a square eye with a loop beneath and a strong Roman nose. In the codices, as noted above, he is distinguished from the aged God D only by the addition of the four-petal *kin* sign—and even that may be omitted—a sort of curly "barbel" dangling from a corner of the mouth, such as the Chacs have, and usually a spiral, decorated with little square-to-round attachments, which protrudes from behind his nose as seen in profile. The incisors of the upper jaw are filed to the shape of a squat T, but that feature is often hard to distinguish in the codices (Fig. 9). Skulls from Maya burials at times show similarly filed teeth, perhaps indicating that those individuals had been dedicated to the sun or perhaps were priests (*ah kin*). The pupil of the eye is set in the upper inner corner of the eye. The first Spaniards encountered Maya who squinted, and from Landa we know that was deliberately arranged in childhood, again, perhaps, to indicate a devotee to the sun or one who would be a future priest.

However, as the personification of the day Ahau, sun is usually shown as a handsome youth with an almond eye. That Ahau, meaning "Lord," is the sun is made clear by the fact that the equivalent name in some highland tongues is Hunahpu, the hero twin who, after his adventures on earth, became the sun. Furthermore, an Ixil name for the day Ahau is Kitix, meaning "Sun God." Ahpu, another name for the sun, means "He with the Blowgun," and, in fact, the youthful sun on earth carried a blowgun. Lastly, since XAhau, "Lady Ahau," was a name for the moon goddess in some highland languages and she was the sun's wife, it is logical that her husband should bear the title Ahau.

Further complicating the situation, the day Ahau may be repre-

Fig. 9—Sun God. Stucco head with typical filed teeth and a curlicue at each corner of the mouth. Pupils in lower, instead of upper, corners of the eyes and suppression of the top part of *kin* sign in the forehead perhaps because of the position of the head high on roof comb. Palace, Palenque. *(After A. Ruz.)*

sented as the head of a vulture, a monkey, or a being with a long nose. To speculate on those variants would take more space than is available.

We are surely dealing with a dual aspect of the sun: the youth who courted the moon and had various adventures before taking up his duties as the sun (p. 355) serving as the day Ahau; and the aged sun god in the sky, associated with Itzam Na (God D) and as such at times called Itzam Na Kinich Ahau, functioning as the *kin* sign (and as the *kin* part of the month Yaxkin and patron of that month).

The glyph of the aged sun god and the symbolic form of the

kin sign usually have a sort of "tail" attached as an affix to the right of or below the head. This may represent a conventionalized bunch of cords standing for *tab*, "cord," for *u tab kin*, "the sun's cords," is a name for the sun's rays. It does not occur with the youthful sun god because, if I am right, the youthful sun was on the stage before the sun rose in the sky.

Sun was more dreaded than loved, undoubtedly because unless the rain gods intervene he will scorch the crops. In the codices, his aspect is always malignant, with drought and bad weather what he has in store for mankind. On the other hand, among the present-day Tzotzil, it is held that sun protects man with his light from the powers of evil which are abroad in the dark (Guiteras, 1961:287, 294, 301). The Tzotzil also pray to the sun for health, and a similar belief probably exists among the Chorti, for they regard him as patron of sorcerers and curers. The Vienna dictionary has an entry which reads: "idol whom they adored who was a man for having discovered the art of writing [*letras*] of this land Ytzamna, Kinchahau." López de Cogolludo, who drew extensively on the Vienna dictionary for his information on Maya gods, dropped the Kinchahau and assigned the discovery to Itzam Na, whereas it was clearly the Kin[i]ch Ahau aspect of the god who should be credited. This is understandable, because days *(kin)* were the basis of divination, and priests were called *ah kin*. Wisdom (1940:399) notes that Ah Kin, the sun god, is in Chorti belief, patron of knowledge and power, which would agree with that role of patron of priesthood and writing.

As previously remarked, there is little evidence of present-day worship of the sun. The Cakchiquel of Panajachel (Tax, 1951: 559) invoked him formerly, for old people uncover or kneel facing him at sunrise, saying as they kiss the earth: "Now you have arrived again, our señor. Then give us permission to eat and drink this day. Do not make us dispirited [*no desmayes*] in our daily work. We hope you will let us live another day." Similarly, Guiteras (1961:97) notes that a few Tzotzil of Chenalho, facing the sun, pray to him at sunrise and sunset for health so that they may be able to work hard. They do not perform this rite on a cloudy or rainy day. The Chamula Tzotzil burn incense to the sun for recovery from sickness, and men pray to him for a wife just as the women pray to the moon for a husband (Pozas, 1947: 452–53). It is interesting that the health aspect is stressed. Perhaps that arose because sun was husband of moon, patroness of illness and medicine. Pilgrimages were made in times of pestilence to the shrine of Kinich Kakmo, who, as we shall see, was an aspect of the sun.

Heads of gods were substituted for the numbers one through thirteen somewhat frequently on the monuments of the Classic period and quite rarely in the Dresden codex, apparently with the ideas of calling attention to the Maya belief that numbers were gods (part of the deification of time which was so important in Maya thought) and of adding to the grandeur or beauty of a text, somewhat like illumination of initials in mediaeval manuscripts. Portraits of numbers fourteen through nineteen combine a jaw-bone and sometimes a "percentage" sign (both symbols of the death god, deity of the number ten) with the head of the god of the second digit. For example, the god of the number eight is the maize god; the head for eighteen is that of the maize god with the death attributes of the god of ten added. The system corresponds to our "teens"—eight and ten—and conforms to the Maya system of expressing those numbers in speech.

In this series of deified numbers, the aged sun god personifies the number four, the association probably having arisen from the fact that four is the number of the four world directions, and four is man's number, man being to a certain extent under the protection of the sun god. Deification of numbers is a very old Maya concept, for there are examples of head numbers on quite early stelae.

There is also a system by which thirteen days in sequence starting with Caban (day seventeen) are similarly associated with the gods of numbers one through thirteen. Thus Caban is the day of the moon goddess who personifies the number one (Thompson, 1950: 88–89). Ahau, which, as we have seen, is the day of the sun god, fits this pattern, for it is the fourth day in the series starting with Caban, and we have seen that four was the number of the sun god.

There is no evidence that the sun god was head of a war cult as he was in Central Mexico in connection with the military orders of Jaguars and Eagles.

At sunset, the sun god descended into the underworld, land of the dead, and, according to Lacandon belief (Amram, 1942), lowering himself from his hammock, was carried on the shoulders of Sucunyum, older brother of Hachacyum, through the underworld. There was a halt at midnight for a snack; at dawn, having reached the eastern side of the world, sun was ready to cross the sky again (in modern belief the vehicle may also be a chariot—European influence). In Mexican belief, he was transformed into a skeleton during the infernal journey and had to be clothed again with flesh and blood to give him strength for his diurnal journey. That view was probably held by the Maya, but confirmation is lacking.

Because of his nocturnal journeys, sun, a celestial deity, was one of the nine lords of the night and the underworld (he was ninth in the series), one of the cases in which a Maya god belonged to two diametrically opposed groups. As lord of the night, he appears in inscriptions commonly with the addition of crosshatching (the method of representing black on the monuments) or other symbols of the underworld.

An aspect of the sun god or a subsidiary solar deity is Kinich Kakmo, "Sun-face (or eye) Fire Macaw." He appears in Codex Dresden with macaw head and human body carrying a burning torch, the symbol of drought or burning heat, in each hand; on the monuments his glyph is the head of a macaw with the *kin*, "sun," glyph before it. On Dresden 40*b*, the number four substitutes for the *kin*, confirmation that the sun is patron of number four.

The early writer Lizana reports that there was a temple of Kinich Kakmo on the north side of the plaza of Izamal (north was associated with the sun god). It was said that this god descended at midday to burn the sacrifice, flying like a macaw. In times of pestilence, men and women flocked to his shrine with offerings. As we have seen, the sun god was a patron of health, so we are probably not far in error in seeing in Kinich Kakmo a manifestation of Kinich Ahau, particularly since the sun is known as *kak*, "fire," in several Maya languages.

I suspect that the solar cult was fostered by the hierarchy; when that disappeared the Maya peasants ceased to pay much attention to the sun god.

The Lacandon have a god called Acan Chob or Chi Chac Chob who is said to have been the husband of Acna, the moon goddess. As the spouse of that lady was the sun, and as *chob* means, according to Tozzer, "squint-eyed," it seems certain that this is a name for the sun god, for he was squint-eyed, being depicted with the pupil in the upper inner corner of his eye. Bruce (1967:98–99) has Ah Kin Chob, which could mean "Lord Sun (or Priest) Squint Eye" as the husband of Ix Chel, that is, the moon goddess in her childbirth aspect. This greatly strengthens the case for identifying this Chob, "Squint-Eye," as the sun god, but Bruce says that he is the lord of the milpa and regards him as probably the same as the young maize god of the Dresden codex! Unfortunately, Lacandon culture and religion are now in complete collapse.

According to other sources (Baer and Baer, 1952:234, 252; Tozzer, 1907:95; and Duby, 1944:32) he helped Hachacyum, his father-in-law, make the heavens and the underworld, making firm the foundations of the earth with huge rocks and crossbeams. He taught the Lacandon to make bows and arrows. During eclipses, men chant to him to persuade Hachacyum to stop the eclipse lest the world end. Can this be a garbled memory of prayer being addressed to him, as sun god, to stop the eclipse (stop fighting with moon)?

THE MOON GODDESS

Names for the moon as a heavenly body are *u* or *uh* in lowland and Chiapan languages; *po* in Kekchi, Pokomchi, and related Pokoman (note: *po'o* in Mixe and *poya* in Zoque, both non-Maya); *ik* in the closely related Quiche, Cakchiquel, and Zutuhil; *ich* in Ixil and Uspanteca; and *kia* in Mam. Titles of respect accorded the moon goddess are: Our Mother (Lacandon, Palencano Chol, Chorti, Tojolabal, and Mam); Holy Mother (Tzotzil and Tzeltal); Mistress (Ix Ahau or Xhau in Mam, Jacaltec, Aguacatec, Tojolabal, and Chuh); and Grandmother (Quiche and Cakchiquel). In Yucatan, Colel, "Mistress," seems to have been shared by the moon goddess, the Virgin Mary, and another deity (p. 272).

As already noted, the moon goddess is widely held to be sun's wife, the exception being with the Tzotzil, who, having confused her with the Virgin Mary and the sun with Jesus, have espoused her to Saint Joseph and consider her to be mother of the sun.

In Yucatan, the moon goddess in her non-lunar aspects was surely called Ix Chel, although the direct evidence for that is non-existent, but her functions make it clear that Ix Chel was the moon goddess. The Lacandon apply that name to Acna, "Our Mother," the moon goddess and wife of the sun, when she functions as patroness of childbirth; in Yucatan, Ix Chel was goddess of child-birth, procreation, and medicine.

Since Ix Chel was one of the leading Putun deities, and considering she had a great shrine at Cozumel at one time under Putun control, it is probable that her name was introduced in Yucatan by the Putun Itza when they conquered Chichen Itza (p. 11). Note, also, that the capital of the Acalan Putun was at one time Tixchel, "at (the place of) Ix Chel." She was also an important deity of the Pokomchi Maya, and there is a report (To-villa, 1960, bk. 2, ch. 3) of a Manche-Chol deity Chuemexchel, almost certainly a garbling of Chuen *e* ("and") Ix Chel, since there is a deity Chuen. I suspect the name originated in the Choloid group of languages, but its meaning is not clear.

Landa notes that there was a festival in honor of Ix Chel, as goddess of medicine, on the sixth day of Zip, but he also states that on the previous day a dance called *okot uil* was performed. This is best translated as "dance of the moon," independent partial confirmation that Ix Chel was the moon goddess also in Yucatan. Elsewhere, he informs us that she was goddess of childbirth, and that it was customary to put her idol beneath the bed of a woman about to be delivered, adding that she was the goddess of making children (*diosa de hacer criaturas*), an apparent euphemism for sexual intercourse.

The Kekchi, Quiche, Tzotzil, and Chorti (under the guise of the Virgin of Esquipulas) are in accord with the Lacandon in regarding the moon as patroness of childbirth; the Tzotzil pray to her as Holy Mother for fertility and for a spouse.[1] Pregnant women are in great danger during eclipses, and the unborn child may develop deformities if they go out of doors when the moon is under attack during an eclipse (p. 235).

As patroness of disease, the moon goddess is invoked in a cure for ulcers under the name Ix U Sihnal, "Lady Moon of Birth" (*Ix . . . nal* is presumably the feminine version of *Ah . . . nal*, "owner") in Ritual of the Bacabs (MS: 107). In present-day Yucatan, certain forms of *kak*, a large group of pustule-forming diseases, including smallpox, are termed "*kak* of the Virgin." As the moon goddess came to be identified with the Virgin Mary (they share the title *colel*, "mistress"), it is highly probable that the moon goddess was once the patron of those diseases. Indeed, I am confident that certain almanacs in the Dresden and Madrid codices, in which the moon goddess, Goddess I, appears in all sections, treat of disease, (Thompson, 1958). In one picture (Plate 11*c* right) she has *kak* (glyph for "fire," rebus for *kak* diseases) on her back (*cuch*, "burden carried on back," rebus for "fate" or "destiny"—the Maya made great use of that kind of punning in their glyphs).

In Quintana Roo, the moon is still thought to have marked influence on the growth of some diseases and disorders (Villa, 1945: 136). The Cakchiquel believed the moon caused disease (Coto dictionary, *fide* Brinton, 1869), and, according to Paul Wirsing, she was regarded as patroness of disease among the Kekchi. On the other hand, she was not the only Maya deity concerned with disease, although, I believe, the most important, as the almanacs in the codices seem to demonstrate.

With regard to her sexual interests, sun and moon were the first persons in the world to have intercourse following the forming of her sexual organs by the cleft hoof of a deer. She was a wanton, having an affair with her brother-in-law, Venus, and eloping with the king vulture. The Quiche, too, regard her as goddess of procreation, and, as we have seen, the Tzotzil pray to her for fertility

---

[1] Letter of Paul Wirsing to Mrs. Elsie McDougall; Schultze-Jena, 1946:29; Wisdom, 1940:360,400; Guiteras, 1961:125,292; Holland, 1936:158.

and to win a spouse. They also regard her as goddess of pro-creation, and believe conception is most likely at full moon when woman is most fertile (Holland, 1963:158).

My Maya foreman from Socotz, British Honduras, Jacinto Cunil, said that his grandfather had told him that in olden times a man had intercourse with a woman only between full moon and its disappearance. Concerning the licentious side of the moon goddess, in a series of riddles recorded in the Chilam Balam of Chu-mayel (Roys, 1933:94), an initiate is ordered to bring the vile (*kaz*, but the word can also have sexual connotations and is applied to a ruined woman) thing or person of the night. The moon is the answer to the riddle.

Despite these laxities, the moon is sometimes addressed as virgin and, as noted, she is confused with the Virgin Mary. The reason for that is simple: the virgin, particularly in Spanish paintings of the Assumption, stands on a crescent. Such representations include the Virgin of Guadalupe and the Virgin of Izamal, patroness of Yucatan, both objects of great veneration by the Maya. The Maya, noting the crescent, not unreasonably decided the Virgin was a moon goddess. Indeed, the Tzotzil recite the Hail Mary to the moon.

The moon goddess is also connected with bodies of water. The Cakchiquel of Panajachel believe that the moon goddess is owner of Lake Atitlan and has her palace beneath its waters (information of Sol Tax). The Tzotzil of Chenalho regard her as goddess of one or more local lakes, offering her prayers and flowers; those of Chamula run to wells and deposits of water during eclipses to see the moon better (Guiteras, 1961:166, 292, Pozas, 1947:475–76). A Yucatec expression for lunar invisibility at conjunction is *binaan u tu ch'en*, "the moon has gone to her well" (Vienna dictionary; variant form in Motul).

Strong confirmation for association of the moon with bodies of water is to be found in the incantation for *anal-kak* ulcers in Ritual of the Bacabs already cited, which seems to have been closely connected with the moon because of mention of the title Ix U Sihnal, "Mistress of Birth," and because *kak* disorders seem to have been particularly under the care of the moon goddess. The passage in question (MS:109) reads: "Mistress Mother [Ix Ahau Na] in the heart of the sky. The child of Lady of the Sea [Ix Kaknab (written Kuknab)]; the child of She in the Middle of the Cenote [Ix Tan Dz'onot]; the child of She who Sits in the Mud, the child of She who Emerges from the Sand." The child appears to be the red *anal-kak* ulcers, object of the incantation. Roys translates Ix Ahau Na as "Palace-lady." *Na* means both "mother" and "house," and that is an alternative, but Roys had not spotted the lunar associations of the incantation and was probably unaware that Ix Ahau was a term for the moon in several Maya languages.

Titles such as Lady of the Sea, She in the Middle of the Cenote, She who Sits in the Mud, and She who Emerges from the Sand are in complete accord with this apparently widespread Maya belief linking the moon goddess with bodies of water.

The awesome cave of Bolonchen, in southern Yucatan, known as XTacunbilxunan, "Hidden or Guarded Lady," served as water supply when the town's wells ran dry. Stephens (1843, 2:148–55) described the festival when, the town's supplies having given out, the cave was first used. A chamber two hundred feet below ground was dressed with branches and lights, and the day was passed in feasting, music, and dancing. As the cave is half a league from the town and access to water requires an arduous descent into the bowels of the earth and a still more fatiguing ascent therefrom burdened with loaded water jars, it is hard to credit Stephens' explanation that the festival manifests the people's joy that a new water supply was available. The name, Hidden or Guarded Lady, was said to refer to an old tradition that a girl was concealed there by her lover, but I conjecture that that was a later explanation to account for the name, and that in fact Stephens witnessed rites formerly in honor of the moon goddess, once resident at the bottom of that stupendous cave, but memory of whom had been lost with three centuries of Christian dominance.

Such associations of the moon goddess with bodies of water find confirmation in the Central Mexican belief that the moon goddess resided in Tlalocan, abode of the rain gods. Indeed, in mainland Mexican art, the moon symbol frequently serves as a container for water.

Taken together, the above points supply good evidence that the moon was closely connected with water. Below are presented

245

arguments for seeing her also as a goddess of the earth and, by extension, of the crops it yields.

Caban, "Earth," is the day of the goddess; indeed, its glyph has as its main element a sort of query mark with a wavy tail, generally accepted as representing a lock of hair, symbol of women in general and of the moon goddess in particular who was *the* woman, first woman in the world, and mother of mankind.

The Kanhobal of San Miguel Acatan apply the title Our Mother to the earth and the maize as well as to the moon goddess, and the three become identified in speech and thought (Siegel, 1941:66). The Chorti believe the moon to have some connection with plant growth; all useful trees are hers, and to her they owe their productivity (Wisdom, 1940:400). The Tzeltal say one must never point a finger at the moon, our mother, or one's milpa will be parched (Castro, 1959). For the Huaxtec, a Maya group long separated from the rest of the Maya, the moon goddess is also goddess of earth and water (Stresser-Péan, 1952:291).

Paralleling Maya beliefs, the Mexican Tlazolteotl, also called Tozi, "Our Grandmother," or Teteo Innan, "Mother of the Gods," who appears to have been originally a Huaxtec moon goddess, was an earth goddess, patroness of childbirth, medicine, and weaving; and among the Cora of west central Mexico, the moon goddess, also called Our Mother, was goddess of the earth and maize and wife of the sun (Preuss, 1912:liv-lxxiv).

I propose that the belief that the moon was also goddess of the earth and its products is very ancient and was probably widespread on the Formative horizon but lost ground in most parts of the Maya area to rival cults of the young maize god and of deified manifestations of the earth reptile.

The moon goddess was the first woman on earth to weave— she was weaving when she first attracted sun's attention—and so is a patroness of that craft. Her connection with weaving is further demonstrated by the Lacandon belief that she carries with her on her nightly journey across the sky her loom sticks to protect herself against possible attack from the jaguars to be let loose from the underworld when this world ends.

However, it is Ix Chebel Yax, wife of the creator (Goddess O), who is the real patroness of weaving. She has a hank of cotton thread in her glyph and sometimes has a spindle of spun cotton set in her headdress.

The sharing of this patronage of weaving by the two goddesses is understandable, for weaving, cooking, and washing are women's chief activities and those which set them apart from men. In times past—in theory at least—every woman wove and every man made milpa.

In that connection, one must consider an incantation in Ritual of the Bacabs (Roys, 1965: 162–63) addressed to Jesus Mary, also termed Ix Hun Ahau, "Lady 1 Ahau" or "Sole Mistress" (the latter seems preferable in view of the name Ix Ahau, "Mistress," applied to the moon goddess in the western highlands). There are references to the raw cotton, the spun yarn, the worked thread, the (gold) weaver's bar, and the (gold) spindle cup of Ix Hun Ahau. The evidence of the names—Mary, confused with the young moon goddess, and Ix Hun Ahau, if read "Sole Mistress"—support the moon as the objective of this invocation, but one cannot rule out her rival, the old Goddess O.

In Ritual of the Bacabs (Roys, 1965: 23–28), four Ix Chels, associated respectively with the world directional colors red, white, black, and yellow, are cited in an incantation for asthma and in association with the four Itzam Na. In another incantation (p. 53), the red and white Ix Chels are mentioned. Here she (they?) is termed "virgin," and her stone needle and thirteen balls of dyed thread are disclosed. The incantation is directed against the spider, which, because of its web, has an obvious affinity with a goddess of weaving; the title "virgin" is probably a borrowing from the cult of the Blessed Virgin Mary.

The composer of Ritual of the Bacabs assigned world colors and sometimes world directions to so many persons and things that one is at a loss how to take the reference to four Ix Chels with their colors. I incline to the view that there was only one Ix Chel, that the mention of four was merely a bit of abracadabra, and that a lot of these associations of objects with world colors similarly were recited to impress the patient but in fact had been manufactured out of whole cloth by the author.

We have noted that the moon goddess was the personification of the day Caban; her youthful head is the head for the number one which she personifies, just as the day Caban is the first of the series of days associated with the gods corresponding to the same sequence of numbers.

To summarize this discursive survey: In the lowland Maya belief the moon was wife of the sun. She was patroness of women in general, of pregnancy, childbirth, and of procreation. She was goddess of medicine and disease and, as such, appears in almanacs treating of disease in codices Dresden and Madrid; she was connected with lakes, wells, and underground water deposits; and she was probably once widely accepted as patroness of the earth and its produce, although that side of her activities appears to have fallen largely into abeyance with the passage of time. She shared patronage of weaving with the old goddess (O of the codices).

She was commonly known by such titles as Our Mother, Holy Mother, Grandmother, Mistress (Ix Ahau, sometimes contracted to Xau) Colel, and probably Mistress of One or One Mistress (Ix Hun Ahau). Her commonest name appears to have been Ix Chel; other names or titles were: Ix U Sihnal, "Moon Patroness of Birth"; Ix Hun Zipit Caan, "Lady One Conjunction of Moon"; She in the Middle of the Cenote; and Lady Sea.

She can be identified without serious question with Schellhas' Goddess I of the codices (Plate 11).

It is strange that this goddess, so important in pre-Columbian days, so vivid and popular a character, should have receded so far into the background in the contemporary scene. She was not a deity imposed on the peasantry by the hierarchy. The rise of the European concepts of evil winds and the evil eye probably had some effect in diminishing her popularity, but I judge there is another explanation. The cult of the rain gods and other milpa deities was concentrated in the milpas, to which the friars did not penetrate. The personifiers of the Chacs could brandish the lightning symbols to their hearts' content, and the small boys tied to the legs of the altar to represent frogs could make as much din as they wished imitating the croaking of frogs; there was little chance that the representatives of the Catholic church and the Spanish crown would know what the men were up to. On the other hand, should their wives, whose environment was the town, hold some festival in honor of Our Mother the Moon in the village, the cura would be down on them like a ton of bricks; they could not carry on the ceremonies *sub rosa* because they never held ceremonies *sub arboribus*.

It is sad that this wanton, vivacious lady, whose doings arouse our interest and excite our sympathy, should now be taking her last curtain calls.

GODS OF THE PLANET VENUS

Information on the cult of Venus derives largely from six pages of Codex Dresden covering tables of heliacal risings of the planet after inferior conjunction and its "stations" together with texts and pictures. The former give prophecies, almost all melancholic, in agreement with Mexican belief that heliacal risings of the planet were extremely dangerous to various categories of humans and their crops.

The material in the codex, apart from closely paralleling data from Central Mexico, shows direct Mexican influence in the names of three of the five Venus gods. Accordingly, it is a fair assumption that these pages in the present edition of the codex were substituted for a different presentation in the original (lost) edition. Here, then, there is probably a break in continuity between the Classic and post-Classic periods. The Mexican influences are probably late and introduced, possibly in the tenth century, by the Putun Itza (p. 11), for the name of another regent, Lahun Chan, "Ten Sky," is not Yucatec, but attributable to the Putun or some other member of the Chol-Tzeltal-Tzotzil group of languages which substitute *ch* for Yucatec *c*, as sky in Yucatec is *caan*, not *chan*. The god's glyph comprises the number ten and the sky sign. As the cult is alien, the material very complex, and identifications of gods difficult, I shall not enter into detail; the material is covered elsewhere (Thompson, 1970).

Of the remaining four deities, suffice it that one, shown blindfolded, is almost surely Itzlacoliuhqui-Ixquimilli, the Mexican blindfolded god of cold who was also Venus as god of dawn. Another has a blue-green plumaged bird in the lobe of one ear, and a snake was probably inserted in the other as it protrudes beyond the god's profile about level with the ear lobe. The two together would form the name Quetzalcoatl, for the bird is probably the quetzal and *coatl* is "snake." The proposal takes on new strength from what appears to be an inverted conch shell, symbol of that god, set in the front of the headdress. Quetzalcoatl was definitely a god of Venus as morning star. Another has the head of a member of the cat family, perhaps a puma. His glyph comprises five elements, an uncommonly rare feature in Maya writing, and I think it is an attempt to write a Nahuatl name, for many Nahuatl names are polysyllabic. One element looks remarkably like a drawing of the constellation Orion.

The last of the five is the black-faced God L, a rare Yucatec god about whom little is known; I hesitatingly identify him as one of the Bacabs. Thus, only one of the five is Yucatec.

There are grounds for the belief that 1 Ahau, the ritualistic day for heliacal rising after inferior conjunction, came to be a collective title of the Venus gods. In a colonial almanac, the regent of a day Lamat, the glyph of which is the Venus sign, is described as "jaguar-faced 1 Ahau with the protruding teeth." Elsewhere Lahun Chan is said to have huge teeth, and a further indirect reference to him speaks of his having the head of a jaguar and the rear parts of a dog. Moreover, on the monuments of the Classic period, appearances of the day 1 Ahau are commonly linked to clauses with Venus glyphs.

This Venus cult exercised the hierarchy, but, because of its astronomical associations, it had little appeal to the Maya peasant as is shown by the very minor role the planet plays in present-day Maya life. The Kekchi Maya, and the Mopan Maya probably under Kekchi influence, regard the planet, whom they call Xulab, "Keeper(?) of Wild Animals," as patron of hunting. He is said to have wild animals in a special pen and to let them loose to be hunted by those who burn copal to him. This aspect of the cult probably arose from the fact that dawn is widely considered to be the best time for hunting. Among known Yucatec hunting gods, the name of the planet does not occur. The Kekchi also refer to the morning star as a (hunting?) dog running ahead of the sun god. Other names are Ah Ahzah Cab, "Awakener" (Yucatec and Lacandon); Xux Ek, "Wasp Star" (Yucatec); Canan Chul Chan,

"Guardian of Holy Sky" (Tzeltal); and, everywhere, terms meaning "big star."

RAIN GODS—THE CHACS

The Chacs or Chaacs, the Yucatec rain gods, are the recipients of more prayers and offerings in a pagan context than any other supernatural being, but one must never forget that the Maya regards himself as a good Catholic and makes no conscious division into opposing Christian and non-Christian groups of those to whom he prays.

The cult is very ancient, as portraits and glyphs of the gods on monuments of the Classic period and in the codices make clear, but it is confined to the lowlands; in the highlands of Guatemala and Chiapas the gift of rain is usually in the hands of mountain or earth gods. The Chacs were worshiped by the Manche Chol, for the vocabulary of their language carries these entries: *relampago* ("lightning") *u lem* or *leem chahac*, "lightning of Chac"; and *rayo* ("thunderbolt"), *chahac*. The Aulies have recorded a Palencano Chol story of Chahc, which they translate "Lightning," who went to stand above the water because it had already rained hard. He sent his servant to ask cloth from his (Chahc's) wife, but the servant found only toads who were her children in the house. The servant found Chahc's wife on returning again. She tore much cotton for Chahc, but it was not really cotton, it was cloud. "It rises for it will hold rain." As will be shown, frogs and toads are closely connected with the Chacs. This story makes clear that the Chac cult was prevalent among the Palencano Chol. Apparently, it did not extend to the Putun, whose term for lightning, *chauuc*, links up with a parallel derivation (with shift to Yucatec *cauac*) in Chiapas and elsewhere.

The Chacs of Yucatan find their first mention in Landa, who calls them gods of the cornfields and of the grains, but one of the ceremonies in which he specifies their participation was for rain. Landa also writes of the four Chacs associated with world directions and colors (East, red; North, white; West, black; South, yellow). Landa, unlike any other writer, inserts the word *xib*, usually "man" but here perhaps from an old root meaning "to scatter," before the word Chac.

Chaac, according to the Motul dictionary, was a man of great stature who taught agriculture and whom the Indians held to be god of bread, water (in the sense of rain), thunder, and lightning. It is quite clear that he was a god of the milpas and their produce only in the sense that unless the Chaacs sent the rains there would be no crops. *Chac*, now the commoner but probably less correct way of writing the gods' name, is an adjective signifying "red," "great," or "severe." The present-day Maya of Yucatan think vaguely of the Chacs as old, white-haired men, often bearded, and, in the opinion of a few people, tall. I think it is taken for granted that their features are human.

In present-day belief, there are four leading Chacs, known as Nucuch Chacob, "The Great Chacs," with the same color and directional associations as Landa reported. There are many other minor Chacs who will be discussed below.

The Chacs are generally accepted as being identical with God B of the codices, a deity who has a long pendulous nose, a scroll beneath the eye (the pupil of which is represented by a volute), a peculiar projection above the nose ending in a curl, and a mouth which is usually toothless but sometimes shows normal teeth. As in the case of the sun god, a thin, ribbonlike object with backward curve projects from a corner of the mouth, and frequently a similar object dangles from below the center of the upper jaw. The identity of these objects is uncertain, but I am inclined to see in them the flickering tongue of the serpent (Plates 4*a*, 8*a–c*, 10 *a*, *b*). Spinden (1913:62–64) and others have demonstrated conclusively that the features of this long-nosed god, who is equally common on the monuments, derive from those of a snake. Indeed, God B's head is sometimes attached to the body of a serpent or, in human form, he rides astride a snake (Plate 10*b*). As we shall see in discussing the rain deities called Chicchans, the Chorti Maya still retain the old tradition that these rain deities were snakes.

In the codices, the Chacs (I drop the name God B in favor of Chac) are associated with precisely the same world directions and colors as reported by Landa and modern investigators in Yucatan; frequently they perch on world directional trees, a feature not reported in modern sources. Both in the codices and on monuments of the Classic period, Chac holds an axe with a stone blade set in a wooden haft (Plates 4*a*, 8*a*), a feature shared with his Mexican cousins, the Tlalocs. The Mopan Maya of southern British Honduras call the small celts of polished stone, which they frequently find in clearing land for milpa, *baatchac*, "Chacs' axes," believing them to be the thunderbolts hurled by the Chacs. Sometimes, in the codices, the Chacs hold burning torches, symbols of burning heat and drought, for the Chacs can both send and withhold the needed rain.

The importance of the Chacs in Maya life is well demonstrated by the many divinatory almanacs covering farming activities in the codices, for in these the Chacs are dominant. Chacs are pictured, according to Schellhas, 141 times in Codex Dresden, just about half the total of all portraits of gods (the most numerous: the moon goddess, 51 times; death god, 33; God D, 19; God C, 17; and the maize god, 14).

A general term for all Chacs is Ah Hoyaob, "the Sprinklers" or "Urinators" (Redfield and Villa, 1934:115). In scenes in the codices, rain falls from between the legs of a Chac or a goddess, seemingly O (Codex Madrid 9*b*, 30*b*, 31*a*, 32*b*), and on Dresden 37*b* a Chac is making water. The urine terminates in the head of a heron, which is probably one of those Maya puns so often used: *bacha* means both "heron" and "to pour water from a narrow-mouthed vessel," in this case the penis.

Other scenes in the codices show Chacs or Goddess O pouring water from inverted bowls (e.g., Codex Dresden 36*c*, 39*b*, 67*a*, 74; Codex Madrid 9*b*, 13*a*, 14*b*); the Tlalocs are similarly pictured in Mexican codices, and in present-day belief the Chacs cause the rains by sprinkling water from gourds (Plates 9, 10).

Tozzer (1907:155) has Adz'enulob as another name for the Chacs, but this must be Ah Tzenulob, "Those who Support or Provide Others with Food," in agreement with the early definition of the Chacs as providers of food through the fructifying rains.

Many names for individual Chacs survive in Yucatan and Quintana Roo (Redfield and Villa, 1934:115–16, 339–55; Villa, 1941: 118), but there is uncertainty as to whether, as is now believed, these are titles of individual Chacs or collective titles. In connection with the association of Chacs with saints of the Catholic church, discussed below, Saint Michael has now become a sort of general of the Chacs, but that he is an intrusive alien is illustrated by the fact that he does not sally forth with the Chacs to pour water on earth.

The real chief Chac is Kunku Chac (*kun* can mean "tender" or "kindly"; *ku* is "god"). When the rains are due at the close of the dry season (around June 1 in Yucatan), the Chacs assemble at *chun caan*, "the bottom of the sky," situated in the east. Thence they ride forth on their horses, issuing from a doorway called *holhun taz muyal* (apparently, "thunder opening in the cloud layer") with Kunku Chac at their head. They ride across the skies, each with a gourd containing the rain water in one hand, brandishing a machetelike implement called *lelem*, "lightning," because it produces that phenomenon, to take up their positions at the four world directions. They are the gathering clouds which sweep westward.

Other Chacs in addition to Kunku Chac are XT'up Chac (*t'up*, "smallest," "youngest") also called Ah Chalen Caan Chac, "Clear Water Sky-chac" (but probably a corruption of the Ah Ch'alelem Caan Chac, "lightning-bringer Sky-chac"), and again Ah Bulen Caan Chac (but surely *buleu* or *buleb*, "jar"), "He with the Jar Sky-chac," a reference to the water jars carried by the Chacs (Plate 9, top). He carries a small gourd known as *zaayam* or *zaayab chu*, and as he rides over cenotes, the water, with a roar, shoots upward to refill the vessel; over milpas the water falls from it in torrents. *Chu* in fact signifies water carrier without specifying material, so the word is also applicable to pottery vessels such as rain gods carry in Maya and Mexican codices.

Ah Bolon Caan Chac, "Nine Sky-chac," "Innumerable Sky-chac," or "Virgin Sky-chac," is yet another of the group. Probably a long tradition lies behind this name, for heads of the long-nosed god with the *caan*, "sky," sign prefixed are common in the Classic-period inscriptions. This Chac is also called Bohol Caan Chac, "Hollow-sounding Sky-chac." As his name implies, he makes much thunder but little rain.

Then there is Ah Hadz'en Caan Chac, "Lash or Blow Sky-chac," for he makes thunderclaps which sound like the crack of a whip.

Perhaps a separate Chac, but I suspect merely a variant of one of the names of XT'up Chac, is Ah Lelem Caan Chac, "Lightning Sky-chac."

Ah T'oxon Caan chac, "Distributor Sky-chac," produces the fine enduring rain; Hopop Caan Chac, "Sets-light-to-the-sky Chac," causes the lightning; Mizen Caan Chac, "Sweeps-the-sky Chac"; Xoc Tun Caan Chaacob, "Keeping-count Sky-chacs" they keep count of the Chacs when they assemble, but *xoc* is also a mythical celestial fish); and Ah Ch'ibal Tun Chaacob, "Chacs of All the Generations," are other names for Chacs.

Bishop Landa writes of four deities, whom he calls the red, white, black, and yellow Pauahtuns, assigned to world directions and sequent years, but his account is confused, for he supposes that both Chacs and Pauahtuns were other names for the Bacabs. He says nothing of the functions of the Pauahtuns. They are next mentioned in the writings, dated 1813, of Granado de Baeza, cura of Yaxcaba (1845). There they are called Pahahtuns, are said to be rain deities, are associated with world directions and colors, and had by then come to be identified with Saint Dominic (east), Saint Gabriel (north), Saint James (west), and XKan Le Ox "Lady Yellow Ramón Leaf," alias Mary Magdalene (south). According to *hmen* informants of Redfield and Villa (1934:116), Pahuatun *(sic)* is an alternative name for Chac; in Quintana Roo the forms Papatun and Babatun occur, and there again they are regarded as alternative names for the Chacs. Indeed, the two occur together: Kan Babatun Chac, Ek Babatun Chac, "Yellow, Black Babatun Chac," and so on (Villa, 1941:118). They may originally have been winds as servants of the Chacs and later identified with them. Villa adds that Red Babatun Chac, in the east, is known also as Cangel (pronounced *canhel*).[2]

---

[2] Bishop Landa, in a somewhat confused passage, writes that in Kan years they set a statue of Bolon Dz'acab (p. 227) on a post and placed on its shoulders an *ángel* as a symbol of water. "And this year had to be good, and these angels they painted and made frightening. They carried it to the chief's house where was the other statue of Bolon Dz'acab." In the corresponding year of the Dresden codex presided over by Bolon Dz'acab, a Chac is carried on the back of a Bacab. There seems, therefore, ground for identifying Chac, who was no beauty, with this *ángel*. Beltran de Santa Rosa, on the other hand, defines *canhel* as "dragon,"

The many names the Chacs bear seemingly reflect the Maya custom of applying many appelatives to a single deity or group of deities, principally to underline his or their functions, a situation already encountered in reciting the designations of the moon goddess.

The chief Chacs, as we have seen, are thought to reside in *chun caan*, "at the foot of the sky," except when they take up their positions at the four points of the compass (or the angles between, as some believe) during the rainy season. On the other hand, the lesser Chacs, when not engaged in rain making, move through the forest and shelter in cenotes or caves (Villa, 1945:103). Indeed, scenes in the Dresden codex picture Chacs in or astride cenotes. One may also note that victims thrown into the cenote at Chichen Itza met and conversed with gods beneath the waters; as the cenote cult was primarily to petition for rain, one may conclude that those deities were Chacs as well as Itzam Na. The

---

suggestive of the celestial or earth dragon-monsters but also associated with good crops. We shall see *anhel* as a name for rain gods among the Chorti and for earth and rain gods among the even more distant Maya of Chiapas. It is therefore difficult to derive the name from the Spanish *ángel*. Apart from the fact that no Maya deities (except the bee gods) had wings, Landa would hardly have applied the Christian term angels to those frightening manifestations of paganism.

To add to the confusion, the four Pauahtun are termed Cangeles Ik, "Wind Canhels," in a creation story in the Chilam Balam of Chumayel (Roys, 1933:110). Note that *cangeles* is given the Spanish plural termination—in Maya, *canhelob*. Can Hel means "Four Succeeding-in-office-ones," and the *hel* glyph occurs in passages dealing with the succession of world directional gods. I think the resemblance of *canhel* to *arcangel*, Spanish for archangel, pronounced exactly the same as *canhel* except for *ar* (close to the Maya masculine prefix *ah*), best explains the identification of Archangels Michael and Gabriel with the Chacs (p. 255).

The only conclusion I can see is that Can Hel or Ah Hel (?) were widespread terms for groups of directional gods who succeeded each other in office at set times, whether they were Chacs, wind gods, or celestial monsters. As to confusion between wind and rain deities, wind gods are of scant importance among the lowland Maya, and wind gods which bring rain storms are closely connected with the Chacs, apparently as their henchmen.

There occur in the Chilam Balam of Tizimin (pp. 1, 10, 11) and of Chumayel (p. 92) yet other names for Chacs and rains. I include them in this footnote in order not to clutter the story of the Chacs with even more names. They are: Vulture Sky-chacs, Rabbit Sky-chacs, Woodpecker Sky-chacs, Deer Chacs, Crested Chacs, Chacs of Little Profit, Jaguar Rains, and *pek* (represented in the codices by pictures and the glyph of the homonym *pek*, "dog"). Some of these for the most part harmful rains are represented in the codices; a vulture stands in pouring rain, and the dog, for *pek* weather, has lighted torches, the symbol of drought, in his paws. See also Ah Chun Caan and Yaxal Chac (pp. 322, 326).

grand scale of offerings at that cenote leads to the further conclusion that the Chacs there were not mere underlings.

A word is in order about the belief that the four great Chacs
ride across the skies on horseback. As noted (p. *xvi*), this could
have arisen because the Maya, at first contact with the Spaniards,
thought horse and rider were a single being and related those New
World centaurs to the Chacs because of the lightning and thunderbolts they hurled (from their guns). A more important reason
for the connection lies, I think, in the story of the Four Horsemen
of the Apocalypse who ride on red, white, black, and pale horses,
almost a duplication of Maya directional colors, which may have
been confused with references to the four angels (the *canhel?*)
standing at the four corners of the earth (D. E. Thompson, 1954:
13). The Book of Revelation was assuredly an irresistible lure to
the Maya mystic.

Corresponding to the many names of Chacs, there are various
appelative and portrait glyphs of the Chacs in codices and on the
monuments of the Classic period. The glyph (668) of the Chacs
in the codices and also at Chichen Itza and Uxmal, but nowhere
else (good evidence that the codices were written in Yucatan),
is the back of a clenched first with the usual "jade bead" at the
wrist. The hand is personified by being provided with mouth and
vestigial nose; the squat T-symbol set in the middle serves as the
eye. Affix 103 is usually present. The T-symbol is the identifying
element of the day Ik, a term meaning in Maya "wind," "breath,"
and, by extension, "life." However, it clearly means also "germination," for plants grow from it (Plate 15*c*, *d*). The hand in
this position is perhaps to be read as *kab*, "hand," but also "to do
or make anything by hand." The whole probably means something like "causer of germination," an apt title for rain gods.

The Tlalocs, the Mexican rain gods, are so close to their cousins
the Chacs[3] that it is at least possible that some feature of the Tlaloc
cult unrecorded in the Maya area may once have been a feature
of the Chac cult. According to Mexican and Zapotec belief, the
rain gods had four great tubs in which they stored the rain; some

---

[3] They share world directional and color associations, have very close connection with snakes, carry axes and zigzag lightning sticks, invert jars to send
rains, send thunderbolts and lightning, comprise four (or five) principal deities
and many minor ones, and prefer child victims.

rain was good, but the contents of other tubs were harmful, causing mildew or frost. No such tradition appears to have survived
in the Maya lowlands, but in almanacs picturing the Chacs in connection with world directions and colors in Codices Madrid (3*a*–
6*a*) and Dresden (31*b*–35*b*), there are bodies of water contained
within the coils of snakes. In Codex Madrid, a Chac stands beside
each of the four ophidian containers; in Dresden, the Chac stands
in, squats on, or emerges from the open jaws of the snake container (Plate 4*a*), of which there are three, that which one would
expect in the first section being unaccountably absent. There
seems every reason to suppose that these snake containers correspond to the four tubs which in Mexican and Zapotec belief held
the rains.

Frogs, because their croaking announces the rains, have an intimate relation to the Chacs. They are the Chacs' musicians and
guests. A charming myth of the Mopan Maya of southern British
Honduras tells of the adventures of a boy who worked for the
Chacs (Thompson, 1930:149). Mischievously, he inverted the
Chacs' rain gourd and almost flooded the whole world; he opened
the wind bag, and the released winds howled and shrieked around
the world; he swept the frogs out of the Chacs' house unaware that
they were their musicians and guests. The Palencano-Chol legend
already cited tells us that the toads were the children of Chac's
wife and so presumably his also.

The special pets of the Chacs are the little black frogs with an
orange line down their backs known as *uo* (*Rhynophrynis dor-
salis*), who also gave their name to the second twenty-day month
in the Yucatec calendar. They burrow underground and, I suppose, hibernate during the dry season, and, as all Maya know,
their bodies are full of new-corn gruel.

In Codex Madrid, page 31*a*, frogs labeled with the four world
directional glyphs and spewing forth water surround Chac, from
whose lower quarters pours a stream of water (Plate 10, top),
and in the great ceremony for drought, *ch'achac*, "summoning
the Chacs," still held in Maya villages of Yucatan, a small boy is
tied to each of the four legs of the temporary altar. They represent
the frogs and imitate the croaking of that creature to attract the
rain by a process of sympathetic magic.

The above must read as a very dry bit of learned information. I wish, instead, that I could convey to readers the jubilant tenderness I have witnessed when a *uo* has been awakened from his sleep by the pick or shovel of one of my Maya boys in an archaeological dry-season dig. In a sense, the interest could be compared to that which a pedigreed bitch with month-old puppies excites, but there is much more to it than that, for there is a profound religious connotation; the *uo* symbolizes man's resistance to the evil forces of drought.

Similarly, the tortoise is an ally of the Chacs, but, unlike the *uo*, he is abroad during the dry season. His eyes fill with tears; he weeps for men's affliction, and, it is said, his tears draw the rains. In return, the pious milpero, when he fires his milpa, shouts first to the tortoise to warn him to save himself. The tortoise has on his plastron the *kan* cross, symbol of rain, and in the glyph of the tortoise carapace the *kan* cross is prominently displayed just as the head of the tortoise, when it serves as the month glyph Kayab, has the same *kan* cross in its eye. These are both elements of the folklore and mysteries of Maya religion.

Priest, noble, and peasant unite in worship of the Chacs, an understandable convergence of beliefs since drought was a constant anxiety of both the peasant and his parasites. The appearance of tortoise and frog in downpours of rain (Madrid 17*c*) demonstrates how elements of folk religion had won a place in the hieroglyphic books which only the hierarchy handled.

As to the Chacs' place in hierarchic religion, they, seemingly, were gods of the number six. The profile of the god corresponding to that number is characterized by a hafted axe set in the eye, and in that connection it will be recalled that the axe is an attribute carried by the Chacs, and that with it they caused thunderbolts. Some glyphs of God B (usually with -*te* postfix) in Classic-period texts show him holding an axe in front of his temple so that the blade almost touches his eye. Indeed, occasionally (e.g., Yaxchilan, L. 33, H1, St. 11, R3) the blade does in fact cover part of the eye. Despite the close connection between Chac and axe, and the axe in the eye of the god of number six, that deity lacks the typical long nose of the Chacs. Notwithstanding that breakdown, the association seems to hold because the day corresponding to the

259

number six in the sequence starting with Caban (p. 239) is Ik, but we have already noted that the Ik sign is the central feature in the codical hand form of the god's appellative.

The many glyphs and pictures of the Chacs in the Classic period (when some are hard to distinguish from those of Bolon Dz'acab) and in the codices demonstrate the outstanding importance of that group of gods, an importance shared by the rain gods in the hierarchic cults of ancient Oaxaca and the Mexican plateau. In all regions, the hierarchy needed to conciliate the peasant on whose labor and support the regime rested; an all-out effort to propitiate the rain gods might be expected to insure the prosperity of the community and certainly contributed to political stability.

The peasant's involvement was more direct and more emotional. Farmers' anxieties that the rains come when needed are worldwide, but, unlike the Old World farmer with a livestock economy of pasture, hay, and root crops to offset cereal loss, the Maya peasant, generally speaking, had all his eggs in one basket; he had no real livestock to spread the risk. For that reason, rites invoking the Chacs, particularly the *ch'achac*, "summoning the Chacs," held in time of drought with the participation of the whole male community, are charged with deep anxiety at famine's lengthening shadow. Those apprehensions find a temporary outlet in communal service.

The *hmen*, prayer-maker, must be engaged to carry out the ceremony; the altar with its four forked corner posts and leafy covering of green *habin* must be built. At noon of the first of the three days, all the men accompany the *hmen* to fetch uncontaminated water (*zuhuy ha*) from a distant cenote from which the Chacs fill their gourds when they water the young maize, reached only by crawling through a dark, slippery tunnel about a hundred feet long, assurance that no woman has contaminated the source by her presence. The difficult entrance and the snakelike movement of the torch-lit procession increase the feeling of awe which attaches to this ritual. In the evening the men return and hang the gourds of virgin water beside the altar; they swing their hammocks in the surrounding cleared space so that the continence of the whole community is insured for the three days of the rite. Incontinence by a single person would bring disaster; women are rigidly excluded from the proceedings, although kept busy enough preparing the food offerings. Oblations are made by the *hmen* at intervals during the second day.

On the third day, the rites reach their climax. Nearly two-score hens are sacrificed after *balche* liquor has been ceremonially poured down each beak; the altar is piled with preparations of maize of every sort and description, usually arranged in multiples of the sacred numbers four, nine, and thirteen: nine pails of soup; four times nine breadstuffs of one variety; nine more special breads; thirteen gourds of *balche*; and two shallow gourds of the same. The boy-frogs are tied to the four altar posts, and then one older man, impersonator of Kunku Chac, leader of the Chacs, is lifted by four men and carried to a cleared space about twenty-five feet east of the altar which represents *chun caan*, abode of the Chacs. This is done with care and reverence so that no bearer turns his back on the altar, where all the gods are now gathered.

The climax of the ceremony is near. The *hmen*, kneeling (a Christian position) before the altar and flanked by his two chief assistants, repeats the prayer summoning the gods; as he prays, assistants sprinkle *balche* on the altar and place more copal on a smoking incense burner. The "frogs" are croaking a special note to summon the rains, and from time to time Kunku Chac imitates with his voice the sound of thunder and brandishes his lightning stick. The various offerings of food are consecrated one by one to the gods and lifted from the altar. Then all retire some distance from the altar and in complete silence wait while the gods partake of the offerings. Later, the food is divided among those present and the ceremony concludes with a feast.

Such, in brief, is the *ch'achac* as performed three decades ago at Chankom, almost in the shadow of Chichen Itza (Redfield and Villa, 1934:138–43). Minor variations occur from village to village. The villagers of Telachaquillo hold their *ch'achac* at the edge of the most easterly cenote within the wall of ancient Mayapan (note that the Chacs' home is in the eastern sky); the *hmen* is reported to throw parts of the offerings into the cenote. At other villages, four men, each with gourd and lightning machete, stand at the four corners of the altar as impersonators of the Chacs; during the prayers they dance nine times around the altar brandishing their lightning machetes. A group of four boys in the surrounding woods imitates the screaming call (like that of a jay) of the *bach* (chachalaca), supposed to presage rain.

This great three-day ceremonial intercession well illustrates the hold of the Chacs on the Maya farmer. It is to be doubted that the *ch'achac* of today differs in essentials from the small-community ceremony of pre-Columbian days. The "state" ceremonies for rain, with sacrifices of children, processions, and offerings to cenotes, are of course long extinct, but over and over again archaeological finds of offerings, for instance eccentric flints (p. 147) in lots of nine or, less frequently, thirteen and twenty (p. 215), show a blessed continuity of rites over a thousand years.

RAIN GODS—THE CHICCHANS AND THE WORKERS

The rain gods of the Chorti Maya of eastern Guatemala and adjacent parts of Honduras and El Salvador (map 3) have been studied by Wisdom (1940: 392–97). They are essentially close relatives of the Chacs, although one could hardly describe the relationship as one of flesh and blood, for the Chicchans' blood is the cold blood of snakes, wherein is demonstrated the evolution of the Chacs from snakes.

The sky Chicchans, in Chorti belief, are four giant snakes (*chan* is "snake" in Chorti) each of which dwells at the bottom of a large body of water at the four points of the compass. The chief Chicchan resides in the north, at the bottom of the Golfo Dulce, now far outside Chorti territory but once within Chol-Chorti lands. A variant belief places both a male and a female Chicchan at each world direction, and an additional pair at the north (confusion with center?). Violent storms and cloudbursts result from collisions of a female Chicchan with a cloud as she rushes across the sky; thunder is the shouting of one Chicchan to another on the opposite horizon. When they shout a lot, the thunder is continuous. For that reason, the sky Chicchans are at times called Ah Ciricnar, "Owner of the Thunder." They also send lightning. There are, in addition, innumerable earth Chicchans living in streams, springs, and lakes, but as the dry season approaches they travel upstream and, entering springs, live during the dry season in the hills from which the springs issue. At the start of the rains, the Chicchans re-enter the streams, the size of their bodies causing the waters to swell; if too many swim downstream at one time, the river overflows its banks. Movements of the Chicchans within the hills cause earthquakes; a tremor indicates the Chicchan is turning in his sleep, and a violent earthquake ensues if the Chicchan turns completely over to lie on his other side.

Chicchan is the name of the fifth day in the Yucatec calendar, and, although meaningless now in Yucatec, it surely derives from a Choloid original meaning some specific snake, partly because this fifth day is Snake in the Middle American sacred almanac, partly because the crosshatched spot on the eyebrow or temple of the day Chicchan is an ophidian symbol, but above all, as noted, because *chan* is "snake" in Choloid tongues.

Besides the sky Chicchans, there are four other giant gods, the Ah Patnar Uinicob, known in Spanish as the "Working Angels," (see *anhel*, p. 255n.) but which in Yucatec could mean "Owners of the Jars Men," a possible reference to the jars from which water was poured on the earth. They are very closely linked with the Chicchans in producing celestial phenomena, and, as Wisdom notes, they are at times confused with them. Like the sky Chicchans, they are set at the four world directions and each acts as the "companion" of a Chicchan; several informants thought them superior to the Chicchans, who act as their assistants. The Ah Patnar Uinic at the north is the most important. In making rain, the earth Chicchans churn up bodies of water, causing the water to ascend to form clouds, whereupon the Ah Patnar Uinicob with their stone axes beat the water out of the clouds and rain falls; they make lightning and so they are sometimes called Lightning Makers.

Lightning is caused by passage through the air of those stone axes; a spot or a tree hit by lightning is said to have been struck by an axe aimed to kill an earth Chicchan beneath. The sometimes dual-sexed Ah Catiyon, whose leaders are at the four compass points, also help make rain by beating the clouds.

During the dry season a group of four junior gods takes over. They are known as Ah Kumix Uinicop, called in Spanish the minor *ángeles*. *Kumix* refers to the smallest or youngest or last of a series, directly comparable to the T'up Chac.

Although there seems at first to be this clear-cut division between Chicchans and the giant men, in fact there are gradations, because although the Chicchans are generally thought of as giant snakes, they are sometimes regarded as having the upper part of the body in human shape but the lower half that of a feathered serpent, or "he may be a gigantic man appearing like a snake to people." Some say that they have two small horns at the front of the head and two large ones at the back (cf. horns on feathered serpent heads at Chichen Itza and celestial dragons with antlers, Fig. 5*c*). The female Chicchan, usually called Chicchan of the Great Water, is a mermaid, the upper part of the body that of a woman, the lower half that of a fish.

The great eight-day rain ceremony concluding on Holy Cross Day, May 3, associated with the coming of the rains over much of the Maya area, starts in a manner reminiscent of the start of the *ch'achac*; four boys or girls are sent secretly to a sacred spring for water to be used in preparing the various maize dishes eaten after the ceremony. The prayer-maker—he must observe continence a week before and a week after the cermonies—first buries maize and cacao gruel in each corner of the town ceremonial hut. Later, the group follows him to the nearest sacred spring or to the foot of the nearest sacred hill in which earth Chicchans dwell during the dry season. Into a hole about two feet deep is poured a jar of blood together with the bodies of the two turkeys and two domestic fowls from which the blood has been drawn. These offerings are for the earth deities. Some two hundred pieces of copal are added as an offering to the rain deities (throughout the Maya area, the black clouds of copal smoke attract the black rain clouds). The ceremony, which concludes with an all-night feast, dance, and bout of drinking, is to induce the Chicchans to come forth and produce rain.

Clearly, the Chicchans and the Ah Patnar Uinicob together equate with the Chacs. The main differences are that the Chacs nowadays have lost their ophidian characteristics and do not inhabit streams and springs or the interiors of hills. Pictures of Chacs in pre-Columbian art, particularly in the codices, make obvious the snake origins of the Chacs; like the Chicchans, they can have a human (or part human) head on a snake's body (Plate 10), so we can be satisfied that the Chacs' association with snakes has been lost only in recent times in Yucatan. As to the absence of Chacs from streams and springs, these do not occur in Yucatan. In other features, notably giant size, world directional associations, the hurling of stone axes as thunderbolts, connection with clouds, and indeed even with frogs, the Chorti and Yucatec rain gods are remarkably close. Apart from such obvious resemblances as the four principal sky rain gods and the innumerable minor ones, apparently earth dwellers, one may note that the Chorti Ah Patnar Uinicob are also conceived as *ángeles* (that is, *anhel*), at least, the Spanish name for them is Angel Workers.

Finally, one may note that whereas the four great Chacs ride horseback and are thought by some to release the winds from special bags, in Chorti belief, the wind gods, Ah Yum Ikar, "Lord of the Wind," carry the rain over the world once it has been beaten out of the clouds as described above, but they ride on horseback (they are now regarded as innumerable or as three Catholic saints). Thus the Chorti divide between three closely related groups of gods functions which the Yucatec assign only to the Chacs.

LACANDON RAIN GODS

Lacandon ideas concerning the rain gods are at complete variance with those reported above; their beliefs find no room for quadruplicity and corresponding assignments to world directions and colors, features which could have been lost in the last century or two. Most attention is paid to Menzabac or Metzabac,[4] both meaning "Black Powder Maker." Yucatec *zabac* is a black dye from a tree of the same name. Menzabac supplies this powder which, when sprinkled on clouds, causes them to release the rain they hold. He is also called Yum Canan Zabac, "Lord Guardian

[4] Some Lacandon, particularly those whom Baer and Baer have studied, have shifted the sound *a* to *u* as in *fur*, a shift found also among the Palencano Chol and Mopan Maya. They also tend to change *l* to *r* like the Chorti. To standardize those pronunciations, I restore the *l*, drop a final *r* which sometimes creeps in, and write the *u* sound as *a*. In conformity with Yucatec usage, *s* is written *z*.

of the Black Powder." He was one of the creation gods, having created Mexicans, Guatemalans, and Tzeltal. He lives in a cave on the edge of a lake of the same name. He sends fever, and is keeper of the good souls, perhaps an indication of a belief in a paradise resembling the Mexican Tlalocan (p. 301).

When Hachacyum, the creator, decides to send rain he dispatches Hahana Ku, "Much-rains-house God," to Menzabac to buy the black powder. The latter always wants to cause great rainstorms and so tries to sell a huge quantity, but Hahana Ku, knowing that this would anger Hachacyum, buys only a small quantity, a gourdful. From his place in the mountains he scatters this over the clouds. He then causes the wind to blow by waving the tail feather of a macaw so that the winds will disperse the powder on the clouds; if he desires lightning, he strikes the edge of his axe (cf. the axes of the Chacs) with this feather. The lightning is personified as U Hahab Ku, "Much Rain Maker God." If Hachacyum wants to send hail, he dispatches Hahana Ku to buy it from Itzan Noh Ku, "Itzam(?) Great God," whose appellative is Ac Net'bat, "Our Gnawer or Cutter of Hail." He is also a god who cares for the sick.

Ah Peku (*Ah*, "he"; *pec*, "thunder"; *ku*, "god"), who resides on hilltops, climbs on the clouds before it rains and causes the thunder which announces the rains. *Pec* is the noise of thunder, drumming, and bellringing; hence the Chac pictured beating a drum on Codex Dresden page 34*c*.

The above (except for some translations of names) derives from Baer and Baer (1952:232, 252). Cline (1944) adds that Menzabac makes clouds by burning copal, the black smoke turning into black clouds, and that he is guardian of all fresh water. Tozzer (1907:98) gives Tan Hadz' Ku as a name for the lightning god. The term is actually a verb, "He is Striking or Lashing-with-a-whip God," and probably should be simply Hadz' Ku. He is said to drive the storm, and the flash of lightning is his whip. That definition must be modern, for the Lacandon have neither horses, carts, nor whips. *Hadz'* can also mean the blow which lightning strikes, and that is clearly the old meaning. Duby (1944) writes that Itzan Noh Ku lives in a lake and sends fevers, Soustelle (1935:

338) specifies his lake as Lake Petha, and Bruce (1967) informs us that he is lord of lakes and crocodiles.

Five rain deities are mentioned. As I have said, there is nothing corresponding to the quadruplicity of the Chacs with their world directions and colors, nor is there any equality between them or *primus inter pares* arrangement. The thunder and lightning deities are somewhat obscure persons, and all take orders from the creator god, something no honest Chac would tolerate. The association of the Lacandon rain gods with hills, caves, and bodies of water is repeated all over Middle America except in Yucatan where there are no mountains.

There are no parallels in Maya mythology to the almost child-like simplicity of these Lacandon beliefs on the relationships and duties of the rain gods—the messenger hurrying with orders from one god to another and those charming pictures of the god buying *zabac* and hail, formerly, one may suppose, with payments of cacao beans. Such details seem to mirror the traditions of a very primitive group and support the opinion that the Lacandon of today are Yucatec only in speech. Rain deities are hardly of prime importance among the Lacandon, perhaps because theirs is a territory of exceptionally high rainfall. One is left with the impression that the Lacandon attitude to their rain gods is more of affection than awe.

RAIN GODS OF THE TZOTZIL

The rain deities of the Tzotzil are known as Chauc or Anhel (*ángel*). *Chauc*, defined in the Delgaty Tzotzil-Spanish vocabulary as "thunder," "lightning," and "thunderbolt" (*rayo*) is undoubtedly the same as Cauac and variant spellings, names of the nineteenth day in various Maya calendars, and Chauoc, nineteenth day of the Chuh calendar. This is the day of rain in the intertribal Middle-American almanac. In Central Mexico, the head of Tlaloc, the rain god, serves as its glyph; in Maya texts various rain or storm symbols constitute the sign.

The Tzotzil of Larrainzar (Holland, 1963:93) hold that the Chauc or Anhel live in caves and control rains and winds. When there are thunderings or lightnings, an Anhel, having issued from a cave, is in the sky. They sprinkle water from a great jar which falls to earth as rain; the blowing of the wind is the breathing of an Anhel in his cave. Other Anhel send hot and cold weather. Every spring, however insignificant, has its Anhel who controls its rate of flow. The Anhel also have dominion over the wild animals and now and then release one to fall victim to a hunter. Other Anhel own great quantities of maize and other produce.

The Tzotzil go to the caves to pray for a happy issue out of all their afflictions at sowing and harvesting and particularly on May 3, Day of the Holy Cross, associated with the coming of the rains over most of the Maya area. Then the people go in procession with incense and pine branches to make altars in front of the crosses of the deep caves. Fireworks are set off and aguardiente is drunk. If San Antonio (!) is satisfied with the offerings, rains will be abundant and crops bountiful.

The belief of the Tzotzil of San Pedro Chenalho (Guiteras, 1961) parallel and supplement the above. Chauc, alias Anhel, is the rain god, god of water, owner of the thunderbolt, lord and owner of the mountains, protector of milpas, particularly those planted on the slopes of his mountain domain, giver of maize, and intimately related to our sustenance (cf. Ah Tzenulob, "Providers of Food," as a title of the Chacs). He is lightning; he lives in the interior of a mountain, the doorway to his home being a cave guarded by a frog. That a snake is Anhel's seat can be deduced from the fact that to avoid naming a snake it may be referred to as "Anhel's seat." The beating of Anhel's drum causes lightning (cf. Ah Peku, the Lacandon thunder god); Chauc's daughter is X'ob, the maize mother. He is not only benign, for he strikes with his thunderbolts those who act evilly. He is subservient to, and less powerful than, the earth god. They share prayers and offerings at hilltops, caves, and water holes in thrice-yearly agricultural rites.

Although Miss Guiteras' informant describes the Chauc as a single person, his description leaves the distinct impression that there were many Anhel, each occupying its own mountain or spring, as is the case among the earth Chicchan of the Chorti. In a footnote (p. 287), Guiteras adds the exceedingly interesting statement that among the Tzotzil of San Bartolomé de los Llanos, lightning is referred to the four world directions and colors (East, red; North, white; West, black; South, yellow),[5] the only evidence I know of quadruple assignment to world colors and directions of rain deities by the Tzotzil, although I surmise that was a conviction once shared by all the Maya of Chiapas.

Material on Tzeltal rain gods is scant, but one can infer a former arrangement of Chauc associated with world directions and colors (including center, green) and with the same thunder and lightning associations from an entry in the Slocum and Gerdel Bachajon-Tzeltal vocabulary which reads: "*chahwuc* (el) rayo (trueno) . . . *saquil chahwuc, tsajal chahwuc, yaxal chahwuc*, rayo blanco, rayo colorado, rayo azul (naguales)."

In the Guatemalan highlands, the sending of rain is largely a function of mountain or earth gods. In some cases, perhaps, these have taken over the duties of rain gods, who, like those of the Chorti and Tzotzil or like the Tlalocs, reside in or on mountains, springs, and lakes.

It is my opinion that the rain cult, with world color and directional features and with quadripartite deities deriving from or fused with snakes, had developed in all its essentials in the Formative period, probably as an Olmec creation. Even allowing for the inborn conservatism of established religion, it is remarkable how uniform the cult remained over such a wide area.

Before leaving these overcast skies, a word is in order on the rather numerous manifestations of Tlalocs in the Maya area. Typical and easily identified heads of Tlaloc appear on Classic-period monuments and pottery at several ceremonial centers of the Central area, particularly at Tikal and Copan. These are attributable, in part, to influence from Teotihuacan, where the

---

[5] Díaz de Salas (1963:257) states that the Tzotzil of San Bartolomé assign blue to the eastern corner and red to the western corner, wtih no recognition of the other two directions. Chenalho has the same Classic arrangement (east, red; etc.) as Guiteras reports for San Bartolomé; Larrainzar (Holland, 1963:92) has for the angles: northeast, white; northwest, white; southwest, black; southeast, red. Apart from assignment of white to two directions and consequent suppression of yellow, red at southeast fails to conform to the classic pattern. In a subsequent paper (Holland, 1964), the colors are assigned not to the angles but the compass points, with green added for the center. Clearly the system is in the ultimate stages of collapse.

Tlaloc cult was supremely important, but other Tlaloc figures appear on monuments of the Central area which were erected after the decline of Teotihuacan. Still other Tlaloc reliefs at Puuc sites, notably Uxmal and Sayil, are attributable to the very close of the Classic period. The recent discovery of the remarkable underground shrines of Tlaloc in Balankanche cave, on the outskirts of Chichen Itza, brought light to an ancient cult center sealed off a millenium ago (Andrews, 1961; 1965:313). Carbon–14 datings of recovered material of A.D. 870, plus or minus a hundred years, would place these offerings within a few years of the conquest of Chichen Itza by Mexican-influenced Putun invaders, dated with reasonable confidence at A.D. 918 (p. 141)

We can, I would suppose, explain these sporadic Tlaloc cults as aberrations of the hierarchy, either forced on them by incursive alien rulers or accepted because foreign cults were fashionable; it would surprise me profoundly to learn that Tlaloc worship ever established even the most slippery of footholds in the milpa rites of the Maya peasant, although, essentially, Chac and Tlaloc are as alike as two water snakes in a pond.

WIND GODS

In some parts, the winds are thought to be under the control of the rain gods. Thus, in Mopan-Maya folklore the mischievous servant of the Chacs opens their windbag and lets loose the winds (Thompson, 1930:149). A passage in Redfield and Villa (1934:164) well illustrates this link between water and wind: "There is, in fact, an idea that it is water that causes wind; that wind arises only from the water. In proof of this it was pointed out that leaves of the plants growing on the sides of the cenote are in motion when everything else is quiet." Even the cool air blowing from a dry cave is explained as coming from unseen waters behind its walls.

In modern Chorti belief, the winds seem to have hived off from the rain gods, taking some of their functions and attributes. Their chief duty is to ride horseback across the skies distributing the rain beaten out of the clouds (Wisdom, 1940:397), a duty which in Yucatan falls to the horse-borne Chacs, but the Lacandon call on the wind to distribute the powder over the clouds to cause rain. The Chorti winds are called Ah Yum Ikar, "Wind Lords."

A passage in the Chilam Balam of Chumayel (Roys, 1933:110) reads: "The [four] angels of the winds [*cangeles ik*] which were set up while he created the star, when the world was not yet lighted, when there was neither heaven nor earth: the Red Pauahtun, the White Pauahtun, the Black Pauahtun, the Yellow Pauahtun." The Pauahtuns are now accepted as Chacs (p. 255), but they could have been winds, servants of the Chacs who later were merged with them.

The Lacandon believe that wind gods are set at the four points of the compass. Under the name Chaob (*ch'aob*, "carriers off"?) they, in conjunction with an earthquake, will bring about the destruction of the world when the last Lacandon dies, and—delightful touch—they will blow so hard they will blast the monkeys out of the trees (below). Their leader, the god in the east, is called Hunaunic (Amram, 1944; Cline, 1944). Bruce (1967:98) writes that the Hanauinicob, which he translates "Servants (or "Men") of the House of Water," correspond to the Chacs, that is, they are rain gods. As noted, some Lacandon pronounce *a* like *u* in *fur*. Accordingly, Amram's Hunaunic doubtlessly can be identified with Bruce's Hanauinic (*-ob* is the plural termination).

Bruce writes that there are six of these beings assigned to the four points of the compass plus northeast and southeast. All bear merely the names of those directions, except the one in the east, who is called Bulhacil u Talkin, "Inundation of the East." Note that Amram has the eastern one as leader. *Bul ik*, according to the Motul dictionary, is "wind storm with earthquakes" and is qualified by the colors red and white (only the entry under white adds that earthquakes are involved). It is probable that there were four, each with its world color and direction, and, as serious earthquakes are unknown in Yucatan, one may surmise that these also played a role in a world destruction, past or yet to come.

Despite Bruce's informant (Lacandon culture has collapsed rapidly in the past decade), we must accept these as wind gods, not merely winds, for Baer and Baer (1952:252) say Chikin Kuh, "West God," lives in the west and sends west winds. Presumably they did nothing in particular and did it very well, but every wind has its day, and theirs will be when, at the Last Trump, they blast the monkeys right out of their trees. Bruce's informant was right to the extent that here also the winds are closely connected with, but subsidiary to, rain gods, as the Lacandon title Servants of the House of Rain indicates. Ah Mac Ik, "Coverer Up of Winds," is appealed to when boisterous winds damage milpas (Tozzer, 1907: 157).

The Ixil Maya of the highlands (Lincoln, 1946:202) address red, white, and yellow winds in prayer.

In a prayer at a *ch'achac* ceremony in northern British Honduras recorded by Gann (1918:47), recipients of the offering who were mentioned included Cichpan Colel XHelik, "Beautiful Lady Succeeding-one-another Wind(s)." A female wind is a strange oddity. *Hel* refers to handing over authority from one to another with the implication that XHel Ik is sole survivor of the Can Hel Ik group (p. 255n.).

In Yucatan, Quintana Roo, and British Honduras, prayers and offerings are made to the winds (Ikob) at milpa firing so that they will fan the flames. Directional winds may be addressed, but most important is Mozon Ik, "Whirlwind," or Kakal Mozon Ik, "Whirlwind of the Fires," because it rapidly spreads the flames. One gets the impression that the winds are addressed primarily as personifications of nature rather than as gods in their own right. Remember, their apparent masters, the Chacs, have not issued from their home when the milpas are burned.

In the Guatemalan highlands there is a similar failure to accord much importance to the winds; the Tzotzil of Chenalho state that there is no wind god (Guiteras, 1961:260).

The concept of evil winds which bring sickness of all kinds is today of tremendous importance throughout Middle America, but appears to be mainly or totally of European origin. It was grafted on a minor pre-Columbian belief in winds that could cause evil, as could certain rains. With the native root, the stock has had a rank growth, and its sour fruit has yielded a surfeit of superstitious evil.

EARTH AND THUNDER GODS—THE TZULTACAH

The concept of gods of the surface of the earth is more developed among the highland than lowland Maya. The Tzultacah, by combining features of earth gods and rain gods, carry the process of identification of rain gods with such natural features as mountains, springs, and rivers farther than do the Chorti, the Maya of Chiapas, or, for that matter, the worshipers of Tlaloc. Kekchi territory being one of heavy rainfall, the rain-giving powers of their gods have lost ground to potency in other spheres. Because the Tzultacah and the Chacs are at the extremes, with Chorti Chicchans and Tzotzil Chaucs in the center, it seems advisable to step momentarily out of the lowlands to examine this cult in the Alta Verapaz, bearing in mind that it may partly derive from the Chol, many of whom the Kekchi absorbed. Material is largely drawn from Sapper (1897:271–83), Burkitt (1902, 1918), and correspondence of Paul Wirsing with Elsie McDougall.

Tzultacah means "Mountain-Plain" or "Mountain-Valley" and so is a poetic term for the surface of the earth. The Tzultacah are innumerable, but Thirteen Tzultacah is a term sometimes used in prayers to embrace the whole body as a single entity. The Tzultacah may live in, and personify, a spring or river, but above all each is lord of a particular mountain, with which he is identified and within which he dwells. A cave within a mountain is that Tzultacah's dwelling; otherwise his home is thought of as underground beneath the mountain. There are male and female Tzultacah; they marry and are given in marriage and a lady Tzultacah may even elope with some mountain swain.

A prayer, recorded by Sapper, by Kekchi from the neighborhood of Coban asking the Tzultacah to protect the maize crop about to be sown, names six. Two of them, Cancuen and Chahmayic, are rivers; Itzam is female; and Pecmo is a mountain with a famous cave, scene of great gatherings to pray to its owner and a pilgrimage not lightly undertaken since it involves a preliminary forty-day period of continence. The Tzultacah of Pecmo has particular power in protecting from fevers and snake bites. Itzam is married to Siete Orejas, a distant mountain on the Pacific side of the country. Tradition has it that she used to eat people until dissuaded from that distressing habit by her far-off husband. This item may derive from folk memory of human sacrifice to that formidable lady.

Although, so far as one can gather, no rain ceremonies are made in honor of the Tzultacah, there are close parallels between them and lowland Maya rain gods. The Tzultacah are lords of water, Sapper informs us without expanding that statement; floods are outward signs of the feasts they celebrate in the interior of the earth; thunder and lightning are their possessions. Indeed, some of the Tzultacah are also known as *truenos*, "thunders," and the rumbling of thunder is one Tzultacah talking to another. They hurl stone axes and often strike men dead with them as punishment for wrongdoing; a thunderclap is the noise made by a Tzultacah striking a tree with his stone axe. Moreover—and I think this is significant—they, like rain deities and controllers of thunder and lightning throughout most of the Maya area, are also called *anhel*.

Snakes are the servants of the Tzultacah who send them to punish man for evil-doing; a light bite (non-poisonous) for a minor offense, a bite from a rattler for real depravity. In some parts, the Indians will not kill snakes for fear of angering their masters, the Tzultacah. The caves and underground homes of the Tzultacah are furnished with hammocks in which the gods rest; the cords of these are rattlesnakes.

At the present time, almost no evidence of a quadripartite arrangement of Tzultacah corresponding to the Chacs, Chicchans, and Tlalocs exists, but one may note that four Tzultacah in turn hurled their thunderbolts at the rock (for the Kekchi, Saclech, north of Chama on the road to Salinas de los Nueve Cerros) beneath which the maize was hidden (p. 350). The Tzultacah are often local, a few outstanding peaks in the vicinity of each town, although some are known and worshiped, or at least paid respect, over very wide areas.

The above details mark the similarities of the Tzultacah with regular rain deities, but they must not be allowed to obscure the other activities of the Tzultacah not shared with Chacs and Chicchans and which largely are those of earth deities, and one must bear in mind that Tzultacah does refer to the surface of the earth, "Mountain-Plain."

The Tzultacah protect the individual from harm, particularly when he is passing through their territory; they nourish and guard his crops, they guard his cattle, as lords of the forest they are the owners of game and all wildlife, and to them one prays for success in hunting. To an unknown extent, they have fevers and disease in their control, possessing the ability to guard people from those afflictions and to chastise the wicked with them.

There is no idea that the Tzultacah ever reside in the sky or pour water from on high onto the earth.

The term Mountain-Valley or Plain (*tacah* means both "plain" and "valley") for earth deities occurs in varying forms among diverse Maya highland groups, and mountains are the recipients of offerings and prayers throughout the whole area. With regard to the tradition that Itzam once ate human beings, Wagley (1949: 55) reports that Mam of Santiago Chimaltenango pay particular attention to three peaks, and turkey blood is offered only to them. It is said that formerly the guardians of those three peaks drank human blood. Habel (1878:13) relates that the Catholic priest of San Juan Sacatepequez, who was well versed in Indian customs, told him that the custom of sacrificing a person to the mountain deity still obtained (nearly a century ago). This took place in the dry season, and for that reason no one ventured out alone from January to March.

Such reports probably reflect folk memory of what happened in "the good old days."

La Farge (letter of 1929) reports Uitzailic, "Mountain-Valley," as a single or group Chuh deity. The Quiche equivalent is Juyutikah with the same meaning but seemingly different functions (Bunzel, 1952:264). The Itacai are Chorti mountain gods (p. 323). (See also under Ancestral and Lineage Gods.)

The hunting prayer addressed to the Tzultacah by Kekchi travelers obtained by Sapper (1893:289–90; English translation in Thompson, 1954) is of moving beauty. Here are a few sentences:

> [The offering] I have brought thee is in truth not much and of little good for thy eating, for thy drinking. Whether it be so or not, what I say and what I think, O God, is that thou art my mother, thou art my father. Now I shall thus sleep beneath thy feet, beneath thy hands, thou lord of the mountains and valleys, thou lord of the trees, thou lord of

the liana vines. Tomorrow is again day, tomorrow is again light of the sun. I do not know where I shall then be. Who is my mother? Who is my father? Only thou, O God, Thou seest me, thou protectest me on every path, in every time of darkness, from every obstacle which thou mayest hide, which thou mayest remove, thou, O God, thou my lord, thou lord of the mountains and valleys.

My thoughts turn to that tender passage in Exodus set to exquisite music by Handel:

Thou shall't bring them in, and plant them in the mountain of thine inheritance, in the place, O Lord, which Thou hast made for Thee to dwell in, in the sanctuary, O Lord, which thy hands have established.

In both prayers there is the same antiphony, with one sentence reiterating the preceding theme, and, of course, the mountains are the sanctuary those gods of the forest—and its lianas and trees —have established.

THE BACABS

Of these gods, so frequently mentioned in early sources but so inadequately explained, Bishop Landa had this to say:

Among the multitude of gods which this people worshiped, they adored four, each one of whom was named Bacab. These were four brothers, they said, whom God placed at the four quarters of the world when he created it, supporting the sky so that it should not fall. They also said of these Bacabs that they escaped when the world was destroyed by the flood. They give to each of them other names, and with these indicate in what quarter of the world God has placed him, holding up the sky, and they appropriate one of the four year bearers to him and the quarter in which he is.

Landa also gives their individual world directions, colors, year bearers, and names as follows: East, red, Kan years, Hobnil; North, white, Muluc years, Can Tzicnal; West, black, Ix years, Zac Cimi; South, yellow, Cauac years, Hozanek. In a fragmentary creation story in the Chilam Balam of Chumayel occurs this passage: "There would be a sudden rush of water when the theft of the insignia (or despoiling of the Can Hel) occurred. Then the sky would fall, it would fall down upon the earth, when the four gods, the four Bacabs (*cantul ti ku, cantul ti Bacab*) were set up who brought about the destruction of the world."

Bacab may mean "water sprinkler," or it may signify "around the world" or "around the hive." Although the term "the four gods, the four Bacabs" is most general, we also find Ah Koh Bacab, "The Masked Bacab," and the Motul dictionary defines *bacab* as "*representante, zingles* (?)." *Representante* is an old Spanish term for actor or impersonator, really the same thing; *zingles*, if that is the word written, may have been intended for *zingales*, a form of *zincalis*, "gipsies" or "strolling players."

These enigmatic titles are explained by the fact that the Bacab are referred to in the books of Chilam Balam as Tolil Och or Ix Toloch, the "Opossum Actors." As Opossum Actors they are prominent on the four pages of Codex Dresden which give the ceremonies and prognostications for the incoming year. Each wears the head of an opossum as a mask and has the prehensile tail of the same marsupial attached behind. Most important, each carries the image of the ruling god of the incoming year on his back, seemingly to indicate that his is the responsibility for the fate of the incoming year (Plate 4*b*).

The Bacabs are also gods of bees and the apiary. In fact, Hobnil, chief Bacab, was the leading patron of beekeepers, and his name is surely a syncopation of *hobonil*, "of the bee-hive." Possibly they are the same as the Ah Muzencab, the bee gods of the present-day Yucatec Maya. One hopes that a Bacab was the Lord of the Bees who tenderly cured all bees which, as a consequence of the hive's destruction by human robbers of its honey, suffered broken wings or legs, had been crushed, or had lost their sight (Thompson, 1930:156), a story which aptly illustrates the Maya view that all creation has its rights and that man must not abuse them.

Men with upraised arms, commonly sculptured at the tops and bottoms of columns of the Mexican period at Chichen Itza, surely represent the Bacabs. Almost invariably, their aged features are emphasized by the addition of long beards; understandably, since they have survived from the era before the flood. They wear distinctive loincloths terminating in elongated ovals with interior crosshatching (Fig. 10 *l–n*). I am reasonably confident that these derive from bees' wings (Thompson, 1970), thereby reinforcing the connection with apiculture.

These Atlantean figures at Chichen Itza have distinctive and prominent attributes; one is shown at the center of a spider's web, another wears a flat spiral shell (*planorbis*) on his breast, the third emerges from a conch shell or wears that shell on his back, and the last has his body encased in the carapace of a turtle. In delineation, these Bacabs show strong Mexican influence. Indeed, sky bearers occur in two Mexican codices (Borgia and Vatican B). Chac Hubil Ahau, "Great Lord of the Conch"; Hub Tun Ahau, "Lord Stone Conch"; and Ah Yax Ac, perhaps "He, Green Turtle" (C. B. Tizimin: 12; Ritual of the Bacabs MS: 170; C. B. Chumayel: 3) may be names of the conch and turtle Bacabs.

The Bacab cult evidently goes back to the Classic period. In a temple at Copan, two seated Bacabs, each with upraised arm, support the heads of a two-headed celestial dragon (Fig. 10*o*). Each Bacab wears a peculiar looped headdress, the ends of which are crosshatched in a manner reminiscent of the loincloth ends of the Chichen Itza Bacabs. This looped headdress, with a central knot or medallion and crosshatching, is the attribute of the Bacabs and can be seen on numerous portraits of the old god emerging from a conch or wearing a turtle carapace as found on polychrome vessels of the Classic period and in the codices (Fig. 10*g–i*). Bacabs are also represented on the façade of the Iglesia, a Classic period building at Chichen Itza; one with conch shell, another with turtle carapace, and one seemingly with wings.

This looped headdress becomes an affix (Catalog Nos. 63, 64) which identifies as a Bacab, or a Bacab association, the main sign to which it is attached (Fig. 10*g–k*). For instance, it may stand above a conch shell, the whole forming the name glyph of the Bacab of the conch shell. Similarly, the *cauac* glyph which stands for the sound *ku*, "god," with the number four and Affix 63 or 64 (they are merely variants of one another) prefixed, reads *Cantul ti ku, cantul ti Bacab*, "the four gods, the four Bacabs" (Fig. 10*a*). Again, this same Affix 63 or 64 over the kin glyph appears on all four pages covering new-year ceremonies in Codex Madrid. As *kin* means "festival," in addition to its more usual meanings of "sun" and "day," the combination reads "Festival of the Bacabs," very appropriate in view of the importance of those gods in the new-year ceremonies.

It is grievously frustrating that although it is clear from what Landa writes, from the many citations in colonial literature, and from appearances in pre-Columbian art that the Bacabs were

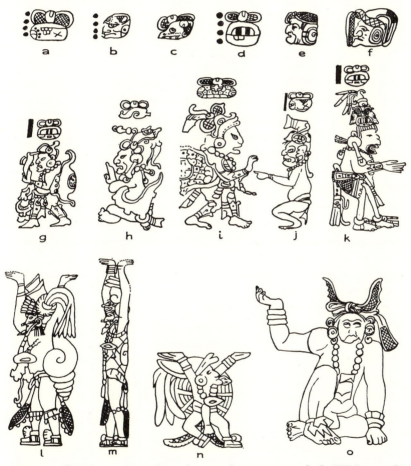

Fig. 10.—Bacabs. *g, i, m*: Wearing turtle carapaces. *h, l*: With conch shells. *n*: With spider web. *j, k*: With tun headdress. *l-o*: Holding up heavens. *a-f*: Additional glyphs of Bacabs.

279

actors (in more senses than one) with leading parts on the Maya stage, we know precious little about them. They exercised very strong influences on the luck of the year; they supported the skies; they were closely associated with bees; they were actors or performers and, as such, disguised themselves as opossums; they may also have personified stars or constellations; and they were four and were associated with world directions and colors. There are hints that they may also have dwelled beneath the earth, supporting it as they did the sky. For fuller discussion of their nature, see Thompson, 1970a.[6]

THIRTEEN GODS AND NINE GODS

In Maya colonial literature there are frequent references to a group of deities known as Oxlahun ti Ku, "Thirteen Gods." As in the case of the Chacs, these thirteen gods can be thought of as so many distinct personalities or collectively as a single personage. In a number of passages they are contrasted with the Bolon ti Ku, "Nine Gods," so as to make it evident that the Thirteen Gods are celestial, the Nine Gods, lords of the underworld. It will be recalled that there are thirteen layers of the skies, and these were and probably still are invoked in prayers (p. 193, 195), just as there are nine layers of the underworld. The Oxlahun ti Ku personify those thirteen heavens just as the Bolon ti Ku personify the nine underworlds, and allegorically they stand in the same relation to one another as light to darkness or good to evil.

We know more about the Nine Gods because, as lords of the underworld and darkness, they ruled in unending sequence over a "cycle" or "week" of nine nights. The Maya of the Classic period normally recorded the glyph of the lord of the night who ruled over the night corresponding to the day of the Initial Series which he inscribed on a monument. Consequently, we have the

---

[6] Landa says that the owners of cacao orchards made a festival to the gods of merchants, Chac and Hobnil, in Muan. At first thought this suggests that Hobnil, as one of the Bacabs, was connected with cacao. However, Hobnil was patron of the year which Landa describes, so his participation in this cacao rite may indicate merely that he received attention as ruler of the year. Note that in the beekeepers' festival that Landa describes as falling in Zec, but which probably was that of the day 1 Kan, Hobnil received special attention, although all the Bacabs were invoked as patrons of apiculture.

glyphs and the sequence of all nine gods. Unfortunately, there is no such certainty about the thirteen gods of the days, although I am convinced that these were the gods who ruled over the numbers one to thirteen, and, of course, they, being attached to the day names, also repeated through all eternity. Strangely, a deity in one group could belong to the other. Thus, the sun god, a celestial creature if there ever was one, is god of number four in the series one through thirteen, but as night sun functions also as one of the nine gods.

An obscure fragment of a creation story in the Books of Chilam Balam records a fight between the two groups, an interesting parallel to the war in which Saint Michael and the heavenly host overcame and cast out the great dragon, Satan, and all the powers of evil and darkness. I reproduce the passage because it well illustrates the obscurities which surround so much of Maya mythology and the difficulties in translating Maya allegorical writing when one is not sure of the unfolding story. The translation is largely that of Roys (1933:99), but I have allowed myself major emendations and have also drawn on Barrera Vásquez and Rendón (1948:153–55).

> It was [Katun] 11 Ahau when the Ah Muzencab, the Bee gods [the Bacabs?] went forth to blindfold the faces of the Oxlahun ti Ku. . . . This was after the creation of the world had been completed. Then the Oxlahun ti Ku were seized by the Bolon ti Ku. Then it was that fire descended, the rope descended. Then war came. There was fighting. Then Oxlahun ti Ku was seized; his head was wounded, his face was buffeted, he was spat on; also he was on his back. He was despoiled of his rain and lightning powers [?, *canhel*], of his cloud-making black powder [*zabac*], [his] quetzal was taken away. Also were taken [from him?] lima beans, our ground daily bread [maize], ground hearts of small squash seeds, ground large seeds of the *ca* squash, ground kidney beans. Green [or the first] Bolon Dz'acab wrapped in a cloth the seed. Then he went to the thirteenth layer of heaven. Then a mass of maize dough with the tips of maize cobs remained here on earth. Then its heart departed by the action of Oxlahun ti Ku, but they did not know that the heart of our daily bread [maize] was gone. After that the fatherless ones,

the miserable ones, and those without husbands disintegrated; they were alive but they had no judgment. Then they were smothered by the sands, in the midst of the sea.

A great flowing and ebbing of the water. There will come the water at the time the despoiling of the rain and lightning powers [of Oxlahun ti Ku] occurred. Then when the sky would sink down, the earth would sink down, the four gods, the four Bacabs are set up who would cause the destruction of the world.

I have taken liberties with the text, particularly in reading *canhel* as "rain and lightning powers" (p. 255n.), and taking *zabac* in the Lacandon sense as the black powder which makes the rain clouds.

This fight is clearly tied to a destruction of the world by flood. The "miserable fatherless ones" without judgment who disintegrated, apparently in water, can surely be equated with the similarly unintelligent mud-men who fell apart in the Popol Vuh creation story (p. 334). The Lacandon myth of a fight between creator and lord of the underworld (p. 344) is also reminiscent of the Chumayel story. One is left with a vague impression that the struggle was for control of the crops and that the Oxlahun ti Ku were the losers.[7]

THE MAIZE GOD

The Maya learned at his father's knee how, after failures with other materials, the gods successfully made man of maize. There is more truth in that than meets the eye, for maize constitutes the

[7] Because the Maya often fail to employ the plural termination *-ob*, one is left in doubt as to whether the author thought of Oxlahun ti Ku as one or thirteen gods. The faces which were blindfolded are in the plural, but unfortunately *uichob* means both "faces" and "eyes." I have followed Roys' usage of single and plural although I suspect that a plural rendition would be closer to Maya intention. *Uiil*, which Roys translates "tubercle," is a ritualistic name for maize used almost as we speak of our daily bread, so the latter is the translation I have used. Barrera Vásquez uses *sustento* and *alimento*, the same thing but without ritualistic connotation. The Mani and Tizimin versions of this myth have *hutlahi*, "disintegrated"; Chumayel, *hullahi*, "pierced." In view of the disintegration of the men of mud in the Popol Vuh, the former is more acceptable. *Minan u puczikalob* translates to "they were without hearts," but *puczikal*, "heart," is, by extension, "judgment," and that makes more sense in the context.

incredible figure of 75 per cent of the daily energy intake of the present-day Yucatec (Benedict and Steggarda, 1936). The percentage is higher in really remote villages and was probably higher in pre-Columbian times when domestic pigs, cattle, plantains, and bananas were unavailable.

Because of his dependence on this one crop and his unending battles to protect it from its natural enemies, the Maya peasant's relationship to maize has an intimacy which we, whose acquaintance with corn is largely confined to packaged corn flakes, corn chowder, or succotash, find hard to understand. There is a mystical relationship between man and his milpa of which anyone who has lived in a Maya village cannot fail to be aware. The milpero and his corn—and this is true of all Middle America—grow together like oak and ivy.

Maya birth ceremonies illustrate how even the newborn child is psychically united to maize; one is the counterpart of the other. These, apparently referable to the Pokoman Maya, have been described by a seventeenth-century writer. To the accompaniment of prayers for his well-being, the child's umbilical cord was cut over a multicolored ear of maize with a brand new obsidian knife (thrown into the river after the ceremony). The bloodstained ear was smoke cured, and at the appropriate season the grain was removed and sown with the utmost care in the name of the child. The yield was harvested and again sown, and the increased yield served, after a share had been given to the temple priest, to maintain the boy until he was old enough to sow his own milpa. They said that thereby he not only ate of the sweat of his brow, but of his own blood. Las Casas (1909, ch. 179) details a similar rite which differs in two respects: the first food the child eats is a gruel made from the first harvest, and some seed is kept so that the boy, when he is of age to do so, plants it himself, and the produce he sacrifices to the gods.

This custom survives to the present day among the Tzotzil (Guiteras, 1960). The blood-spattered grains from the ear on which the umbilical cord is cut are sown by the father in a tiny milpa called "the child's blood." The growth of the little crop is carefully watched over by all, for from it one augurs the child's future. The eating of the "blood crop" by all members of the family constitutes a sort of communion which links all to this new member of the family.

In fact, union of child with maize is prenatal, at least in Central Mexico. There it was believed that if a woman ate tamales which stuck to the cooking pot, her child would similarly adhere to her womb and would die. They also said that if a mother who had just given birth to a child were to burn maize cobs, the child's face would become pock marked; to avoid that, she had to pass with them before the child's face.

The maize not only influences the child's life, it guards it. Among the Bachajon Tzeltal, it is customary to leave an ear of yellow maize with a baby which has to be left unattended so that the child's soul will not be stolen. A similar custom exists among the Jacalteca Maya. There, if the child is left for any reason, an ear of corn of any color is placed on each side of it. The reason is not explained (Blom and La Farge, 1926–27:360; La Farge and Byers, 1931:80).

In Yucatec, a youth of marriageable age was known as "maize plant coming into flower." I had once considered this to be merely figurative speech, but in view of the above discussion, I am not sure that it does not reflect a definite relationship.

The Chilam Balam of Chumayel (pp. 48–54) has a mystical account of the release of the maize from its hiding place below the mountain (p. 349) full of allegory and abracadabra in broken Latin. The maize is called *tun*, the word for stone in general and jade in particular. Jade, because it was green and, above all, because it was precious, symbolized maize. That this refers to maize is made additionally clear by inclusion of the term *gracia*, "divine grace." A section reads: "There occurred the birth of the first jade of divine grace, the first infinite divine grace when there was infinite night, when God was not. Not yet had [the maize] received his divinity. Then he remained alone within the divine grace, within the night, when neither heaven nor earth existed. Then it was pulverized at the completion of the katun; then his birth was not possible in one katun. There were his locks of hair. His divinity came about; then he departed." Later we read: " 'How was the grain of maize born? How, indeed, father?' 'Thou knowest. Ah Mun was born in the sky'."

The old Chac or thunder god smashed to pieces the rock under which the maize was hidden, and the maize was released, that is, it was born. The maize god normally has long hair, presumably derived from the tassel of the ear of corn. Ah Mun, I feel sure, is a name for the young maize god. It means an unripe fruit or crop and is also applied to an adolescent, providing another term applicable to growing corn and growing youth.

Generally speaking, the maize god is a passive being. Agricultural almanacs in Codex Madrid show the maize, either as the god or its glyph, as the victim of assaults—eaten by birds, raccoons, or weevils or burned up by drought—or the beneficiary of rains sent by the Chacs. Man is the plant's ally in repulsing many of the attacks—all, one might say—for with his intercessions and offerings to the Chacs he brings rain to his thirsty partner. He drives off wild animals, he clears away choking weeds, and, of course, by the mere act of planting he allows the maize to spring to life. In return the maize feeds him and his family. Each depends on the other, and with dependence grows love.

Man's need to protect and cherish maize is well brought out in another practice reported by Sahagún of Aztec women:

> If they saw dry grains of maize scattered on the ground, they quickly gathered them up, saying "Our Sustenance suffereth: it lieth weeping. If we should not gather it up, it would accuse us before our Lord. It would say 'O, Our Lord, this vassal picked me not up when I lay scattered upon the ground. Punish him!' Or perhaps we should starve."

A very similar idea exists among the Tzotzil of Chenalho. According to one informant:

> Black hunger is brought about by the sin of women; they are careless when they grind; pieces of meal fall to the ground and are burned or stepped on. . . . Red hunger is caused by the little tots who throw their corn around, who play with their tortilla instead of eating it.

Drought is said to be caused by drunken quarrels arising because maize or beans have been exchanged for liquor. "It is sinful to exchange one's maize, one's life for *trago* [liquor]." Again, gophers, rats, birds, dogs, and so on eat part of one's maize crop.

285

The soul of all the eaten part must be called back. One prays to the corn spirit (here female): "Señora X'ob, Señora Anhel, bring back the soul of the maize that has been carried away; do not allow its soul to forsake us because animals have eaten it; call your companions together so that the soul of corn be undivided, so that we have strength to eat of it." When a man is ill, five ears of corn are placed at the head of the bed or under it. They protect him from *Tentación*, the evil spirit.

The widely held idea, brought out above, that it is sacrilegious not to cherish our friend and ally, maize, is beautifully illustrated by a Lacandon belief that in the underworld evildoers become dogs and mules which have no rest from work. The bad category comprises those who marry women of a forbidden group, homosexuals, murderers, and those who waste food (maize, presumably).

Even the maize can be jealous of its friends. The Mam of Chiapas often come upon little talking ears of corn. They threaten to abandon man if he insists on giving up the cultivation of maize for that of coffee. Localities where the little ears have thus appeared become regular places of pilgrimage; men bring them offerings and promise not to abandon them for coffee.

Everywhere in Middle America, double ears of corn are regarded as emblems of fertility and have special honors paid them. In some parts of Guatemala they are regarded as the spirit of the corn and an assurance of a good crop for the following year. One ear is kept for seed; the other is placed as a thank offering before the household saint, for if carefully guarded it brings luck to the family. In other parts of the Guatemalan highlands, the largest ear of the harvest is fastened to a rocket; if it attains a great height, that is a good omen. The Mam of Chiapas similarly regard twin ears of maize as symbols of fertility. Dressed in paper, they are held by persons dancing to the music of a marimba, and later, placed on a candlelit altar, they are censed with copal.

Again, in the Cakchiquel village of San Pedro Sacatepequez, during a dance called the Dance of the Ears of Corn, unmarried girls in turn take from the altar a sort of corn doll made of ears and husks of corn and corn tassels. Each is dressed in a miniature replica of the women's costume of that village. The grain from these ears is used for next season's planting.

The Mopan Maya of southern British Honduras believe that the maize spirit takes refuge in the last ears of maize to be gathered. These the owner of the milpa himself gathers; they are sprinkled with the blood of a chicken, set aside, and at the next sowing mixed with the rest of the seed. Thereby the maize spirit's presence in the new crop is insured. This presents remarkable parallels to Old World ideas about the corn spirit, but on reflection one sees how, given the idea of a maize god or spirit, this belief could arise as readily as those to do with double ears or, for that matter, with corn dollies, also an Old World tradition.

To conclude this discussion of the Maya in relation to maize, I shall repeat a quotation I have used elsewhere. It is from the pen of a Franciscan missionary, writing 250 years ago, and refers to the highland Maya. "Everything they did and said so concerned maize that they almost regarded it as a god. The enchantment and rapture with which they look upon their milpas is such that on their account they forget children, wife, and any other pleasure, as though the milpas were their final purpose in life and source of their felicity." That is a fair assessment, although the good friar was wrong in one respect: the Maya did regard maize as a god.

In conversation with colleagues who have been in close contact with the Maya, we have agreed that among the lowland Maya the sex instinct is not strongly developed. One observed that the impulse seemed so weak that he often wondered how the race was perpetuated. Gann, who spent most of his life as a medical officer among the Maya of British Honduras, bemoaning the fact that when it came time to make milpa the Maya laborers deserted the dig, remarked, "The spring is in his blood, and being but feebly sexed, and almost completely lacking in sensuality, his thoughts, instead of turning to love, turn to the milpa, whither his steps turn also, charm the archaeologist never so wisely with offers of high wages."

That last observation any archaeologist who has used Maya labor would confirm. When milpa clearing time comes, the Maya slips away like any lover off to dally with his mistress. It has seemed to me that the sex instinct is somehow channeled into love and anxious brooding over the young maize as it produces its first leaves. It is a New World version of the mystic marriage of Saint Catherine, and it turns the Maya peasant into a mystic.

Such attitudes to maize, as I see it, alone explain the various customs noted above and make sense of, for instance, the practice of setting an ear of corn to guard a sleeping child. The Indian would say, "We and maize are of the same substance; our creators made us of maize, and our strength comes from the maize we have eaten at sunrise, noon, and sunset almost from birth."[8]

From the above presentation, one gets the impression, as I have remarked, that maize and man are allies in their fight for survival against stronger forces of aggression, and that maize has power to protect man only in a mild magico-religious way (as ears beside a child). All the same, material in the Maya codices, as well as the very full data on cults of maize deities from one end of Middle America to another, make it obvious that the relationship was not quite so casual, at least in the eyes of the hierarchy.

The maize god appears on the monuments and in the codices as a very youthful and handsome individual, at times with even a touch of effeminacy. His head may be set amid maize foliage to indicate the ear growing from the plant (Fig. 2), or maize leaves often set with grains of maize and frequently shaped like the *bil*, "growth," affix (Catalog No. 130), may rise from his head (Plates 4*b*, 5*a*, *b*, 8*g*, 13, 14*c*, 15, 17). In the Dresden codex, a *kan* ("maize") sign is often set in his headdress; in Codex Madrid, a line from the front of the maize headdress through eye to chin suggests the god wears a mask. In contrast, the corncob headdress with huge tassel of Piedras Negras Stela 40 (Plate 12) conveys arrogance, but the wearer is apparently a royal impersonator.

The maize god is the governing influence in many divisions of divinatory almanacs in the codices, and on Codex Dresden, page 34*a*, is a sacrificial scene (Plate 5*a*) in which, apparently, an impersonator of the maize god has been beheaded (beheading is especially associated with deities of vegetation in Central Mexico). One may also note that an impersonator of the maize god is the central figure in the group of performers on the famed murals in

[8] Sources: Fuentes y Guzmán, 1932–33, pt. 1, bk. 12, ch. 3; Sahagún, 1950–69, bk. 5, app. chs. 4, 8, 18; Guiteras, 1960, 1961:243, 251; Blom and La Farge, 1926–27:360; La Farge and Byers, 1931:80; Pozas, 1952:260; Kelsey and Osborne, 1939:45; Osborne, 1965:167; Thompson, 1930:48; Vásquez, 1937–44; Gann, 1926:234.

Room 1, Bonampak. Moreover, as we shall see, the maize god is ruler of one of the thirteen numbers and its corresponding day, a distinction not granted to a nonentity.

As to names of the maize god, colonial sources mention a god Kauil and other deities incorporating that word—Ah Uaxac Yol Kauil and Itzam Na Kauil. *Uil* is an old term for "sustenance" and is used as the equivalent of "our daily bread." *Kaa* is the root of words signifying "surplus" or "abundance"; Surplus of Our Daily Bread seems a reasonable term for a maize deity. (Cauil, "Double Ration of Food," a near homonym, is another of his names.) As we shall see, the number eight is the number of the maize god; *yol* signifies "heart of," so He Eight Heart of Abundance of Our Sustenance is a reasonable title for the maize god.

I have already suggested that Ah Mun, "The Unripe Maize," is a suitable name for the maize god, as are also Zac Uac Nal, "White Bursting Forth [or Six] New Corn," countenance of Katun 9 Ahau (Roys, 1954: 47, note 27), and Uac Chuaac Nal, "Bursting Forth [or Six] Tall New Corn." Brinton (1895:41) wrote of Yum Kaax, "Lord of the Harvest Fields." Morley (1915: 18) writes of the "Maize god, Yum Kaax, 'Lord of the Harvest Fields'," identifying him with God E, the maize god of the codices. Others, including, I fear, myself, followed this lead. Yum Kaax means "Lord of the Forest," and, so far as I can see, no early source supports this identification as a maize god, which seems to have been Brinton's invention.

The head of the maize god stands for the number eight, of which the god is patron, and, by extension, the maize god is lord of the eighth day starting with Caban. This is the day Kan, which, in fact, is the day "maize," the Kan sign being the well-known symbol for maize which is often set in the maize god's headdress. A representation of the number eight carved on Stela I, Copan, neatly seals the connection between the number eight and maize, for there a bar and three dots within a cartouche are surmounted by the maize affix (86), a sign resembling, and perhaps deriving from, the *bil*, "growth," affix (130).

The Nahuatl people of the Mexican plateau had both male (Centeotl) and female (Xilonen, alias Chicomecoatl) corn deities in addition to goddesses such as Tlazolteotl, alias Tozi, who, through functioning as earth deities, came to have definite responsibilities for maize. I see no evidence among most Maya groups of a goddess who directly personifies the maize.[9] However, the Tzotzil of Chenalho have a corn mother named X'ob (*ob* is a ritualistic term for maize in Tzotzil). She is the daughter of the thunder and rain Anhel and was unhappily married to a man subsequently converted into lightning, by whom she had children. That notwithstanding, she is regarded as a beautiful little virgin. She took an ear of corn from each corner of her husband's milpa, and these miraculously multiplied. She lives (with her father?) in a hill (Guiteras, 1961:192, 216, 268). There is also in Chenalho an *anhel* called Ohob. Can he be a masculine form of X'ob?

The moon goddess being in Maya legend daughter of the thunder god and, as we have seen, identified with the Virgin Mary, it seems possible that X'ob originally was the local moon goddess, who may have conformed to the pattern of being also an earth and maize deity, but that is speculation. It is also worth bearing in mind that there was an Aztec trading post, and possibly a garrison as well, at Tzinacantan, in Tzotzil territory. It is, therefore, possible that this concept of a maize goddess was borrowed from Mexican beliefs, although I know of nothing in Mexican myth corresponding to the four miraculous ears of maize.

In keeping with the peasant's view that the maize spirit is first and foremost his friend and ally, offerings are not made to him, to the best of my knowledge, by present-day Maya. On the other hand, the Maya priests, who did not share their anxieties and daily watching of the growing crop under enemy attack, raised the

[9] Siegel (1941:66) writes that the Kanhobal Maya of San Miguel Acatan speak of the maize as "Our Mother Corn" who "gives us our lives," and the maize spirit as "the spirit of Our Mother Corn," but—and it is an important but—in the same paragraph Siegel tells us: "the moon, earth and corn become identified in thought and speech," so here too we are probably dealing with a maize goddess as such, but with an extension of the functions of a moon-earth goddess.

Barrera Vásquez (1939) develops an interesting thesis that Ix Kan Le Ox, a fourth and sole female of the four Chacs or Pauahtuns, is the maize goddess and corresponds to God E of the codices. However, God E wears masculine dress and shows no female characteristics (goddesses in the codices normally display, as identificatory feature, a prominent breast). We have noted (p. 207) sources which make it tolerably certain that she was Goddess O, wife of Itzam Na. As she functions as an active rain goddess in codices Dresden and Madrid (Plate 9, top) it is understandable that she should consort with the Chacs. Certainly the Chorti maize spirit is masculine, for the bean spirit is his wife (Wisdom, 1940:402).

corn spirit to a god. One may conjecture that a similar dichotomy existed in the Old World in attitudes toward Ceres and Demeter.

THE INVISIBLE GUARDIANS

There are ill-defined groups of guardian spirits who protect the Yucatec Maya in his daily life.

Every Maya village and town theoretically has four entrances oriented to the world directions. In actuality there may be half a dozen or more paths leading into a village, none of which is aligned with the four points of the compass, but there are four "official" entries thus oriented, and at each a Balam stands guard to protect the village. Some hold that a fifth Balam is at the center of the settlement. The Balam are also called Nucuch Uinic or Nucuch Macob, both meaning "the Huge Men." They are protectors against dangerous animals, probably in ancient times against raiding enemies, and nowadays against evil winds (a Spanish introduction in all probability). This they do by shooting fragments of flint or obsidian at the attackers. When people find these fragments or bits of animal fur, they know the Balams have been active in their defense.

Four Balams also stand guard at the four sides of one's milpa to protect it from robbers. They are also known as Yumi[l]col, Lord of the Milpa." The Balams are usually thought of as without definite form; sometimes as giants, as their names indicate, sometimes as dwarfs. *Balam* means "jaguar," and the word was also used to designate the rulers and priests of the town "who with their valor keep guard over it." The jaguar was a symbol of fierceness and valor, so the Balams are really the valiant ones. I suspect that the little pottery jaguar sometimes found in excavations (p. 211) represent them, and that in pre-Columbian thought the Balam were regarded as having had the forms of jaguars or, at least, were metaphorically jaguars. Somewhat similar are the Kuil Kaxob, "Gods of the Forest," and I think Brinton's Yum Kaax, "Forest Lord," is another name for this ill-defined group who protect one in the forest. There are, too, the Ah Beob, "They of the Roads," who go before to open the trail and protect one from harm— falling branches, snakes, and perhaps robbers.

All these beings are known collectively as Yuntzilob, with a meaning something like "Worthy Lords." They also partake of the duality which permeates Maya religion, for the Balams can be harmful, too. They will return a changeling for a lost boy; if one fails to make them offerings, they will send sickness; and their cries at night are a sign of imminent death in the village.

They receive token offerings from milpa makers and are mentioned in prayers during milpa ceremonies. They are very real to the villagers—on a par with the little folk of bygone Ireland—but one suspects that the hierarchy paid them little attention. (Principal sources: Redfield and Villa, 1934; Villa, 1945.)

THE JAGUAR GOD

A jaguar god, his features often displayed by an impersonator, is very prominent in the art of the Classic period, and he appears frequently on the fronts of incense burners from Chiapas and the highlands of Guatemala. His most readily recognizable attributes, even when he serves as the disguise of an impersonator, are a large conventionalized jaguar ear complete with circular jaguar-hide markings; a loop passing beneath both eyes and twisted into a design resembling our number eight above the bridge of the nose; round eyes (denoting a god's animal derivation); "whiskers" in the form of a curving line from level with the nose to the chin, almost certainly representing the jaguar's whiskers; prominent filed central incisors in the upper jaw, symbolic of the sun god, or a fang, such as distinguishes representations of the jaguar, at each corner of the mouth; occasionally, but of uncommon importance, a bar and two dots, that is, the number seven on the cheek (the god's glyph [Catalog No. 1018] at times shows this number above the earplug); and, at times, the water lily, a well-recognized attribute of the jaguar. Figure 1*b* is a somewhat atypical portrait, but note the jaguar ear; water lily dangling behind; ill-formed, twisted number eight; and jaguar skin.

As this deity does not appear in the hieroglyphic codices (unless he is God L), we have few guides to his activities. However, he not only wears the number seven at times, he is in fact god of the number seven and god of the day Akbal, seventh in the series of days beginning with Caban. Indeed, in glyphic representations of the Yaxchilan leader Jaguar Shield, the shield which is affixed to the head of a jaguar has the Akbal sign set in it. To close the circle, the big shield so prominent on the Tablet of the Sun, Palenque, is decorated with this selfsame jaguar god.

The day name Akbal means "night" or "darkness" in various Maya languages, and the equivalent day in the Zapotec calendar has the same meanings. The equivalent Nahuatl day name signifies "house," but its ruler was the jaguar god Tepeyollotl, "Heart of the Mountain," a deity of caves and the interior of the earth. Moreover, Beyer (1921:43) has noted that, on the Mexican plateau, not only did the jaguar stand for night and darkness, but a spread-out jaguar skin was thought to symbolize the starry night.

The Maya had precisely the same idea. On a sculpture at Copan the lord of the night carries as his "burden" a rolled-up jaguar skin symbolizing the night, and glyphs derived from a jaguar skin function in the same way as the realm ruled by the lords of the night. With the so-called Ben Ich prefix, which very probably stands for *ah*, the masculine prefix, this same jaguar-skin sign appears to mean "He of the Starry Sky," or—less probably—"He of the Jaguar Mat," that being a symbol of high rank (Thompson, 1968).

The material is uncommonly complex, as is so often the case when one explores the byways of mythology; for a full discussion see Uotan (p. 326) and Thompson (1950:73–75). Suffice it that the jaguar is intimately leagued with the underworld, land of darkness, and with the night sky. Thereby he becomes yet another case of duality, for he reigns in the sky and on or under the earth. The Lacandon belief that the world will be ended by jaguars ascending from the underworld to eat the sun and moon (p. 345) well illustrates the interrelationship between sky and earth.

Among the peoples of the Mexican plateau, the jaguar was also a god of war, and in the highlands of Guatemala he is associated with sorcery. Perhaps such a connection with war finds some support in jaguar and Akbal designs on shields, but there may enter other associations, for the jaguar skin is a symbol of chieftainship and was used to cover his seat of office.

The whole concept was surely hierarchic and so has not survived in peasant cultures.

Maya gods of the earth are of both human and reptilian nature. The latter have been reviewed under Itzam Cab (Ain) and Bolon Dz'acab, as have other deities—the moon goddess, the earth Chicchan, and the Tzultacah—whose functions as terrestrial powers are additional to their main powers.

The only anthropomorphic god primarily a deity of the soil worshiped to this day is the Chorti god Ih P'en or Tulanta', personification of the earth and patron of plant growth, fertility, family life, property, and other wealth. This being is both male and female, and their union causes the cultivated plants, their offspring, to grow. Here again, we are dealing with separate individuals who in union form a single personality. Wisdom (1940: 402), source of this information, translates their appellative U Uincirop ca Rum as "Guardians of Our Earth," but the term literally means "Men of Our Earth." *P'en* is an old root for the male generative principle (cf. Yucatec *p'en*, "penis," *xp'en*, "hermaphrodite," and, with relationship suffix *-el*, *p'enel*, "son," in Putun and Palencano; *pen*, "fornication," and *ah pen*, "fornicator," in the Manche-Chol vocabulary which fails to distinguish between *p* and *p'*).

Ih P'en, as the passive spirit of maize, is male and the consort of Ix Kanan, female spirit of the bean. I think one can deduce that the two are thought of as human in form from the fact that the saints of each family, usually Manuel and the Virgin Mary, are regarded as their representations. The Virgin Mary is Manuel's woman or companion; a virgin well past puberty is a bit of a freak in an Indian community, so although she may have the Spanish title of virgin, she is not really expected to behave like one.

At the ceremony to summon rain at sowing, turkeys and chickens are offered to the earth couple at the same time that offerings are made to the Chicchans (p. 264).

There is archaeological evidence for an earth god in human form. The god of number eleven in the series of gods of numbers one through thirteen has the earth (query-mark) symbol as his distinguishing attribute, and so surely must be an earth god. He is certainly the same person as the benevolent God R of the codices, who has this mark on his cheek (Plate 15*a*) and has the number eleven as part of his name glyph.

The upper part of Stela 40, Piedras Negras, has a serenely beautiful representation of the maize god or his impersonator sowing maize—the grains falling from his hand are visible. The lower part of the stela shows the bust of a god on whom the seed is about to fall; he must accordingly represent the earth. (Plate 12).

The same personage, recognizable by the earth symbol, is one of a group engaged in a penitential blood-drawing ceremony on a vase now in University Museum, Philadelphia. This deity, God R, has been tentatively, but, I am now sure, correctly identified with Buluc Ch'abtan (Thompson, 1950:135; 1961:14).

Buluc Ch'abtan (*buluc* means "eleven") is prominent in the tun prophecies in the Chilam Balam of Tizimin (Roys, 1949), but it is hard to make out what were his activities and powers. Although *ch'abtan* means "penance," Eleven Penances hardly fits an earth god, and I am sure has nothing to do with the meaning of the god's name.

In Ritual of the Bacabs, *ch'ab*, "creation," and *akab*, "darkness," are paired over two dozen times, usually qualified by the words *col*, *cool*, or *coil*, the principal meanings of which are "lust" or "madness"; *kazil*, "evil"; and *kazal*, "sexual organs," "sperm," or "roguery." Roys (1965: xv) believed that *ch'ab* is the male principle and *akab*, the female, and cites good evidence for his conclusion. This is undoubtedly so, but I would take the matter a step farther and suppose that the two forces, male and female, were united in one person, and that an earth deity. We have just seen that the Chorti unite male and female in their dual-sexed earth god Ih P'en. I would conjecture that *ch'ab* and *akab* are similarly united. Moreover, we have seen that *p'en* is a term for the male organ which supplies an almost exact parallel to the expressions noted above: lust of creation, lust of darkness; sexual organs of creation and darkness; and the evil of creation and darkness, since coition is regarded as sinful (p. 175). That *ch'ab* and *akab* are looked on not only as a personage but as a place (the earth) I infer from the use with them, once, of the word *yol*, "in the midst of," "in the heart of," not normally (never?) used with persons.

Apparently the earth did give birth to humans, for on the sarcophagus of the tomb under the Temple of the Inscriptions, Palenque, persons emerge from the earth carefully labeled with the query-mark earth sign, and this is confirmed by legendary ancestors emerging from under the earth (p. 195).

Ch'ab, as the male principle, creation, corresponds to Ih P'en (*Ih* may be a corruption of the masculine prefix *ah*; Ah Ch'ab is also given as a name of the creator, p. 205). Eleven, as we have seen, is personified as the god with the query-mark earth symbol. What of the remaining element, *tan*?

Tan has several meanings. One possibility is that it is a directional suffix, as in *chikintan*, "westward"; *xamantan*, "northward"; *citan*, "more onward"; and so on. Related to this usage is *tan* in the sense of "front," "face," or "chest," perhaps referable to the face of the stretched-out, personified earth common in the Mexican period at Chichen Itza (e.g., Marquina, 1951, Fig. 439). Note in that connection the apology to the mountain-valley earth god for damaging his face (*uich*) and heart (*yol*) when felling forest, given in Mopan-Maya prayers (p. 194). I think the *tan* element is best explained in that way. However, no linguistic connection between *cab*, "earth," and *ch'ab* can exist; no Choloid group has the form *chab* for "world," and even if they had, such shifts practically never involve the dropping of a glottal stop.

One last point: Ritual of the Bacabs twice speaks of the snakes of (*u canil*) *ch'ab* and *akab*; in the above-mentioned sculptures, snakes rise from the stomach of the recumbent earth gods, and once (MS:69) we read, "Thirteen the stoppers of the nostrils of *ch'ab*, of the lewdness of *akab*"; on the manuscript page 81 is given *mac u hol cab*, "the stopper of the opening (or head) of the earth." I suggest these are the same thing.

At Chichen Itza, during the Mexican period, earth monsters

commonly have a bone (?) plug inserted in each nostril (Seler, 1902–23, vol. 5, pt. 3, Figs. 110–19, 181, 188, 192, 193), but this same strange arrangement occurs also in the Central area during the Classic period (Spinden, 1913, Figs. 15*e*, 138), and in many profiles similar plugs protrude from where a nose should be. I would suggest that the thirteen stoppers of the nostrils of *ch'ab* and *akab* refer to these, again linking their possessor to representations of the earth; thirteen, presumably, is used in a ritualistic sense.

I believe there is not much doubt that Buluc Ch'abtan is an earth deity, but whether he is an anthropomorphic form of the earth monster, as God D appears to be of the celestial monsters, I would not hazard a guess. Although he is portrayed as a handsome young man, I infer from the points set forth above that, like Ih P'en, he was a dual-sexed being.

There was surely confusion in Maya thought between the reptilian and personified forms of the earth, so it is not surprising to find the *ch'ab* and *akab* male and female conceptions applied to both, but whereas the lizard pair are male and female, sky and earth, these personified earth gods appear to be dual sexed and confined to the earth.

Ah Uuc ti Cab and U Yum Cap (pp. 228, 327) presumably are earth gods. The concept of a personified earth deity or deities is important among the present-day Maya of the highlands, but they are outside the scope of this chapter. There is also overlapping with mountain gods who are also rain deities, such as the Tzultacah. It is not easy to arrange religious beliefs in tight categories.

MAM, GOD OF EVIL

López de Cogolludo (1867–68, bk. 4, ch. 8) writes that the Yucatec Maya had a piece of wood which they dressed like a *dominguillo* (straw figure of a boy used in bull fights to frighten bulls), and to it, set on a stool, they offered food and drink during Uayeb, the five evil and unlucky days at the end of the year. At the close of Uayeb they undressed the idol and threw the pieces on the ground without troubling to offer it any more reverence.

While the five days lasted, they called it Mam, "Grandfather" (it must not be confused with the quite unrelated Mams, another name for the Tzultacah, p. 315).

Pío Pérez (in Stephens, 1843, 1:437), quoting a lost source (?), says that on the first day of Uayeb they carried Mam about, feasting him with all magnificence; on the second they used less solemnity; on the third they moved him from the altar to the middle of the temple; on the fourth, thence to the doorway; and on the last day they had the ceremony of taking leave or dismissal.

Those five days were a period of fasting, gloom, and extreme danger; during them no unnecessary activity was undertaken.

This same being is very much alive to this day in the Zutuhil town of Santiago Atitlan, where his principal duty is to preside over the period from Wednesday to Friday afternoon of Holy Week, which covers the agony in the garden of Gethsemane and the arrest, trial, and crucifixion of Jesus; it ends as the church ceremony of lowering the figure of Jesus from the cross is completed, which, for Christians, marks the end of sorrow and fasting. This period, like that of Uayeb, is not only one of sorrow and tension, it is also the prelude to a new cycle of life.

This personage is also called Mam. He is, as well—particularly in conversation with non-Indians—called Maximon, generally thought to be derived from Simon (Peter); he is also identified with Judas Iscariot, the other betrayer of Christ.

The body of this Mam is also of wood. It is a flat piece, said to be of *palo de pito*, about fifty-four inches high and seven inches broad. Another piece of wood or perhaps a gourd forms the head, and over it is placed a crude mask; the legs are also of wood. There are unconfirmed reports that an idol is hidden in the body. When dressed for ceremonies, the core is wrapped in rags and corn husks, over which are placed two or three sets of local men's costumes. The Atitlan Mam, like his Yucatec counterpart, resembles a scarecrow.

At the start of his reign he is carried, after a pause at the town hall for offerings and ceremonies, to a position outside the church where he is tied to a post before which stands a sort of altar. He receives offerings of incense, candles, cigars, silk kerchiefs, and huge quantities of bananas and cacao beans which are then hung up on the reredos of the main altar of the church. Previously, he had passed under an arch decorated with produce specially fetched from the Pacific coast. Crowds wait patiently before Mam, and nearly everyone makes him an offering before passing into the church.

On Good Friday afternoon, as soon as the figure of Christ has been lowered from the cross, Mam's treatment alters abruptly: he is ignominiously hurried off to the *cofradía* house, where he is undressed and hidden in the "attic," where he remains, untouched and uncared for, except for appearances on the feasts of Saint Michael and Saint Andrew (but, note, not on the festival of the patron of the village).

The Mam is thought to be very evil and to be closely associated with sexual depravity; he is said to have been married to a prostitute at one time (McDougall, 1955; Mendelson, 1959).

Clearly, the Yucatec and Atitlan Mams are the same personage. The main difference is that the Atitlan personage is closely connected with agricultural produce and vegetation in general whereas there is no such information from Yucatan, but that may well be due to the brevity of the account of the Yucatec ceremony.

Mam is also of some importance to the present day among the Kekchi of the Alta Verapaz. In a letter (1932) to the late Mrs. McDougall, one of the two sources for the above account, Gustav Helmrich wrote: "He [Mam] is old, malignant, a destroyer of live things, but handicapped because he is tied in the interior of the earth. At the start of the rainy season, rumblings are audible and the people say 'Listen, the Mam wants to come out.' 'Don't worry, he is well bound,' is the reply." Helmrich went on to write that the Mam is only mentioned with fear; people are afraid that if they mention him, he will carry them off. He holds power only during the nameless days, but Helmrich also wrote that the Kekchi have the custom of burying a Mam figure during those five days which have been transferred to Easter (for the Kekchi no longer have a native calendar).

Mam, then, is a feared god of evil, who is loosed from his home below the surface of the earth only in set times of crisis, at the conclusion of which he is no longer held in awe and is rudely banished. There is a ready explanation for his connection with vegetation; there is a widespread Maya belief that darkness and the underworld are evil (p. 296), but as the latter reaches up to immediately below the surface of the earth, it also produces crops, and so its gods carry emblems of vegetal growth (p. 219).

No certain pre-Columbian representations of Mam have been identified, but possibly the ugly, dumpy little fellow held aloft by a large crowd of attendants in a detached scene of the murals of Room 3, Bonampak, is Mam.

Mendelson illustrates a modern Mam mask from Atitlan, but without recognizable attributes, for old symbolism is lost. Mam, then, is the spirit of evil from beneath the earth who was abroad in times of mourning and tension—in the five unlucky days in ancient times, in the great period of sorrow in Holy Week in his new Christian context—but joyfully spurned when his reign ends.

DEATH GODS

The Maya recognized three abodes of the dead: the underworld, final resting place of most persons; a paradise located in one of the heavens; and a celestial home to which were admitted warriors who had died in war or on the sacrificial block and their feminine counterparts, those who died in childbirth.

In Yucatec, the underworld was called Metnal, certainly derived from Mictlan, Nahuatl term for that region; to some lowland Maya it was known as Xibalba, a term found also in the Popol Vuh, perhaps a borrowing from lowlanders, for it was located on the edge of lowland territory in the Alta Verapaz. This land was situated in the bottommost of the nine underworlds, presumably the fifth, since they were almost certainly in a stepped arrangement.

The road to Metnal is lengthy and hazardous. The Chamula Tzotzil, whose name for the underworld is *olontic*, "down below," place with a dead person a pair of new shoes to stand up to the journey. There are three gates to be passed and a lake to be crossed with the aid of dogs before the destination is reached (Pozas, 1959:203). The belief that dogs aid one to cross a body of water was widespread from the Valley of Mexico to central Honduras; it survives among other Tzotzil groups, the Tzeltal, and the Lacandon. The last place a small palm figure to represent a dog at each corner of the burial mound, and these guard the soul on its last journey. In the hands of the dead are placed a bone of a howler monkey and a lock cut from each side of the deceased's head. The first is for defense against fierce dogs on the journey; the second, to drive off birds of prey. Tortillas, an ear of corn, and a gourdful of *posol* are buried with the dead as food on the journey (Leonard, 1955). Ancient Maya tombs have yielded skeletons of dogs and, in one instance, a flint carving of an alert dog.

Landa writes that evildoers went to Metnal, where they were tormented, and the good to the paradise, but in that he is surely echoing Christian beliefs.

As to that paradise, Landa described it as a land of milk and honey where the dead passed a life of happy leisure with all imaginable delights beneath the shade of a giant ceiba tree (the sacred *yaxche*). This place equates with Tlalocan, the Mexican paradise and home of the Tlaloc rain gods, to which were admitted those who had died from lightning (under the Tlalocs' control), drowning, and certain diseases connected with water, such as pleurisy. A fresco of Tlalocan at Teotihuacan shows people playing games and a sort of leapfrog.

Unweaned children of the Tzotzil of Chamula who die are placed, wrapped in a mantle, in a great tree in the sky. This tree has many women's breasts at which the children are constantly suckled. This blissful paradise for children must surely be the same as Landa described beneath the ceiba tree, and what a delightful example of poetic imagination it is.

Again according to Landa, suicides went to this paradise, conducted thither by Ix Tab, "She of the Cord," whom he designates as goddess of the hanged. I doubt that a goddess with that sole function existed. More probably that duty was undertaken by the moon goddess for these reasons: a goddess with rope around her neck is pictured in the eclipse tables of Codex Dresden, and a goddess of hanging would have no place there, whereas a picture of the moon goddess is relevant to a table of eclipses. There is good evidence that a Mexican moon goddess resided in the equivalent Tlalocan (Thompson, 1939:144), and the Maya moon goddess took up residence in a body of water at conjunction, which is precisely when solar eclipses occur.

Early sources do not mention a third place of the dead, but

there is a belief current in Yucatan that the dead, after a temporary residence in the underworld, go to the highest (seventh) heaven, but men who have died in war and women in childbirth go straight there. The Tzotzil of Chamula have the strange idea that murdered people (a confused remembrance of the fate of those sacrificed?) go to be with the sun. There are conflicting ideas among the Lacandon that the death god punishes the wicked; another that after the body has been burned by the death god, the soul can go where it wishes; and that at the end of the world all the dead will ascend to the highest heaven. These views are discussed more fully below, but I am tolerably certain Christian ideas concerning hell and purgatory have influenced them. It is often said that the Lacandon have never been exposed to Christianity, but that is not so. Priests, notably Fathers Vico, Lorenzo, Margil, and Calderón, were inculcating Christianity among them from the mid-sixteenth to the opening years of the nineteenth century.

The Yucatec belief cited above concerning warriors and women dead in childbirth is certainly aboriginal, and finds support in the words spoken on one occasion by a Maya priest to the victim he was about to sacrifice: "We are not sending you to hell, but to glory in the sky, as our forefathers used to do."

There are various death gods and more appelatives. Cizin—the root of the word means "stench"—is the most important and widespread, his worship extending from Yucatan to Pokoman territory. I feel confident that he is the death god (A) most commonly found in the codices and the almost jolly one on the vase in the Museum of Primitive Art (Plates 4c, d, 8d, 14d). Another death god whom Landa calls Uac Mitun Ahau was patron of years assigned to the days Kan, the south, and the color yellow. He appears on a page of new-year ceremonies in the Dresden codex, and his glyph (Catalog No. 1042) occurs on monuments of the Classic period. I think his name may have been miscopied in the surviving copy of Landa; an expression *chacmitan ch'oc*, "great hellish (?) putrescence," occurs in the Chilam Balam of Tizimin; Chac Mitan Ahau would make more sense.

Landa also gives Hunhau (Hun Ahau) as a death god. Hun Ahau (1 Ahau) appears to have been a calendar name for Venus at heliacal rising. Lucifer denotes both devil and morning star; Middle American representations of Venus often carry death symbols to show they have just emerged from the underworld. Nevertheless, in mythology 4 Ahau and 1 Ahau seem to be associated respectively with the celestial light and terrestrial darkness aspects of creation.

Yum Cimil, "Lord of Death," Xibalba (Palencano Xiba), and Cumhau are other names for the death god(s); the Kekchi of Chamelco call him Ma Us Amkuinic, "No Good Man." Brinton (1895:44) cites Father Hernández, quoted in Las Casas, as the source for Ah Puch as a name of the death god, and that name has been accepted by most modern writers, including myself. In fact, no such name occurs in the source; it is written Eopuco, probably Ah Pucu, which is surely the same as Pucuh, name for the lord of the underworld in Tzeltal, Tzotzil, and Tojolabal. Hernández' informant was probably Putun speaking. Ikal Ahau and Oxlahun Tox are other death gods (pp. 323, 325).

According to one Lacandon informant, Cizin, as lord of the underworld, burns the soul of the dead first on the mouth and anus. When the soul complains, Cizin douses him in cold water, causing further protest, whereupon Cizin burns more and more till all the soul is gone. The soul then goes to Sucunyum, who, spitting on his hand, cleans the soul, which may then go where it likes. This burning may have arisen from infiltration of Christion ideas about hell.

Sucunyum, "Lord Elder Brother," looks after Cizin and inspects souls before passing them on to Cizin for punishment. He feeds and cares for the sun on his journey through the underworld, carrying him on his shoulders. He keeps Cizin from causing earthquakes, for Cizin is also an earthquake god (Amram, 1940; Baer and Baer, 1952:232–33).

Amram also was informed that Sucunyum sends the souls of good people to Menzabac, the rain god, instead of turning them over to Cizin. This substantiates the view expressed above that the Maya paradise was, like Tlalocan, the home of the rain gods. An informant told the Baers (1952:236) that four cabbage palms (did he mean ceibas?) grew in heaven, support for a Lacandon paradise concept.

In the belief of the Tzotzil of Chamula, the ruler of Olontic, their underworld, is the father of the sun god, a most unorthodox view. The sun goes to visit him each night, and the dead are buried at sunset so that they can journey to the underworld with him. The Chorti Maya recognize as death god a giant being called Chamer, "Connected with Death," a skeleton in white robes. Either he has a female consort or his clothes are a woman's. Following European ideas, he is armed with a scythe with a bone blade. Mexicans recognized a death goddess, spouse of the ruler of Mictlan, and, according to one source, the Lacandon name Cizin's spouse as XTabai (cf. Ix Tab), nowadays an evil spirit who, in Yucatec belief, lures men to embrace her and then drives them mad or kills them. A death goddess also appears in the Dresden codex, and as weaving is women's work, the death weaver in Codex Madrid (Plate 4*d*) is surely a death goddess, so we can rest assured that Cizin was married and his wife ruled with him over the underworld, both sadly bereft of carnal joys.

As depicted in the codices, Cizin is represented with fleshless nose, lower jaw, and spine and often with his ribs showing. He wears a collar with death eyes between lines of hair, an attribute found with his Mexican equivalent, and his body usually has black or yellow spots. A long bone hangs from the lobe of his ear. Sometimes the whole of his head is converted into a skull (Plates 4*c*, 8*d*, 14*d*). A common attribute is a sort of percentage sign on face or body in Classic sculpture. He is associated with Cauac years, the south, and the yellow directional color. Yellow is a symbol of death and, as noted, he has yellow spots. Yellow flowers are used to decorate graves, and in the Guatemalan highlands mourners painted their bodies yellow. On the Mexican plateau, the death god ruled over the north, in contrast to his relegation to the south by the Maya.

The death god is the personification of the number ten and lord of the tenth day counted from Caban, which is Cimi, "death," and is represented by the death god's head. Oddly, he is not one of the lords of the night.

As is to be expected, his influences are always evil, and the days he rules are unfavorable to every activity.

CHAPTER 8

Lowland Maya Religion:
Less Known and Alien Gods

As a consequence of the suppression of much of Maya culture and religion by the Spaniards and the rarity, in that incurious age, of observers interested in recording their fast-waning charms, uncommonly little is known of some deities and cults which were once important but which quickly submerged beneath the incoming tide of the Conquest. Among them should be numbered the gods and rites of idol makers, tattooers, merchants (their old commerce was swept away), and warriors and lineages of the nobility as well as deified ancestors of family and perhaps clan. Sometimes merely a name remains without information as to whether it is of a separate deity or merely one aspect of a divine power well known in some other field. With the old nobility laid low, cults of their ancestors, possibly once very prominent features of Maya religion, withered on the vine.

Such cults did not pass into oblivion quite undefended. As late as twenty years after the Spanish Conquest, Maya chiefs were touring Yucatan in an underground campaign of resistance, performing pagan ceremonies and telling the people that the Roman Catholic faith, baptism, the mass, and friars' preachings meant naught. *Ma bin bal xchristianoil*, "Christianity is nothing," was their cry, but it availed them nothing; the tide could not be turned back. Not a few who tried to do so suffered physical torment for their efforts.

It is less understandable why so little is known about certain cults, notably those of fishing and hunting, having nothing to do with either the ruling class or crafts condemned to extinction, Fishing is a community occupation, so one would have expected its cult to have gone underground. Plausibly, nothing is known of such rites because no interested observer ever chanced to be in a Maya coastal village. As to hunting, that being a secondary occupation of the commonalty, enthusiasm may not have been enough for its special rites and patrons to endure some four centuries underground.

There are, then, reasons for supposing that the distinction between less known gods and lesser gods may not be very real. As to cults of alien gods, they owed their introduction to the ruling class and perished with it.

GODS OF OCCUPATIONS AND OTHER CULTS

Merchant gods. The pre-eminent Maya god of merchants was Ek Chuah (*ek* means both "black" and "star" in Yucatec), who was also god of cacao. The connection lies in the fact that cacao beans were the currency of all Middle America, and so were the foundation of all commercial transactions.

This deity may be of Putun origin, for the Putun, the great traders of the Maya area, called him Ik Chaua (*ik* signifying, again, "black" or "star"). He is perhaps the same as Chua of the Putun-influenced Lacandon of eastern Acalan (p. 40). Meanings of *chuah* or *chaua* are unknown; Ah or Ix Chuah are Yucatec names for certain wild bees, but a connection between bees and merchants is not obvious.

Students are agreed that Schellhas' God M of the codices is this god. He is normally painted black, except for a red area around lips, chin, and a peculiar downward projection of lower lip or chin which is very characteristic. He has a markedly elongated nose which is near horizontal or retroussé, reminding us that the Aztec applied the term "sharp-nosed" to their chief god of merchants. This distinctive feature I have named the Pinocchio nose (Plate 11*a*). He wears a plaited carrying strap, the mark of merchants, in his headdress and often has a pack on his back. Usually a sort of white, elongated horseshoe with outcurving ends is around each eye, and he may hold a spearlike object which probably represents the staff which all porters use. He appears often in Codex Madrid, frequently as a traveler. Twice he is entirely white except for red lips and chin projection and blue horseshoes.

On murals at Santa Rita, British Honduras, and on incense burners from Mayapan and from Nebaj, in the Guatemalan highlands, his body and face are painted half blue and half red or striped in those colors. There are representations of him in copper and stone, and he almost surely appears on turquoise mosaic figures now in museums in Copenhagen and Rome. Note the projecting chin, black skin, spear, and fan of a merchant on a vase (Plate 3*b*).

On mainland Mexico there were six merchant gods, each distinguished by his own attributes; among the Maya there is some evidence of five. At least the different coloring of Maya gods—black, white, and blue and red—indicates that there were more than one Maya merchant god (Thompson, 1966*a*). Appropriately, the glyph of this god is the merchant's pack.

Merchant gods and their pack glyphs appear on monuments of the Classic period. On a monument at Pomona, at the bend of the Usumacinta River above Tenosique, and so at some time or other in Putun territory (p. 26), the pack glyph replaces the normal head of the jaguar god of number seven as patron of the month Uo (Lizardi, 1963, Fig. 5).

This last fact makes one wonder whether the Ek (Putun Ik) of the god's name refers not to his black color, but to *ek* or *ik*, "star," particularly as the Motul dictionary defines *xaman ek* as "north star," guide of merchants. Such an interpretation sorts reasonably well with the jaguar god of number seven as lord of the starry sky, but is purely speculative.

Landa writes that travelers, by which he surely means merchants, carried incense and censers with them. Each night they set up three stones on which they placed several grains of incense, and they also put incense on three other flat stones arranged before the former, praying to Ek Chuah for a safe return home.

This nocturnal ceremony—the merchants of Central Mexico did likewise—gives minor support to the suggested stellar connection of the god.

Merchant gods do not rule over any number or day, but the presence of the pack glyph among heads of gods who are connected with lunations (Glyph C of the lunar series) raises Ek Chuah another step to a stellar home. Should Ah Bolon Yocte (p. 320) be the name of a merchant god, Katun 11 Ahau was under their patronage.

Although these merchant gods were uncommonly important, particularly among the Putun Maya, nothing more is known of their cult; with the collapse of the merchant class they ceased to be worshiped.

Gods of hunting and fishing. Helpful Landa writes that hunters held their festival on the seventh day of the month Zip, the chief event being a dance in which each participant held a deer skull colored the sacred blue and an arrow. Blood from ears and tongues and other offerings were made, and everyone finished up roaring drunk. Deer dances are still performed by the Maya, but without pagan associations.

A number of pages of Codex Madrid are devoted to hunting and trapping rites, the hunters being distinguished by a peculiar headdress. Deer are most prominent, but trapped armadillos and turkeys have their place.

Landa names the hunting gods as Acanum, Zuhuy Zip, Tabai, and others; the Vienna dictionary gives Ah (?) Cancum, Ah Tabai, Ku Bolay, and Ceh Lac. The first is Landa's Acanum of unknown derivation; *ceh* is "deer," *lac* is a pottery idol.

To the present-day Yucatec Maya of Quintana Roo, Zip is the name of certain forest beings who protect the deer from hunters; they take the form of small deer, the most important having wasps' nests between their antlers. A Zip sometimes deceives a hunter by inducing him to shoot, say, an iguana, believing it to be a deer (presumably the Zip operate also in the United States causing hunters to shoot cows and men in mistake for deer). In Yucatan similar ideas prevail: the Zip guard the deer from hunters, watching over them as men guard their cattle; they cause a hunter to miss his aim; and should a hunter pursue a Zip, wasps would issue from the antler nest and sting him. A hunter hangs the head, stomach, and liver of a shot deer from a tree for about an hour, a symbolic offering to the Zip and certain Christian saints now patrons of hunting. Before hunting, one should make an offering of maize gruel to those personages so that they will allow one to shoot one of their creatures. Sometimes they are addressed as Ek Zip, Black Zip (Villa, 1945:103; Redfield and Villa, 1934: 117, 127, 350).

The *zuhuy* prefixed to Zip in Landa's list means "uncontaminated," "free from contact with the world," or "virgin"; it does not mean that the Zip are female.

In the Chilam Balam of Tizimin and Ritual of the Bacabs appear several references to Ah Uuc Yol Zip, "He Seven Heart of Zip." The meaning of Zip is obscure (the suggested "miss the target" hardly stands up), but one wonders if the above title cannot refer to 7 Zip, day of the deer festival. Can these deer spirits have been thus named because their festival fell in Zip, or was Zip so named because of the festival? The year prophecies of the Chilam Balam of Tizimin mention also Uuc Zuhuy Zip, "Seven Virgin Zip," undoubtedly the same personage.

Tabai or, with the masculine prefix, Ah Tabai survives today as the name of evil spirits who inhabit ceiba trees; their female counterparts, the XTabai, are beautiful beings (but their backs are like hollow tree trunks) who lure young men to embrace them, thereby driving them to madness and death (Thompson, 1930: 110, 156–60). Note another connection with trees: the offerings to the Zip are hung from trees. Ku Bolai means "God of Preying Animals."

The Chorti deer god is dual sexed: the male protects stags, the female, does. He inhabits a hill. Hunters burn copal to him, asking permission to shoot a deer and where to find it. Copal is also burned before the carcass (Wisdom, 1940:72, 400).

As noted (p. 250), the Mopan Maya regard the planet Venus as patron of hunting; the Tzeltal and Kekchi cut off a deer's head and burn copal before it, the latter say that is to appease the Tzultacah. On pages 40 and 47 of Codex Madrid, deer lie on planetary bands, indicating celestial connections, and this is reinforced by an obscure reference in the Chilam Balam of Chumayel to the deer "which hooks the sky." (See also p. 369).

Yucatec fishermen, again on Landa's authority, held their celebration on 8 Zip, the day after the hunters' festival. It started inland with anointment of fishing tackle, drawing of blood, and setting up of a tall pole. The participants then adjourned to the seashore where with nets and fishhooks they caught many fish. Only one of Landa's names for fish gods can be reconstituted—Kak Ne Xoc, "Fire-tailed Shark." Another name appears to be Chac Uayab Xoc (p. 321).

The Mopan Maya, in a communal water-poisoning to stun fish, make use of some interesting rites, but the prayer they recite is addressed to the water; they have no fish god (Thompson, 1930: 90–91).

Pottery models of fish, perhaps idols, were found by Gann (1900, Plate 34) at Santa Rita, British Honduras, a coastal site and probably the ancient Chetumal.

A head of a god closely resembling D, but with prominent barbules (Catalog No. 1011) occurs in the Classic period, particularly at Palenque, and this same head is attached to a fish painted on a bowl from Caracol, British Honduras, now in the Museum of Archaeology and Ethnology, Cambridge University (Plate 14*b*). Another fish god, but with a long snout (Catalog No. 1012), is patron of the month Zotz', "bat." The connection is not apparent.

Gods of cacao growers. Owners of cacao trees—our source is again Landa—made a festival in the month Muan to Ek Chuah, Chac, and Hobnil, sacrificing a dog with cacao-colored spots, blue iguanas, feathers (the color of cacao?), and copal. This ended with a banquet at which no one was allowed more than three cups of liquor—for obvious reasons manufacturers of chocolate to this day strongly support temperance. Ek Chuah, as we have seen, was god of merchants; Hobnil was one of the Bacabs.

Gods of apiarists. Owners of hives had their feast in honor of their gods, the Bacabs and especially Hobnil (p. 280n.), in the month Zec according to Landa. In fact, in Landa's year the day 1 Kan fell in the month Zec, and the series of years starting with

1 Kan, which included Landa's year, were under the special protection of Hobnil and the other Bacabs. Accordingly, I am inclined to think that 1 Kan was the day of the festival and it just chanced to fall during Zec in Landa's year. In any case, the Bacabs were closely associated with bees. Balche flowed freely, hardly surprising since honey is its main constituent.

Several pages of Codex Madrid are given over to apiculture, with bees, hives, and offerings depicted, as well as a scattering of gods with antennae.

The Yucatec Maya today recognize bee gods called XMulzencab who appear in the story of the creation, each with world color and directional associations in the Chilam Balam of Chumayel. Roys (1933:63–64) believed that a deity who appears head down and is popularly known as the diving god is, in fact, a representation of the XMulzencab. This being, modeled in stucco on façades, is particularly common on the east coast of Yucatan, a region famed at the time of the Spanish Conquest for its production of honey, particularly on Cozumel Island and in the province of Chetumal. The figure is prominent on a building at Coba, and in that connection, as Roys pointed out, it is of interest that the Yucatec Maya believe that the XMulzencab dwell at that site.

The diving god is part human, but he has winglike attachments to his arms and at times wears what seem to be antennae (Lothrop, 1924, Figure 22, Plates 3, 23). This diving position is that in which bees are usually shown in the apiculture section of Codex Madrid. This identification is reasonable, but one should bear in mind that a swallow god, Tel Cuzan, was the principal deity of Cozumel.

God of balche. The Motul dictionary lists Acan as god of wine, a term applied to *balche* by early writers. *Acan* means, *inter alia*, "bellowing." Anyone who has heard the shouts of drunken Maya might be inclined to see a connection. Probably the gods of apiary were also patrons of *balche*, for this is fermented honey made with bark of the *balche* tree added. The Lacandon patron is Bohr or Bol. If he is angry, the *balche* will not be good. He is Cacoch's aid (Cline, 1944; Bruce, 1967).

Gods of medicine and its practitioners. As already noted, the moon goddess, Ix Chel, was patroness of disease and medicine.

Landa describes the festival in detail: "The doctors and shamans and their wives gathered in the house of one of their number, where the priests, after driving out the devil, brought out their medicine bundles in which they carried around many trifles and various little idols of the goddess of medicine, Ix Chel (for which reason they called this festival Ihcil Ix Chel) and some little divination stones which they cast called *am*. With their great devotion they invoked in prayer the gods of medicine: Itzam Na, Cit Bolon Tun ["Father Virgin Jade?"] and Ahau Chamahez ["Lord Death Causer," probably a Putun deity, as *chami* is "death" in some Choloid languages including Putun; cf. Manche *chamel* and Palencano *chümel*, "sickness" or "to die"]."

The ceremonies concluded with everyone dancing with the rewrapped bundles on their backs, and, the sexes then separated, a banquet with everyone except the priests as drunk as lords.

Other patrons of medicine or disease are the sun god (p. 238) and Kinich Kakmo. The Lacandon believe Kaak, the fire god, Itzan Noh Ku, and Menzabac send fever, the two last probably because malaria is rife in the rainy season, and they are rain gods. Probably most gods sent diseases, and there is inconclusive evidence that, as among the Mexicans, individual gods were connected with specific categories of disease (Thompson, 1958:305–306). The many almanacs touching on disease, over which the moon goddess, Ix Chel, presides in the Dresden codex, attest to her pre-eminence in that field.

The Chorti god of remedies, Ah Uincir Dz'acar, "Remedy Man," patron of herbalists, is said to be the owner of all remedial plants. He is dual sexed, the male being responsible for the curing of men, the female for women (the Chorti lean heavily toward dual-sexed gods). He is angered if any waste or misuse his remedies (Wisdom, 1940:401). Ah Uincir Kopot is another name. (See also Pozlom and Dz'iban Na, pp. 325, 327).

Gods of war. Landa describes a ceremony in the month Pax by warriors in honor of Cit Chac Coh, "Father Red (or Great) Puma." This is perhaps a deity of Mexican origin, for a puma is prominent in the friezes of jaguars and eagles, commemorating the military orders of those names at Chichen Itza. López de Cogolludo (1867–68, bk. 4, ch. 8) states that in war four captains carried (on a litter?)

an idol of Ah Chuy Kak, perhaps Ah Ch'uy Kak, "Kite (bird) Fire." The Itza of Tayasal had two war gods, Pakoc (Ximénez says Pecoc, and that he was in a cave) and Hexchunchan, to whom they burned copal before beginning a war; they may be tribal ancestors. López de Cogolludo also mentions a god Kakupacat, "Fiery Glance," who bore in battle a shield of fire with which he protected himself. Ah Hulneb (*hul* is "spear," with instrumental *-eb*, perhaps "He of the Spear Thrower"), a god of Cozumel, was pictured spear in hand. Hun Pic Tok, "Eight thousand Flints," who had a shrine of Izamal, sounds as though he were a man of war.

Gods of poetry and music. Kai Yum, "Singing Lord," is the Lacandon god of music; his brazier is shaped as a pottery drum. Pottery drums used in rites are whitened and carry a head of this god in relief. Kai Yum is said to dwell in the sky (Tozzer, 1907: 97, 111). He is an assistant of Cacoch, a creation god (p. 202) according to Bruce (1967:96).

Ah Kin Xoc (*ah kin*, "priest"; *xoc*, "to count or read," here "to recite?"), a great singer, and musician, and god of poetry (most Maya "poetry" was probably sung), was also called P'izlimtec, defined in the Vienna dictionary as "to compete in a trial of strength" (a sort of Maya *eisteddfod*?). In a Maya creation story in the Chilam Balam of Chumayel he appears in the guise of a hummingbird and marries the five-petaled *plumeria* flower. This suggests that he is an aspect of the sun god, who in guise of a hummingbird wooed and won the moon goddess (p. 364; for *plumeria* see p. 202). However, one should bear in mind that Piltzintecutli was a name for the Mexican god Xochipilli. Ah Kin Xocbiltun was another name for this god. There is no information on rites in honor of this muse.

God of tattooing. There is mention of Acat, a god of tattooers. Acat is a Nahuatl day name meaning "reed"; Ah Cat would be "He of the Storage Jar."

God of ball-game players. See Macuil Xochitl under Mexican gods.

God of fire. As noted, the Maya regarded Itzam Cab, earth aspect of Itzam Na, as god of fire, and that deity sometimes has the fire glyph as his headdress (p. 230), but no information on a fire cult has come down to us although the fire god was extremely important on the Mexican plateau.

The Lacandon have a god Kaak, "Fire," who, besides being a god of fire, sends and protects from diseases, presumably because a number of pox diseases are also called *kaak* or *kak* in Yucatec (p. 243). Kaak is said to be patron of trails, protecting travelers from jaguars and snakes, and he sees that arrows which have missed their mark are found. He lives in a cave at Lake Metzabac in which many braziers, skulls, and human bones are found. The most recent writer on the subject, unlike his predecessors, says Kaak is also a war god; the Lacandon have not fought for a couple of centuries.

That fire is personified is brought out by a Cakchiquel view that it is a great sin to have sexual intercourse before a fire, for fire is a very fastidious being (Tax, 1951:802).

Drilling new fire with wood was the occasion for an important ritual particularly in connection with the start of a new period of time; fire glyphs often accompany period endings on monuments. The Mopan Maya have a tale that fire was first obtained by a dog which, swimming a river, stealthily lit a wax candle at a neighbor's fire and swam back with it alight (Thompson, 1930: 151). The candle in the myth is post-Columbian, for the Maya had no candles until the Spaniards introduced them.

Ancestral and lineage gods. Recent field work has shown the importance of deified ancestors in the lives of some Maya groups, particularly the Tzotzil (e.g., Guiteras, 1961; Holland, 1963; Vogt *et al.*, 1966). These beings, known as Totilme'iletic, "Fathers and Mothers," live in the sacred mountains which surround their towns and in hills which dominate springs and smaller residential groups. They meet, in the case of Zinacantan, to deliberate on the Calvary hill and there await offerings of black fowl and white candles (both of European origin—because the place is identified with Christianity?). They supply the people with their food and they reward and punish their people according to their deserts; punishment is sometimes by means of a thunderbolt. They have large corrals in the interior of a great mountain in which are penned wild animals—jaguars, ocelots, coyotes, and others—one for each living member of the community, and these are cared for by aides of the Totilme'iletic. If a person commits some evil, his particular animal or nagual is loosed from the corral, a dangerous matter because any harm that befalls the nagual befalls him. The nagual is returned to the corral when its *alter ego* performs a propitiatory rite.

Apart from the nagual element, rampant in Chiapas (p. 167), these ancestral deities are close to earth gods such as the Tzultacah (p. 272) found over much of the Guatemalan highlands, the entrances to whose homes beneath mountains are caves or sink holes, who send thunder and lightning, who are particularly associated with mountains around their worshipers' homes, who have the care of wild animals which they keep in pens beneath a mountain (Thompson, 1930:141), and to whom prayers are offered for good crops.

The Tzultacah are addressed in prayers as My Father, My Mother, and, in southern British Honduras, My Grandfather, My Grandmother, and also Mam, "Grandfather," but no one has suggested that they are ancestral deities. Indeed, the Christian God is named as My Mother, My Father in Kekchi prayers offered in church (Sapper, 1897:294), and there seems to be no reason to suppose that He is regarded as an ancestral god. Similarly, in Yucatan various gods have *cit*, "father," prefixed to their names.

Are we to assume that deities such as the Tzultacah and the Cit gods of Yucatan were ancestors but that the relationship has now been lost? Or should we suppose that Totilme'iletic was once an honorific but now is taken in a literal sense? The evidence of the application of the honorific title to the Christian God is a strong argument for the second alternative.

In support of the second alternative, I would advance three other reasons. First, it seems a more logical explanation. Secondly, one might suppose that pride would demand personal and named ancestors with whom families and clans (in the broadest sense) could identify themselves. That is particularly true if one accepts that Maya society had a strong class basis, by and large, for most of its history (probable chief exception was the temporary reversion to village units in many parts at the close of the Classic period; p. 51). American ethnologists often seem under a compulsion to identify themselves with the national drive to export democracy, if only by wishful thinking. Nameless ancestors naturally fit this postulated Maya democracy; named lineage ancestors smell of decadent aristocracy driven from the New World—retroactively where necessary—circa 1780.

Thirdly, as is brought out below—abominable Toryism—ancestral deities, at least in Yucatan, were named and definitely associated with certain lineages.

All things considered, I conjecture that the Tzotzil always had an ancestor cult, but probably once based on lineage; that personified ancestors of the nobility disappeared (at the close of the Classic period or with the Spanish Conquest?); and that a general ancestor cult took its place and finally merged with Our Fathers, Our Mothers, the mountain gods. In that connection, the Kanhobal pattern at Santa Eulalia is of interest: the village ancestral pair lives and is worshiped devoutly in a cave close by the village, and there is a separate mountain cult (La Farge, 1947:127–28).

In Yucatan there is evidence of lineage cults, perhaps confined to the aristocracy. Landa again comes to the rescue on this:

> They burned the bodies of the lords and those of high esteem and placed the ashes in great urns, building temples over them [the common people were buried]. . . . At the present time, it was learned, they put the ashes of very important lords in hollow pottery statues. The rest of the nobility made for their fathers wooden statues, leaving a hollow in the occiput, in which they place the ashes of part of the body, well plugged. They removed the occipital skin of the deceased and stuck it over the entrance. They buried the rest [of the body] as was the custom. They kept these statues with much reverence among their idols.
>
> They cut off the heads of the former lords, the Cocoms [one of the greatest families of Yucatan], and having boiled them, they removed the flesh, they sawed off the crown from the middle toward the rear, leaving the front with jawbone and teeth. They replaced the missing flesh of these half skulls with a certain bitumen, modeling the features of the deceased. These they kept with the statues with the ashes in their house oratories, together with their idols, holding them in great reverence and esteem and making them offerings of

food on every feast day so that they should not lack food in the other life.

The above is clear evidence of an ancestor cult among the aristocracy in Yucatan, and a somewhat similarly treated skull from Nebaj points to a comparable situation in the Alta Verapaz. The shrines in many important residences, particularly at Mayapan where the Cocoms ruled, are probably evidence for the prevalence of such ideas.

Few names of lineage gods have survived in Yucatan. Zacal Puc, "White Hill(?)," one of the early invaders of Yucatan, may have been a Putun Maya. It is said that he was the first to offer *posol* to the Chacs; he seems to have been the god of the Cupul, rulers of the province of that name (Roys, 1939:5). Chocum Kin Chac was god of those called Kumum, and Hun Ix Kin Chac of people named Puc (Scholes and Adams, 1938, 1:153). The Chilam Balam of Chumayel lists four founders of lineages, including Zacal Puc, without indication that they were deified, but as Zacal Puc was so honored, it is probable the others were. A cryptic remark in the Putun *relación* of Paxbolon (Scholes and Roys, 1948, facsimile p. 157, line 6) may perhaps refer to ancestor worship. After a listing of the rulers of Acalan from the founder appears the statement, in the Spanish version, that only these were the kings and they guarded the towns. The Putun term for "guarded the towns" is *u canan ti bel cahob*, "their watching over the matters of the towns." *Canan* in Yucatec is a general term for guarding things, such as houses and cattle, but it is also a ritualist term applied to various deities, specifying what they guard. Its appearance in this *relación* leaves one with the impression that it may well have been a ritualistic term applied to dead rulers with the implication that they still watch over their people, that is, that they are ancestral deities of the royal lineage.

On the other hand, all Quiche families believe their ancestors have a lively interest in the affairs of their descendants. Their consent is sought, with offerings, to a contemplated marriage, and they are even asked to send a specified number of children. They prevent marriages from breaking up by punishing an adulterer with sickness or even death and also castigating the wife if she has not played her part by keeping her man content (Schultze-Jena, 1946:1–4). These, clearly, are ancestors of individual families invoked only by direct descendants.

To summarize material on lineage and ancestral cults, the following may be listed:

In pre-Columbian Yucatan, lineage gods appear to have been successful invading warriors. At least the ones we know most about—Zacal Puc and his companions—are described as the four lineages from heaven and seem to have been the leaders of the four groups of invading Itza. I would suppose that the Maya peasant made no claim to participate in these cults, which surely were linked to the ruling class, who, of course, needed the prestige of a valorous and specifically named ancestor as much as any Old World aristocrat holding up his end at the walls of Jaffa or on Sunset Boulevard.

The absence of any traces of ancestor worship in present-day Yucatan or among related peoples of British Honduras supports the above conclusion; as a feature of the old nobility, such cults would have disappeared just as did the worship of other gods of the aristocracy—Itzam Na, Kukulcan, and so on.

A study of the Popol Vuh leaves one with the impression that among the Quiche, too, there were cults in honor of the founding fathers. These also appear to have been swept away with their practitioners, the ruling class, when Spanish rule was established. Yet today ancestor worship among the Quiche is on a family basis. One prays to one's immediate ancestors, but anonymously, for help in family matters. They are ready to perpetuate the family, but take no interest in anyone else. Indeed, there must be friction and serious rivalries in the land of the dead, with the ancestors of Family A warning against marriage with a member of Family B, and the ancestors of Family B doing all they can to support their descendant, the despised swain.

Finally, we have the peculiar situation among the Tzotzil in which anonymous ancestors of the whole community appear to have merged with the local mountain-valley earth deities. Perhaps it is just as well that they did so, for anonymous ancestors

318

shared by the whole community are pretty uninspiring objects of worship.

Phallic cult. Phallicism seems to be absent from all ceremonial centers of the Central area. In the Puuc area of Yucatan and adjacent Campeche, stone phalli are numerous. They are reported from Chacmultun, near Loltun, Nohcahcab, San Pedro, Uxmal, Xkichmook, Xkoben Haltun and Xkonchen (both near Xul), and Xul. They are found at Chichen Itza (stucco, now in the Field Museum of Natural History, Chicago); Hampopol, Campeche; Nizucte, Quintana Roo; Santa Rita, British Honduras (clay); and on a pottery incense burner from a cave at the foot of the Maya Mountains (Gann, letter, Dec., 1929).

Related full-figure sculptures are reported from Sayil, Yucatan; Telantunich, Quintana Roo; and Pustunich, Campeche, but these are of a most unusual style and probably not contemporaries of the first lot.

I would conjecture that the phallic cults are due to influences from Veracruz.

OTHER LOWLAND MAYA GODS

Many names of apparent gods in the Books of Chilam Balam and Ritual of the Bacabs, as well as others in ethnological reports, are omitted unless there is valuable information on their functions, as are names of all animal and insect gods, specters, hobgoblins, and such like beings. A few gods previously mentioned in passing are included to record fuller data concerning them. The index will prove useful in tracing secondary names of gods, and readers may also consult Anders (1963), but bearing in mind that his spellings of Maya names are unstandardized and so at sixes and sevens.

Acante, Acantun, "Set-up Post," "Set-up Stone." Four with directional colors, they are prominent in new-year rites and in idol making (p. 191). There are many references to them in Ritual of the Bacabs.

Ach Bilam. Lord of Yaxchilan. His statue is a stone figure from a temple façade now before a temple. Lacandon make pilgrimages to it before burning their milpas. He is also called Nohoch

Bilam. One source says this is a ritualistic name for Nohoch Ac Yum (J. Soustelle, 1933:338; G. Soustelle, 1961:416; Cline, 1944; Duby, 1944:32).

Ac Yanto, "Our Helper." Brother of Hachacyum. This deity made white men and their products—metals, domestic animals, and so on. The same story is told of him as of Acanchop; that he intercedes with Hachacyum to stop eclipses (Baer and Baer, 1952:232–34, 251).

Ac Zac Iual. Idol of Valladolid, Yucatan. Every four years there was a fight for the honor of carrying his standard, kept on top of his pyramid (*Relaciones de Yucatán,* 1898–1900, 2:5).

Bolomac (Bolon Mac?, "Nine Men"). Nagual of the Manche Chol (Manche Chol vocabulary). He is perhaps the same as Bolon ti Ku.

Bolon Mayel, "Most Fragrant." In the Chilam Balam of Chumayel creation legend (MS: 45), he came to earth. His associations are with flowers and honey.

Ah Bolon Yocte, "He of Nine (or Many) Strides." He is linked to Katun 11 Ahau both in the Books of Chilam Balam and on the Dresden codex, page 60, probably as its ruler or countenance. A passage reads: "The drum and rattle of Ah Bolon Yocte shall resound." At Santa Rita, the merchant god is beating a drum and shaking a rattle. As, furthermore, Ah Bolon Yocte's name suggests travel and he is the only god mentioned (in two places) in connection with drum and rattle, I conjecture that he is one of the merchant gods.

Ah Buluc Balam, "Lord Eleven Jaguar." One of four gods called in to counteract the evils of Cauac years (Landa). The prefix *ah* suggests he was in human form.

Bulucte ti Chuen, "Eleven Chuen (or Chuens)." He is paired with Buluc Ch'abtan as ruler of a tun in the Chilam Balam of Tizimin, page 11. See Chuen.

Cabtanilcabtan. He is god of one of the wards of the Putun capital of Itzamkanac (Scholes and Roys, 1948:395).

Cacoch. One of four Lacandon creation gods (p. 202), he carries offerings to some gods and lives on east shore of Lake Petha (Tozzer, 1907:96, 107–108; Baer and Baer, 1952:250).

Canan, "Guardian," was a title applied to various deities, for example: Canan Balche, "Guardian of the Wild Life of the Forest"; Canan Kax, "Guardian of the Forests"; Canan Cacab, "Guardians of the Village"; Canan Era, "Guardian of the Milpas" (*era* is a Spanish term taken over by the Maya); and Canan Semillaob, "Guardian of the Seed," a delightful example of the Maya plural termination *ob* added to a Spanish word. All the above are Lacandon or Yucatec terms. Canan Chul Chan, "Guardian of Holy Sky," was a Tzeltal name for the morning star. Canam (*sic*) Lum, "Guardian of the Soil," was a Chiapan appellative.

Chacam Pat was a Lacandon god supposed to have lived in a palace structure at the archaeological site of Yaxchilan (J. Soustelle, 1935:338).

Ah Chac Mitan Ch'oc, "He of the Great Rotten Stench." Apparently, this was a name for Venus as morning star. He is linked to the day 1 Ahau, the day of the planet, and once to 8 Ahau (C. B. Tizimin: 12, 41, 48, 50). I suggest that Landa's Uac Mitun Ahau, as patron of the years starting with Cauac, may have been a miscopying of Chac Mitan.

Chac Uayab Xoc, "Great Demon Shark." "When he cleanses himself, Ah Xixteel U, Chac Uayab Xoc. At that time the fire is set, it is set to the tail of the shark. When it is set, it clings to the sky, to the clouds; at that time it is beheld everywhere. At that time the face of the sun is covered, the face of the moon is covered." (C. B. Tizimin:9, Roys translation). *Xix* is "to cleanse," yet another case of Maya punning. Apparently this same fish god is mentioned by Landa under the name Ah Kak Ne Xoc (miscopied as Xoi). He is twice paired with Chac Mumul Ain (p. 218). A portrait of Xoc is used as a rebus for *xoc*, "to count," in inscriptions dealing with the passage of time.

Chicchan god. He is god of number nine, and perhaps the same as the Chicchan of the Chorti (p. 262). By extension, he is lord of day Chicchan, ninth day counted from Caban. His portrait (Glyph 1003) is of a youth with jaguar spots around his mouth and often with jaguar whiskers added. In the codices he has on his temple the crosshatched snake marking of the day Chicchan, and his forehead carries the *yax* sign which is the symbolic form of the day Chicchan. Tlaloc also has jaguar features. Accordingly, there can be no doubt that this important god is a rain god (Plate 8*h*).

Chuen is the name of the eleventh day in the Yucatan calendar, corresponding to Monkey in most Middle American calendars. The name is surely related to 1 Chouen, "1 Spider Monkey," brother of 1 Batz, "1 Howler Monkey." Both were skilled in all arts and crafts. The Motul dictionary gives Ah Chuen, "Artificer, Craftsman of Some Art." It is probable that craftsmanship rather than the monkey is the god's métier. Yet in rebus portraiture he might be shown as a monkey, and so it is probable that the monkey-faced God C represents him. He is listed by Tovilla (1960, bk. 2, ch. 3) as Chuemexchel, separable into Chuen e ("and") Ix Chel, as one of the chief gods of the Manche Chol, and is listed in a Pokoman dictionary of Moran as Hun Cheuen, "1 Cheuen" (Miles, 1957:748). The same name is given by Las Casas (1909, ch. 235) as brother of Hun Ahau. He created the sky, planets, land, water, fire, and, together with his brother, man. The people who had this myth are not named, but probably the story came from Alta Verapaz. He is clearly an important god. See also Bulucte Chuen and Yaxal Chuen.

Ah Chun Caan, "He of the Base (or Trunk) of the Sky." His idol was adored by the people of Mérida (Vienna dictionary). As *chun caan* was the place where the Chacs gathered and where their leader lived, this may be a title of the chief Chac.

Chul Tatic Chites Vaneg (Uinic), "Holy Father, Creator (*ch'ihtez*, "to create") of Man." He is the Tzeltal creator (Pineda, 1883, pt. 2, p. 38) and perhaps the Christian God.

Ah Ciliz. The Chorti believe he causes eclipses by getting angry and eating the sun. The Lacandon say he serves meals to the sun (Wisdom, 1940:399; Amram, 1944).

Ah Cuxtal, "Come to Life(?)," is Lacandon god of birth (Tozzer, 1907:157).

Cit Bolon, "Father Nine (Many or Uncontaminated)." Seemingly a countenance of Katun 10 Ahau on the katun wheel in the Chilam Balam of Kaua, he is probably an incomplete version of the next entry.

Cit Bolon Ua, "Father Nine (Many or Uncontaminated) Liar

or Ensnarer." An evil force, he is the countenance or patron of katuns 8 Ahau and 10 Ahau.

Ikal Ahau, "Black Lord." His fierce soot-covered image in the church of Oxchuc, a Tzeltal town, suffered the same fate as that of Poslom (see below). For the Tzotzil of Larrainzar he is a feared death god of child size who wanders at night attacking people. He enjoys raw human flesh. By day he lives in a cave, but is also thought to inhabit the towers of the churches of Chamula and Santo Domingo, San Cristóbal. According to Castro, Ikal Ahau is an abbreviation of Ikal Ahau Chaan, "Swift Serpent," lord of a powerful mountain near Oxchuc (Núñez de la Vega, 1702, 9: 133; Holland, 1963: 125–27; Guiteras, 1961: 189; Castro, 1965:29–31).

Itacai are Chorti mountain spirits. They are giants of human shape said to live in a town composed of mountains, each one the home of an Itacai (Wisdom, 1940:403).

Itzanal is the first assistant of Cacoch. Bruce (1967:96) distinguishes him from Itzan Noh Ku.

Kakal Ku, "Fire God" or perhaps "Sun God" (*kak* is a term for the sun in some Maya languages, but not Yucatec). A Yucatec prayer addressed to him at the sacrifice of two children was: "Lord God all powerful, provide us with what we need. Give us water and what we need for our sustenance." This suggests a rain god (but perhaps the fire aspect of Itzam Cab, p. 230). López de Cogolludo (1867–68, bk. 1, ch. 4) gives Kakal Ku (written Rakalku, but *r* and *k* are frequently mistaken for one another) as a god of death at Isla de Sacrificios, Veracruz. I have found this in no early source. If it is correct, which one may doubt, the name must have been supplied by a Maya interpreter on an early expedition, for Isla de Sacrificios is far outside Maya territory.

Ix Kanan was Chorti spirit of beans and wife of the maize spirit (Wisdom, 1940: 402).

Kin Cobo was legendary hero of Lacandon. He was probably an ancestral god of Cobo lineage (Tozzer writes this *couo*; Couoh, "Tarantula," is a common Yucatec surname. I suspect the Lacandon name was once Couoh). He had many adventures in the underworld. U Zucun Yum changed his son into four pairs of gophers, setting a pair at each world direction (J. Soustelle, 1935: 339; G. Soustelle, 1961: 50). *Kin* here may mean "priest."

Kinchil Coba, "Chachalaca Bird of the Sun." As a sentinel he stood guard over the Itza of Tayasal. His concrete statue crowned a nearby small hill (Avendaño y Loyola, 1896:29v). The name occurs also in the Books of Chilam Balam. Chachalacas start screaming loudly at the approach of anyone, so the name is apt for a divine guard. They supply an interesting parallel to the geese of ancient Rome.

Kinich Chante, "Sun-faced Showy One" (C. B. Tizimin: 1, 9).

Ah Kohk Nar were Chorti guardians of the new corn. They are four ears of corn modeled in copal and put in the granary with the maize to guard it from an evil spirit. Three have Spanish names, but the fourth is Kumix, "The Little One" (Wisdom, 1940: 403).

Ah Mahen Tok, "He with Flint Knife in Chest," is the showiness or capacity (*chan*) of the katun (C. B. Tizimin: 12).

Mer Chor was Chorti guardian of the milpa (*chor*). He is sometimes confused with the earth god, and is said to be dual sexed and to live in the west (Wisdom, 1940: 401).

Muialha, "Rain Cloud," is god of the Lacandon of the Jataté River (Duby, 1944: 92). Compare to Oxlahun taz Muyal, "Thirteen Layers of Clouds" (below).

Multun Tzek, "Stone Mound of Skulls," is possibly the countenance of Katun 2 Ahau in the Chilam Balam of Kaua. López de Cogolludo (1867–68, bk. 4, ch. 8) writes that Mul Tul Tzec (*sic*) ruled in evil times of misfortune. I have thought the name may refer to the skull platforms as at Chichen Itza and Uxmal, Maya equivalents of the Aztec *tzompantli*, in which case this may not be a personified deity. The name occurs in the Chilam Balam of Tizimin, pages 4, 9, and 10, sometimes with the *ox*, "very, much, or important," prefix. Roys, in a letter (1947), wrote: "Re the Ox Multun Tzek glyph in the Chilam Balam of Mani, an Indian told me the word meant three graves, one for the *dz'ulob*, the whites, one for the mestizos, and one for the Indians. It sounds childish, but could the glyph be three graves with circles of worms around them?" *Ox* also means "three."

Muur, "Mound." G. Soustelle (1943) gives this as the name for the forest and its god. As the word means "mound," one wonders whether she was given the term *monte* which can mean in Central America both forest and small hill.

Oi Yum Cap, "Oi Lords of Earth," is from the Yocotan Putun (Blom and La Farge, 1926–27: 142). (Mishearing of U Yum Cap? q.v.).

Oxlahun taz Muyal, "Thirteen Layers of Clouds," is addressed in a Yucatec prayer (p. 193).

Oxlahun Tox, "Thirteen Death," a day name, is a Tzeltal demon, presumably a death god, who was portrayed seated with horns like those of a ram (Núñez de la Vega, 1702:9).

Pacat Pach, "Look Behind," created the first hills, the Puuc, in Yucatan (Pérez dictionary).

U Pal Ac Yum, "Our Lord's Boy," also called Ah T'up, "The Smallest." Youngest son of Hach Ac Yum, alias Nohoch Ac Yum (p. 344). (Baer and Baer, 1952:251).

P'a P'ol Chac. Lizana (1893, ch. 4) gives this as a name for the building on top of a pyramid at Izamal in which the priests dwelled, translating it "House of the Heads and Lightnings." Pa Pol Chac would be the "Head Smashing Chac." In any case, this is probably a title of the Chacs.

Piltec or *Ah P'iltec* were four deities with world directional and color associations who, in the Chilam Balam of Chumayel creation story, conducted people to their lord, suggesting that they were inferior beings. In the Chilam Balam of Tizimin, the name is written Ah P'iltec.

Poxlom or *Pozlom* was a god seemingly of disease, particularly venerated by the Tzeltal, who appeared as a ball of fire or in the sky as a star (Núñez de la Vega, 1702:137). The bishop describes the discovery in 1687 of his and other idols in the church of Oxchuc. All the Indians were made to recite the creed, listen to a sermon on their iniquities, and spit on the idol, after which it was publicly burned. With that, the good bishop optimistically thought the cult had been extirpated, but, nearly three centuries later, Pozlom (Holmes has Pozlob) still attracts much attention among the Tzotzil as a manifestation of evil powers, particularly illness, and as a destroyer (he eats souls); balls of fire are still one of his manifestations (Guiteras, 1961:340, etc.; Holland, 1963: 124, etc.).

HT'ubtun, "He who Spits Precious Stones" (López de Cogolludo, 1867–68, bk. 4, ch. 8).

Ah T'up, "Youngest" or "Smallest" is a frequent character in Maya religion and folklore. Almost invariably, he was the strongest or wisest of a group of gods or of divine brothers.

Uac Lom Chaan, "Six Stretched-out Glorious One(?)," was god of the ancient (pre-Spanish?) people of Mérida (Vienna dictionary). López de Cogolludo copied the last word as Chaam, "Molars," giving rise to wrong interpretations.

Ah Uaynih, "The Sleeper," was Chorti god of sleep. He aids the death god who can only bring death when the person is asleep or in a coma. This being is dual sexed, the male bringing sleep to women, the female to men (Wisdom, 1940:398).

Uotan is the third day in the Tzeltal calendar corresponding to Yucatec Akbal. He is "The Heart of the Town or People," "Lord of the Horizontal Wooden Drum," and the first man whom God sent to divide the land among the Indians. He placed treasures in a sealed jar and mantles (*mantas*; the text has *dantas*, "tapirs," probably a *lapsus calami*) in a dark cave. Almost certainly he is the equivalent of the jaguar god of darkness and number seven, lord of the day Akbal (p. 292).

Ah Xuce, alias Yum Cap (q.v.), is the spirit which causes the rainbow (Baer and Baer, 1952: 238).

Ah Yax Ac, "Lord Green (or New) Turtle (or Dwarf)," was guarded with other gods at Cozumel (C. B. Chumayel MS:3). Perhaps he is the Bacab who wears a turtle shell.

Yaxal Chac, "Green Chac," is a countenance of Katun 7 Ahau and perhaps of Katun 13 Ahau. Possibly he was a Chac connected with the zenith, the associated color of which, like all middle points, was green.

Yaxal Chuen, "Green (or New?) Chuen," is the countenance of Katun 12 Ahau (see Chuen).

Yax Bolay Ul, "Green (or New) Wild Beast or Snake." A passage in the Chilam Balam of Tizimin, page 6, reads: "At that time is the setting in order of the mat [symbol of rule] for Yax Bolay Ul." This is followed by a reference to serpents following one another nose to tail. As *bolay* is a common name for dangerous serpents, I think this personage is a snake being. There are also references to Chac Bolay Ul. *Chac* is "red"; *ul* is a frequent termination of names of gods.

U Yum Cap, "Lord(s) of the Earth," were dwarf beings of the Putun (Russell, 1947). This is also a Lacandon name for the spirit of the rainbow, alias Ah Xuce (Baer and Baer, 1952:232, 238; see also Oi Yum Cap).

Zac Talah (Zac T'ahlah?, "White Water Drip Appearance,") was worshiped with much ceremony in a cave or *sascab* mine near Chichen Itza before firing, planting, and harvesting milpas. This is a kneeling Atlantean altar support, bearded and with upraised hands, apparently similar to Bacabs at Chichen Itza. (Le Plongeon, 1886:88–91). Clearly, taken from the ruins, given new functions, and at last renamed (with reference to stalactitic changes?), he is ecclesiastically a most reprehensible but ethnologically a very engaging instance of relapse into heathenism.

Dz'ibaan Na, "Written House(?)," cures diseases. He is the younger brother of Menzabac and lives on an island in Lake Metzabac (Baer and Baer, 1952:232). Another source has him as guardian of the mountains and hunting (Amram, 1942:22).

MEXICAN GODS IN THE MAYA LOWLANDS

Below are listed Mexican gods certainly or possibly represented in Maya art or mentioned in literature.

Chacmol was a fanciful name bestowed by the no less fanciful Le Plongeon—the real name of these beings remains unknown—on reclining figures of considerable size, with knees raised and usually with a hollow or a plaque on the stomach, presumed to be for offerings. Over a dozen of these, in stone, have been found at Chichen Itza, where they normally stand before the entrances to temples. One of stucco is at the small site of Chacmool, Quintana Roo, and a small one (2 feet, 5 inches long) is at Canicab, Yucatan. A small one was found near Quirigua. They occur all over Central Mexico from one coast to the other, including Tula (fairly common in western Mexico), but not in Oaxaca or farther east. Distribution strongly supports a non-Maya origin, as do Mexican style ornaments of those at Chichen Itza. It has, however, been claimed that the concept spread from Yucatan to Mexico.

I am inclined to accept them as representing an earth deity because of recumbency with raised knees and shoulders.

Ix Chante Kak is cited in an incantation for ulcers (Ritual of the Bacabs, MS:107). Roys translates "Lady Notable Fire or Ulcers." Perhaps she is Chantico, Aztec goddess of fire according to Seler and others, with the Maya termination *kak*, "fire."

Ixquimilli is identified as god of the planet Venus (p. 249).

Kukulcan is the feathered serpent. Identity of this god with Quetzalcoatl is too well known to call for discussion.

Macuil Xochitl, "Five Flower," is god of the dance, gambling, and sport mentioned in the Chilam Balam of Chumayel (MS:46). The figure of a player on a ball-court marker at Copan probably represents this god, as like him he has a hand across his mouth (Strömsvik, 1952, Fig. 20a).

Tezcatlipoca is depicted five times on columns in the Warriors complex at Chichen Itza, in all cases with one leg amputated and four times with the recognizable smoking-mirror attribute (Thompson, 1942).

Tepecthic is one of ten principal idols of the Putun-inspired Lacandon of Dolores. The name is un-Maya, and, as some leaders of this group had Mexican names, it is probable that the god's name is connected with *tepec*, "mountain."

Ix Pic Tzab. Roys translates the name of this goddess (Ritual of the Bacabs MS:154) as "Lady Eight Thousand Rattles," but it could be alternatively "Lady Rattle(snake) Skirt," perhaps equivalent of Coatlicue, "Serpent Skirt," her skirt being of rattlesnakes.

Tlalchitonatiuh, "Sun Near Earth," the rising run, is generally depicted as an individual combining the features of the sun as a skeleton rising from the underworld (p. 240) with those of Tlaloc. He appears over and over again as a recipient of human hearts offered by warriors in the guise of jaguars, eagles, pumas, and so on at Chichen Itza. These represent warriors of the military orders, and the concept is a direct importation from Tula (Thompson, 1943a).

Tlaloc portraits are common in the Classic period at Copan, the Petén, and Puuc sites of Yucatan, and in the more recent Mexican period at Chichen Itza as well as in the great shrine of Tlaloc at Balankanche (p. 270).

Tlazolteotl appears with her unusual facial painting on an incense burner at Mayapan (Thompson, 1957:614).

Xipe, the unpleasant god of flaying, may not have originated on the Mexican mainland, but his cult was most developed there. He is represented on incensarios at Mayapan (Thompson, 1957: 612–13), there are statements probably referable to his cult in the literature, and God Q may be he or a closely allied god. Xipe is presented on a column at Oxkintok and as an Atlantean figure at Xculoc, Campeche. A fragment from Piste, near Chichen Itza (Seler, 1902–23, 5:384) may also be his portrait. There are possible Xipe heads at Classic sites in the Central area.

CHAPTER 9

Maya Creation Myths:

Creation and Destruction of Worlds

INTRODUCTION

Some changes to the original version (p. *xx*) have been made in this chapter mainly to delete material given elsewhere and, by reducing headings, to bring the format into line with the rest of the book. A few details are new.

Assemblage of the many fragments of creation myths recorded within the Maya area can be of value not only for the insight they allow into pagan thought, but also because of the information they can supply on relations both between Maya highlands and lowlands and also between each of those areas and other parts of Mexico. The material is widely scattered and in some cases difficult of access, and clearly what has been recovered represents but a small fragment of the lore on the subject current in Middle America when Cortés stepped ashore on Good Friday of 1519. Chance has largely decided what should or should not be preserved. It is a sad thought that perhaps only one European was sufficiently interested to collect and set down in detail such legends as the lowland Maya told their families in their homes or recited to strangers around the campfires of some group of itinerant merchants. He was Fray Andrés de Avendaño y Loyola, and his treatise on the priests and prophecies, idols, and calendar of the Yucatec is lost.

The effect of time and degree of European contact on the rate of loss of pagan detail to European elements in myths is a matter of some interest. Old World influence is apparent in Mexican myth very soon, for the story of people with ears so long that they wrap themselves up in them when they go to sleep appears in a native source, *Histoyre du Mechique*, probably composed in 1543, two decades after the Spanish Conquest. Naturally, myths were never frozen into immutable patterns of words and incidents in pre-Columbian times, but some present-day creation myths show complete mestization.

Other problems raised concern the center of diffusion of the concept of multiple creations and destructions of the world and the period or periods when specific incidents came to be shared by peoples of the Mexican plateau and the lowland Maya. No doubt many myths were spread by merchants.

Because they are the most detailed, legends of the various creations from the Valley of Mexico and its environs are first presented for points of comparison with Maya myths.

VALLEY OF MEXICO

The reason for the fullness of data from this region probably lies in the fact that there were persons interested in putting the different versions in writing soon after the Spanish Conquest, before the attrition which all paganism had to face had become serious.

There are five main Nahuatl sources: written in the Codex Chimalpopoca (two versions) and the *Historia de los mexicanos por sus pinturas*, painted in Codex Vatican A with commentary, and sculptured on the famous Aztec calendar stone and other stone objects (Beyer, 1921).

Codex Chimalpopoca comprises three distinct manuscripts, the first being the *Anales de Cuauhtitlan* and the last, *Leyenda de los soles*. Both, written in Nahuatl, come from independent sources. The *Anales*, by an unidentified author, dates from about

331

1570; the *Leyenda* is dated 1558; the *Historia . . . por sus pinturas* survives in a Spanish version of 1547, a copy of a lost original. Codex Vatican A, a pictorial and hieroglyphic book, derives from a lost original of about 1550. All, accordingly, are largely uncontaminated by European ideas.

Minor variations, notably in the succession of world creations and destructions, will not be discussed in view of the fact that the Valley of Mexico material is presented primarily for comparative purposes. The scheme here followed seems most likely to be the original, but the variants may well have been current before the Spanish Conquest. All are essentially uniform. Each creation is known as a sun. In outline they are:

First Creation. 4 Ocelotl ("jaguar") was its name. Tezcatlipoca was the sun. The world was inhabited by giants. After thirteen times fifty-two years it was ended by jaguars devouring the giants.

Second Creation. 4 Eecatl ("wind") was its name. Quetzalcoatl was the sun. After seven times fifty-two years it was ended by terrible winds which swept away houses, trees, and people. The few survivors were turned into monkeys.

Third Creation. 4 Quiauitl ("rain") was its name. Tlaloc was the sun. After six times fifty-two years it was ended by fire raining down from the sky and the forming of lava (volcanic eruptions). The sun burned all the houses. The people were children. The survivors were turned into birds.

Fourth Creation. 4 Atl ("water") was its name. Chalchihuitlicue was the sun. After thirteen times fifty-two years it was ended by floods. The mountains disappeared, and the people were turned into fish. According to one version, two persons survived because Tezcatlipoca ordered them to bore a hole in the trunk of a very large *ahuehuetl* tree and to crawl inside when the skies fell. The pair entered and survived the floods. Later they annoyed Tezcatlipoca, who changed them into dogs by cutting off their heads and sticking them on their buttocks.

Fifth Creation. 4 Ollin ("movement") was its name. Tonatiuh, the sun god, was its sun. Eventually an earthquake will bring it to an end. Men were created from bones rescued from the underworld realm of the death god by Quetzalcoatl. Blood which he drew from his body dripped on the bones, bringing them to life.

The gods created four men, and Tezcatlipoca and Quetzal-coatl turned themselves into great trees. "With the men and trees and gods they raised the sky with its stars as it now is. When the sky was raised Tezcatlipoca and Quetzalcoatl walked across it, and made the road which appears in the sky, and they were there and ever after are there with their abode there."

In the sixth year after the flood, Centeotl, the maize god, was born, and two years later the gods created men. In the fourteenth year, the gods decided to make the sun because the world was still in darkness, but this did not happen till the twenty-sixth year after the flood.

Deities supporting the heavens and trees set at the (four) points of the compass appear in codices Borgia and Vatican B, and world directional trees are a conspicuous feature of Codex Fejérváry-Mayer. All three codices are pre-Columbian and certainly origi-nated outside the Valley of Mexico, probably somewhere in the area embracing Puebla, northern Oaxaca, and southern Veracruz, so those two elements clearly had a far wider distribution than the Valley of Mexico.

So much for Central Mexico.

QUICHE, CAKCHIQUEL, AND ZUTUHIL

A large part of the Popol Vuh recounts the adventures of the sun and his brother on earth before the former took up his duties as the present sun; a smaller part tells of the creations and destruc-tions of the world (Recinos, 1950). The book was written in Quiche employing European script in the second half of the six-teenth century, and so is somewhat later in date than the Valley of Mexico sources. On the other hand, the more isolated Quiche were presumably less exposed to Spanish influence than the natives of the Valley of Mexico. Certainly the Popol Vuh is easily the best authority for highland Maya mythology. The creations ac-cording to this source are:

First Creation. Man was made of mud. Consequently, the figure "melted away, it was soft, did not move, had no strength; it fell down, it was limp, it could not move its head; its face fell to one side, its sight was blurred, it could not look behind. At first it

333

spoke, but it had no mind. Quickly it soaked in the water and could not stand." The gods were so dissatisfied that "they broke up and destroyed their work and their creation." It is not clear whether the whole world was destroyed at that time, but man was created afresh.

Second Creation. Men were made of wood of the *pito* tree and women of reed after an augury by the old pair of gods of divination had shown that *pito* wood, the beans of which, like maize grain, were used in divination, was a better substance than maize. The people looked, talked, and multiplied like men, but they lacked souls and minds, their faces were without expression, and their flesh was yellow. They did not remember their lord and creator, and for that reason they were destroyed.

A heavy resin fell from the sky, the face of the earth was darkened, and a black rain fell day and night. Animal demons killed the people, breaking and devouring their flesh. The domestic animals and the utensils attacked their owners. The dogs asked the wooden men why they had not fed them but instead always had a stick handy to beat them. The turkeys and the dogs kept for eating said, "You ate us, now we shall kill you." The metates complained that they had suffered when the maize was ground on them; but now it was their turn, they said. The pots and griddles accused man of burning them and clamored for revenge. The stones of the hearth did likewise. When the wooden men tried to escape to the roof crests, the houses collapsed; the trees and the caves refused them shelter. The race was annihilated, and from the survivors descend the monkeys.

Third Creation. Next, the ancestors of the present race were made of dough of yellow and white maize—first four men and then four women. They pleased their creators by thanking them for their creation, preservation, and all the blessings of this life. They were too wise; there was danger that they would equal the gods in wisdom. Consequently, Heart of Heaven blew mist into their eyes, diminishing their knowledge and wisdom. The world was still in darkness. Finally, the morning star rose before the assembled people. The priests burned copal and then the sun appeared, even the animals turning to face it. It rose with unbearable heat, drying the muddy surface of the earth. Certain gods,

334

deified animals, and hobgoblins (*zaqui coxol*, "little men of the forest") were turned to stone.

That the present world would end in destruction is not indicated in the Popol Vuh, but there is an extraordinary reference to that event in testimony given in 1563 by the Mercedarian Friar Luis Carrillo de San Vicente. The area to which this relates is not specified, but it is definitely in the highlands of Guatemala and quite probably that part occupied by the Quiche. According to this friar, old Indians on the point of death pass their idols on to others, bidding the recipients guard, honor, and venerate them because those who follow their law and custom will prevail, whereas the Spaniards, who were upstarts, must come to an end, and "when they were dead, these gods must send another new sun which would give light to him who followed them, and the people would recover in their generation and would possess their land in peace and tranquility." (Scholes and Adams, 1938, Document 46.)

Thus, for the Quiche, we have three races of man created and two destructions of man in the past, with a third destruction and a fourth creation promised for the future. In connection with the divination of the old pair (Xpiyacoc and Xmucane) to decide whether man should be of *pito* wood or of maize, it should be noted that the equivalent pair in the Nahuatl pantheon, Oxomoco and Cipactonal, made a divination to find out who should break open the mountain to obtain maize (p. 348).

In the Annals of the Cakchiquels, the book of the neighbors but enemies of the Quiche, there are very brief references to this same series of traditions (Recinos, 1953:46–47). One race of man was made of earth but was useless. He was fed with wood and leaves (confused recollection of the creation of men of wood?) but neither walked nor talked; he had neither blood nor flesh. Subsequently, man was made of maize dough mixed with blood of the tapir and the serpent. Thirteen men, but fourteen women, were created. "Then they talked. They had blood, they had flesh. They married and multiplied."

The Zutuhil conserve memories of a flood, at which time men were turned into animals (Rosales, 1948:801).

MAM, KANHOBAL, AND JACALTECA

The Mam Maya of Santiago Chimaltenango, in the western highlands of Guatemala, retain memories of three creations, a mixture of Maya and Christian themes (Wagley, 1949:51).

First Creation. People were said to have been monkeys. They were destroyed by a flood of burning pitch.

Second Creation. Some say the second race comprised gophers. A flood destroyed it.

Third Creation. The first people were Saint Joseph and the Blessed Virgin Mary. Saint Joseph made the earth, which was perfectly flat. As it was always dark, Saint Joseph made the sun and, later, the moon. Jesus was born and in four days grew to full size. He said to his father, "Do not be troubled, father, for I am going to make another world and you will be able to help me."

Then Jesus began to make the mountains and valleys and canyons for the rivers. He made the moon less bright than the sun so that people could sleep at night.

In the Kanhobal town of San Miguel Acatan, a cycle of stories, some of which refer to the creation, also attach to Jesus (Siegel, 1943:125). The Jews caught and crucified God, but He set a ladder on the cross and climbed to heaven. The cock crew and the world became clear. In the last sentence it seems possible that the author's use of the word "clear" rises from a misunderstanding of the Spanish *se aclaró*, "became bright." Clearly, the ladder as a symbol of the Passion, the denial of Saint Peter, and the darkness at noon have modified this version of the coming of light to the world, a favorite motif in all these Middle American creation stories.

The Jacalteca recount (La Farge and Byers, 1931:113) that the world was once in darkness. When the sun (apparently Jesus) rose, the Spaniards hid in caves and under the water, but were killed. Perhaps we may presume that those under the water were drowned. We are reminded of the belief recorded by Fray Luis Carrillo de San Vicente that the present world would end with the destruction of the Spaniards.

MAYA LOWLANDS: PRE-COLUMBIAN

Archaeological evidence for the cosmological beliefs of the

Maya is not plentiful but does point to world directional trees and Atlantean figures upholding the sky as ideas current during the Classic period.

The so-called crosses of the Tablet of the Cross and Foliated Cross at Palenque have long been regarded as probable world directional trees. They are either maize plants or trees of abundance. Dating from around A.D. 700, both are superb reliefs (Figs. 2, 3). To these should be added the scene on the lid of the sarcophagus of the burial of the Temple of the Inscriptions at the same site (Ruz, 1954, Fig. 8). A conventionalized tree rises from immediately behind a person in an awkward half-reclining position. Beneath, and probably serving as base of the tree, is a head of the Earth Lizard; perched on the tree is a bird.

In codices Borgia (pp. 49–53) and Vatican B (pp. 17–18), the world directional trees similarly rise from or from immediately behind figures reclining in similar awkward positions, and also have birds perched on them. The figures are gods or god impersonators. With the group must belong the scene on the Dresden codex, page 3, of a tree rising from or from behind a sacrificial victim with a gaping incision for the removal of his heart. On the tree perches a vulture who apparently has removed one eye of the victim, reminding us of the Maya expression *colop u ich*, "pulling out of the eye," which occurs so frequently in the Ritual of the Bacabs, frequently as the title of a god (Plate 5*b*).

Possibly scenes on the reliefs of the Temple of the Panels, Chichen Itza (Ruppert, 1931, Plate 11), treat of directional trees, for there are four of them in the south panel with a bird perched on each one. At the bottom of the panel there is a line of monkeys.

In Codex Dresden, Chacs perch on trees associated with the four world directions (Plate 8).

YUCATEC: COLONIAL PERIOD AND PRESENT DAY

Material on creations and destructions of the world is found in the Books of Chilam Balam of Chumayel (Roys, 1933:99), Mani, and Tizimin (Barrera Vásquez and Rendón, 1948: 153), reduced to writing in the Colonial period.

First Creation. This took place in a katun 11 Ahau, which is the first in the round of thirteen katuns (20-year periods) which together form the Maya ritualistic cycle of 260 years of 360 days, the framework of all Maya mythology, history, and prophecy.

The principal actors are Oxlahun ti Ku ("Thirteen God" or "Thirteen Gods") and Bolon ti Ku ("Nine God" or "Nine Gods"). The former apparently is a collective term for a group of sky gods, the latter for a group of gods of the underworld, night, and darkness. A translation of the relevant passage has been given (p. 281). The meaning is not completely clear, but there is a suggestion of a parallel with the Lacandon account of the creation (immediately below), in which the creator god, a celestial being, is killed and buried by Cizin, lord of the underworld, and his two sons. The strife between the celestial powers and the infernal powers of darkness finds a strange reflection in the Book of Revelation, but I feel sure that these Maya legends are pre-Columbian, and the resemblances are fortuitous.

There follows the only reference to a human (?) race of this creation: "After that the fatherless ones and those without husbands disintegrated. They were alive, but they had no judgment. Then they were smothered by the sand in the midst of the sea. There would be a coming and going of water. The water will come at the time the despoiling of the rain and lightning powers [of Oxlahun ti Ku] occurred. Then the sky would sink down, the earth would sink down when the four gods, the four Bacabs, are set up who would cause the destruction of the world."

The above account clearly shares features with the version in the Popol Vuh of the first creation and destruction in which the men of mud, without intelligence or judgment, disintegrated. In the Yucatec version we are not told the composition of the men, but they were without judgment and they disintegrated, so it is a fair deduction that they, too, were of mud.

The Bacabs and their task of upholding the sky and Landa's important statement on their part in creation and destruction of the world have been discussed (p. 276).

Second Creation. Immediately following the statement about the setting up of the Bacabs, the Chilam Balam of Chumayel and of Tizimin (Barrera Vásquez and Rendon, 1948:155) continue:

338

Then after the destruction of the world was completed, they set up the red tree of abundance [to the east], pillar of the sky, sign of the dawn of the world, tree of the Bacab, for the yellow cock oriole to perch on.

Then the white tree of abundance was set up to the north for the white bunting to perch on. Support of the sky, sign of destruction was the white tree of abundance.

Then the black tree of abundance was set up to the west of the flat land, as a memorial of the destruction of the world, for the black-breasted *pidz'oy* bird to perch on.

Then the yellow tree of abundance was set up to the south of the flat land, a memorial of the destruction of the world, for the yellow-breasted *pidz'oy* bird to perch on, for the yellow cock oriole to perch on, the timid yellow bird.

Then the green tree of abundance was set up in the center of the land, a memorial of the destruction of the world.

Following this, the plate of another katun was erected, and the red, white, black, and yellow Piltec were placed respectively to the east, north, west, and south of the world. The account continues:

> However, Ah Uuc Cheknal was set up for all the earth. He came from the seventh layer of the earth. Then he descended to fecundate [or trample on the back of] Itzam Cab Ain ["Iguana Earth Crocodile"]. Then he descended to the abutment of the angle between heaven and earth. They traveled to the four waxes [?], to the four layers of stars. There was no light in the world; there was no sun; there was no night; there was no moon. Then they saw that the dawn was coming. Then the dawn came. During the dawn thirteen infinite series and seven was the count of the creation of the world. And then it dawned for them.

Itzam Cab Ain, the manifestation of Itzam as the earth, has been discussed at length (p. 218). Ah Uuc Cheknal is unknown outside this context. His name means something like "Seven Times Stud Animal Owner" or "He who Fertilizes the Young Growing Maize Seven Times," but to have the latter meaning the growing maize must be regarded as an animal or bird. It is in this sense that Ah Uuc Cheknal copulates with Itzam Cab Ain, mounting on his back. Thus the mating of the celestial lizard with the earth

339

lizard is the beginning of the world. Creation as a result of pairing of a celestial deity of light with a terrestrial goddess of darkness, with frequent references to "the lust" of creation, is narrated in passages in the Ritual of the Bacabs (p. 295), and a similar pairing of the sun god with the moon goddess, who is also a deity of the soil and the crops, is a feature of the Mopan myth of the creation outlined below.

A sixteenth-century source (*Relaciones de Yucatán*, 1:51) says the Maya knew of the flood and the fall of Lucifer (the downfall of Oxlahun ti Ku?) and that the present world would end with fire.

In support of the suggestion made above that the men of the first creation, according to the Books of Chilam Balam, were of clay because they disintegrated, another sixteenth-century source (*Relaciones de Yucatán*, 1:79) informs us that God made the first man of earth, and he was called Anom; and in confirmation of this the Motul dictionary has the entry "Anom, the first man, Adam." However, Ritual of the Bacabs has Anom in the plural, indicating that the creation was not of a single man, and that is in agreement with most pre-Columbian myths.

Another source (López de Cogolludo, 1867, bk. 4, ch. 7) says that the flesh and bones of the first man were of earth mixed with dry grass, and his hair was of the same dry grass.

From present-day material collected by Tozzer (1907:153–54) and Redfield and Villa (1934:330–31), a Yucatec series of four creations and three destructions of the world may be reconstructed:

First Creation. The *zayamuincob* built the now-ruined archaeological sites and the great stone roads while the world was still in darkness, before the sun was created. They were dwarfs, but they could carry great loads on their backs. They were also called *p'uz*, "hunchback" or "bent" in Yucatec, but in other Maya languages, such as Tzotzil, the word signifies "dwarf." They had magical powers and needed only to whistle to bring together stones in their correct positions in buildings or to cause firewood to come from the bush to the hearth by itself. The people became wicked and it was announced that there would be a flood. The little people built great stone tanks like the underground storage reservoirs as boats, but as they did not float the people were drowned. According to the version recorded by Tozzer, there was then a great road suspended in the sky stretching from Tulum and Coba to Chichen Itza and Uxmal, a detail reminiscent of the great Coba-Yaxuna road. When the sun appeared, the dwarfs were turned to stone. Their images are to be seen today in many of the ruins. Tozzer illustrates one of these. It is an Atlantean figure from Chichen Itza and is of short stature.

The story of the *p'uz* is told also in Socotz, British Honduras (Thompson, 1930: 166). On old village sites in the forest, one comes upon old metates worn by use to troughlike *pilas*. These are the boats of the *p'uz*, the tiny folk. They forgot to worship God and He told them He would send a flood to destroy them. They decided not to make boats of wood, for they might rot before they were needed, but of stone. When the flood came, the *p'uz* embarked and, naturally, were drowned.

Zayanuincob (*sic*) is translated as "the adjusters" by Tozzer, but I suspect that was due to his misunderstanding of the Spanish word *"ajustar"* given in the Pío Pérez dictionary for *zay*. *Zay-amuincob* can be translated as "the twisted men" or "the disjointed men," suggesting a connection with "hunchback." The word may also be connected with *zay*, "ant," for there is also a Yucatec tradition of an ancient race called *chac zay uincob*, "red ant men." They were industrious like the ants which take out the red earth and make straight roads through the forest. The old people also spoke of those people as *yichobe bei yichob colelcab*, "those with eyes like those of bees," or *canal ubaacilob*, the meaning of which is uncertain, although *canal* would be "on high." The flood which ended this creation was *haiyokocab*, "water over the earth," comparable to the terms *haycabal* and *haycabil* used in the Books of Chilam Balam.

The belief that the dwarfs were turned to stone reminds us of the gods, animals, and "little men of the forest" who suffered the same fate in the creation story in the Popol Vuh (p. 335).

"Those with eyes like bees" is suggestive of the Bacabs who were closely associated with bees (p. 277). A fragment of a Quiche creation story from Chichicastenango (Tax, 1949:129) may bear on the matter. It is told that before the flood, the people

341

decided to go underground to save themselves. God, in disapproval, changed them into bees.

Second Creation. Next there lived the *dz'olob*, a term Tozzer renders as "the offenders." I have not succeeded in finding that meaning. A flood also ended this age.

Third Creation. The *macehual* came into being. The age ended with yet another flood, this one called *hunyecil* or *bulcabal*. *Macehual*, a Nahuatl loan word, means "the common people," and here probably indicates that the people were the same as the present-day Maya. The Motul dictionary, a sixteenth-century source, says of *hunyecil*, "general flood, in which, the Indians used to say, only a *maguey* [henequen] point separated the water from the sky." In fact, *hunyeci* means "one point of a henequen (leaf)." *Bul ik* is a hurricane with earthquakes, and that is probably the meaning here (p. 271).

Fourth Creation. This is the present world in which we live. It contains a mixture of all previous peoples to inhabit Yucatan. According to an early source, the *Relación de Mérida* (*Relaciones de Yucatán*, 1898–1900, 1:51), the present world will end in fire.

MOPAN AND KEKCHI

The Mopan of southern British Honduras have a long story of the life of the sun and moon on earth in which there are references to the creation of the world. The Kekchi have the same cycle of legends.

According to the Mopan version (Thompson, 1930:119–40), the son of Adam and Eve was placed in heaven and wore the sun's crown, but it was too hot for him. At the end of seven years, he caused a flood into which he plunged to cool off. Once more cool, he resumed his solar duties. The people complained to Adam that many had been drowned, and they feared the same thing would happen again. Adam suggested that one of three brothers living with their grandmother XKitza might take on the job. The second son was agreeable and was sent to travel across the sky to see how he liked it. He did not like it at all, for he found the landscape very monotonous; it was a dull, flat plain without hills or valleys, seas or rivers. Were the world more interesting, he said, he would be happy to be the sun forever. The messenger reported this.

The world became dark for a short while; the hills, valleys, rivers, and seas were made. The boy tried again, and at journey's end he was enthusiastic. "Now the world is beautiful. I will be the sun forever; I will never grow old, but will always be strong and do my work." The messenger told him the time had not yet come; for the present, the first sun would continue to do his work.

Sun wooed the girl who was to become the moon. They were the first people to have sexual intercourse, and for that reason the moon is mother of mankind, goddess of love and of childbirth. After many adventures on earth, sun and his wife and brothers ascended to the sky to take up their duties, the two brothers becoming morning and evening stars. However, in contradiction, we are also told that the younger brother was turned into a monkey.

Another Mopan story (Thompson, 1930:150) narrates that jaguar existed before man was made. The creator, taking mud, started to fashion men. The jaguar was watching, but the creator did not wish him to observe the process. He gave the jaguar a jar and a calabash full of holes and sent him to fetch water from the river, hoping to finish the creation while the jaguar tried to fill the jar with water scooped up with the leaking calabash. The jaguar was unsuccessful in filling the jar till the frog called to him, "*Chohac, chohac, chohac.* Smear mud over the holes." By the time the jaguar had thus filled the jar, the creator had made thirteen men and twelve guns. The jaguar learned, after being shot twice in the paw, that man was to be the master.

The incident of the leaking calabash has a parallel in the Popol Vuh; the twins send their grandmother with a leaking jar to fetch water while they search for the ball-game equipment.

Almost the same stories of sun and moon as are given for the Mopan Maya are current among the Kekchi (Gordon, 1915; Burkitt, 1918; Dieseldorff, 1926–33, 1:4–5). Burkitt was the author, whose name was withheld, of the myths published by Gordon. Dieseldorff obtained his version from the German, Paul Wirsing, who lived among the Kekchi for very many years. There are some grounds for thinking that the Kekchi borrowed these stories from the Manche Chol, a large part of whom they absorbed in the sixteenth and seventeenth centuries.

The late Mrs. Elsie McDougall passed on to me information of Señor Viaux, resident in Alta Verapaz, that an old Kekchi woman attributed skulls in a cave near Coban to people living before the creation of the sun. When the sun appeared they stayed in caves, for the light was so bright they could not see. By day they made pots; at night they came to the surface.

Creation myths of the Lacandon have been recorded by Baer and Baer (1952:233–36). According to these stories, the gods once lived on earth and built the great buildings now in ruins.

As for the first creation, Hachacyum, the creator, made the Lacandon men; his wife made the women. Ah Metzabac, collector of black dye to form the rain clouds, made the Tzeltal Maya, the Mexicans, and the Guatemalans; and Acyanto, "Our Helper," created the Americans. These people were of clay, and Hachacyum made the people of each totem of a different clay. The figures had red eyebrows and green beards and were dressed like the gods. Cizin, god of the underworld, in mischief made their eyebrows and beards black. He also made figures in imitation of those of Hachacyum. Hachacyum passed a palm leaf over the fire and waved it over the clay figures. Thereupon, all came to life, but those Cizin had made turned into the totemic animals of the Lacandon.

The world was then flat. Cizin and his two sons killed Hachacyum and buried him, but Hachacyum came to life and created the underworld with the aid of two other gods. One of them, Acanchop, made secure the foundations of the earth (*acan* means "founded") with huge rocks and crossbeams. When the underworld was completed, Hachacyum burst open the ground beneath Cizin so that as the former ascended to make the heavens, the latter fell through into the underworld.

Ah T'up, alias U Pal Ac Yum, Hachacyum's youngest son, also made some clay figurines which came to life. His brothers were provoked and shot and killed them, but they came alive again. After this had happened about five times, the brothers beheaded them, whereupon they stayed dead. When Ah T'up saw the people he had created, they had become palm trees, *xaan (Sabal mexi-cana)*. The father said the trees would remain on earth and grow here. One informant said there were four such trees in heaven.

The present world will be ended, after the last Lacandon dies, by the jaguars of Cizin eating the sun and moon (Cline, 1944). According to another version (Baer and Baer, 1949), at the end of the world all the Lacandon will gather at Yaxchilan. The gods will behead all single men, hang them by their heels, and gather their blood in bowls to paint their house. The final resting place of souls where the world ends will be in the highest of the seven heavens, that of Ah Chembekur, which is in complete darkness (Baer and Baer, 1952). The gods will then rebuild Yaxchilan.

The mention of trees, and the other informant's mention of four trees in heaven, makes it reasonably certain that this is a broken-down memory of the world directional trees.

According to Cline (1944), Hachacyum was buried by his brother-in-law. On the fourth day, the body had so swollen that it split the earth, forming a big crevasse by which Hachacyum, who was not really dead, climbed out. He was now more power-ful than Cizin, whom he banished to the middle of the earth. As noted (p. 282), these details supply an interesting commentary on, perhaps an amplification of, the fight between Oxlahun ti Ku and Bolon ti Ku. One is also reminded of the incident in the Popol Vuh in which Zipacna, believed to lie dead at the bottom of a deep pit, frees himself after three days and kills his opponents (Recinos, 1950:101).

Cline also writes that when, with the death of the last Lacandon, no one remains to make offerings to sun and moon and other gods, these will fall to earth causing an earthquake, which with terrific winds borne by the Chaob (Ch'aob?, "Carriers off"), led by the one in the east, will destroy the world.

A fragment of a Palencano-Chol creation myth has been re-corded by Arabella Anderson (1957). God wanted to destroy men and replace them with a new race. Therefore, he made dark-ness. The jaguars would go forth to kill men; they would not sleep because it was always night, and thus they would kill all men. One man closed his house very carefully with thick wall boards and went up to the ridge of the house. When the god

345

found him there alive, he tore off the man's head and stuck it on his anus, and the man was changed into a spider monkey; perhaps the Spaniards were changed into howler monkeys. There follows the incident of Pandora's box to be discussed later. Destruction of all men by jaguars we have noted in Nahuatl creation myths and, set in the future, among the Lacandon. The beheading and sticking of the head on the rump to form a new being we found in the *Leyenda de los soles* version of the fourth creation.

TZOTZIL AND TZELTAL

The Tzotzil of Larrainzar retain a myth recording three creations of the world (Holland, 1963: 71–72).

First Creation. The world was completely flat; there was no sun, only a feeble light. The people were imperfect because they did not die. This angered the gods, who sent a flood to end the world. Only the priests escaped death because they were monkeys, both spider and howler monkeys, and so were able to save themselves by climbing the tallest trees.

Second Creation. People were again imperfect because they did not remain dead. After three days they came to life again and lived forever. This also displeased God, who determined to destroy the world with a torrent of hot water. When the water began to fall, some people took refuge in caves, but all died. The human bones often found in caves are their remains.

Third Creation. God decided to try again, and sent his son, Jesus Christ, to earth to create the third world. The first inhabitants were three ladino couples who were wealthy and occupied themselves in reading and writing. God then created the Indians to do the hard work.

The Tzotzil of San Andrés Larrainzar retain belief in four gods who sustain the world on their shoulders. Known as Cuch Uinahel Balumil, "Sky (and) Earth Bearers," they are set at the corners of the world. Their slightest movement produces an earth tremor or even an earthquake. The gods of the four cardinal points occupy positions intermediate between those of the Cuch Uinahel Balumil. They are associated with world directional colors, but not in the arrangement of those in Yucatan and the Maya codices (Holland, 1963:92).

Material from another Tzotzil village, San Pedro Chenalho, amplifies the above material (Guiteras, 1961:156–57, 176, 182, 186–87, 194, 253–54, 282, 287).

First Creation. The world was once overrun with jaguars; it belonged to them, and that is why God the Father had to kill them. This seems to have been before man was first created. The first men were of mud. They could not stand erect, and at first they could not talk. Someone, seemingly a Jew, came to teach them, but he taught them to sin. The people died from a flood, but some escaped in a box floating on the water. They turned into monkeys because they ate charcoal when their food gave out.

Second Creation. People of this (?) creation stayed dead only three days.

Third Creation. God made Adam and Eve of clay. There are ladinos in the world because the woman sinned with a white dog, and Indians because she sinned with a yellow dog and gave birth to Indians. Long ago (in this creation?) there was another sun, Lucibel (Lucifer?) He gave little heat; soil and vegetation did not dry, so man could not burn the felled land to make milpa. The child Jesus offered to be the sun, promising to give more heat. He and his mother ascended to heaven, He to be the sun, she the moon.

The earth is square and surrounded by sea. The sky rests on four posts. Beneath is another square on which the dwarf people, the *yohob*, live. The sun is drawn in his cart across the sky by (dead?) human beings. They hand it over at sunset to the dwarfs underneath. The sun continues his journey below the earth but just above the dwarfs, and the latter protect themselves from his heat by covering their heads with mud.

Information from the Tzeltal village of Oxchuc (Villa, 1946: 570) closely parallels the above Tzotzil world view. In Oxchuc belief, the flat earth is supported by four thick columns, at the bases of which live dwarfs only a foot tall and black because the sun passes so close to them (in his journey through the underworld). Four more columns, set on the earth, hold up the heavens. There is some doubt about whether these are at the cardinal points or at the northwest, northeast, southwest and southeast "corners" of the earth.

347

From Tenejapa, another Tzeltal town, a fragmentary creation legend has been recovered by Cámara (1946:34). The first men were without clothes, and, not knowing how to make fire, they were cold. They could not talk. The creator ordered Mam to make a flood. God, in a subsequent creation, made fruit trees so that man could have food, and he took maize from the ants who took it out of hills. When man began to eat, he began to talk.

The above covers published material on creations of the world to the best of my knowledge.

The Discovery of Maize

The same myth of the discovery of maize beneath the rocky peak of a mountain is found on the Mexican plateau and among various Maya groups.

MEXICAN PLATEAU

The previously cited *Leyenda de los soles* (Chimalpopoca, 1945:121; Lehmann, 1906) is alone in ascribing the discovery of maize, apart from the smashing of the rock under which it lay, to divine intervention. Quetzalcoatl asked the ant where he obtained the maize which he was carrying. At first the ant would not tell, but finally indicated as the place the Cerro de Tonacatepetl (Maize Mountain). Quetzalcoatl turned himself into a black ant and accompanied the red ant to the deposit beneath the mountain, and, taking some grains, he carried it to the other gods in Tamoanchan. Quetzalcoatl tried to carry the mountain away on his back, but he could not. Divination with maize grains by Oxomoco and Cipactonal revealed that only Nanahuatl could pulverize the mountain. The Tlalocs—the blue Tlalocs, the white Tlalocs, the yellow Tlalocs, and the red Tlalocs—prepared themselves. Nanahuatl it was who broke open the mountain, but the Tlalocs stole the food, white, black, yellow, and red maize, beans, amaranth, and *chia* (*Salvia hispanica*).

In Maya versions which follow, the other gods steal the maize after the old infirm one faints from the effort. Nanahuatl, the syphilitic god, was rickety and without strength, so we may

348

perhaps infer that he also fainted, giving the Tlalocs their opportunity. The incident must have been thought important, for it survives in several versions of the myth.

MOPAN, KEKCHI, AND POKOMCHI

The most detailed version of this myth circulates among the Mopan of San Antonio, British Honduras (Thompson, 1930: 132–34), and is also current among the Kekchi, who may have taken the story from the Manche Chol.

Maize lay hidden beneath a great rock, only the leaf-cutting ants which had found a small crack on the rock leading to the supply knew of it. One day the fox found and tasted some grains of maize dropped by the ants as they carried them off from beneath the rock. He ate them and found them delicious. When the ants returned at night, he followed them, but the crack in the rock was too small to let him reach the maize, and he had again to content himself with grains the ants dropped.

Back among the other animals, fox broke wind; they wanted to know what he had eaten that even his wind smelled sweet. Fox denied that he had found a new food, but the other animals, unbelieving, followed secretly and saw what he was eating. They too ate the maize and liked it; they asked the ants to fetch them more grains. The ants at first were agreeable, but, finding they could not keep all the animals supplied, they refused to bring out more maize except for themselves. The animals asked the large red ants and then the rat to help, but neither could get through the crack. Finally, they gave man the secret of this wonderful food.

Man asked the help of the mountain-valley gods, the Mams, the thunder gods who send the rain. There are four principal Mams and others of lesser importance. Yaluk, oldest and greatest, was not present when man asked their help. In turn, the three others hurled a thunderbolt at the rock, but failed to break it open. Finally, they had to send to ask Yaluk's help.

Yaluk sent the woodpecker to tap the rock to find where it was thinnest (hollow?). When the woodpecker had done this, Yaluk told him to hide behind a ledge of the rock and not thrust out his

349

head. Yaluk, gathering all his strength, hurled his thunderbolt at the spot the woodpecker had indicated and pulverized the rock. He was an old man; the effort was too much for him and he fainted. Disobeying orders, the woodpecker had thrust out his head. It was cut by a flying piece of rock and bled profusely; ever since the woodpecker has had a red poll.

All the maize had been white, but Yaluk's thunderbolt had burned some grain which turned red, and had smoked other grain which turned yellow, so now there is red, yellow, and white maize (the informant surely forgot to mention black maize, charred by the thunderbolt). Before Yaluk recovered from his fainting, the three younger Mams seized all the white maize, leaving only the damaged red and yellow for Yaluk. Yaluk was very angry.

Yaluk's maize grew well, but the white maize the other Mams had stolen did not germinate. They came to Yaluk to ask his advice. He told them to steep their maize in lime for three days and then plant it. Naturally, the crop failed again. Finally, a small crop of white maize was obtained. The Mams gave the maize to man to sow.

A Kekchi version, similar in all major details to the above but lacking some minor items, has been published by Burkitt (1918).

The legend of the maize hidden beneath the rock must have been current among the Pokomchi, for Narciso (1960:106) recounts how the twelve thunders, sent to smash the rock within which the maize was kept, failed. Then the thirteenth, the weakest and most ill, inspired by the woodpecker who had spied through a hole the rich legacy of the gods, smashed the rock, thus giving that wonderful food to man.

YUCATEC: COLONIAL PERIOD

In mystic language which probably had little meaning for the transcriber or compiler of the present edition, the Book of Chilam Balam of Chumayel refers to the above myth in a lengthy chapter. A small part (Roys, 1933:107–12, with minor amendments by Thompson) tells us that the maize spirit or deity "remained alone within the *gracia* [a ritualistic term adopted by the Maya for maize], within the night when there was neither heaven nor earth. Then he was pulverized [*buki*. Roys, unaware of the story of the freezing of the maize, changed this to *luki*, "he departed"] at the end of the katun because he could not be born in the first katun. There were his long locks of hair [presumably, as Roys notes, the corn silk usually shown on the cheek in portraits of the maize god]. His divinity came to him when he came forth. He was hidden within the stone." There is mention in an obscure passage of the macaw doing something behind the *acantun*, "the stone column." One is reminded of the part played by the woodpecker in the Mopan and Bachajon-Tzeltal versions. The rock beneath which the maize lay is called *chac ye tun*, "great pointed rock," *ocontun*, "stone pillar," and *zuhuy tun*, "virgin, uncontaminated rock." In a play on words, the maize is called *tun*, which means not only stone in general, but specifically "jade," in turn a symbol for "precious." These terms are applied to maize almost throughout Middle America.

BACHAJON TZELTAL

A Bachajon-Tzeltal myth of the finding of maize (Slocum, 1965) retains the essentials of the Mopan version. The Jews, apparently regarded as the first people in the world, saw a large black ant (*xolop*) carrying maize. When it would not say where it had obtained the grains, they tied it tightly round the middle until its stomach was almost cut in half to make it tell, and that is why the ant's body looks as though it were cut in two. Finally, the ant was forced to reveal that the maize was within a rock. The Jews got the woodpecker to tap the rock to see where it was thin, giving him a special beak to do the job. Two of the lightnings, the *rayos*, the Chahuuc, failed to smash the rock, but the third, the red Chahuuc, split the rock open but fainted with the effort. The Jews hastily gathered and hid the big ears of maize; when red Chahuuc came to, he was surprised to see how little corn there was. He planted what was left and it grew well; the stolen corn did not grow. When the Jews asked him why theirs did not grow, he told them to cook it before sowing. When it again failed to sprout, they again went to Chahuuc for advice. This time he told them to put lime in it. Again it failed to grow. He did this to teach them that it is wrong to steal.

The cooking or steeping in lime of the seed is a typical example of the Maya love of a practical joke. Note how the steeping in lime occurs also in the Mopan version.

The Tzeltal of Tenejapa say that God took maize from the ants who had obtained it from *anheles* (caves, hills, or springs, but also their owners, the thunders). When man began to eat, he began to talk (Cámara, 1946:34).

MAM, QUICHE, AND CAKCHIQUEL

The Mam of Colotenango (Valladares, 1957:239–41) have different traditions of the origin of maize, one of which is a version of that already noted, but with important elements, notably the parts played by the ant and the thunder gods, missing.

In ancient times there was no maize; people fed on the roots of a plant called *txetxina*, "mother maize," with a large root and a single stalk. People noted that the dung of the wildcat, the *uech*, contained maize. They asked him where he had obtained it, and at his suggestion they sent a louse to travel on his shoulders, but the louse fell off en route. Next, they sent a flea. The flea also fell off the wildcat, but he managed to jump on again and thus locate the source of maize. The people went to the spot. It was a rock on a mountain called Paxil, "Water Beneath," in the *municipio* of La Libertad, department of Huehuetenango. The ancients asked the woodpecker to break open the rock with his beak, and this the bird did. Thus the people obtained maize and ceased to eat *txetxina*. In La Libertad, the informant said, there is always an abundance of maize.

According to another legend recovered in the same town, maize came first from a milpa in a high spot near Nebaj and was the property of the woman owner of the place. In a time of famine, men sent the crow to rob grain, but the crow was surprised by the woman and never returned. The *zompopo* ant was next sent, and he managed to rob grain which he gave to the people. Soon it was growing everywhere. One day the woman who owned the maize came down to the lands occupied by humans, and, seeing the growing maize, she called out "Who stole my maize?" No one answered. Suspecting it was the ant, she caught it and squeezed its waist to make it answer. Ever since, the ant has had a very narrow waist. As the ants brought man maize, it is not good to kill them. But what is one to do? One must destroy them, otherwise they will eat up the milpa.

Maud Oakes (1951:244) recounts a story of the Mam of Todos Santos that maize grew untended on the mountain called Xepaxa, about twelve miles in a direct line west of Todos Santos. A man once brought some home. His family did not know how to cook it; they roasted it and liked the taste. He collected more and finally brought back seed to sow. Omak, near Nebaj, is another source of wild maize, and there are others.

According to the Popol Vuh (Recinos, 1950:165–67), the yellow and white ears of maize came from Paxil and Cayala, and from them was made the present human race. The mountain cat, the coyote, the small parrot, and the crow were the animals which brought the maize. They told the gods to go to Paxil and Cayala and showed them the road to those villages. This land yielded other food plants of every description. Maize hidden beneath the rock does not seem to be a Quiche tradition, but one incident, how colored maize originated, appears in a story of an old Quiche of Quezaltenango (Termer, 1957:240). A spirit living in the volcano of Siete Orejas had the only supply of maize in the world, but some evil spirits burned his maize so that the grain on the outside was charred black, that part-way in was scorched, and that in the center remained untouched. Since then, there have been black, yellow, and white maize in the world.

In present-day Santo Tomás Chichicastenango, it is told that when Jesus was crucified, He miraculously turned, exposing his back. From it came white, yellow, and black maize, beans, potatoes, and all other food plants. Then He died. This legend (Tax, 1947:580) may have arisen from Jesus' words, "I am the bread of life."

The *Annals of the Cakchiquels* (Recinos, 1953:46) notes "only two animals knew there was food [maize] in Paxil, the place where those animals, the coyote and the crow, are found. The coyote was killed, and in his remains, when he was quartered, corn was discovered." This maize was kneaded with the blood of the tapir and the serpent to make men.

The episode of maize hidden beneath a rock is current among the present-day Cakchiquel of San Antonio Palopo. Palikwala smashed the rock with a thunderbolt and got the maize through a crack (Redfield, 1946:36).

COMMENT

Clearly, this story once had a very wide distribution throughout the Maya area, and no doubt investigation would reveal its presence in areas from which it has not yet been reported. It would be hard to say whether it originated in or outside the Maya area.

The traditions current among both Mam and Quiche that maize grew wild near Nebaj, which is in Ixil territory, and those among the Mam, Quiche, and Cakchiquel that it grew wild in northwestern Huehuetenango are of particular interest in view of the recent discoveries of the first domestication of corn in the Coxcatlan caves, not so very far west of the above-mentioned areas. It is possible that these traditions have a basis in fact. In the Kekchi myth, the maize was hidden beneath Saclech Mountain, two days' travel north of Chama on the road to Salinas de los Nueve Cerros, well north of ancient Kekchi territory. Note that all these locations are in the extreme north of the highlands, close by the abrupt drop to the lowland rain forest.

The Mopan tell of a tree with branches on which grew all fruits and vegetables other than maize (Thompson, 1930:134–135). Men tried to fell it, but by nightfall it was not completely cut down. Next day, the cut was not visible. The second day, the men hid to see what happened. The animals collected all the chips and put them back in the cut so that it healed. Then the men worked day and night till the tree was felled; since then, man has had all such vegetables. A similar myth is current in British Guiana, and one is reminded how the felled trees and shrubs in the twins' milpa were set up by the animals in the Popol Vuh (Recinos, 1950.133).

Sun as Culture Hero: Deception and Death of Old Woman

Below are given a series of incidents in the life of the sun on earth before he assumed his solar duties. Sometimes he is alone, but more often he is accompanied by a brother who later becomes the planet Venus or, in Quiche and Cakchiquel tradition, the moon. This last, however, is contradicted by modern legends and belief which have the moon a woman and the wife of the sun (Bunzel, 1952:428).

In outline, the boys or sun alone hunt, but the old woman gives all the meat they bring home to her lover. The children learn this, slay her lover, and trick the old woman into eating part of his body. She tries to kill the children, but they triumph, generally after a contest of riddles, and kill her.

MOPAN AND KEKCHI

The Mopan version is perhaps the most detailed (Thompson, 1930:120–23).

There were three brothers who lived before the (present?) sun was made. The future planet Venus was the eldest, the future sun was the second, and the one who was later turned into a monkey and became another planet was the youngest. They lived with their grandmother, XKitza. The boys hunted birds with their blowguns and gave the meat to the old woman, but she gave it to her lover, a huge monster, some say a tapir, who visited her every night. When the boys were asleep, she smeared fat on their lips and threw the bones of the birds under their hammocks. When the boys woke hungry and asked for meat, the old woman told them they had eaten it and called attention to the fat on their lips and cheeks and the bones beneath their hammocks. They believed her until one day the trogon told them the trick XKitza played on them.

They made a deadfall trap, setting sharp stakes in the bottom. XKitza's lover fell in and was killed. The boys cut off and roasted the animal's penis, and, taking it home, gave it to XKitza to eat. She said it was tasty. The boys laughed and some birds called out, "Look at her; she has eaten her lover's penis." XKitza was suspicious.

She sent the boys to sleep and went down to the river to sharpen her claws. The boys asked the toad and then the big crested lizard to spy on her. The latter warned the boys that XKitza planned to kill them. Each put a wooden stool and a calabash, to represent body and head, in his hammock with a blanket over both, so it looked as though all were asleep. Then they hid in the rafters of the hut. XKitza crept in and dug her freshly-sharpened claws into each calabash in turn, believing each was a boy's head. The boys laughed in the rafters. XKitza looked up. "I was only playing," she replied to their questions.

The boys decided to kill the old woman, but as the youngest brother did not agree with this plan, they turned him into a monkey (see below). The boys and XKitza took turns asking each other riddles. She could not answer those posed to her, and so the boys killed her; sun shot her with an arrow.

A Kekchi version of the above, with minor variations, is recorded from San Juan Chamelco, Alta Verapaz (Goubaud, 1949: 126–28).

The old lady starved the children, putting fat on their lips and fingernails while they slept. The boys set machetes, knives, and pieces of broken bottles along the path followed by her lover when he came to visit the old woman. He died of the wounds he received, and the boys cut up his body and gave the meat to grandmother. "How tasty," she exclaimed as she ate the meat. They saved a leg for her lover, but, not unexpectedly, he did not appear to eat it. Next day the boys, while hunting with their uncle, told him how they had killed the man. Later, the old woman learned of her lover's death and how she had been tricked into eating part of him. She scolded them and tried to kill them as they slept. In this version, the boys place bunches of bananas in their beds. The old woman drives a knife into each as the boys watch from the attic. Finally, old woman threw herself into a well. The boys cut her in pieces, buried her head and clothes, and roasted her arms, legs, and ribs. As on previous occasions, a bird sang, "Died, died." "Who died?" asked the boys' uncle. When he learned, they had a big feast of the meat and danced. Everyone was happy at the old woman's death.

356

CAKCHIQUEL

The Cakchiquel of San Antonio Palopo (Redfield, 1945: 252) have a version of sun's boyhood, which involves a *temascal* (sweat house), not reported from elsewhere in the Maya area but prominent in the parallel myths from southern Mexico given below.

There were three brothers; the elder ones became the sun and moon, and the youngest they turned into a monkey because he told stories on them. The brothers worked their milpa by magic; they prayed and the hoes did the work. The youngest boy told grandmother. She scolded the brothers, and since then the hoes have not worked unaided. After the youngest had been turned into a monkey, sun and moon threw their grandparents into the *temascal* and then threw them in the fire. Grandfather, turning himself into a *pisote*, escaped to the coast. Later, the brothers took up their celestial duties.

The *pisote, inter alia,* functions as a creator god, and that might have significance in this passage, but *pisotes* are also regarded as clowns, and grandfather had just suffered the indignity in the *temascal* of having an ear of maize thrust in his anus. Accordingly, the clown aspect seems to fit better.

MAZATEC POPOLOCA, MIXE, AND ZAPOTEC

Incidents of this same myth occur among various Indian groups of south Mexico.

Johnson and Johnson (1939) record a Mazatec-Popoloca story of sun and moon as children when the world was still dark, before the present sun and moon undertook their duties. A number of the incidents are unrelated to those found in the Maya area, but the following parallel Maya motives:

The boy who was later to become the sun liked to hunt, but the meat he brought home the old woman gave to her husband. Sun learned this. He killed the old woman's husband, who had the form of a deer, and filled the skin with all animals which bite and sting—serpents and so forth. Sun left the swollen, stuffed carcass lying there; the kidneys he took and gave to old woman. She ate them. Going to the well, she was greeted by the birds, who, at the instance of sun, cried "You have eaten your husband's kidneys." Angrily, she hit the parrot with some plants; since then it has been green. She trod on the toad and that is why he is flat.

Her husband she found snoring (in a parallel passage, the buzzing of bees and wasps is likened to the sound of snoring). She hit him with a stick to wake him so that he would come and eat. Instead, the animals poured out to sting her. The old woman said the children had won, for there had been other contests. She went to live in a volcano. When clouds cover the volcano, it is sun putting the old woman's skirt over the volcano to annoy her.

Miller (1956:71–99) relates Mixe stories which contain elements of the childhood of sun and moon. Indeed, in the last two stories, the boy and girl are called sun and moon. They killed their grandfather and gave his flesh (in one case, his testicles) to his wife to eat. The water in which the meat was cooking called out to her "You are boiling your husband." The children filled the old man's *petate* (sleeping mat) with stinging insects; the old woman hit it and got stung. The dummy-in-bed episode appears in a different context and with a pleasant twist to it; the dummy contains bean soup, and when it flows from the "wound" the "murderer" supposes it to be the victim's blood.

The bird (hummingbird in one version; *salta-pared* in others) appears while the old woman is arranging her loom to weave. She takes it in her bosom and becomes pregnant.

In a fragmentary version (Carrasco, 1952), the two children—boy and girl—killed the old man. As they cooked some beans, they heard a voice saying, "You killed your grandfather; now you eat him." The old woman chased them, and after adventures they ascended to the sky to become sun and moon.

The Zapotec of Mitla tell of a childless woman married to a lazy old man (Parsons, 1936: 324–28), with whom lived an orphan boy and his sister, later to become respectively the sun and the moon. Every day they hunted; the boy with his blowgun killed birds and hares, and sometimes a deer. They brought the meat to the old woman, but she gave it all to the old man; the

358

children were very hungry. San Antón told them where to find two deer, but again they were given no meat. San Antón next told them to kill and skin two more deer and stuff them with every sort of stinging insect.

They killed the old man, took out the heart, and filled his corpse with stinging insects. They gave the heart to the old woman, saying it was the heart of a deer they had killed. While it cooked, she went to the river to wash. The frog called to her, "Eater of your own family." She shook the old man to wake him for his meal, the stinging creatures came out and stung her, and she realized the old man was dead. Her brother told her to build a fire in the *temascal*, the sweat house, to kill the children. However, San Antón told the children of the plan and bade the boy make an escape hole on the far side of the *temascal* and put thorns and maguey leaves on the fire to make it spark so the woman would think they had burned.

The children escaped from the *temascal*; with chile smoke from the blowgun (In the Mopan version of the escape of sun and moon, sun fills the old man's blowgun with ground chile which temporarily incapacitates him when he draws in his breath to shoot them as they flee) they suffocated the old woman but were pursued by her brother. There follow various incidents of the well-known tale of the Magic Flight. Finally, they killed the pursuing brother and took out his eyes. By a trick, the boy got the stronger right eye, the girl, the weaker left eye. The sun had offered her a rabbit for her stronger eye, suggestive of the rabbit-in-the-moon belief. God made the boy the sun because he had the stronger eye. His sister was made the moon. They still quarrel about the eyes.

Other tales of the hero children incorporating motifs already discussed are in Chinanteca (Weitlaner, 1952), Mixtec (Cruz, 1946:217–19), and, to a lesser extent, in Sierra Popoluca (Elson, 1947). Slaying of the deer lover and filling of his skin with wasps and other stinging insects is recorded from Miahuatlan, Puebla (Barlow and Ramírez, 1962), the Mixtec (Cruz, 1946:218–19), and the Chatino (Cicco and Horcasitas, 1962). The last has the old woman burned to death in the *temascal*.

Perils of Tree Climbing

In these stories, sun, while still on earth, gets rid of unwanted brothers. They are turned into monkeys, or from their dead bodies other animals are created. In some versions, their fate is apparently sealed when their grandmother laughs at them.

QUICHE, CAKCHIQUEL, AND KANHOBAL

In the Popol Vuh (Recinos, 1950:126–27), the twin heroes Hunahpu and Xbalanque, who later become the moon (morning star?) and sun, were mistreated by their elder half-brothers, Hun Batz and Hun Chouen, and by their grandmother. They were given almost no food. Their half-brothers even tried to kill them. The four brothers went out hunting. Hunahpu and Xbalanque, with their blowguns, shot many birds in the top of a tree, but the dead birds were caught in the branches. They persuaded Hun Batz and Hun Chouen to climb the tree to retrieve them. As the elder pair climbed, the tree grew taller and bigger; they called out in fright for they could not climb down. Hunahpu and Xbalanque told them to loosen their loincloths, tie them below their stomachs, and pull the long ends from behind. They did so, but the loincloth ends became tails, and they were turned into monkeys. Indeed, *batz* is the general Maya name for howler monkey, and *chuen* is a day name in the Maya calendar corresponding to the Aztec day name Ozomatli, "Spider Monkey."

When the youngsters returned, their grandmother was anxious and sad. They told her Hun Batz and Hun Chouen would return, but with animal faces, and on no account must she laugh at them. The twins began to beat the drum, play the flute, and sing. Soon Hun Batz and Hun Chouen arrived and started dancing to the music. The old lady began to laugh and the monkeys ran off. Three times they danced and three times she laughed. The fourth time they ran off, they did not return. They stayed in the trees.

The Cakchiquel of Palopo (Redfield, 1946:252) tell the incident of the youngest brother being turned into a monkey after being sent to climb a tree.

Among the Kanhobal of San Miguel Acatan (Siegel, 1942), Jesus got his elder brothers to climb a tree which grew taller as they climbed. They also were turned into monkeys. Jesus stripped bark off the tree and with it formed a lake at the base of the tree.

MOPAN AND KEKCHI

The Mopan version is very similar (Thompson, 1930:122–23). The boys who were to become the sun and Venus wanted to get rid of their youngest brother. They shot a bird, which stuck in the top branch of a tree. They tied a blanket around the waist of the youngest boy (surely a loincloth in earlier recountings of the tale), and sent him up the tree to retrieve the bird. When he was almost at the top, the sun told him to call out *"wac-wac-wac-wac-wac,"* imitating the chatter of spider monkeys. The boy did so, and, climbing higher, began to chatter like a spider monkey and to swing from tree to tree. The blanket turned into the animal's fur and the dangling end into its tail. Sun told him he must remain there. From him are descended all monkeys. Later he became a planet or the evening star (the present-day Mopan think of morning and evening stars as unrelated).

A somewhat decultured version of the creation of monkeys is current among the Kekchi (Dieseldorff, 1926–33, 1:5–6). A sick man sent his children to work in the milpa, but they played. They set fire to thirteen gourds of tobacco to make their father think they were burning the milpa. When they saw him coming to see what they were doing, the boys climbed a tree and began to chatter like monkeys. Night overtook them in the tree and they turned into monkeys.

BACHAJON TZELTAL AND PALENCANO CHOL

In these versions, the tree is brought down and the climbers killed. The Tzeltal story (Slocum, 1965:7–18) tells of two brothers who lived with an old woman, "grandmother." Each day, the elder, Yax Kahkal, "Green or First Sun," killed his brother, Youngest of the Family. He chopped the body in pieces, but the wasps and bees collected the pieces and restored the child to life. (Compare this with the collection of the pieces of moon after she had been hit by her father's thunderbolt in the Mopan story.

The collectors then were dragonflies [Thompson, 1930:128].)
Younger brother watched the old lady spinning cotton thread.
He took a handful of the cotton seed piled beside her—presumably she had been carding the cotton—and, going into the forest,
threw it up into a tree, where it turned into a beehive. From that
all our honey derives, but some fell to the ground, and from that
came the hives which certain bees make on the ground.

Younger brother persuaded older brother to climb to the top
of the tree to get the honey. Older brother greedily ate it, but
when younger brother asked him to throw some down, he
dropped, three times in succession, only wax. Younger brother
molded the wax and in the top set pieces of palm wood which he
had sharpened. The wax turned into gophers, the sharpened wood
becoming the teeth. For that reason, the old people say the gopher
has no bones. Younger brother started to cut down the tree. Older
brother told him to stop. Younger brother showed older brother
his tiny machete and asked him how he could possibly cut down
the tree with such a small blade. The tree fell, but it was because
the gophers gnawed through all the roots, and elder brother was
smashed in pieces. The larger pieces became large animals such
as deer, peccary, and *tepescuintli*; the smaller pieces became birds.
His clotted blood (*stonch'ich'el*) became a bird, the *xtonch'ich'*
(a pun).

Grandmother accused younger brother of having killed his
brother when the latter failed to return home, but he denied it.
He told her to shell corn to feed the animals which would come
to the hut, and she must grab those she liked to keep as pets in
the hut. Animals and birds which eat corn were those that came.
She caught them by their tails. The boy told her that if she laughed
at them they would escape, leaving their tails behind. Nevertheless, she could not help laughing, and the pets ran off, leaving their
tails behind. That is why deer, rabbit, and peccary have no proper
tails. The only one she caught again was the rabbit. This our
heavenly mother, the moon, still holds. It can be seen even today
in the middle of the moon.

The Palencano Chol version closely resembles the Tzeltal
(Aulie and Aulie, 1951), which is understandable since the two
groups are neighbors.

Our mother, the moon, had seven children by her first husband, who died. Our father, the sun, wanted to have intercourse with her, so she used to send the children away each evening to work in the milpa, and they returned next day. She became pregnant. When the baby, son of sun, was born, she tried to hide him, sending the other boys each day to work in the milpa, but they suspected, and, hiding, they saw their half brother come out. He wore a small hat, red like fire it was, and red were his small trousers, and he had a tiny machete. When the boys came, the mother was making tortillas; son of sun was hidden in a large pottery jar. Later, the boys took their young half brother to the milpa. On his fifth trip to the milpa, they killed him. After they had been home a short while, the dead boy arrived carrying a peccary on his back; his brothers were amazed. The same thing happened next day. On the third day, all went to the forest. There was a hive at the top of a high tree. Son of sun told his brothers to climb up to fetch the honey. He asked them to throw some down, but they threw down only wax. Four times they hit him on the head with the wax. He grew angry. He made ten little gophers and put them in the ground. They ate the roots, the tree fell, and the brothers were smashed in pieces. Son of sun went home. His mother asked what had happened to his brothers. On the fourth day, he told her to shell four baskets of corn. He went to the milpa and returned with his brothers who had been converted into tame animals: one peccary, two ducks, two male turkeys, two raccoons (?), two pigs, two chickens, two armadillos, two deer, and two hen turkeys. Our mother fed the animals. She did not weep much, but sun's son said nothing; he was angry.

Sun Courts Moon

This myth has a more limited circulation and is not reported, except for isolated details, outside the Maya area.

MOPAN AND KEKCHI

The Mopan story is given in full by Thompson (1930:126–29). The future sun fell in love with XT'actani, a fine weaver, who lived with her grandfather, T'actani. To impress her, he passed by her hut carrying a deer he had hunted. As deer were scarce, he stuffed the skin with ashes, grass, and leaves, and each day paraded past her hut with it on his shoulder to give the impression he killed a deer every day. T'actani, suspicious, told his daughter to throw water on the path. Sun slipped; the skin burst, the ashes and grass poured out, and XT'actani laughed at him. Sun changed into a hummingbird and darted from flower to flower of a tobacco plant before the hut. At XT'actani's request, the old man shot the hummingbird with his blowgun. She took it into her room, where it revived, and in the night, reassuming his human shape, sun persuaded her to flee with him. She later became the moon. To delay pursuit, sun covered the old man's *sastun* ("jade" or "crystal"), in which he could see everything, with soot and filled his blowgun with ground chile. When the old man drew breath to blow the pellet, he nearly choked to death.

Nevertheless, Chac was persuaded to hurl a thunderbolt at the couple fleeing in a canoe. Sun turned into a turtle and moon into a crab to escape the blow, but the bolt killed moon. Sun collected her remains in thirteen hollow logs with the aid of dragonflies. When they were opened thirteen days later, twelve contained snakes and noxious insects. They escaped, and since then those stinging and biting things have been in the world. (A Palencano-Chol myth [Anderson, 1957] has the Pandora's box incident. The dog was responsible for loosing all those pests on mankind.) The thirteenth log contained XT'actani. The deer trampled on her and with his hoof formed her vagina. Sun cohabited with her, the first sexual intercourse in the world.

Dieseldorff (1926–33, 1:4–5) gives almost the same story as the Mopan in a version collected, I understand, by Paul Wirsing. The informant was one of the Kekchi-speaking Cuculs, supposed to belong to the large body of Manche Chol absorbed by the Kekchi. The sun is called Xbalamque, "Jaguar Sun" (cf. Xbalanque of the Popol Vuh). The blood of the girl is gathered in twelve jars. There follow the incidents of the noxious insects and the trampling by the deer.

Further material was communicated by Paul Wirsing to the late Mrs. Elsie McDougall. When the old man inhaled the powdered chile, he writhed in pain, and that caused the first earth-quake. Moon did not change into a crab but slipped into an armadillo shell. Her blood was gathered in thirteen pottery jars.

In another version, collected by Burkitt (Gordon, 1915:120–21), the girl is called Matactin and the sun, Li Cagua Saque, "Our Lord Sun." The dragonflies collected the girl's blood in thirteen jars. Thirteen days later, sun poured their contents into a fountain. From twelve came snakes, worms, and reptiles; the thirteenth held Matactin. Sun ordered deer to conduct her to the sky.

In still another variant, also collected by Burkitt (Gordon, 1915:116–17), sun, attracted by the girl, borrowed turtle's shell and held it before his face so that it cast a shadow over the girl. While she rested in the shade, sun threw the shell over her and captured her. After the stealing of his daughter, the old man constructed an enormous blowgun so that its pellet would reach even the sun on high. Sun threw powdered chile into the blowgun as the old man drew breath; his hard coughing was the beginning of whooping cough in the world.

When the old man finally fired, the clay ball struck sun, causing him to let go of the girl. She fell in the sea, smashed to pieces. Small fish gathered the pieces and patched them with their silvery scales. Then, each holding in his mouth the tail of another, they made themselves into a net and tried to lift the girl to the sun. Because of his heat, they could not reach sun. Instead, they left the girl in the sky, where, as the moon, she still tries to overtake her lover. The fish became the Milky Way.

CAKCHIQUEL

A long tale from Palopo, written in Cakchiquel with Spanish translation, is given by Redfield (1946:292–370). The old man Mataktani had two daughters. One caught a hummingbird who turned into human shape and became her lover. Every evening when sun set, he came to be with her. Her conversation with him was overheard by her father, but she denied that there was a man with her.

Mataktani sent the louse to get two hairs from each as evidence of the man's presence, but the louse was too heavy (with blood?)

to climb. Next, the old man sent the flea on the same mission, but the hummingbird hid in a gourd, and flea had to report failure. A mouse, sent on the same mission, got the hairs, but climbing up to the rafters he knocked against a gourd which fell on the sleeping couple and awoke them. They realized what had happened. Next morning, on being taxed, the girl confessed. Mataktani agreed to accept the hummingbird as his son-in-law but set him several tests. These, being outside the theme, will not be summarized.

Later, the couple decided to move away to escape the domination of the old man. He had a magic blowgun, and by sucking through it he could bring back anyone at which it was aimed. The hummingbird put lime, chile, and soot in the blowgun before the couple fled. Mataktani, incapacitated by the intake of these, sought the aid of his *capitanes*. He asked one to thunder and strike his daughter with a thunderbolt. When the girl was thus killed, the hummingbird placed her bones in a pottery jar which he left in charge of an old woman, promising to return for them. A week later there was much noise in the jar, and the old lady was frightened and closed it. Hummingbird returned after two weeks. Opening the jar, he found the bones had turned into those animals which work the honey and the wax to make the candles which serve the glory of God.

Sun is not mentioned save for the passage which implies that it is the sun who joins the girl as soon as he completes his day's work at sunset. Clearly, any idea that these events predate the appearance of the present sun is lost.

Moon's Adultery

These incidents in sun's and moon's story appear to be of limited distribution today, but they are of particular interest because there is archaeological evidence for their currency during the Classic period.

MOPAN AND KEKCHI

The following events are also referable to the period before sun and moon took up their duties in the sky (Thompson, 1930:130–32). Sun built a hut for himself and moon, and his elder brother

Xulab, the future morning star, came to live with them. Sun suspected an intrigue between his wife and morning star. He had an old woman make him a tamale with a center of chile, gall of birds, and annatto. He put it under his arm so that the heat of his body would cook it (anticipation of solar heat?). He gave it to the guilty couple, who, on starting to eat it, vomited and drank all available water trying to get the taste out of their mouths.

His wife, XT'actani, was so unhappy she was persuaded to fly on the back of a *zopilote* (vulture) to become the mistress of the king vulture. Sun borrowed deer's skin and hid under it, feigning to be a dead deer. The *zopilotes* came to feed on the carcass. When the one who had carried off XT'actani came close to peck out his eye, sun caught him and forced the bird to carry him on his back to the white stone "palace" of the king vulture (it was his nest, white with bird droppings). Finally, he persuaded XT'actani to return to earth with him.

The time had come for sun to take up his duties. He, his wife, and his elder brother, morning star, ascended into heaven. XT'actani, as the moon, was as bright as sun; it was perpetual day, and the people complained that they could not sleep. Sun took out one of her eyes, and since then she has given only a soft light.

A Kekchi version given to Mrs. Elsie McDougall by Paul Wirsing follows in the main the Mopan account. Not an affair with morning star, sun's elder brother, but the action of Chocl, "Cloud," sun's younger brother, caused the breakup of sun's and moon's marriage. Cloud used to pass to and fro while moon sat bathing herself in her washtrough (*batea*). Sun could not see his wife and suspected that cloud's interest was more than fraternal. He struck moon, and her crying drew the interest of the *zopilote*. When sun borrowed deer's skin, he tied a cloak in its place, but it was too short to cover deer's hindquarters and these became bleached. Similarly, the *zopilote's* feathers became bleached at the extremes which were not covered by sun's body as he rode on that bird.

CLASSIC PERIOD: LOWLANDS

Various scenes on pottery vessels of the Classic period certainly depict sun's ruse of hiding under the deer's skin. The best example is on a painted Tepeu 2 vase from Yalloch (Gann, 1918, Plate 19a; Thompson, 1939a, Fig. 3). The deer's front legs are bent forward like human arms, a position impossible for a deer; human hands and legs are visible; beside the sun under the deer is a hummingbird, sun's guise; beyond is a vulture. Above the hidden sun hovers an insect with extended proboscis, surely to represent the blowfly which, at sun's request, sent word to the vultures of the deer carcass. Another example is the Cámara vase now in the Bliss collection (Lothrop, Foshag, and Mahler, 1957, Plate 81). Here, again, the deer's forefeet are bent the wrong way, and the outline of the rear legs is human, not that of a stag. A sort of blanket with crossbones on the animal's back may indicate that he is supposed to be dead. Above, a king vulture flies down. One personage blows a conch trumpet; another holds an antler in his hand as though he had just wrenched it off the animal's head. If that refers to some incident in the legend, it has not survived. This vessel, too, is referable to Tepeu 2.

A carved brown jar from San Agustín, but probably of Copan manufacture (Smith and Kidder, 1943, Fig. 27b), shows a kneeling figure with a deer draped around him. As a hummingbird also appears in the scene, it is a reasonable assumption that sun is in the act of hiding beneath the deer skin. This is also late Classic.

QUICHE

The hero brothers Hunahpu and Xbalanque, after their adventures on earth and after vanquishing the rulers of the underworld, Xibalba, ascend to the sky to become the sun and moon (Recinos, 1950:163). The same is the fate of the hero brothers in the stories of the Cakchiquel of Palopo (Redfield, 1946:252). This is difficult to understand, since elsewhere throughout the Maya area the moon is female and almost invariably the wife of the sun. Moreover, as Xbalanque is the name of the sun (borrowed from the Kekchi?), Hunahpu, "1 Ahau," must be the moon. However, there is good evidence that 1 Ahau was the morning star in Yucatan (Thompson, 1950:219). One can only suppose that at some time this identification of the younger brother with the moon was made, perhaps as a result of non-Maya influences, for among both the present-day Quiche and Cakchiquel the moon is feminine and, apparently, wife of the sun.

General Considerations

There are a number of dominant motifs which are worth re-capitulating: the boys are mistreated by the old woman and are kept hungry; they kill her lover who is in the shape of a deer or a monster; and by subterfuge they get the old woman to eat part of her lover, although the animals tell her of this jeeringly or as a warning. Alternatively, the boys fill the deer carcass with sting-ing creatures which sting the old woman when she strikes the carcass; in revenge, she tries to kill the children; they, warned by animals, place dummies in their beds. Another plot involves old woman's smothering in a *temascal*; the boys kill her after she fails to answer riddles.

There is an emphasis on blowguns: the boys hunt with them; moon's father-grandfather has a magic one which sucks people in or will send a pellet to hit the sun in the sky; sun, in the Mopan legend, hurls his blowgun at mountains to make a tunnel through which he can crawl instead of climbing over the peak; and the hero brothers of the Popol Vuh use their blowguns as bridges over streams and to hide in during their night in the house of bats. The insertion of chile pepper in the blowgun is a rather widely dis-tributed motif.

The unwanted brother or brothers are sent to climb a tree to get a bird or honey and are changed into monkeys, or the tree is toppled over and the smashed pieces of their bodies are changed into various animals; they return to the old woman's hut in their new forms, and, as she cannot refrain from laughing at them, they are forced to keep their animal forms forever.

In sun's courtship of moon and subsequent life, the deer plays many roles. These are so varied and intimate that they suggest some now lost religious notions on the relationship of deer to the moon and sun. The old woman's lover is seemingly a deer, at least his carcass is that of a deer; sun deceives moon about his prowess as a hunter by carrying a stuffed deerskin on his shoulder; he crouches under a deerskin as part of his scheme to recover his wife; and a deer forms moon's sex organs. According to a Tzeltal tale (Castro, 1959), the deer loses his antlers every year because he put his head under a woman's skirt and the woman's heat burned them off. The nature of the incident suggests that moon was the woman. In one Kekchi version, sun orders the deer to conduct moon to the sky. A Cakchiquel story recorded by Otto Stoll relates that on a short day the sun is drawn across the sky by two deer, whereas on long days two *jabali* pull him.

The young moon was a keen weaver, and she was weaving when sun visited her. According to Wirsing, she brocaded a hummingbird on the cloth when sun came in that guise. This is of interest, for the moon goddess is a patroness of weaving.

The Pandora's box episode could represent a post-Columbian introduction, but the considerable variation in details (the Mazatec deerskin as substitute) suggests the possibility that this is a very ancient story brought from the Old World in pre-Columbian times. As noted, the capture of the vulture motif is represented on pottery of the Classic period, but the story seems to survive only in the lowlands and among the neighboring Kekchi who probably obtained it from the Manche Chol they absorbed.

The deprivation of one eye suffered by moon so that she will give less light is widespread, although accounts of how the eye was lost vary. Rabbit in the moon, often considered a Nahuatl concept, is ubiquitous. It is reported from the Mopan (Thompson, 1930:64) and the Zapotec (above). Bernard Bevan (personal letter) informs that he found rabbit-in-moon belief among the Chinantec, Mixtec, Zapotec, Mixe, Chiapanec, Quiche (at Chichicastenango among many Guatemalan highland towns), in Nicaragua, and even Panama. Quarrels between sun and moon, widely believed to cause eclipses, are omitted from the discussion since they are subsequent to the creation.

The hummingbird is important in Middle American mythology. We have seen that sun disguised himself as a hummingbird to court moon in the Mopan, Kekchi, and Cakchiquel myths, and a hummingbird is represented in two scenes on pottery showing sun hidden under deer's skin and clearly refers to this incident. In a Chatino myth of sun and moon (Cicco and Horcasitas, 1962: 74) the mother of the twins becomes pregnant from fondling in her bosom a brightly colored (humming?) bird. The Mixe have the same myth, as noted. A ball of bright feathers tucked under her huipil caused Coatlicue's pregnancy. There is a case for identifying her son, Huitzilopochtli, "Hummingbird on Left," outcome of that pregnancy, as the sun.

Scornful laughter could have strange effects. In the Bachajón tale, such laughter allowed the animals to escape, leaving their tails behind them. In the Mopan myth (Thompson, 1930:124), Venus had the animals penned in. When his wife laughed at him because he was so ugly, the animals broke out and scattered. Venus grabbed some, such as deer, brocket, rabbit, and peccary, but, their tails breaking off short, they escaped. In the Popol Vuh, the monkey twins took refuge in the tree tops when their grandmother laughed at their antics as they tried to dance.

The Palencano-Chol incident of hiding sun's son in a large pottery jar occurs also in a creation legend of the Pipil of Izalco. Sun, when a child, was similarly hidden (Schultze-Jena, 1935).

It will be recalled that the child in the same Palencano-Chol story wore a fiery red hat and red trousers. Red is the color of the sun god in Mexican codices. Mendelson (1958) reports that in times past, the Zutuhil of Santiago Atitlan used to dress Santiago and San Juan in green cloaks when rain was needed and in red cloaks when they wanted the sun to shine.

The many explanations of how animals got their characteristic features are of interest—almost parallels to Kipling's *Just So Stories:* why the woodpecker has a red poll, parrots are green, toads flat, ants pinch-waisted, some animals very short tailed, deer white tailed, vultures white on the wings, iguanas crested, and so on.

The theme of idle boys in the milpa with some trick to deceive (p. 361 and Thompson, 1930:163–65) or with magical aid (p. 357, and the hoes which do the work in the Popol Vuh) are widespread.

There can be little doubt that material on the subject which would have widened the distribution of motifs has been overlooked. Isolated motifs unrelated to the cycle of creation myths have not been cited, and stories in the Popol Vuh concerning the hero brothers not found in the folk tales of other groups—the journey to Xibalba, the trials, the ball game, and so on—have also been excluded.

The names of individuals deserve investigation. Note, for instance, XT'actani, Matactin, and Mataktani. Xbalanque of the Popol Vuh clearly is the same as the Kekchi Xbalamque. Dieseldorff tells of a half-civilized Kekchi who, on being accused of theft, swore his innocence by the sun which he pointed at and called *li cagua* Xbalamque, "Our Lord Sun." This is good evidence for supposing that the Quiche obtained their cycle of legends of the two heroes from the Kekchi. Indeed, the entrance to Xibalba is said to have been near Coban. However, it seems likely that the Kekchi, in turn, received these stories from the Manche Chol whom they absorbed in such large numbers as they expanded northeastward.

The stories we have reviewed vouchsafe us deep insight into Maya thought and poetry, for who but a poet could paint us that word picture of the little fish, each holding his companion's tail in his mouth to form a net to lift moon to the sky. They are a welcome respite from the aridity of so many present-day methods in archaeology. G. K. Chesterton came near the truth when in *The Everlasting Man* he wrote:

> We do not submit a sonnet to a mathematician or a song to a calculating boy; but we do indulge the equally fantastic idea that folklore can be treated as a science. Unless these things are appreciated artistically, they are not appreciated at all. When the professor is told by the barbarian that once there was nothing except a great feathered serpent, unless the learned man feels a thrill and half a temptation to wish it were true, he is no judge of such things at all. When he is assured, on the best Red Indian authority, that a primitive hero carried the sun and moon and stars in a box, unless he claps his hands and almost kicks his legs as a child would at such a charming fancy, he knows nothing about the matter.

I at least feel moved to clap my hands and—but for age—to kick my legs when I pass in memory those stories of the creation and the doings of the heroes before sun took up his duties. That is the reason I do not tabulate the motifs. Chesterton has a good point, but it must not be carried too far: clap hands at the myths

372

because they entertain, but also—a matter which did not interest him—because they inform. They shower gentle rain on the somewhat arid analyses of the three previous chapters; they are the Chacs of this book.

I could not leave it in better hands.

References

The following abbreviations are additional to normal usage:

A. Anthr.: *American Anthropologist*

A. Antiq.: *American Antiquity*

A. S. G. H.: *Anales de la Sociedad de Geografía e Historia de Guatemala*

B. A. E.: United States Bureau of American Ethnology

B. Goath.: Biblioteca Goathemala de la Sociedad de Geografía e Historia

C. I. W.: Carnegie Institution of Washington

C. I. W. Notes: *C. I. W. Notes on Middle American Archaeology and Ethnology, Division of Historical Research* (later, *Department of Archaeology*)

E. C. M.: *Estudios de Cultura Maya*, Seminario de Cultura Maya

I. C. A.: *Proceedings, International Congress of Americanists.*

I. N. A. H.: Instituto Nacional de Antropología e Historia

I. N. I.: Instituto Nacional Indigenista

J. S. A. P.: *Journal de la Société des Américanistes de Paris*

M. A. R. I.: Middle American Research Institute, Tulane University

Micro.: Microfilm Collection of Manuscripts of Middle American Cultural Anthropology, University of Chicago Library

374

P. M.: Peabody Museum of Archaeology and Ethnology, Harvard
  University
R. M. E. A.: *Revista Mexicana de Estudios Antropológicos*

AMRAM, D. W.
1942 "The Lacandon, last of the Maya," *El México Antiguo*, 6:15–
  26. Mexico.
1944 "Notes on Lacandon religion and astronomy." Unpublished MS.

ANDERS, F.
1963 *Das Pantheon der Maya*. Akademische Druck- und Verlagsanstalt, Graz.

ANDERSON, A.
1957 "Two Chol texts," *Tlalocan*, 3:313–16. Mexico.

ANDERSON, A. H., AND H. J. COOK
1944 *Archaeological finds near Douglas, British Honduras. C. I. W.
  Notes 40*. Cambridge.

ANDREWS, E. W.
1939 "A group of related structures from Yucatán," *C. I. W. Pub.
  509*, Contrib. 26. Washington.
1941 "Pustunich, Campeche. Some further related sculptures," *Los
  Mayas Antiguos*, pp. 127–38. Mexico.
1943 "The archaeology of southwestern Campeche," *C. I. W. Pub.
  546*, Contrib. 40. Washington.
1961 *Preliminary report on the 1959–60 field season. National Geo-
  graphic Society—Tulane University. Dzibilchaltun program.
  M. A. R. I. Miscellaneous Ser.*, No. 11. New Orleans.
1965 "Archaeology and prehistory in the northern Maya lowlands,"
  Handbook of Middle American Indians, 2:288–330. Austin.

ANGUIANO, R. DE
1908 "*Proyecto para reducir a la fe a los indios xicakes*," *Colección
  de libros y documentos referentes a la historia de América*, 8:
  389–414. Madrid.

ANNALS OF THE CAKCHIQUELS: *See* Recinos, 1953

AULIE, W., AND E. AULIE
1951 "Palencano-Chol vocabulary and folk-tales with English translation." MS.

AVENDAÑO Y LOYOLA, A. DE
1696 *"Relación de las entradas que hizé a la conversión de los géntiles Ytzaex."* MS. Original in Newberry Library, Chicago.

BAER, P., AND M. BAER
1949 "Notes on Lacandon marriage," *Southwestern Journ. of Anthropol.*, 5: 101–106. Albuquerque.
1952 "Materials on Lacandon culture of the Petha (Pelha) region." Micro., No. 34. Chicago.

BARLOW, R. H., AND V. RAMÍREZ
1962 *"Tonatiw iwan meetstli," Tlalocan*, 4:55–61. Mexico.

BARRERA VÁSQUEZ, A.
1939 *La identificación de la deidad "E" de Schellhas. Cuadernos Mayas*, No. 2. Mérida.

———, AND S. RENDÓN
1948 *El libro de los libros de Chilam Balam.* Mexico.

BARTRES, L.
1908 *Civilización prehistórica de las riberas del Papaloapam y costa de Sotavento, Estado de Veracruz.* Mexico.

BELTRAN DE SANTA ROSA, P.
1859 *Arte del idioma maya reducido á sucintas reglas y semilexicon yucateco.* Mérida.

BENEDICT, F. G., AND M. STEGGERDA
1936 "The food of the present-day Maya Indians of Yucatan," *C. I. W. Pub. 456*, Contrib. 18. Washington.

BERENDT, C. H.
No date *Lengua maya, miscelanea.* 3 vols. MS in Univ. Mus., Philadelphia.

BERLIN, H.
1956 "Late pottery horizons of Tabasco, Mexico," *C. I. W. Pub. 606*, Contrib. 59. Washington.

Beyer, H.
1921 *El llamado "calendario azteca."* Mexico.

Blom, F.
1932 "Commerce, trade and monetary units of the Maya," *M. A. R. I.*, 4:531–56. New Orleans.
1959 "Historical notes relating to the pre-Columbian amber trade from Chiapas," *Mitteilungen aus dem Mus. für Völkerkunde in Hamburg*, 25:24–27. Hamburg.

———, and G. Duby
1955–57 *La selva lacandona.* 2 vols. Mexico.

———, and O. La Farge
1926–27 *Tribes and temples. M. A. R. I.* Pub. 1. 2 vols. New Orleans.

Borah, W., and S. F. Cooke
1963 *The aboriginal population of central Mexico on the eve of the Spanish conquest. Univ. of Cal. Ibero-Americana*, Vol. 45. Berkeley & Los Angeles.

Borhegyi, S. F. de
1961 "Shark teeth, stingray spines and shark fishing in ancient Mexico and Central America," *Southwestern Journ. of Anthrop.*, 17:273–96. Albuquerque.

Brainerd, G. W.
1958 *The archaeological ceramics of Yucatán. Univ. of Cal. Anthropol. Records*, Vol. 19. Berkeley & Los Angeles.

Brasseur de Bourbourg, C. E.
1867 *"Rapport sur les ruines de Mayapan et d'Uxmal au Yucatan," Archives de la Commission scientifique de Mexique*, 2:234–88. Paris.

Brinton, D. G.
1869 "A notice of some manuscripts in Central American languages," *Amer. Journ. of Science and Arts*, 50:222–30. New Haven.
1882 *The Maya chronicles.* Philadelphia.
1887 "On the so-called Alaguilac language of Guatemala," *Proc. Amer. Philosophical Soc.*, 24:366–77. Philadelphia.

1890 *Essays of an Americanist*. Philadelphia.
1895 "A primer of Maya hieroglyphics," *Univ. of Pa. Philology, Literature, and Archaeology Ser.*, Vol. 3, No. 2. Philadelphia.

BRUCE, R. D.
1967 "*Jerarquía maya entre los dioses lacandones*," *Anales del I. N. A. H.*, 18:93–108. Mexico.

BUNZEL, R.
1952 *Chichicastenango, a Guatemalan village. Amer. Ethnological Soc. Pub. 22.* Locust Valley, N.Y.

BURKITT, R. J.
1902 "Notes on the Kekchi language," *A. Anthr.*, 4:441–63. New York.
1918 "The hils [*sic*] and the corn," *The Mus. Journ.*, Vol. 9, Nos. 3–4. Philadelphia.

CÁMARA BARBACHANO, F.
1946 "*Monografía sobre los tzeltales de Tenejapa.*" Micro., No. 5. Chicago.

CARDÓS DE MÉNDEZ, A.
1959 *El comercio de los mayas antiguos. Acta Anthropológica, Época 2*, Vol. 2, No. 1. Mexico.

CARRASCO, P.
1952 "*El sol y la luna. 1. Versión mixe*," *Tlalocan*, 3:168–69. Mexico.

CASTRO, C. A.
1959 *Los hombres verdaderos. Universidad Veracruzana, Serie Ficción*, 7. Jalapa.
1965 *Narraciones tzeltales de Chiapas. Universidad Veracruzana, Cuardernos*, 27. Jalapa.

CERDA SILVA, R. DE LA
1940 "*Los zoque*," *Revista Mexicana de Sociología*, Vol. 2, No. 4, pp. 61–96. Mexico.

CHAMBERLAIN, R. S.
1948 *The conquest and colonization of Yucatan. C. I. W. Pub. 582.* Washington.

1953 *The conquest and colonization of Honduras. C. I. W. Pub. 598.* Washington.

Chapman, A. M.
1959 *Puertos de intercambio en mesoamérica prehistórica. I.N.A.H. Serie Historia, 3.* Mexico.

Chilam Balam of Chumayel, Book of: *See* Roys, 1933.

Chilam Balam of Kaua
No date. Reproduction by W. Gates.

Chilam Balam of Mani
No date. Part of Codex Pérez.

Chilam Balam of Tizimin
No date. Original in Mexico, D. F. Reproductions by Gates and others. Transcription by R. L. Roys. Part translation in Roys, 1949.

Chimalpopoca (Códice de)
1945 *Anales de Cuauhtitlán y leyenda de los soles.* Translated by P. F. Velásquez. Universidad Nacional Autónoma, Mexico.

Cicco, G. de, and F. Horcasitas
1962 *"Los cuates: un mito chatino,"* Tlalocan, 4:74–79. Mexico.

[Ciudad Real, A. de]
1873 *Relación breve y verdadera de algunas cosas . . . que sucedieron al Padre Fray Alonso Ponce en . . . la Nueva España.* 2 vols. Madrid.

Cline, H.
1944 "Lore and deities of the Lacandon Indians, Chiapas, Mexico," *Journ. Amer. Folklore,* 57:107–15.

Codex Borgia
1898 *Il manoscritto messicano borgiano del Museo Etnografico della S. Congregazione di Propaganda Fide. Riprodotto fotocromografia.* Rome.

CODEX DRESDEN

1892 *Die Maya-handschrift der Königlichen Bibliothek zu Dresden. Herausgegeben von Prof. Dr. E. Förstemann.* Dresden. (Also, Berlin, 1962.)

CODEX MADRID

1967 *Codex Tro-cortesianus (Codex Madrid). Einleitung und Summary von F. Anders.* Akademische Druck- und Verlagsanstalt, Graz.

CODEX PARIS

1969 *Codex Peresianus. Einleitung und Summary von F. Anders.* Akademische Druck- und Verlagsanstalt, Graz.

CODEX PÉREZ

1949 *Códice Pérez. Traducción libre del maya al castellano por el Dr. E. Solís Alcalá.* Mérida. With Maya text. Contains C. B. Mani.

CODEX VATICAN B

1896 *Il manoscritto messicano vaticano 3773.* Rome.

COE, M. D.

1961 *La Victoria, an early site on the Pacific coast of Guatemala. P. M. Papers,* Vol. 53. Cambridge.

COE, W. R.

1959 *Piedras Negras archaeology: artifacts, caches and burials.* Univ. Mus., Univ. of Pa. Monographs. Philadelphia.

1962 "A summary of excavation and research at Tikal, Guatemala: 1956–61," *A. Antiq.,* 27:479–507. Salt Lake City.

CONTRERAS GUEBARA, A. DE

1946 "Relación hecha a su majestad por el Gobernador de Honduras de todos los pueblos de dicha gobernación," *Boletín Archivo General del Gobierno,* 11:5–19. Guatemala.

COOK, S. F., AND L. B. SIMPSON

1948 *The population of central Mexico in the sixteenth century. Univ. of Cal. Ibero-Americana,* Vol. 31. Berkeley & Los Angeles.

CORTÉS, H.: *See* MacNutt.

CORTÉS Y LARRAZ, P.
1958 *Descripción geográfico-moral de la diócesis de Goathemala. B. Goath.*, Vol. 20. 2 vols. Guatemala.

CRESPO, A.
1935 "*Relación geográfica del Partido de Escuintla*," *Boletín Archivo General del Gobierno*, 1:9–15. Guatemala.

CRUZ, W.
1946 *Oaxaca recóndita. Razas, idiomas, costumbres, leyendas y tradiciones del Estado de Oaxaca.* Mexico.

CURIOSO, UN
1845 "*Cocom*," *Registro Yucateco*, 1:349–50. Mérida.

DESCRIPCIÓN DE SAN BARTOLOMÉ
1965 "*Descripción de San Bartolomé del Partido de Atitlán, año 1585*," *A. S. G. H.*, 38:262–76. Guatemala.

DÍAZ, J.
1958 *La primera noticia del descubrimiento de la Nueva España, en Europa: El itinerario de la expedición del Capitán Juan de Grijalva (año de 1518), escrito por el capellán de su armada.* With notes by C. R. Menéndez. Mérida.

DÍAZ DEL CASTILLO, B.
1908–16 *The true history of the conquest of New Spain.* Translated by A. P. Maudslay. 5 vols. The Hakluyt Soc., London.

DÍAZ DE SALAS, M.
1963 "*Notas sobre la visión del mundo entre los tzotziles de Venustiano Carranza, Chiapas*," *La Palabra y El Hombre*, 26:253–67. Jalapa.

DIESELDORFF, E. P.
1909 "*Klassifizierung seiner archäologischen Funden im nördlichen Guatemala*," *Zeitschrift für Ethnologie*, 41:862–74. Berlin.

1926–33 *Kunst und Religion der Mayavölker im alten und heutigen Mittelamerika.* Berlin.

Diez de Navarro, L.
1946 *"Fortificación de la costa de Honduras y la reorganización de la división administrativa de la Provincia de Guatemala,"* Boletín Archivo General del Gobierno, 11:58–65. Guatemala.

Douglass, A. E.
1889 "A portrait pipe from San Salvador, Central America," *Amer. Antiquarian*, 11:348–53. Chicago.

Duby, G.
1944 *Los lacandones, su pasado y su presente. Secretaría de Educación Pública. Biblioteca Enciclopédica Popular*, No. 30. Mexico.

Durán, D.
1867–80 *Historia de las Indias de Nueva España y islas de tierra firme.* Edited by J. F. Ramírez. 3 vols. Mexico.

Ekholm, G. F.
1961 "Some collar-shaped shell pendants from Mesoamerica." In *Homenaje a Pablo Martínez del Río*, pp. 287–93. Mexico.

Elson, B.
1947 "The Homshuk: a Sierra Popoluca text," *Tlalocan*, 2:193–214. Mexico.

Foshag, W. F.
1954 *"Estudios mineralógicos sobre el jade de Guatemala,"* Antropología e Historia de Guatemala, Vol. 6, No. 1, pp. 3–47. Guatemala.

———, and R. Leslie
1955 "Jadeite from Manzanal, Guatemala," *A. Antiq.*, 21:81–83. Salt Lake City.

Foster, G. M.
1945 "Sierra Popoluca folklore and beliefs," *Univ. of Cal. Pubs. on Amer. Archaeology and Ethnology*, Vol. 42, No. 2. San Francisco & Los Angeles.

Fuentes y Guzmán, F. A.
1882–83 *Historia de Guatemala ó recordación florida.* Edited with notes by J. Zaragoza. Biblioteca de los Americanistas, Madrid.

1932–33 *Recordación florida. Discurso historial . . . del Reyno de Guatemala. B. Goath.*, Vol. 6. 3 vols. Guatemala.

GAGE, T.
1958 *Thomas Gage's travels in the New World.* Edited and with an introduction by J. E. S. Thompson. Norman.

GALINDO, J.
1833 "Description of the River Usumasinta in Guatemala," *Journ. Royal Geog. Soc.*, 3:59–64. London.
1920 "A description of the ruins of Copan." In Morley, 1920, pp. 593–604. Original in Spanish, 1834.

GANN, T. W. F.
1895–97 "On the contents of some ancient mounds in Central America," *Proc. Soc. of Antiquaries*, 16:308–17. London.
1900 "Mounds in northern Honduras," *B. A. E. Annual Report*, 19: 655–92. Washington.
1918 *The Maya Indians of southern Yucatan and northern British Honduras. B. A. E. Bulletin 64.* Washington.
1925 *Mystery cities: exploration and adventure in Lubaantun.* London and New York.
1926 *Ancient cities and modern tribes.* London and New York.
1927 *Maya cities: a record of exploration and adventure in Middle America.* London and New York.

GARCÍA DE PALACIO, D.
1860 *Carta dirijida al Rey de España. Año 1576.* Edited with translation, introduction, maps, and notes by E. G. Squier. New York.

GARCÍA DE PELÁEZ, F. DE P.
1968 *Memorias para la historia del antiguo reino de Guatemala. B. Goath.*, Vol. 21. Guatemala.

GARIBAY K., A. M.
1958 *Veinte himnos sacros de los nahuas.* Universidad Nacional Autonóma, Mexico.

GATES, W.
1920 "The distribution of the several branches of the Mayance linguistic stock." In Morley, 1920, pp. 605–15.

GILLIN, J.

1951 *The culture of security in San Carlos, a study of a Guatemalan community of Indians and ladinos. M. A. R. I. Pub. 16.* New Orleans.

GORDON, G. B.

1915 "Guatemala myths," *The Mus. Journ.*, 6:103–44. Philadelphia.

——, AND J. A. MASON

1925–28 *Examples of Maya pottery in the museum and other collections.* 3 vols. Univ. Mus., Philadelphia.

GOUBAUD C., A.

1949 "Notes on San Juan Chamelco, Alta Vera Paz." Micro., No. 23. Chicago.

GRAHAM, I.

1963 "Juan Galindo, enthusiast." *E. C. M.*, 3:11–35. Mexico.

GRANADO BAEZA, B. DEL

1845 "Informe dado . . . en contestación al interrogatorio de 36 preguntas," *Registro Yucateco*, 1:165–78. Mérida.

GUITERAS H., C.

1960 *La familia tzotzil en la salud y en la enfermedad. Tlatoani*, 13. Mexico.

1961 *Perils of the soul. The world view of a Tzotzil Indian.* Glencoe & New York.

HABEL, S.

1878 *The sculptures of Santa Lucia Cozumalhuapa in Guatemala, with an account of travels in Central America and on the west coast of South America. Smithsonian Contrib. to Knowledge*, Vol. 23, No. 269. Washington.

HERRERA T., A. DE

1728 *Historia general de las Indias Occidentales.* 4 vols. Antwerp.

HISTORIA DE LOS MEXICANOS

1891 *Historia de los mexicanos por sus pinturas. Nueva colección de documentos para la historia de México*, Part 3, No. 1. Mexico.

HISTOYRE DU MECHIQUE
1905 *"Histoyre du Mechique."* Edited with notes by E. de Jonghe. *J. S. A. P.*, (o. s.) 2:1–41. Paris.

HOLLAND, W. R.
1963 *Medicina maya en los altos de Chiapas.* I. N. I., Mexico.
1964 *"Conceptos cosmológicos tzotziles como una base para interpretar la civilización maya prehispánica,"* *América Indígena*, 24:11–28. Mexico.

JIMÉNEZ MORENO, W.
1954–55 *"Síntesis de la historia precolonial del Valle de México,"* *R. M. E. A.*, 14:219–36. Mexico.

JOHNSON, F.
1940 "The linguistic map of Mexico and Central America," In *The Maya and their Neighbors*, pp. 88–114. New York.

JOHNSON, I. WEITLANER, AND J. B. JOHNSON
1939 *"Un cuento mazateco-popoloca,"* *R. M. E. A.*, 3:217–26. Mexico.

JOYCE, T. A.
1914 *Mexican archaeology.* London.

JUARROS, D.
1823 *A statistical and commercial history of the kingdom of Guatemala in Spanish America.* London.

KELEMEN, P.
1943 *Medieval american art.* 2 vols. New York.

KELLY, I., AND A. PALERM
1952 *The Tajin Totonac, Part 1. Smithsonian Institution Institute of Social Anthropology Pub. 13.* Washington.

KELSEY, V., AND L. DE JONGH OSBORNE
1939 *Four keys to Guatemala.* New York.

KIDDER, A. V.
1947 *The artifacts of Uaxactun, Guatemala. C. I. W. Pub. 576.* Washington.

———, J. D. Jennings, and E. M. Shook
1946 *Excavations at Kaminaljuyu, Guatemala. C. I. W. Pub. 561.* Washington.

La Farge, O.
1947 *Santa Eulalia. The religion of a Cuchumatan Indian town.* Univ. of Chicago, Chicago.

———, and D. Byers
1931 *The year bearer's people. M. A. R. I. Pub. 3.* New Orleans.

Landa, D. de
1938 *See* Pérez Martínez
1940 *See* Tozzer

Las Casas, B. de
1877 *Historia de las Indias.* 2 vols. Mexico.
1909 *Apologética historia de las Indias.* Madrid.

Lebrón de Quiñones, L.
1951 *Relación breve y sumaria de la visita hecha por el ... Oidor del Nuevo Reino de Galicia, por mandado de Su Alteza.* Guadalajara, Jal.

Lehmann, W.
1906 *"Traditions des anciens mexicains. Texte inédit ... avec traduction en latin,"* J. S. A. P., 3:239–97. Paris.
1920 *Zentral-Amerika.* 2 vols. Berlin.

León Pinelo, A.
1958 *Relación sobre la pacificación y población de las provincias del Manché i Lacandón.* Madrid. Also in Scholes and Adams, 1960.

Le Plongeon, A.
1886 *Here and there in Yucatan.* New York.

Lincoln, J. S.
1942 *"The Maya calendar of the Ixil Indians of the Guatemalan highlands,"* C. I. W. Pub. 528, Contrib. 38. Washington.
1946 *"An ethnological study of the Ixil Indians of the Guatemala highlands."* Micro., No. 1. Chicago.

LIZANA, B. DE
1893 *Historia de Yucatán. Devocionario de Ntra. Sra. de Izamal y conquista espiritual.* Mexico.

LIZARDI R., C.
1956 *"Otro dios maya de maíz,"* Miscelánea de Estudios Dedicados al Dr. Fernando Ortiz, pp. 945–50. Havana.
1963 *"Inscripciones de Pomoná, Tabasco, México,"* E. C. M., 3:187–202. Mexico.

LONGYEAR, J. M.
1944 *Archaeological investigations in El Salvador.* P. M. Mem., Vol. 9, No. 2. Cambridge.
1947 *Cultures and peoples of the southeastern Maya frontier. C. I. W. Theoretical Approaches to Problems Ser.* No. 3. Cambridge.

LÓPEZ DE COGOLLUDO, D.
1867–68 *Historia de Yucatán, escrita en el siglo xvii.* Mérida.

LOTHROP, S. K.
1921 "The stone statues of Nicaragua," *A. Anthr.,* 23:311–21. Lancaster.
1939 "The southeastern frontier of the Maya," *A. Anthr.,* 41:42–54. Menasha.

———, W. F. FOSHAG, AND J. MAHLER
1957 *Pre-Columbian art. Robert Woods Bliss collection.* London and New York.

LUNARDI, F.
1946 *"Miscelánea maya,"* Honduras Maya, 1:76. Tegucigalpa.

MACKIE, E. W.
1961 "New light on the end of classic Maya culture at Benque Viejo, British Honduras," *A. Antiq.,* 27:216–24. Salt Lake City.

MACNUTT, F. A.
1908 *Hernando Cortés: His five letters of relation to the Emperor Charles V.* Translated and edited with introduction and notes. London and New York.

McBRYDE, F. W.

1947 *Cultural and historical geography of southwest Guatemala.*
Smithsonian Institution Institute of Social Anthropology Pub. 4.
Washington.

McDOUGALL, E.

1955 *Easter ceremonies at Santiago Atitlan in 1930. C. I. W. Notes*
123. Cambridge.

MALER, T.

1910 *Explorations in the Department of Peten, Guatemala and adja-*
cent region: Motul de San Jose; Peten Itza. P. M. Mem., Vol.
4, No. 3. Cambridge.

MANCHE-CHOL VOCABULARY

1935 *Arte, vocabulario y doctrina en lengua cholti, 1685. Maya Soc.*
Pub. 9. Facsimile. Baltimore.

MARQUINA, I.

1951 *Arquitectura prehispánica. I. N. A. H. Memorias,* 1. Mexico.

MARTÍNEZ HERNÁNDEZ, J.

1913 *"La creación del mundo según los mayas. Páginas inéditas del*
manuscrito de Chumayel," 18th I. C. A., London, *1912,* pp. 164–
71. London.

MARTYR OF ANGHIERA, P. [PETER MARTYR]

1612 *The history of the West Indies containing the actes* [*sic*] *and*
adventures of the Spaniards. London.

MAUDSLAY, A. P.

1889–1902 *Archaeology. Biologia Centrali-Americana.* 5 vols.
London.

MENDELSON, E. M.

1958 "A Guatemalan sacred bundle," *Man,* Vol. 58, No. 170. London.
1959 "Maximon: an iconographical introduction," *Man,* Vol. 59, No.
87. London.
1965 *Los escándalos de Maximón.* Guatemala.

MENDIETA, G. DE

1870 *Historia eclesiástica indiana.* Mexico.

MERWIN, R. E., AND G. C. VAILLANT
1932 *The ruins of Holmul, Guatemala. P. M. Mem.*, Vol. 3, No. 2. Cambridge.

MILES, S. W.
1957 "The sixteenth-century Pokom-Maya: a documentary analysis of social structure and archaeological setting," *Transactions of the Amer. Philosophical Soc.*, Vol. 47, Part 4. Philadelphia.

MILLER, W. S.
1956 *Cuentos mixes.* I. N. I., Mexico.

MORALES VILLA VICENCIO, J. DE
1937 "*Fee de la llegada al peñol y autos de lo que en la jornada zusedió,*" *Boletín Archivo General del Gobierno,* 2:133–84. Guatemala.

MORLEY, S. G.
1920 *The inscriptions at Copan. C. I. W. Pub. 219.* Washington.
1937–38 *The inscriptions of Peten. C. I. W. Pub. 437.* 5 vols. Washington.
1946 *The ancient Maya.* Stanford.

MORRIS, E. H., J. CHARLOT, AND A. A. MORRIS
1931 *The Temple of the Warriors at Chichen Itza, Yucatan. C. I. W. Pub. 406.* Washington.

MOTUL DICTIONARY
1939 *Diccionario de Motul, maya-español, atribuido a Fray Antonio de Ciudad Real y Arte de la lengua maya por Fray Juan Coronel.* Edited by J. Martínez Hernández. Mérida.

MUÑOZ CAMARGO, D.
1892 *Historia de Tlaxcala.* Edited with notes by A. Chavero. Mexico.

NARCISO, V. A.
1960 "*Los indios pokonchies,*" *Boletín del Instituto Indigenista Nacional, Época 2,* Vol. 3, pp. 83–111. Guatemala.

NÚÑEZ DE LA VEGA, F.
1702 *Constituciones dioecesanos del obispado de Chiappa.* Rome.

NUTTALL, Z.
1909 "A curious survival in Mexico of the use of the Purpura shell fish for dyeing," *Putnam Anniversary Volume*, pp. 363–84. New York.

OAKES, M.
1951 *The two crosses of Todos Santos. Survivals of Mayan religious ritual.* New York.

OVIEDO Y VALDÉS, G. FERNÁNDEZ DE
1851–55 *Historia general y natural de las Indias, islas, y tierra-firme del mar océano.* 4 vols. Madrid.

PAPELES DE NUEVA ESPAÑA
1905 *Segunda serie. Geografía y estadística.* Edited by F. del Paso y Troncoso. 6 vols. Madrid.

PARSONS, E. C.
1936 *Mitla, town of the souls.* Chicago.

PÉREZ DICTIONARY
1866–77 *Diccionario de la lengua maya por D. Juan Pío Pérez.* Mérida.

PÉREZ MARTÍNEZ H.
1938 *Relación de las cosas de Yucatán por el P. Fray Diego de Landa.* With introduction, notes and various related documents. Mexico.

PINEDA, V.
1888 *Historia de las sublevaciones indígenas . . . de Chiapas; gramática de la lengua tzel-tal . . . y diccionario.* Chiapas.

POMAR, J. B.
1891 *Relación de Tezcoco. Nueva colección de documentos para la historia de México*, Part 1. Mexico.

PONCE DE LEÓN, L.
1882 *"Relación de la Provincia de Soconusco."* In Fuentes y Guzmán, 1882–83, 1:425–28.

POPOL VUH: *See* Recinos, 1950.

PORTER, M. N.
1948 *Pipas precortesianas. Acta Anthropológica*, Vol. 3, No. 2.
Mexico.

POZAS A., R.
1947 *"Monografía de Chamula."* Micro., No. 15. Chicago.
1952 *"Los mames de la región oncocercosa del Estado de Chiapas,"*
Anales del I. N. A. H., 4:253–61. Mexico.
1959 *Chamula, un pueblo indio de los altos de Chiapas. I. N. I.*
Memorias, No. 8. Mexico.

PREUSS, K. T.
1912 *Die Nayarit Expedition: Die Religion des Cora Indianer.* Leipzig.

PROSKOURIAKOFF, T.
1951 "Some non-classic traits in the sculpture of Yucatan," *29th I. C.*
A., New York, 1949, 1:108–18. Chicago.
———, AND J. E. S. THOMPSON
1947 *Maya calendar round dates such as 9 Ahau 17 Mol. C. I. W.*
Notes 79. Cambridge.

RECINOS, A.
1950 *Popol Vuh: The sacred book of the ancient Quiche Maya.*
Norman.
1953 *The Annals of the Cakchiquels and Title of the Lords of Totoni-*
capan. Norman.

REDFIELD, R.
1946 "Notes on San Antonio Palopo." Micro., No. 4. Chicago.

———, AND A. VILLA R.
1934 *Chan Kom, a Maya village. C. I. W. Pub. 448.* Washington.
1939 "Notes on the ethnography of Tzeltal communities of Chiapas,"
C. I. W. Pub. 509. Contrib. 28. Washington.

RELACIÓN DE ZAPOTITLÁN AND SUCHITEPÉQUEZ
1955 *"Memorial de las advertencias y cosas . . . y particulares . . . de*
Çapotitlan y Suchitepeques," *A. S. G. H.*, 28:68–84. Guatemala.

RELACIONES DE YUCATÁN
1898–1900 *Colección de Documentos inéditos relativos al descubri-*

miento, conquista y organización de las antiguas posesiones españolas de ultramar, Vols. 11 and 13. Madrid.

REMESAL, A. DE
1932 *Historia general de las Indias occidentales y particular de la gobernación de Chiapa y Guatemala. B. Goath.*, Vols. 4 and 5. Guatemala.

RITUAL OF THE BACABS: *See* Roys, 1965

ROSALES, J. DE DIOS
1949 "Notes on San Pedro la Laguna." Micro., No. 25. Chicago.

ROYS, R. L.
1931 *The ethno-botany of the Maya. M. A. R. I. Pub. 2.* New Orleans.
1933 *The book of Chilam Balam of Chumayel. C. I. W. Pub. 438.* Washington; Norman, 1967.
1939 *The titles of Ebtun. C. I. W. Pub. 505.* Washington.
1943 *The Indian background of colonial Yucatan. C. I. W. Pub. 548.* Washington.
1949 "The prophecies for the Maya tuns or years in the books of Chilam Balam of Tizimin and Mani," *C. I. W. Pub. 585,* Contrib. 51. Washington.
1954 "The Maya katun prophecies of the books of Chilam Balam, Series 1," *C. I. W. Pub. 606,* Contrib. 57. Washington.
1957 *The political geography of the Yucatan Maya. C. I. W. Pub. 613.* Washington.
1965 *Ritual of the Bacabs.* Translation with introduction and notes. Norman.

RUÍZ DE ALARCÓN, H.
1892 *"Tratado de las supersticiones y costumbres gentílicas que oy viven entre los indios naturales desta Nueva España,"* Anales del Museo Nacional de México, Época 1, Vol. 6, pp. 123–223. Mexico.

RUPPERT, K.
1931 "Temple of the wall panels, Chichen Itza," *C. I. W. Pub. 403,* Contrib. 3. Washington.
1952 *Chichen Itza: architectural notes and plans. C. I. W. Pub. 595.* Washington.

RUSSELL, V.

1947 *"Los dioses enanos chontales, uyumkap,"* Esta Semana, No. 28. Mexico.

RUZ L., A.

1944 *Extensión geográfica del dialecto maya-chontal. Escuela Nacional de Antropología Pub. 2.* Mexico.

1945 *Campeche en la arquelogía maya. Acta Anthropológica,* Vol. 1, Nos. 2–3.

1954 *"Exploraciones en Palenque: 1952,"* Anales del I. N. A. H., 6: 79–110. Mexico.

SABLOFF, J. A., AND G. R. WILLEY

1967 "The collapse of Maya civilization in the southern lowlands: a consideration of history and process," *Southwestern Journ. of Anthropol.,* 23:311–36. Albuquerque.

SAHAGÚN, B. DE

1938 *Historia general de las cosas de Nueva España.* 5 vols. Mexico.

1950–69 *Florentine codex. General history of the things of New Spain.* Translated from the Nahuatl with notes by A. J. O. Anderson and C. E. Dibble. *Monographs of the School of American Research,* 14. 12 vols. Santa Fe.

SAMAYOA GUEVARA, H. H.

1947 *"Historia del establecimiento de la Orden Mercedaria en el Reino de Guatemala, desde en año de 1537 hasta 1632,"* Antropologia e Historia de Guatemala, Vol. 9, No. 2, pp. 30–43. Guatemala.

SANDERS, W.

1960 "Prehistoric ceramics and settlement patterns in Quintana Roo," *C. I. W. Pub. 606,* Contrib. 60. Washington.

SAN FRANCISCO DICTIONARY

1870 *Diccionario Maya-español y español-maya del convento de San Francisco en Mérida. Copiado por C. Hermann Berendt, M. D.* 2 vols. Mérida. Original lost.

SAPPER, K.

1897 *Das nördliche Mittel-Amerika nebst einem Ausflug nach dem Hochland von Anahuac.* Brunswick.

1901 *"Speise und Trank der Kekchi Indianer,"* *Globus,* 80:259–63. Brunswick.

1904 *"Der gegenwärtige Stand der ethnographischen Kenntnis von Mittel Amerika,"* *Archiv für Anthropologie,* 3:1–38. Brunswick.

SCHELLHAS, P.
1904 *Representations of deities of the Maya manuscripts.* P. M. *Papers,* Vol. 4, No. 1. Cambridge.

SCHOLES, F. V., AND E. B. ADAMS
1938 *Don Diego Quijada, Alcalde Mayor de Yucatán, 1561–65. Biblioteca Histórica Mexicana de Obras Inéditas,* Vols. 14, 15, Mexico.

1960 *Relaciones histórico-descriptivas de La Verapaz, El Manché y Lacandón, en Guatemala.* Universidad de San Carlos, Guatemala.

———, AND R. L. ROYS
1948 *The Maya Chontal Indians of Acalan-Tixchel, a contribution to the history and ethnography of the Yucatan peninsula.* C. I. W. *Pub. 560.* Washington.

———, ET AL.
1936–38 *Documentos para la historia de Yucatán.* 3 vols. Mérida.

1945 "History of the Maya area," *C. I. W. Yearbook 44,* pp. 177–83. Washington.

SCHULLER, R.
1924 "Notes on the Huaxteca Indians of San Luis Potosi," *El México Antiguo,* 2:129–40. Mexico.

SCHULTZE-JENA, L.
1935 *Indiana II. Mythen in der Muttersprache der Pipil von Izalco in El Salvador.* Jena.

1946 *La vida y las creencias de los indios quichés de Guatemala.* Translated by A. Goubaud and H. D. Sapper. Guatemala.

SELER, E.
1902–23 *Gesammelte Abhandlungen zur amerikanischen Sprach- und Alterthumskunde.* 6 vols. Berlin; Graz, 1959.

1904 "The Mexican picture writings of Alexander von Humboldt," *B. A. E. Bulletin 28,* pp. 123–229.

394

SHATTUCK, G. C. ET AL.

1933 *The peninsula of Yucatan. Medical, biological, meteorological and sociological studies. C. I. W. Pub. 431.* Washington.

1938 *A medical survey of the Republic of Guatemala. C. I. W. Pub. 499.* Washington.

SHOOK, E. M., AND A. V. KIDDER

1953 "Mound E–III–3, Kaminaljuyu, Guatemala," *C. I. W. Pub. 596,* Contrib. 53. Washington.

SIEGEL, M.

1941 "Religion in western Guatemala, a product of acculturation," *A. Anthr.,* 43:62–76. Menasha.

1943 "The creation myth in Acatan, Guatemala," *Journ. Amer. Folklore,* 56:120–26. Philadelphia.

SLOCUM, M. C.

1965 "The origin of corn and other Tzeltal myths," *Tlalocan,* 5: 1–45. Mexico.

SMITH, A. L., AND A. V. KIDDER

1943 "Explorations in the Motagua Valley, Guatemala," *C. I. W. Pub. 546,* Contrib. 41. Washington.

1951 *Excavations at Nebaj, Guatemala. C. I. W. Pub. 594.* Washington.

SMITH, A. L., AND K. RUPPERT

1956 *Excavations in house mounds at Mayapan, IV. C. I. W. Current Reports 36.* Cambridge.

SMITH, R. E.

1955 *Ceramic sequence at Uaxactun, Guatemala. M. A. R. I.,* Vol. 20. New Orleans.

1958 "The place of Fine Orange pottery in Mesoamerican archaeology," *A. Antiq.,* 24: 151–60. Salt Lake City.

SOLIER, M., W. DU

1945 "*Estudio arquitectónico de los edificios huaxtecas,*" *Anales del I. N. A. H.,* 1:121–45. Mexico.

SOUSTELLE, G.

1943 "*Notes sur le rituel religieux chez les lacandons du Chiapas,*" *27th I. C. A., Mexico, 1939,* Part 2, pp. 408–18. Mexico.

1961 *"Observaciones sobre la religión de los lacandones del sur de México."* Translated by J. L. Arriola. *Guatemala Indígena,* Vol. 1, No. 1, pp. 31–105. Guatemala.

SOUSTELLE, J.
1933 *"Notes sur les lacandons du Lac Pelja et du Rio Jetja,"* J. S. A. P., 25:153–80. Paris.
1935 *"Le totemisme des lacandons,"* *Maya Research,* 2:325–44. New Orleans.
1937 *"La culture matérielle des indiens lacandons,"* J. S. A. P., 29: 1–95. Paris.

SPINDEN, H. J.
1913 *A study of Maya art, its subject matter and historical development.* P. M. Mem., Vol. 6. Cambridge.

SQUIER, E. G.
1855 *Notes on Central America, particularly the states of Honduras and San Salvador.* New York.
1860 *See* García de Palacio.

STARR, F.
1900–1901 "Notes upon the ethnography of southern Mexico," *Proc. Davenport Academy of Natural Sciences,* 8:102–98; 9:63–172. Davenport.
1908 In *Indian Mexico.* Chicago.

STEPHENS, J. L.
1843 *Incidents of travel in Yucatan.* 2 vols. New York & London.

STONE, D. Z.
1941 *Archaeology of the north coast of Honduras.* P. M. Mem., Vol. 9, No. 1. Cambridge.
1942 "A delimitation of the area and some of the archaeology of the Sula Jicaque Indians of Honduras," *A. Antiq.,* 7:376–88. Menasha.
1957 *The archaeology of central and southern Honduras.* P. M. Papers, Vol. 49, No. 3. Cambridge.
1959 "The eastern frontier of Mesoamerica," *Mitteilungen aus dem Mus. für Völkerkunde in Hamburg,* 25:118–21. Hamburg.

STREBEL, H.

1885–89 *Alt Mexiko. Archaelogische Beiträge zur Kultgeschichte seiner Bewohner.* Hamburg and Leipzig.

STRESSER-PÉAN, G.

1952 *"Montagnes calcaires et sources vauclusiennes dans la religion des indiens huastèques de la région de Tampico,"* Revue de l'Histoire des religions *141*, No. 1. Paris.

STRÖMSVIK, G.

1931 "Notes on the metates of Chichen Itza, Yucatan," *C. I. W. Pub. 403*, Contrib. 4. Washington.

1941 "Substela caches and stela foundations at Copan and Quirigua," *C. I. W. Pub. 528*, Contrib. 37. Washington.

1950 *"Las ruinas de Asunción Mita. Informe de su reconocimiento," Antropología e historia de Guatemala,* Vol. 2, No. 1, pp. 23–29. Guatemala.

1952 "The ball courts at Copan, with notes on courts at La Union, Quirigua, San Pedro Pinula and Asuncion Mita," *C. I. W. Pub. 596*, Contrib. 55. Washington.

STRONG, W. D., A. KIDDER II, AND A. J. D. PAUL

1938 *Preliminary report on the Smithsonian Institution–Harvard University archaeological expedition to northwestern Honduras, 1936. Smithsonian Miscellaneous Collections,* Vol. 97, No. 1. Washington.

SUERO DE CANGAS Y QUIÑONES

1928 *"Descripción de la Villa de Espíritu Santo (1581),"* R. M. E. A., 2:176–80. Mexico.

TAX, S.

1947 "Notes on Santo Tomás Chichicastenango." Micro. No. 16. Chicago.

1951 "Panajachel field notes." Micro. No. 29. Chicago.

TERMER, F.

1957 *Etnología Etnografía de Guatemala. Seminario de Integración Social Guatemalteca. Pub. 5.* Guatemala.

THOMAS, C., AND J. R. SWANTON

1911 *Indian languages of Mexico and Central America and their geographical distribution. B. A. E. Bulletin 44.* Washington.

Maya History and Religion

THOMPSON, D. E.

1954 "Maya paganism and Christianity: a history of the fusion of two religions," *M. A. R. I. Pub. 19*, pp. 1–36. New Orleans.

THOMPSON, J. E. S.

1930 *Ethnology of the Mayas of southern and central British Honduras. Field Mus. Natural History, Anthropological Ser.*, Vol. 17, No. 1. Chicago.

1931 *Archaeological investigations in the southern Cayo District, British Honduras. Field Mus. Natural History, Anthropological Ser.*, Vol. 17, No. 2. Chicago.

1934 "Sky bearers, colors and directions in Maya and Mexican religion," *C. I. W. Pub. 436*, Contrib. 10. Washington.

1937 "A new method of deciphering Yucatecan dates with special reference to Chichen Itza," *C. I. W. Pub. 483*, Contrib. 22. Washington.

1938 "Sixteenth and seventeenth century reports on the Chol Mayas," *A. Anthr.*, 40:584–604. Menasha.

1939 *Excavations at San Jose, British Honduras. C. I. W. Pub. 506.* Washington.

1939a "The moon goddess in Middle America, with notes on related deities," *C. I. W. Pub. 509*, Contrib. 29. Washington.

1941 "A coordination of the history of Chichen Itza with ceramic sequences in central Mexico," *R. M. E. A.*, 5:97–111. Mexico.

1941a "*Apuntes sobre las supersticiones de los mayas de Socotz, Honduras Británica*," *Los mayas antiguos*, pp. 101–10. Mexico.

1942 *Representations of Tezcatlipoca at Chichen Itza. C. I. W. Notes 12.* Washington.

1943 "*Las llamadas 'Fachadas de Quetzalcouatl*'," *27th I.C.A., Mexico, 1939*, Vol. 1, pp. 391–400. Mexico.

1943a *Representations of Tlalchitonatiuh at Chichen Itza, Yucatan, and El Baul, Escuintla. C. I. W. Notes 19.* Cambridge.

1945 "A survey of the northern Maya area," *A. Antiq.*, 11:2–24. Menasha.

1946 *Some uses of tobacco among the Maya. C. I. W. Notes 61.* Cambridge.

1948 "An archaeological reconnaissance in the Cotzumalhuapa region, Escuintla, Guatemala," *C. I. W. Pub. 574*, Contrib. 44. Washington.

1950 *Maya hieroglyphic writing: introduction. C. I. W. Pub. 589.* Washington; Norman, 1960.

398

1951 "Canoes and navigation of the Maya and their neighbours," *Journ. Royal Anthropological Institute*, 79:69–78. London.

1952 *The introduction of Puuc style of dating at Yaxchilan. C. I. W. Notes 109*. Cambridge.

1954 *The rise and fall of Maya civilization*. Norman (and 1966).

1956 *Notes on the use of cacao in Middle America. C. I. W. Notes 128*. Cambridge.

1957 *Deities portrayed on censers at Mayapan. C. I. W. Current Reports 40*. Cambridge.

1958 "Symbols, glyphs and divinatory almanacs for diseases in the Maya Dresden and Madrid codices," *A. Antiq.*, 23:297–308. Salt Lake City.

1962 *A catalog of Maya hieroglyphs*. Norman.

1965 *Preliminary decipherments of Maya glyphs 1*. Saffron Walden.

1966 *The rise and fall of Maya civilization*. 2nd, enlarged edition. Norman.

1966a "Merchant gods of Middle America," *Summa Anthropológica*, pp. 159–72. Mexico.

1968 *Deciphering Maya glyphs. Cranbrook Institute of Science News Letter*, Vol. 37, No. 7. Bloomfield Hills.

1970 "A commentary on the Dresden codex, a Maya hieroglyphic book." In press.

1970a "The Bacabs: their portraits and their glyphs." In press.

THOMPSON, R. H.

1962 "Un espejo de pirita con respaldo tallado de Uayma, Yucatán," *E. C. M.*, 2:239–49. Mexico.

TORQUEMADA, J. DE

1723 *Los veinte i un libros rituales i monarchía indiana*. Madrid.

TOVILLA, M. A. DE: *See* Scholes and Adams, 1960.

TOZZER, A. M.

1907 *A comparative study of the Mayas and the Lacandones*. New York.

1913 "A Spanish manuscript letter on the Lacandones in the Archives of the Indies in Seville," *18th I. C. A., London, 1912*, pp. 497–509. London.

1941 *Landa's Relación de las cosas de Yucatán. A translation*. Edited with notes. *P. M. Papers*, Vol. 18. Cambridge.

1957 *Chichen Itza and its cenote of sacrifice. A comparative study of contemporaneous Maya and Toltec. P. M. Mem.,* Vols. 11, 12. Cambridge.

UCHMANY DE DE LA PEÑA, E. A.
1967 *"Cuatro casos de idolatría en el área maya ante el tribunal de Anthr. Assoc. Mem. 71.* Menasha.

VAILLANT, G. C.
1933 "Hidden history," *Natural History,* 33:618–28. New York.

VALLADARES, L. A.
1957 *El hombre y el maíz.* Mexico.

VÁSQUEZ, F.
1937–44 *Chrónica de la provincia del Santísimo nombre de Jesús de Guatemala de la Orden de nuestro seráfico Padre San Francisco. B. Goath.,* Vols. 14–17. Guatemala.

VÁSQUEZ DE ESPINOSA, A.
1942 *Compendium and description of the West Indies. Smithsonian Institution Miscellaneous Collection, 102.* Washington.

VIANA, F. DE, L. GALLEGO, AND G. CADENA
1955 *"Relación de la Provincia de la Verapaz hecha por los religiosos de Santo Domingo de Coban, 1574," A. S. G. H.,* 28:18–31. Guatemala.

VIENNA DICTIONARY
No date *Bocabulario de mayathan por su abeceario.* Original in Vienna.

VILLA R., A.
1945 *The Maya of east central Quintana Roo. C. I. W. Pub. 559.* Washington.
1946 *"Notas sobre la etnografía de los indios tzeltales de Oxchuc."* Micro. No. 7. Chicago.
1955 *Los mazatecos y el problema indígena de la cuenca del Papaloapan. I. N. I. Memorias,* No. 7. Mexico.
1962 *"Los quejaches: tribu olvidada del antiguo Yucatán," R. M. E. A.,* 18:97–116. Mexico.

VILLAGUTIERRE Y SOTO-MAYOR, J. DE
1933 *Historia de la conquista de la provincia de el Itza, reducción y progresos de la de el Lacandón. B. Goath.*, Vol. 9. Guatemala.

VOGT, E. Z. ET AL.
1966 *Los zinacantecos. Un pueblo Tzotzil de los altos de Chiapas.* I. N. I., Mexico.

WAGLEY, C.
1949 *The social and religious life of a Guatemalan village. Amer. Anthr. Assoc. Mem. 71.* Menasha.

WAUCHOPE, R.
1938 *Modern Maya houses. A study of their archaeological significance. C. I. W. Pub. 502.* Washington.
1948 *Excavations at Zacualpa, Guatemala. M. A. R. I. Pub. 14.* New Orleans.

WEITLANER, R. J.
1952 *El sol y la luna, II. Versión Chinanteca," Tlalocan.* 3:169–74. Mexico.

———, AND C. A. CASTRO
1954 *Papeles de la Chinantla 1. I. N. A. H. Serie Científica,* 3. Mexico.

WILLARD, T. A.
1926 *The city of the sacred well.* New York.

WILLEY, G. R. ET AL.
1965 *Prehistoric Maya settlements in the Belize Valley. P. M. Papers,* Vol. 54. Cambridge.

WILLEY, G. R., AND A. L. SMITH
1963 "New discoveries at Altar de Sacrificios, Guatemala," *Archaeology,* 16: 83–90. New York.

WILSON, C. H.
1886 *Notes on river surveys.* Belize.

WISDOM, C.
1940 *The Chorti Indians of Guatemala.* Univ. of Chicago, Chicago.

WOODBURY, R. B., AND A. S. TRIK
1953 *The ruins of Zaculeu, Guatemala.* 2 vols. Boston.

XIMÉNEZ, F.
1929–31 *Historia de la Provincia de San Vicente de Chiapa y Guatemala de la Orden de Predicadores. B. Goath.,* Vols. 1–3. Guatemala.

ZURITA, A. DE
1891 *Breve y sumaria relación de los señores y maneras y diferencias . . . en la Nueva España. Nueva colección de documentos para la historia de México,* Part 2. Mexico.

Index

Citations of Maya codices, the Books of Chilam Balam, Ritual of the Bacabs, the Popol Vuh, and Yucatec Maya are too numerous to have value. They are, therefore, omitted, as are also passing references to archaeological sites. The following place-name abbreviations are used:

A.V.P. Alta Verapas
B.H.   British Honduras
Camp.   Campeche
Chis.   Chiapas
Guat.   Guatemala
Mex.   Mexico or Mexican

Q.R.   Quintana Roo
Salv. El Salvador
Tab.   Tabasco
VC   Veracruz
Yuc.   Yucatan

Hobgoblins: 186, 335
Holtun Zuiua: 23
Homosexuality: 21, 46, 286
Hondo River (B.H.): 60, 127, 129–30
Honduras: 87–93, 98–100, 128, 145
Honey: 60, 75, 109, 128, 152, 182–83; in myth, 362, 363
Hookworm: 54, 58, 65
Horses: deified, *xvi;* Chacs', 164, 254, 257; wind gods', 265
"Hours": 195
House types: distribution of, 17–20; multiple-family, 29, 55, 60, 65, 67; men's, 172, 175; ceremonial, 68, 76, 264
Huaxtec Maya: 19, 217, 246
Hummingbird: 166, 202, 235, 313, 358 ff.
Hunac Ceel: 12, 16, 24, 180
Hunting and hunters: 199, 234, 235, 250, 268, 275, 308–10

Idols: 68, 70, 187–91, 242, 308, 325; absence of, 76, 187; feeding of, 181; making of, 190–91
Iguanas: 152; offering of, 182, 310; *kan,* 214; *see also itzam*
Imagery, word: 372
Incense burners: 76, 112, 180, 187–89, 191, 292, 307, 313
Influenza: 53
Insect offerings: 122, 182
Iron pyrites: 183
Itza: *see* Putun Maya, Tayasal (Peten)
Itzam (iguana): 21, 196, 205, 212
Itzamkanac (Camp.): 5, 7, 8, 13, 21, 26
Ixil Maya: 29, 73, 135; religion and myth of, 174, 175, 237, 272
Iximche (El Quiche): 175, 179
Izamal (Yuc.): 240, 325

Jacalteca Maya: 110; religion and myth of, 161, 165, 175, 203, 284, 336
Jade: 139–41, 183, 187, 190, 284
Jaguars: 166, 188, 197, 202, 215, 220, 235, 246, 291, 332, 343, 345, 347; pelts of, 151–52, 293; and eagles, 179, 312, 328; sacrifice of, 182; sun, 234, 236; rain, 256 n.
Jesus: in Maya myth, 23, 108, 336, 346, 347, 353, 360; in Maya religion, 162, 199, 234
Jicaque Indians: 87–91, 112
Johnson, Samuel: *xx*
Jokes and tricks: 350, 351–52, 359, 364–67

Jonuta, (Tab.): 38, 39, 131

Kan: iguana, 214; cross, 222–23, 259
Kanhobal Maya: religion and myth of, 174, 203, 235, 246, 267, 290 n., 316, 336, 360
Katun: count of, 10, 12, 22–25; prophecy, 22, 186; patron or countenance of, 229, 308, 322–24, 326
Kekchi Maya: 73, 100, 110, 135, 150, 152; religion and myth of, 21, 170, 173, 234, 236, 242–43, 250, 273–76, 299, 303, 343, 361
Kelly, I.: 82
Kidder, A. V.: 140, 141
Kukulcan (person): 4, 10 ff., 44–45

Lacandon: colonial, 4, 27–37, 67–68, 109–10, 122, 126, 135, 167, 328; present-day, 32, 68–70, 111, 112, 265 n.; religion and myth of, 162, 181, 193, 202, 207, 234, 236, 240–42, 246, 265–67, 270–72, 286, 300, 302, 303, 314, 338, 344–45
Lacantun River (Chis.): 4, 27–28, 37
La Farge, O.: *xi, xix,* 161, 165
Lakes: offerings to, 180; below earth, 216; and moon, 244–45; lord of, 267
Landa, D. de: *xix, xx,* 13
Language: *xxiii,* 265 n.; tenacity of, *ix–x;* numerical classifiers in, *xii;* historical deductions from, *xiii,* 72–73; distribution of, 72–73
La Union, (Honduras): 92, 94, 100
Lava products: 128, 141
Lehmann, W.: 87
Lempa River (Salv.): 87–88, 95–96, 102, 139
Lenca Indians: 88, 92 n., 96, 100
Lice: 352, 365; abstention from removal of, 174
Light and darkness: 196, 276, 280, 303, 340
Lightning: 113, 251 ff., 315; "machete," 254, 261
Lime: with tobacco, 110–13; traded, 150
Litter: 137
Lizards: 356
Lizardi R., C.: 222
Locen Maya: 69
Longyear, J.: 88–89
López Mateos ruins (Tab.): 90
Lothrop, S. K.: 87–88, 95–98, 102
Lubaantun (B.H.): 128

Macaw: 152, 240, 266; stone, 92, 94